The Life-changing Impact of Viktor Logotherapy

Teria Shantall

The Life-changing Impact of Viktor Frankl's Logotherapy

Springer

Teria Shantall
Modi'in, Israel

ISBN 978-3-030-30772-1   ISBN 978-3-030-30770-7   (eBook)
https://doi.org/10.1007/978-3-030-30770-7

This Springer imprint is published by the registered company Springer Nature Switzerland AG.
The registered company address is: Gewerbestrasse 11, 6330 Cham, Switzerland

*This book is dedicated to **Dr. Robert C. Barnes**, the President of the Viktor Frankl Institute of Logotherapy of the United States. During Dr. Barnes presidency, the Institute's membership has extended into more than 40 countries in 6 continents of the world. With his encouragement and the official backing of the Institute's Board of Directors, I was able, personally trained by Viktor Frankl as I was, to continue his work and vision by establishing logotherapy centers in South Africa, Israel, and Turkey and training hundreds of logotherapy students from all walks of life.*

Preface

Despite the remarkable progress of Logotherapy in the past two decades in Russia, Kazakhstan, and elsewhere in the world, there is a recognized vacuum in the education of logo-therapists, namely, the neglect of their own spiritual dimension. Shantall's book fills this vacuum remarkably well. Her book deals with the fundamental principles of what it means to be a human being. And particularly with how a person looks upon the world, whether as a meaningless or as a meaningful place. For absence of meaning in life makes existence miserable.

This book reflects and enlivens the author's struggle to turn many meaningless lives into productive and meaningful ones. And her life serves as illustration to this struggle and to its positive outcome.

Shantall's book is based on her long, rich, and distinguished background in Logotherapy, and on her teaching Frankl's theory and method of Logotherapy in different parts and cultures in the world. She is one of Professor Frankl's students in the United States who were fortunate to study under the guidance of the founder of Logotherapy. And this explains her positive and lively approach to the spiritual, philosophical, and particularly to the applied aspects of Logotherapy.

As she so convincingly shows, a logo-therapist is a human being with strengths and weaknesses similar to his or her clients. This means that a logo-therapist is not above the characteristics common to all people. In her lengthy exposition of Logotherapy, she manages to show in great detail how to conduct ourselves so that we may be able to overcome pain, sorrow, frustration, sickness, and even death.

Shantall demonstrates that nobody is beyond hope, beyond redemption. The more one experiences lack of meaning in his or her life, the more he or she may benefit from using Logotherapy to combat feelings of distress and helplessness. As all therapists know, the caring and curing function of Logotherapy is vested in establishing a close emotional bond between therapist and client. This bond is called trust. Trust is a central condition of therapy, of all therapy. It plays a crucial role in individual and social well-being.

According to Shantall, trust in the hands of a logo-therapist means recognition and responsibility for the potential of changing a person's entire life for good or bad. There is an explicit agreement about the expectations of what each party has to do.

And if this trust is damaged and lost, then the whole practice is gone. Therefore, both parties should be equally interested in the outcome of the therapeutic work.

The encounters in Shantall's book between client and therapist are based on the "Socratic Dialogue." Socrates, the ancient Greek philosopher, is generally regarded as the "father of ethics." His method of teaching is commonly known as "midwifery." Similar to the midwife who helps the mother to give birth, Socrates helped his listeners and students to give birth to the truth that resided in their souls. Socrates used "provocative questions" to elicit answers from his opponents in order to awaken in their hearts a sense of personal responsibility for their attitudes to life and truth.

The "Socratic Dialogue" was developed by Frankl as a helping and teaching technique for the practice of Logotherapy. It teaches the seeker of help how to use his or her power, fantasy, dreams, and caring for another person to find meaning in life. This method is basic in the encounter with a client. When the encounter has a positive value for the client, it leads to trust.

In order to achieve trust, a logo-therapist needs to be a person of virtues. As Shantall notes, Logotherapy is based on moral requirements. First and foremost among them are integrity and decency of the practitioner. A logo-therapist must be an individual with honesty and authenticity. For intervening in another person's life needs courage, wisdom, life experience, and a great measure of responsibility. And above all, a logo-therapist must realize that he or she is a worker.

Shantall's book is a work of love. All works of love benefit the giver and the receiver. Viktor Frankl has said that life revolves around work. People fulfill a meaning when they create something, when through their work they improve the world. And Voltaire the French philosopher said that, rather than philosophizing about the purpose of life, one has to understand what life demands from all of us, namely work for the sake of other people – not only for my own sake.

There are many books written on the various facets of Logotherapy by well-known logo-therapists. Yet, none gives such detailed account, nor goes to such lengths to demonstrate the actual work requested from the practitioner to advance the well-being of a client.

Shantall built her book mainly on the spiritual dimension of a human being. This dimension, as Frankl said, is the most important among the three dimensions, namely the biological and the psychological dimensions. The spiritual dimension includes wisdom, which in turn is based on freedom of choice that's unique to human beings. Wisdom is not open to scientific measurements or to analysis. Wisdom can be approached only by philosophy, which in turn deals with personal experience. As Shantall shows in the personal experiences of her own life and in the cases she presents in her book, these lives can't be repeated, but they can be changed for the better.

She begins each chapter in her book with an exposition of the main subject. This is followed with a discussion of the important concepts contained in the chapter, including case illustrations, and ends with a series of questions that she raises for the reader. The questions provide an opportunity for the reader to verify that she or he has grasped the meaning of that chapter and its implications for his or her own life. This approach to the applied aspect Logotherapy is most valuable and refreshing.

Logo-therapists must help their clients to use inner resources when confronting a difficult challenge. Pain and suffering are integral parts of life. And when suffering is extreme, it can destroy the quality of life. Frankl spoke about suffering as a normal part of human experience in life. He maintained that the human spirit is able to triumph over evil for it is capable of elevating itself to unimagined heights for the sake of another human being one truly loves, or for an idea in which one truly believes.

The subject of pain and suffering is well-known to Shantall from her own personal experience and from her dedicated work with many clients, especially with survivors of the Holocaust, who have suffered a lot. In her book, *Life's meaning in the Face of Suffering* (2002), she emphasizes that suffering is always a challenge. What matters is one's attitude to pain and suffering.

Logo-therapists need to differentiate between two kinds of pain: acute and chronic pain. Acute pain may be compared to a venomous snake that attacks you and should be eliminated by all available means. Chronic pain resembles an ox that carries its burden patiently. Chronic pain that's impossible to eliminate by medicine and psycho-therapeutic intervention must be tolerated. Comforting the sufferer is a human and professional necessity in such cases.

Logotherapy teaches us that when we are no longer able to change a situation, we are challenged to change ourselves. And we should always remember what Kant the philosopher said, namely, that we should never treat a person merely as a means to an end.

Shantall uses literary sources and especially stories and wisdoms contained in the Old and the New Testament to support her thesis. Stories may be very useful to all therapists. Let's take for example the Biblical meeting of Jacob with his brother Esau as illustration. According to the story, Jacob stole the rights of the first born from his brother Esau and fled to Babylon. He spent there many years and returned to the Land of Canaan as a rich person. But he had to meet Esau on the way. Jacob was afraid very much that his brother Esau would avenge the wrong he did to him. Thus he prepared for the meeting in three ways: with a prayer, with a gift, and with a readiness to fight.

The encounter with a client requires similar preparations by a logo-therapist. The prayer is for strength in facing the client, especially when the client may have unstable and unpredictable, or aggressive and demanding behavior. Contemplation, prayer, and planning the appropriate steps how to counteract such behavior can help a lot in the encounter.

The fight resembles the struggle with the client in the search for meaning. It is accompanied by pain that's inevitable in any encounter. And the gift is a reward. Jacob was rewarded by the angel with whom he struggled throughout the night with a new name, Israel.

A logo-therapist – if successful in the encounter with the client – may gain a different reward: A feeling that the struggle was worth, that something valuable and meaningful has happened, that there is a feeling of change for the better by the client, and that the encounter was not in vain. This feeling may be perceived by both client and therapist as a gift, as a turning point, and as a foundation for positive encounters in the future.

Shantall's book is more than an exposition of Logotherapy. It is more than a description and explanation of Logotherapy's theory, methods, and philosophy. This is a most valuable and much needed book, a welcome addition to the applied aspects of Logotherapy. The book is practice oriented and comprehensive. It clarifies Frankl's ideas regarding the purpose of all logo-therapeutic work. Her book is well-organized and clear.

The focus of this book is on the life-changing impact of Frankl's meaning-centered approach in counseling and psychotherapy, called Logotherapy. This book seeks to illuminate meaningful interaction between logo-therapist and client in a face-to-face interaction between them, emphasizing the uniqueness of both. This interaction has important ramifications outside the counseling context as well.

Shantall makes it clear that her book is not "religious," even if it uses some examples from major world religions. Her book is universal in its aim and focus. She supports Frankl's approach to the place of religion in logo-therapeutic work as explicated in his *Man's Search for Ultimate Meaning*. Accordingly, logo-therapists must make a clear differentiation between medical and religious ministry. Logotherapy is a philosophical and spiritual outlook on life. It refrains from missionary spirit and zeal. Logotherapy leaves the saving of souls to religious ministry.

Logotherapy is interested in helping human beings in emotional or mental distress to live responsible and meaningful lives. While Logotherapy is anchored in values, and in spirituality, these do not necessarily have to be religious ones. Logotherapy leaves to the individual the option for what, to what, or to whom he or she understands himself or herself to be responsible.

Frankl emphasized many times the need to re-humanize medicine. The re-humanization of all psychotherapies is even more important today in our terror-ridden world. It is the main task of Logotherapy. And Shantall's book is most valuable in this respect. She elevates humanness in helping people in sickness and distress to a spiritual height.

A great advantage of Shantall's book is that you don't have to be a logo-therapist to benefit from reading it. Any reader seeking to enhance the meaning quality of their own lives will find in this kind of therapy a treasure for improving their mental health. This book will help them to navigate successfully the troubled waters of life. This book will enable them to make intelligent and informed decisions about what is valuable and applicable to their situations in life, what appeals to their souls and spirit, and what may give meaning to their own lives.

Shantall's book will appeal particularly to practicing logo-therapists and to students of Logotherapy at all educational levels, and especially to those holding advanced degrees in academia. Her book will enrich the knowledge base of psycho-therapists in religious and pastoral care and counseling too, for it provides a much needed spiritual depth to their professional work.

I am most happy to recommend this book wholeheartedly and without reservations to logo-therapists, to members of the helping professions, and to the general public.

Faculty of Welfare and Health Sciences   David Guttmann
School of Social Work
University of Haifa
Mount Carmel, Israel

Prologue

Adam, Where Are You?

There is a call addressed to all of us, one we can hardly escape. It is a call recorded in the story of creation (Genesis 3:9).

Where are we?

What are we doing with our lives? How are we living it? Are we hiding somewhere, shying away from the challenge to come out, step into our lives, and live it in a way we can really feel good about? Are we prepared to take full responsibility for the way we are living our lives, or is there a sense of shame, guilt, and uneasiness if we have to give an honest account of it?

Are our lives going somewhere? Has it got a worthy purpose? Do we have a sense of direction and destiny? Do we feel we are where we should be, doing what we should be doing with a sense of satisfaction and contentment? Do we sense that we have a calling, a reason why we are alive, and a mission or tasks in life to fulfill? Or are we just floundering about, maybe even badly off course?

We may be refusing to look into such issues, merely taking life as it comes or doing what we feel like doing without any thought of tomorrow or where what we are doing may take us. We may even be set on a path we have carved out for ourselves, stubbornly discounting any way other than the one we have worked out as best suited to ourselves.

But can we escape the scrutiny of conscience?

What kind of people are we? If we fully look at ourselves, what do we see? Are we living up to what we *can*, and, in a deeper sense, what we hope and really *want* to be? Can we escape the uncanny feeling of what we *ought to be?* Do we really like ourselves, approve of ourselves, and feel good, contented, and even happy about ourselves? If we had to judge ourselves from an outsider point of view, will we be pleased about ourselves or ashamed? If ashamed, who will we be shaming?

We will be shaming ourselves!

What do we do about this restlessness we have about ourselves, the feeling that we do not really want to face ourselves; look at our face in the mirror? Is it just a question of being moralistic? Or is the feeling deeper, like an inescapable feeling of *dissatisfaction* about ourselves? Is it that we *know* that we, and we alone, are failing to be the kind of person that we very well know we *could* be?

We may realize that we are not fully ourselves, not really "at home" with who we are!

And what about our lives? Do we feel we are misdirecting it, throwing it away, or wasting it, just letting it pass by? Or do we feel that there is more to life, that we can be further along the road going somewhere?

We may have to sit down with ourselves and truthfully think things through, take the way we are living our lives to its logical conclusion. Is what we have settled for enough or even right? Is it good or bad for us? Does it, in the long run, make any real sense?

We may need to come to a point of saying: "Enough is enough. I am not making sense. Where I am, what I am doing, the way I am living, does not appeal to me. I'm restless. Some things have to change and change quickly, not tomorrow, not the next day, but *now*. I want to be in the moment, be *me* in all that I experience and have to deal with in a way that makes me feel good about myself. I want *this* kind of feeling of connectedness: to be an active agent in my own life, a life I can shamelessly account for. I want to be in the real flow of things, part of all that really matters in life. I want to be in vital touch with myself and what I stand for. I want to be out there, making a difference, making my own and meaningful mark on the world. I want to play my part!"

The only sensible answer to the call "Adam, where are you?" is to say "Here I am, *send me*. I am ready to go and be on my appointed way!"

Life must have a destination. Life must be a mission, have a goal and a purpose, and we must be *in it*, giving it shape. Otherwise, where will we be but nowhere, not anywhere special at all? Without a destination, we are rudderless, rootless, not amounting to much. We remain on the fringes of things, playing around with life in the shallow waters, outside of ourselves, doing little, effecting even less. We may even be in dark and dangerous waters, our lives sinking to the bottom. We may be losing all grip on ourselves as we gulp for air. We may be in great need to breathe freely, have some solid ground under our feet, and have something good in sight.

Our lives must have outcomes and results and good ones; otherwise, what is it all for?

What is life all about? How do I make sense of it? Who and why am I? What am I expected to do and be?

These are the questions that we all, at some time or another, should ask ourselves. The answers would determine whether we would feel in tune with ourselves and with life or not.

The logotherapy of Viktor Frankl (1905–1997) is a school of thought that addresses such questions.

Viktor Frankl was born, lived, worked, and died in Vienna. He was a medical doctor who specialized in psychiatry and neurology. He also held a doctorate in philosophy. As a Jew and Holocaust survivor, he became world famous after the publication of his book, *Man's Search for Meaning*, a book about his experiences in the concentration and death camps of Nazi Europe. This book, originally written in

German, got translated into English and, with its rise in popularity, it was translated into many other languages of the world. This opened the door to travelling the world to lecture and teach his particular approach to life and human suffering and what we, as human beings, are called to do in the face of it.

Life may be tragic in so many ways, but the essential thrust of it is positive. The latter Frankl came to deeply believe. Life *has* purpose and meaning, and we are challenged to find it. Furthermore, life has meaning not just in a general sense or abstract way. No. Its meaning is to be experienced in a *profoundly personal* sense. *Our* lives have meaning. *We* were destined to be. There is a unique purpose in life, an irreplaceable role to play for every one of us. And we are assigned the task to find and realize the unique meaning and destiny of our own lives. We can hardly do less since we really *want* to experience our lives as meaningful and worthwhile! Without a sense of meaning in our lives, we feel unfulfilled. Something is amiss or lacking or seriously wrong. We may even lose our will to live!

Logotherapy seeks to illuminate what *is* meaningful in life and how we can realize the meaning, purpose, or destiny of our own lives. In its focus on how we can experience life as meaningful and worthwhile and ourselves as a worthy part of it, logotherapy illuminates the art of living. This explains its special appeal to all of us, whether we study it as professional therapists and counselors or explore its significance in our own lives as a way of enriching our understanding of life and of ourselves. In fact, it is to the degree that the core principles of meaningful living, as expounded by logotherapy, impact on our own lives and person, that we will be able to apply these principles in ways that will be highly beneficial and of supreme benefit not only to ourselves but also to others.

"Each man is questioned by life; and he can only answer to life by answering for his own life; to life he can only respond by being responsible" (Viktor Frankl 2006:109).

Keywords

Life-changing impact
Meaning-centered
Logotherapy
Viktor Frankl

Contents

Chapter 1
What Is Logotherapy?

Abstract In answering the question set as the heading of this chapter, the reader is first of all provided with the basic tenets of logotherapy, namely, that as human beings we have freedom of will, an inherent will to find meaning in our lives and that the meaning we are searching for is there to be found. How are these fundamental human yearnings challenged by suffering and disaster; how free do we feel in the face of the pain and tragedies that we experience in our own lives; what do we make of the meaning of life in the face of so much evil and violence, sufferings and disasters that we witness in the world around us? What about Frankl's own life? How did he manage to survive his internment in Nazi concentration and death camps and come out of it with the belief that life still holds meaning?

Keywords Logotherapy · Freedom of will · The will to meaning · Meaning in life · The meaning of suffering · Frankl's Holocaust experiences

Healing Through Meaning

"Logos" is the Greek word for "meaning". Logotherapy is therefore healing (or therapy) through meaning. Logotherapy is the term coined by Viktor Frankl to describe his particular approach to life and human suffering and who we are called to be and what we are to do in the face of it.

Logotherapy is based on the following three tenets, principles or concepts: (1) the freedom of will; (2) the will to meaning; and (3) the meaning of life. Taken together, it says the following:

We have the freedom to search for, find and realize the meaning of our lives.

1. *Freedom of will*

As human beings we have *freedom of choice*. This is the **first tenet.** We are not haplessly driven, compelled to act in a certain way, pushed and pulled this way and that. Or, at least, we need not be! We are not determined by inherent inclinations, good or bad, which we have no power to direct or control. We are not automatically good without effort and dedication on our part. Nor are we helplessly fallen creatures, unable to say "No" to what proves to be bad or destructive behavior.

We have a self determining part to play in the shaping of our own lives.

2. *The will to meaning*

We all want to make sense of our lives. This is **the second tenet.** What makes sense is when one thing connects meaningfully to another. Things hold together, they do not fall apart. There is harmony, things are related to one another; parts fit together in a greater whole. Cohesion is the basis of understanding and grasp: "this makes sense, it has meaning, I can see how it works; I understand it!" Disconnected, conflicting, contradictory parts hostile to and set against each other (things that tear apart and destroy), do not make sense to us. They are disordered and create confusion and unrest.

Meaning is something that is inherently lawful, something we fundamentally need and want. It brings order and harmony into our lives. We feel at peace. It appeals and speaks to us, draws us to it in a good way. We experience a sense of connectedness, of being related to and included as an inherent part of a greater whole. What is meaningless *disturbs* our feelings of connectedness. We feel threatened by what feels *alien* to our nature; by something that severs, breaks up our connection to one another; makes us feel at a loss, uncertain and confused. Such a situation is *not* what we want; not what we are striving after and seek to attain. We *will* something *other* than and different to this. We want to experience *meaning* in our lives.

Our deepest desire, need or want, therefore, is to reach out to and connect with what is meaningful to us in the most fundamental sense of the word. We seek connection with something or someone outside of ourselves. We want to be linked to, harmoniously part of some greater whole where everything is held together in a good, non-disruptive and life-enhancing way. We want to be called out of ourselves and into some kind of enlivening interaction with others and with our world.

We feel good, happy about and at peace with ourselves when we have something or someone to live for, something of *worth* to contribute to the common good. We are doing our share for the good of the world around us. This forms the basis of a feeling of *self-worth*, of being a person in our own right. We are *needed:* we *belong* somewhere, have a unique space to fill or role to play.

We *fit* into the greater picture!

3. *The meaning of life*

It would make little sense if we had the freedom to search for, and a fundamental will to find meaning in our lives, if such meaning in life did not exist in any real way; if it was just a case of fantasy, a mere projection of what we desire life to be. This is the **third tenet:** life must be meaningful in and of itself. It must hold meaning outside and beyond us. Its meaning must be *incontestable*. Only if life is *objectively* meaningful is it *there* for us to become part of, embrace, appreciate and enjoy.

Life must have enduring worth beyond human caprice, beyond being something of our own making or something that we can shape to our own liking; this one in this way, and that one in that way. If my answer is as good as yours and anybody else's, whose answer will hold? Life will remain a question with no definite answer, nothing to find in any ultimate sense. So why strive for anything beyond what I may make of life, no matter if it is diametrically opposed to what you or others choose to make of it? Why even try? Life will be a conflict without resolution. What a depressing thought!

Only if the meaning of life is something beyond human speculation and manipulation is its meaning indestructible. Only then can nothing and no-one arbitrarily change or nullify life's meaning. Life's meaning will remain, be unassailable, beyond spoiling, always there to be found by anyone, at anytime, anywhere, no matter what anyone does or tries to do to darken its horizons.

Consider this: what meaning is there in life if everything is arbitrary or happenstance, if we are in this world through some freak accident, soon to slip into oblivion as if we never lived and if, in the end, it makes little difference whether we were here or not?

Furthermore: for life to be real to us, something we can trust and really believe in, ourselves as meaningfully part of, it must be e*verlasting*. It must have been in existence *before* us and go on *after* us. Our present lives must be a vital link in the chain of time. If there is a roster, a timing of what is to happen and when, there is *progress*. Without a beginning of intent towards an envisaged goal, no progress is possible. History will be haphazard, without meaning, a mindless repetition of ·he same old story, a going around in circles. We will simply be swallowed up in this whirlpool of unrelated happenings, floating about as one piece amongst myriads of other broken pieces on the surface of meaningless events.

Meaning is meaning *because* if it has purpose and direction!

Missing and Finding the Mark

Lives that are lived meaninglessly are arbitrary, given over to chance. Such lives fall away from, fail to find and miss out on what is meaningful in life. They *disconnect,* lose anchor and continuity. But once directed towards finding and fulfilling meaning, these lives take on significance, fall into line. Then the truth starts to operate, also retroactively and even to former generations that may have missed the mark!

The truth is this: we are *meant* to have a history, an origin and a genealogical line. We have a prophetic destiny, one we are meant to embrace. How else can we lay hold of life to live it in the way we are called to do if there was no such coherence of a beginning towards an end; if there was not an original plan and an ultimate purpose to the life given to us all?

Our individual lives must feature in the greater scheme of things, be recorded as significant for posterity and as part on an *ongoing* story. We must be players, the characters, in life's unfolding story.

The most optimal place to be, one earmarked by mental and spiritual well-being, is to have *unconditional faith in the unconditional meaningfulness of life*. Coupled to this, Frankl contested, is the awed awareness of our own *unconditional worth:* our capability to achieve and live a most meaningful life, a life that contributes to the quality of life of others and to the betterment of the world.

We have the dignity of personal responsibility!

True Happiness

Life is beautiful. But why do we not always see it, realize it, embrace and enjoy it with the awe, the wonder, the joy, the gratitude it should evoke? Self-absorption and fear are our greatest drawbacks. Optimal being is optimal *well-being*. The stressors are removed, the veil lifted. We are completely *open* to the beauty that surrounds us: we *see* the flowers, the trees, the fields, skies and mountains, the seas and rivers, the magnificence of creation, its creatures; every wondrous aspect of nature.

We live in an awesomely beautiful world.

Nature is a statement of fact: the world is here for *us*. It is *our* domain. How important that makes us! It affirms our worth, our having *to be* here. It is the backdrop to the scene of which we are the front figures. The world is at our feet, not to trample it under foot, but for us to take center stage, find our rightful place in it.

The more we learn about the wonders of nature, the awesome harmony and order of our universe, the more we begin to grasp the potential of human greatness in a world designed for togetherness and peace.

We experience, in ever greater measure, that it is *good* to be alive!

But Why Then Do We Suffer?

What about suffering? The world can look so ugly, so frightening, its face of beauty hidden from us. We can be so full of insecurities, uncertainties; doubts about ourselves. Life can be so painful, others so insensitive and cruel. We may be plagued with anxiety; frightened by what we experience, what we see out there in the world. Life can seem like a tragic affair.

So much of its tragedy is precisely *because* it is spurned, not appreciated for what it can give. Things are in disarray and *unnatural*. We fail to understand and appreciate each other. We do not believe in ourselves or in one another. We nurture our hurts, are self-defensive, full of resentment, feel at a distance from and at odds with one another. Brother fights brother. Communities are torn apart by factionalism. One opinion is hostile and opposed to the next. The world is a place of uprisings, wars and violent conflicts. There is blood-shed and misery, lewd ways of living, lawlessness and corruption almost everywhere. Tyrannical regimes oppress their peoples and seek to dominate the entire world and subject it to its will; terrorist groups even compete for power among themselves.

How do we make sense of the world, of life in the face of so much anguish, turmoil and strife?

There Is Evil in the World

Are we inherently evil creatures, inclined towards falling into unspeakable depths of depravity and cruelty, and is there very little, if anything at all that can be done about it?.

How can anyone believe in life as just and fair if evil holds such sway, has such a free hand, is so rampant and common place that there is no stopping of it, no force strong enough in the world to effectively resist and eradicate it?

We can still see the sense of having to put something right if we did something wrong, if we are faced with the miserable consequences of our own foolish actions. But how does life retain its meaning if we are subjected to injustice, to suffering we have not brought upon ourselves, when we are faced with that which, at the moment of happening, is beyond our power to prevent or change? There is an inherent injustice to falling ill, to becoming a prey of some or other mortal physical affliction. Such tragedies happen to us beyond our ability to safeguard ourselves against it. And can we stop ourselves from growing older; can we prevent our eventual and inevitable deaths?

Victims of Injustice

It is the answer to all the above questions that has made *Man's Search for Meaning,* Frankl's book that captured his own experiences of suffering as a Jew in the Nazi concentration and death camps, a best-seller to this day.

Frankl was a survivor of what became known as the Holocaust, the systematic slaughter of over six million Jews, including one and a half million Jewish children, by a power seeking National Socialist Regime in Germany during the Second World War. Millions of other victims also died in the camps or were killed during the course of the war.

Frankl wrote over 30 books in his lifetime, all expounding the truths he captured in the first two books he wrote soon after his release from the camps. The first was the rewriting of the lost manuscript of his book entitled: *The Doctor and the Soul,* a book he hastily wrote just before he was captured and sent to the concentration camps. The second, *Man's Search for Meaning,* written shortly after the rewriting of his first book, not only contains the story of his Holocaust experiences, but also captures the essence of all he expounded in his unique school of psychotherapy, namely, logotherapy.

Since its first publication, *Man's Search for Meaning* has been read and continues to be read by millions of people all over the world. The book impacts on the reader in a life-changing way. Why? Frankl posed this question himself. Is it that people *are* in fact trying to make sense of their lives and of life itself? There is so much hurt and tragedy and disaster in the world and it also finds its way into our personal lives. This is where we suffer the most. For indeed, Frankl observed, none of us can really claim that we have remained untouched, unhurt and unshaken by the tragic facts of life.

Existential Frustration

Frankl spoke about *the tragic triad of human existence: pain, guilt and death*. Who of us can say that we will never suffer, always get things right and never fail or make mistakes? We are all going to die! He also spoke about suffering *boredom*. There is a particular anguish about feeling what he described as an inner state of *emptiness*. A logotherapist, Genrich Krasko (2004), entitled his book: *The Unbearable Boredom of Being*. If nothing much matters, if there seems to be little to really be excited about, not much reason for anything, we *suffer*. There is, as Frankl called it, an *existential vacuum*, a feeling that nothing much matters in life.

The Call to Come Out of Hiding

But it is in the very face of life's tragedies and disappointments, pain and hardships, its losses, anguish and grief, in the experience of an intolerable feeling of *meaninglessness* that we are most keenly provoked to search for answers. Not only do we yearn for a different kind of world but we also seek to live life in a different and more fulfilling way. From within the very depths of our being, we experience a longing, even a *loneliness*; something that tells us that we want to be lovingly restored to what we feel we were originally given, something we had or *could have had;* something that was given to us as a potential or a promise of what life could have been or was meant to be like.

It was something meant to be ours, but that somehow got lost.

When Meaning Becomes a Mission: The Story of Viktor Frankl

A study of the life of Viktor Frankl, someone who had found what we sense we are all looking for, holds great meaning for us.

There is a golden thread of meaning in his life; a destined path that can be traced throughout it. All of his life's experiences, from the most meaningful to the most painful, had a shaping influence upon his thinking. It was as if there was a preparation taking place towards a point of readiness which launched his life into a very much more vividly clarified direction.

Viktor Emil Frankl was born in Vienna in 1905 to a devout and morally enlightened Jewish family and died in that same city in September 1997. Between those two dates there is a space of life that contains all the struggles, challenges and triumphs of what it means to be human.

It is a story that addresses all of us.

An Innocent Childhood

In his autobiography, *Viktor Frankl: Recollections* (1997), published a few months before his death, Frankl recalled a few major experiences and events in his life. Two of his earliest recollections vividly illustrate what later became the cornerstones of his thinking.

He described the first event, when only a 4 year old, as follows: "One evening, just before falling asleep, I was startled by the unexpected thought that one day I too would have to die. What troubled me then – as it has done throughout my life – was not the fear of dying, but the question of whether the transitory nature of life might destroy its meaning" (1997: 27). What was the meaning of life if it comes to an end, if death, a total end to it, is what inevitably awaits us all?

Little did he know that soon afterwards he would be given an answer to this painful question in the following and second significant event: "One sunny morning, I was awakened. With my eyes still closed, I was flooded by the utterly rapturous sense of being guarded, sheltered. When I opened my eyes my father was standing there, bending over me and smiling" (1997: 31).

A Lasting Impression

The impression left with him was that there *is* meaning in life waiting for us to awaken and reach out to and that this meaning is hidden in the very fact of life's transitory nature.

Time does not stretch out endlessly. It passes and it ends. Birth and death enclose us within a limited space of time. Time is therefore extremely precious. Every moment is a space waiting for us to step into and *fill* with meaningful content. Time asks something from us. We seem called to do something with and about it. Indeed, each day, every moment of time, presents us with something to do or someone to respond to - something is expected us of us in each and every situation.

The Meaning of the Moment

Every situation offers us something unique, comes to us but once and never again. The encounter with every such a moment changes us. We do not meet the next moment in exactly the same way. We change with time, become more of who we will prove to be. Every situation is a chance to show ourselves, to give expression to ourselves in ways that all the more define us. "This is so and so. This is what he or she is like."

We make ourselves known in the world.

Do we want to stay in hiding, tucked away in some kind of enclosure of our own making, not facing life at all? To be unknown in this way, to have never really lived and made our impression on the world or, even worse, to have made a false impression on the world, leaves us with feelings of sadness and regret. Not to have *lived* our lives, is to not have really existed. We can easily be replaced by another. We will not really be missed and will be quickly forgotten. But even more tragic than this type of non-existence is to have lived a wasted, even a bad life, to have damaged what could have been precious in our lives, to have thrown our lives away. How will we be remembered then? Do we want to leave a bad impression, have the way we have lived our lives speak against our person? Do we want to be riddled with guilt and shame, in a state of humiliation and defeat, with no hope of being saved out of it? No one in their right mind would want to leave the kind of legacy that people would like to erase from memory!

The truth of the matter is that we want to be missed. We want to be remembered with love, admiration and respect.

We want to live a life that matters.

Time is meant for progress. It is not to be wasted or thrown away, but it is meant to achieve something of worth. Time indeed waits for no man. We will all come to the end of the time allotted to us. Time will go on without us. When our time is up, we would want to feel satisfied with the way we have lived our lives. We would want to see that we needed to be here and to have done and experienced what we did. Our lives had impact. It meant something. It formed a meaningful part of the whole, of some bigger picture or story, a story that started long before we were born and that will continue its narrative after we have gone, but a story we were part of! We had a say in its plot. We were part of history; a history that started with magnificent intent and works towards an ordained end: a good and meaningful, a benevolent, and yes, a glorious conclusion. It was all very worthwhile!

Death, therefore, gives life its meaning as a once given precious gift of opportunity.

Life is for living it in the way it is meant to be lived!

The Teenage Years

When Frankl was 14 and a science teacher asserted that life, in the final analysis, was nothing but a process of combustion, the young Viktor jumped up and exclaimed: "If that is so, then what meaning does life have?" If life was just a matter of mere and mechanical existence, or of blind evolution; if it was a matter of the survival of only the fittest, the most fortunate, the most successful, the most famous and the most powerful, we could lapse into a state of futility and despair. Where am I in this scheme of things? Is my life but a pointer towards a better end for the future of mankind or towards an outcome I will have no part in? I would be just a forgotten step along the way. Am I just a detail of a plot that swallows me up? When I look at so many wasted and empty lives around me with only a few reaching the top and that, among these few lucky ones, only a few that I can really admire and respect, what is it all for? Everything seems so senseless and cruel, terribly unjust. I am pushed to a point of giving up on life.

The sense of senselessness in life can also be filled with anger and violent protest - an anger that in its extremity wreaks vengeance on a meaningless world and that becomes ruthless and uncaring about the plight of others. A philosophy of: "let us take out of life what we can get out of it" is behind drug-addiction, alcoholism, a crazed seeking after pleasure and power. It is also at the basis of a lawless, violent and crime-ridden way of life.

The Shaping of a Life Task

Frankl felt it was his life's task to *oppose* nihilism, the belief in *non-meaning* (that there is no ultimate meaning to life) that, he believed, was the root cause of human misery. Frankl set out on a career in psychiatry in which he introduced the concepts of meanings and values to psychiatric thought. People were not just their miserable illnesses, mental afflictions and emotional problems or messed up lives. People want to find meaning in their lives, make some sense of their sufferings, know how to deal with it and somehow overcome it, get the better of it and, in the process, become better human beings with a future of hope ahead of them. Frankl therefore sought to *rehumanize* psychiatry.

But what a challenge he was about to face at the very outset of what he saw as his mission in life! Could he have known what was ahead of him in being taken captive and sent to four different Nazi concentration and death camps? His life was to be brought to a sudden halt. Frankl's fundamental belief that life has meaning, expounded in his teachings and writings, was to be severely tested in the years of suffering that followed.

He had already gained stature as an exceptional human being. As a young medical student, he developed programs to help to reduce the number of suicides in the pre-war Austria. He interacted with and participated in the associations of both Sigmund Freud and Alfred Adler, world famous therapists whose views on human nature he dared to question! He received his medical degree in 1930. From 1933–1937 he was head of the Vienna Psychiatric Hospital's female suicide prevention section and worked with thousands of women who were in danger of committing suicide. In 1937 he opened his own private and flourishing practice.

When the Germans invaded Austria in 1938 he, as a Jew, was not allowed to treat Aryan patients. He consequently took a post as head of the neurological department of the Rothchild Hospital in Vienna, the only place where Jewish patients could still be treated. Adolf Hitler, the infamous leader of the Nazi regime, had ordered the euthanasia of the mentally retarded and mentally ill of his own people in an effort to "purify" the blood of the German or Aryan race. Frankl risked his life and saved the lives of such patients under his care by giving them false diagnoses.

But even greater choices were ahead of him.

Crucial Choices

Frankl sought to relocate to the United States to escape what became an increasingly dangerous situation, especially for Jews. Shortly before the United States entered World War II, he was at last invited to come to the American Consulate to pick up his visa. He hesitated. The visa applied to him alone.

Could he leave his elderly parents behind?

Undecided, he took a walk and had this thought: "Isn't this the kind of situation that requires some hint from heaven?" When he returned home, his eyes fell on a little piece of marble lying on the table. When he asked his father about it, his father explained that he had found it among the rubble of a synagogue that the National Socialists had burnt down. He had taken it home because it was a part of the tablets which contained the Ten Commandments. This particular piece had one letter engraved upon it, the fifth letter of the alphabet with the numerical value of five. It stood for the fifth of the Ten Commandments, namely, to honor your father and your mother. Frankl had his hint from heaven! He stayed, letting his American visa lapse (Frankl 1967: 34).

As the situation in Vienna grew even more ominous, Frankl sat down and wrote the draft of his first book, entitled: *Arztliche Seelsorge (Doctor and the Soul)*. His work, that he termed: logotherapy, had already become known as the Third Viennese School of Psychotherapy, the first and second being the schools of Freud and Adler. Frankl had some protection, one he could also extend to his parents, due to his position at the Rothchild hospital. Jews were being rounded up and sent to the Nazi concentration camps that had sprung up over the occupied countries of Europe. But how long was that protection to last? It seemed imperative to capture his views on paper. If he was to perish, the essentials of logotherapy might at least survive him.

Frankl met and married Tilly Grossen In 1941. Together with one other couple they were the last of the Viennese Jews to obtain permission from the National Socialist authorities to wed. By then, Jews were forbidden to have children. A decree was issued that pregnant Jewish women would be immediately deported to a concentration camp. They would face a certain death. Frankl and Tilly decided to abort the fetus she was carrying. Frankl's book, *The Unheard Cry for Meaning,* was dedicated to their unborn child.

Nine months after their wedding day the couple, along with their families, were deported to Theresienstadt where Frankl did what he could to help others. He ran a clinic and helped new prisoners deal with the drastic shock of entry into the camp. He also established a suicide watch. Six months after their arrival in Therensienstadt his father died of starvation and pneumonia, despite Frankl's devoted care. Frankl was ordered to be transferred to Auschwitz. Although Tilly had been granted a 2-year exemption from the transfer because she was working in a munitions factory deemed important to the war effort, she joined him, despite Frankl's efforts to dissuade her.

In the last minutes they were together at Auschwitz and just before the men and women were separated from each other, Frankl (1997: 90) urged her: "Tilly, stay alive at any price. Do you hear? At any price!" He was trying to tell her that if she found herself in a situation where she was selected to be a partner for sex of some or other Nazi or else be killed, she should not refuse out of a sense of loyalty to him. The choice to stay alive in the hope of being with him again would in no way contradict their marriage vows of staying faithful to each other.

However, Frankl was to never see Tilly again. She died in Bergen-Belsen. Frankl's mother was sent to Auschwitz and, being elderly, was sent to the gas chambers. Frankl's brother, Walter, also died there.

On one of his first days back in Vienna after his liberation, Frankl looked up a trusted friend and told him about the news of the deaths of Tilly, his parents and his brother. Only his sister survived, having made her way to Australia before the outbreak of the war. After sharing all of these tragic events with his friend, Frankl burst into tears and said:

> I must tell you that when all this happens to someone, to be tested in such a way, that it must have some meaning. I have a feeling – and I don't know how else to say it – that something waits for me; that something is expected of me, that I am destined for something (1997: 104).

To Be a Jew: The Bigger Picture

As a Jew in Nazi occupied Austria, Frankl was a victim of the Nazi movement's leader, Adolf Hitler, in his unequalled hatred of the Jew. Hatred seeks to obliterate the very existence of the object of hatred, especially if that hatred is driven by vicious envy. Thus Hitler's appeasement of his own violent hatred of the Jew got

formulated as "the final solution of the Jewish problem" – namely, the dehumaniza-
tion and eventual annihilation of the entire Jewish race.

How are we to understand Hitler's obsession with the Jew?

A study of history will show that the Jew holds an uncanny and special position
in this world, a position that provoked envy and hatred by tyrant leaders, nations and
groups throughout history and still does and all the more so in our own day. No matter what the religious persuasions, philosophies or political views of people are, the
Jews find themselves the focus of critical attention. No other nation or group is
singled out in quite the same way. Robert Wistrich, renowned historian and expert
on antisemitism, called two of his works on Jew-hatred: *A Lethal Obsession* (2010)
and *Antisemitism, The Longest Hatred* (1991).

Why? What is the reason for this?

The Bible, for those who are familiar with it, describes the Jews as set apart or
chosen. They were designated as chosen, the Bible tells us, not because of their
superiority over other nations but because they were entrusted with a task, a mission
to fulfill: to live by and instruct the world in the Law of God.

In the mind of people like Hitler and all the unrighteous men before him, such
laws place discomforting limits on the unbridled and barbaric ambition of man to do
"his own thing" and to be uncurbed in his bid to be elevated to positions of absolute
power and boundless pleasure according to concepts of a deity that is pleasing to
him. Such distorted concepts of God, the Bible called: idolatry. "Yes, we are barbarians", Hitler raged. "We want to be barbarians! It is an honorable title. Providence
has ordained that I should be the greatest liberator of humanity. I am freeing man
from the dirty and degrading self-mortification of a false vision (a Jewish invention)
called 'conscience' and 'morality'" (quoted in Spiro 2002: 346).

According to Hitler, the Jews gave the world two curses: circumcision and conscience. Who, argued Hitler, is to lay claim to our lives, set us apart (by the symbolic
act of circumcision) to be accountable (through a conscientious obedience to the
injunctions of the Law) for all we think, say and do? Man will be answerable to no-
one but himself! He will be his own god, set up his own system of beliefs according
to *his* understanding and liking. He will set up his own ideas of God; create his own
religion or godless philosophy of life. Hitler, like the tyrants and dictators before
and after him, sought to cast off the yoke of accountability that the Jewish presence
in the world represents. The place the nation of Israel occupies in the world is to be
usurped and replaced by another.

"There can be no two chosen people, only one!" Hitler raged.

In fact, in the brutish and twisted mind of dictators and fanatical leaders such as
Hitler, Jewish presence in the world must be obliterated. The sense of accountability, so discomfortingly there in the bosom of man, must be eradicated. Genocide, the
annihilation of the entire Jewish race, is the objective. The Jews must be placed in a
position, not of being chosen, but of being despised. They are to bear their shame as
a sinful, failing and unworthy people. Other people, especially their usurpers, are to
be elevated above and be declared to be much more worthy than they. To obtain this
objective, the Jews must be humiliated and shamed, robbed of respect and stature.
Through propaganda and slander, the indoctrination of the mind of the masses, the

Jews are to be seen as evil and as rejected by God. Jews are to be cursed as vermin, pigs, descendants of apes, a cancer that must be excised, removed from the body of mankind.

At the other extreme, the Jews are to be seen as a threat to the existence of other nations. The Jews must be suspected of plotting to take over the world; to be steering the course of history their way. They are to be judged as a people who abuse, dominate, are cruelly insensitive to human rights; a people who exert evil power over the innocent and hapless lives of those they victimize. The world must be made to see Jews as a danger to them and learn to fear and hate them.

"Die Juden sind unser Ungluck" (the Jews are our misfortune"), read a propaganda poster during the Nazi regime.

If the Jews can be made to bend the knee in acknowledgement of the superior power of their adversaries and of their beliefs and way of life; if they, through torture and terror, can be cut down to size, be brought to a position where they would be begging for their lives and, like starved animals, would be fighting over a morsel of food, then they would no longer pose such a threat. They would then prove to be no better than other men, no, inferior to other men!

If the Jew can be accused and held responsible for all that is wrong in the world, their accusers could be freed of guilt, from their own sense of shame and humiliation!

What a convenient scapegoat for the ills of the world Jews are, Hitler, with evil genius, realized! "If there was no Jew," he said, "it would be necessary to invent him" (in Dimsdale 1980: 67).

Like Sheep to the Slaughter?

At Hitler's orders, Jews were rounded up, crammed into cattle cars of German trains and transported like sheep to the slaughter. Joined by others similarly inspired by Jew-hatred throughout Nazi occupied Europe, the possessions of Jews were confiscated, their communities and institutions devastated. If not rounded up on the spot, shot and thrown into mass graves, they were herded into ghettos and from there transported to concentration and extermination camps. Upon arrival at the death camps, equipped with gas chambers and crematoria, pregnant women, children and the elderly were immediately sent to the gas chambers; beautiful women were set aside to be raped. Children who were twins and other children, also adults, were selected for barbaric medical experimentation. Men and women who were fit enough for the slave labor ahead of them, were separated from each other. Before assigned to their barracks, they were stripped naked, shaved, pushed into showers and deloused, given prison uniforms or rags for clothing, and then crowded into their barracks. Life consisted of a near starvation diet, being exposed to the elements and to the outbreak of disease among the camp inmates. They were beaten, tortured, terrorized, starved and worked to death. There was a daily quota of those to be shot and gassed, their bodies thrown in mass graves or just piled up or shoved into ovens to be burnt. Hundreds of thousands of dissidents, Jehovah's witnesses, Communists,

Christians who sought to save Jews, along with gypsies, homosexuals and those not deemed fit for life, faced the same doom; millions of others, especially Poles and the Slavic peoples, were killed as targets of war. Two thirds of European Jewry, the object of intentional murder, were eradicated before this greatest crime in human history was brought to a shaky halt.

Chosen in the Fire of Affliction

How utterly amazing, therefore, that it was there, in the white heat of the most unimaginable suffering, that Frankl found the most powerful clarification of his mission in life - namely, to teach through personal witness and experience of the truth of it, that life holds *unconditional* meaning! Everything that gave life a sense of meaning may well have been stripped from him. But one thing remained. Frankl called this "the last of the human freedoms", a freedom we are never deprived of – namely, the freedom to choose how we will behave, the stand we will take for what is right and decent, humane and just, in the face of that which tries to destroy it. Not only are we able to *retain* our decency and worth as human beings in the most vile conditions imaginable, but we can also grow into most exemplary human beings not only despite it, but *because* of it. Good has the power to overcome evil! How graphically this was voiced by another triumphant survivor, one of the research participants of my doctorate research, after release from a 3 year imprisonment in Auschwitz:

> They wanted to prove to themselves that they could break the Jewish nation, that they could break our spirit, our values, to break anything which is human. To convert us to the level of nothingness, that is what their aim was. Shall I tell you something? They did not succeed! Morally, spiritually, no matter how much we were skeletons, still we had the human touch in us. We were heaps of skin and bone, heaps of dead bodies, but they could not somehow get at us. We remain! (In Shantall 2002: 267).

Suffering as a Task

Frankl entered Auschwitz with only his hastily written manuscript hidden in the inner pocket of his coat. When ordered to strip and despite his plea to retain his manuscript, his coat plus the manuscript were taken from him.

> Thus I had to undergo and to overcome the loss of my spiritual child. And now it seemed as if nothing and no one would survive me; neither a physical nor a spiritual child of my own. I found myself confronted with the question whether under such circumstances my life was ultimately void of meaning.
>
> Not yet did I notice that an answer to this question with which I was wrestling so passionately was already in store for me and that soon thereafter this answer would be given to me. This was the case when I had to surrender my clothes and in turn inherited the worn-out

rags of an inmate who had already been sent to the gas chamber. Instead of the many pages of my manuscript, I found in a pocket of the newly acquired coat one single page torn out of a Hebrew prayer book, containing the main Jewish prayer, Shema Yisrael ("Hear, O Israel"), i.e. the command: 'Love thy God with all thy heart, and with all thy soul, and with all thy might', or, as one might interpret it as well, the command to say 'Yes' to life despite whatever one has to face, be it suffering or even dying.

How should I have interpreted such a 'coincidence' other than as a challenge to live my thoughts instead of putting them on paper? (Frankl 1967: 25–26).

Frankl made a decision right there and then "to not run into the wire" (commit suicide by running into the electric fences around the camp).

The Sustaining Power of Right Choices

Life was no longer showering its blessings of which he had in the past been such a fortunate recipient. A much more active orientation was being called for.

Everything that ordinarily made life worth the living was being taken from Frankl and from those who shared his tragic fate. Now - more than ever, he had to practice what he preached; give expression to what he had already formulated as a truth before his deportation to the camps, namely that it was not what we expected from life but what life expected from us.

Woe to him who saw no more sense in his life, no aim, no purpose, and therefore no point in carrying on. He was soon lost. The typical reply with which such a man rejected all encouraging arguments was, 'I have nothing to expect from life anymore'. What sort of answer can one give to that? What was really needed was a fundamental change in our attitude toward life. We had to learn ourselves and, furthermore, we had to teach the despairing men, that it did not really matter what we expected from life, but rather what life expected from us. We needed to stop asking about the meaning of life, and instead to think of ourselves as those who were being questioned by life – daily and hourly. Our answer must consist, not in talk and meditation, but in right action and in right conduct (Frankl 1968: 78).

Breaking Through to the Dimension of Meaning

Dramatic were those incidences during Frankl's internment when, in his fierce struggle against feelings of total despair and meaninglessness brought upon him by the force of circumstances he was powerless to change, he could break through to spiritual victory.

When it seemed to him that he would die in the near future, his concern was different from that of most of his comrades. Their question was, ""Will we survive the camp? For if not, all this suffering has no meaning." The question that beset him was, "Has all this suffering, this dying around us, a meaning? For, if not, then ultimately there is no meaning to survival; for a life whose meaning depends upon such a happenstance – as whether one escapes or not – ultimately would not be worth living at all" (Frankl 1968:103). How graphically he captured this struggle in the following experience:

> The dawn was grey around us; grey was the sky above; grey the snow in the pale light of dawn; grey the ragses in which my fellow prisoners were clad, and grey their faces. I was struggling to find the reason for my sufferings, my slow dying. In a last violent protest against the hopelessness of imminent death, I sensed my spirit piercing through the enveloping gloom. I felt it transcend that hopeless, meaningless world, and from somewhere I heard a victorious 'Yes!' in answer to my question of the existence of an ultimate purpose. At that moment a light was lit in a distant farmhouse, which stood on the horizon as if painted there, in the midst of the miserable grey of a dawning morning in Bavaria (Frankl 1968: 39–40).

At that very moment a bird flew down and perched on the mound of soil he had dug up. It steadily looked at him. Frankl felt flooded with the sensation that his beloved wife, Tilly, was right there with him, encouraging him. Communing with her in his own mind, he could hear her answering him. He saw her smile, her frank and encouraging look. "Real or not, her look was then more luminous than the sun which was beginning to rise" (Frankl 1968: 36).

How often since then he communed with her in his mind, pouring over the memories of their times together, their love for each other! So strong was the sensation of love that it did not even seem to matter whether she was still alive or not. A truth dawned on him. "Set me as a seal upon your heart, as a seal upon your arm; for love is as strong as death" (Song of Solomon 8:6).

Love is the ultimate and the highest goal to which man can aspire!

A new day was beginning to dawn for him, right there in the concentration camp.

A Vision for the Future

When on one occasion he realized just how his thoughts were being caught up with the endless little problems of the miserable life they were forced to lead, he had the following experience:

> I became disgusted with the state of affairs which compelled me, daily and hourly, to think only of such trivial things. I forced my thoughts to turn to another subject. Suddenly I saw myself standing on the platform of a well-lit, warm and pleasant lecture room. In front of me sat an attentive audience on comfortable upholstered seats. I was giving a lecture on the psychology of the concentration camp (Frankl 1968: 74)!

Frankl's life had come full circle. The choice to stay with his parents and let his American visa lapse, foregoing the chance to have escaped what lay in store for him, ended in a most powerful authentication of the views he had pinned down in his manuscript before he was deported to the camps. His "hint from heaven" at that time of critical choice was the fifth injunction from the Ten Commandments, one that contained a powerful promise: "Honor your father and your mother, as the Lord your God has commanded you, that your days may be long, and that it may be well with you in the land which the Lord your God is giving you" (Deuteronomy 5:16). Frankl died at the ripe old age of 92.

Part of the long life promised him in what he believed was his hint from heaven, was spent with his beloved second wife, Elly. She was the great support of his life and work, as was his family: his daughter, Gabrielle, her husband, Professor Franz Vesely, and their two children, Katharina and Alexander. Between 1946 and 1950 Frankl published 12 books, before his death he had produced 30, which have been translated into 22 languages. His best-known work, *Man's Search for Meaning,* has run into 80 editions, and in the United States alone more than five million copies have been sold. In addition to Frankl, hundreds of authors have published books and articles on logotherapy. There are teaching institutions and societies devoted to logotherapy on every continent. Frankl was awarded many prizes in appreciation of his work. Twenty-four honorary doctorates were conferred on him by universities all over the world. Through his life and work, Frankl brought consolation and hope to millions of people worldwide. Up to a few years before his death he still travelled the world, giving lectures on "the psychology of the death camps" to attentive audiences seated comfortably in well-lit, warm and pleasant auditoriums and lecture rooms!

What man becomes, he has made out of himself, Frankl contended. Swine or saint, man, given his freedom of choice, can be one or the other. Which one he becomes depends on decisions but not on conditions. It is with this truth that Frankl concludes *Man's Search for Meaning,* the book on his Holocaust experiences:

> Our generation is realistic, for we have come to know man as he really is. After all, man is that being who invented the gas chambers of Auschwitz; however, he is also that being who entered those gas chambers upright, with a prayer on his lips.

The Remaining Question

What is the meaning of life in the face of man's inhumanity to man, in the face of so much suffering, injustice, violence, war and terror not only during those dark years, but also now in all situations of senselessness, tragedy and disaster?

The famous father of psychoanalysis, Sigmund Freud, addressed the problem of violence and lawlessness in his analysis of the causes of human suffering in one of his last works: *Civilization and its Discontents* (1930) pointed out that we are to combat suffering caused by the forces of nature; by the feebleness of our own bodies which are doomed to decay and dissolution; and by the inadequacy of the regulations which adjust the mutual relationships of human beings in the family, the state and society. The suffering which comes from this last source is perhaps more painful to us than any other.

How are we to understand human nature? How are we to deal with tragedies that befall us, the hardships and hurts we are subjected to in life, the void and emptiness and confusion we experience and that leave us with feelings of such futility and despair?

What must we make of our world, what attitudes are we to have, how do we approach the lawlessness, the crime, the lies and deceit, the slander, cruelty and senseless violence, also the ruthless ambition for power and success, wealth and good fortune that cares little for the plight or need of others, that we witness all around us? What are we to do in the face of so much evil and selfishness in our world?

What about our own lives? How do we measure up? What are our roles in the lives of others, the situations in which we find ourselves and in the bigger scheme of things?

In short, how do we find meaning in our lives?

Exercise for You, The Reader: What Is Man?

Read the full story of Frankl's experiences in the Nazi concentration and death camps recorded in his best-seller: ***Man's Search for Meaning***, available in many languages and most countries of the world. It can be ordered via the internet. Then answer the following questions:
- What horrified you about Frankl's experiences?
- What impressed you about his story?
- How do *you* understand human nature? What is it like?

References

Dimsdale, J. E. (1980). The coping behavior of Nazi concentration camp survivors. In J. E. Dimsdale (Ed.), *Survivors, victims, and perpetrators: Essays on the Nazi Holocaust* (pp. 163–174). New York: Hemisphere.

Frankl, V. E. (1967). *Psychotherapy and existentialism: Selected papers on logotherapy*. New York: Simon and Schuster.

Frankl, V. E. (1968). *Man's search for meaning: An introduction to logotherapy*. London: Hodder & Stroughton.

Frankl, V. E. (1986). *The doctor and the soul: From psychotherapy to logotherapy*. New York: Bantam Books.

Frankl, V. E. (1997). *Viktor Frankl recollections: An autobiography*. New York: Plenum Press.

Freud, S. (1930). *Civilization and its discontents: The standard edition* (Vol. XX1). London: Hogarth Press.

Krasko, G. (2004). *The unbearable boredom of being: A crisis of meaning in America*. New York: Universe Press.

Shantall, T. (2002). *Life's meaning in the face of suffering: Testimonies of holocaust survivors*. Jerusalem: The Hebrew University Magnes Press.

Spiro, K. (2002). *World Perfect: The Jewish Impact on Civilization*. Bookdepository.com

Wistrich, R. (1991). *Antisemitism: The longest hatred*. New York: Pantheon Books.

Wistrich, R. (2010). *A lethal obsession*. New York: Random House.

Chapter 2
An Existential Analysis of the Human Condition

Abstract Our capacities of thought and choice beset us with many questions. We find that we are evaluating creatures; that we uncannily have a sense of what is right and pleasing, and wrong and horrifying in life. In this chapter, the reader is challenged to consider this reality by way of reflective thought about the prime and fundamental aspects of logotherapy, namely, *self-transcendence* as the essence of human existence; *conscience* as a moral compass in evaluating and judging actions or events as either life-enhancing and meaningful or life-destructive and meaningless; Frankl's concept of the *Unconscious God* as a deep sense of being accountable before something or Someone other than ourselves; the *meaning of meaning* as the attitude, choice or action that is required of us in each and every situation of life; entering into meaningful dialogue with life in creatively making our personal contributions to the betterment of the lives of others (*the creative values*); becoming appreciatively responsive to all that is good, true and beautiful about life (*the experiential values*); and courageously taking a stand and having the right attitude in the face of the tragic situations we face in life (*the attitudinal values*). The reader is brought under the strong impression of the truth of Frankl's statement that *what man is, he is not yet, but ought to be and should become.*

Keywords Self-transcendence · Conscience · The Unconscious God · The meaning of meaning · Finding meaning in life · The creative values · The experiential values · The attitudinal values

An Inescapable Truth

It is evident to all of us that we are beset by many questions; questions we sense we are challenged to answer for ourselves. To run from the facts, so evident before us, is to run from life.

We are challenged to think, to make up our own minds.

© Springer Nature Switzerland AG 2020   19
T. Shantall, *The Life-changing Impact of Viktor Frankl's Logotherapy*,
https://doi.org/10.1007/978-3-030-30770-7_2

This is the most evident feature of the human condition: we are questioning and answer-seeking creatures. Unlike any other form of life, human existence is earmarked by *reflective thought*. In fact, we cannot else but think!

Thought has freedom. We do not merely exist in a mindless way. Nor are we patterned by instinct that adjusts our behavior to the demands of the environment in order to perpetuate our existence. We are *aware* that we exist (we have *self-awareness*). We *evaluate* our experiences. We form impressions, that is, have *critical thought* about whatever confronts us or happens to us. Unlike the animal that is instinct-driven and *not able* to be confronted by questions that provoke the search to make sense of the life given to it, human existence is earmarked by ***self-distancing*** and ***self-transcendence***.

We are not closed systems. We can detach or distance ourselves from ourselves, have a questioning and critical look at ourselves, try to make sense of who we are. We need not be self-absorbed, wrapped up in and concerned only with ourselves, impervious to (defensively afraid of) the demands and challenges of our own lives. We can step out, consider our lives for its meaning and destination. We can transcend or rise above what pulls us down; take a stand, make a decision, change the way we look of things; take control of our lives and live it more meaningfully. We can view things from an objective perspective, and come to grips with what we are faced with in life. We can study events, look at our world with a critical eye, form considered opinions about what is happening in it and determine what role it is that we are called to play in it.

"Self-transcendence," said Frankl, "is the essence of human existence."

Why try to escape it?

Unlike Any Other

The human face has a *spiritually* intelligent look about it. It reflects *a given and extra awareness*, not found in the features of the animal or in the features of what scientists have dubbed pre-historic man. The human story, and civilization as we know it, started with Adam. Into him was breathed *spirit,* an awareness of being *addressed.* He could be *spoken to* and he could *hear.* He had *response-ability,* that is, he could comprehend that he could be expected to give an account of himself. Adam was called to task. A Cain was to become his brother's keeper, live by values that *transcend* the animalistic instinct of mere survival. To be human, is to be *humane*, to care for more than yourself or for more than your own.

Human existence is *commissioned* existence.

Only humans, therefore, have a *face*. We alone are called to face things, are brought face to face with the very purpose of our existence. No other creature on earth is called to account, confronted with choice, given the challenge to take control of its life and do something out of the ordinary and exceptional with it!

A call is made upon human life. As humans we are restless. There is the tension of a search. We have to *find* what we are looking for. We seek answers to the quest provoked by our freedom of thought. Who and why are we and what for? We feel *confronted* by these questions and are therefore *answerable* creatures.

Unlike the animal that simply has its existence, our purpose for existing must be *achieved*. It is not a natural given, fallen in the lap, but a *potential* we have the commission to realize.

How distinct we are; how awesomely different! How lifted above and freed from the constrictions of animal or pre-historic existence; what possibility for greatness has been opened up to us!

Why not think about it?

A Deeper Injunction

Our freedom of thought has a compelling focus, one we *cannot* escape: We have *conscience*, a consciousness of what ought and what ought not to be. We uncannily know, have an inherent sense of what is expected of us, what kind of people we are meant to be, what others and what our world are supposed to be like. We all have imprinted within the depths of our knowing an *idea* of what we must be like, something like an i*mage* of what we ought to be like, a kind of *ideal self* that we feel we should live up to in some way. Failing this image fills us with feelings of guilt and shame, an uncanny sense of *unease*. We cannot really sanction what we sense is wrong about us, not right about our behavior. And so too with our world, with what is happening around us. We have a moral yardstick, a critical awareness that evaluates both ourselves and the world we live in. This sense of knowing is inherent to us, is an essential part of our formation as human beings.

None of us can really escape the awareness of what we are *pre-destined* or *ordained,* that is, *created* and therefore *commanded* to be. We are *expected* to be what we are called upon and well able to be. It is something put before us, something that confronts us, given to us to consider. What will we do about it?

The choice to become what we were preordained to be, is ours!

The Freedom of Responsibility

Frankl described our freedom of thought and decision as *the freedom of responsibility.* We are free to be responsible. This is our *only* freedom. "All freedom is a 'from what' and a 'to what.' The 'from what' of man's freedom is his being driven, and the 'to what' is his being responsible, his having conscience" (Frankl 2000: 59).

Freedom outside of the context of our ability and therefore injunction to be responsible is sheer lawlessness. It is the chaos of arbitrariness expressed in sayings such as "who's to say, who knows, your opinion is as good as the next man's" and "anything goes," right down to "nothing matters much at all." It is the cynicism expressed as "who cares?" And "who is to tell me what to do?" It is the callous attitude behind such statements as "every man for himself" and "who is my neigh-bor?" or "am I my brother's keeper?" It also expresses itself as an intolerance of divergent points of view. Taking a belligerent stand, it disallows others the right to their own points of view. Arrogance is an exercised dictatorship over our own minds and an oppressive, judgmental and rejectionist orientation towards others.

Freedom without responsibility is either an indulgence in freedom or an intoler-ance of freedom itself!

The misuse and abuse of freedom is the outcome of a life without true purpose and direction, leading nowhere but to the dead end of abject futility and meaning-lessness. It is a *nihilism* (the belief in *non-meaning* in the abrogation of any real meaning or enduring values in life) that Frankl sought to combat all his life long. It is in a very real sense a *self-destructive* existence.

To turn our back on what we are meant to be, is sheer folly!

But where does our search to get out of a situation devoid of any purpose: a *free-dom for nothing*, towards purposefulness: *a freedom for something*, lead us to? What is it that we really need and want, and yes, if it is a sense of meaning (something stable, enduring, self-affirming and good), where and how is this found?

What do we mean by meaning?

The Meaning of Meaning

Frankl (1988) categorically stated that meaning cannot be created but must be *found*. "Meanings are discovered but not invented." Frankl contended that we expe-rience or find meaning in three ways or in three sets of common meanings which, because they are common to us all, are called *values*. Frankl singled out what he called: the **creative values** – that which we contribute to life; the **experiential val-ues** – that which we receive from life; and, the greatest of all, the **attitudinal values** – the stand we take in the face of unavoidable suffering.

All of these values are achievements of *finding* meaning in life, meanings that are *there to be found*. Any effort to create such meaning for ourselves will prove futile. Let us explore the truth of the aforementioned statement in the experiences of our own lives, starting with the experiential values first.

1. *Experiential values*

Most of this will concede the fact that meaning is found in an experience of something beautiful, sublime, awesome, inspirational and uplifting. All of these features are found in love. "Man is saved in and through love", Frankl exclaimed! Love *enlivens* us, comes to us as a boundless treasure and blessing. Is love for the taking? Can you force someone to love you, or force yourself to love, or do you *find* love or come to love someone in your life? How wonderful, what a miracle it is, if someone loves you!

Love is *awakened* in you towards someone *other* than yourself.

How do you come to love someone beyond just physical attraction or romantic notions?

Love is deeply and profoundly *spiritual* and has very little to do with mere sexual attraction and the emotional fantasies attached to that. It is very far removed from sexual lust. Lusting after another is to use the body of another for the sole purpose of satisfying pressing sexual urges. In humans, this type of animalistic intercourse is rape. On a more than just a physical level, the desire to "make love" is to fulfil a psychological need: the need to be loved. This kind of attraction to someone is an excitement about yourself as someone that is being loved, found attractive or needed. Such romantic feelings are very self-focused. It can come and go and attach itself to various partners that can fill the same role. But between loving partners, their sexual union is about *oneness.* It is a union of love that has *more* physical pleasure and *deeper* emotional satisfaction as outcomes of their love for one another. This is a sexuality of *joy* so profound that it often causes *weeping* because of the beauty of it!

You come to really love someone because you see the beauty, the specialness, the admirable and exemplary in them. You see them in all that they uniquely are, have the capacity to be and to become, you see their unique being, their potential for greatness, the unscathed beauty of the human spirit, the divine spark of being that they have so impressively realized or are busy realizing or have the potential to realize in their lives. You love someone you respect, someone singular, someone that personifies or reflects what you truly admire and desire to see not only in others but in yourself also. It is something good, of great worth and magnificence, something you cannot command to have but are overwhelmed by when you find it! Very much beyond need-love, it is *gift-love,* something precious, something to treasure. Need-love can attach itself to anyone. Not so real love. **Real love is a covenantal relationship of supreme commitment and devotion, a pledge of faithfulness and loyalty one to the other**. This love never dies and is felt even after the death of the loved one. The person who is truly loved remains beloved, and irreplaceably so, forever!

Similarly, that which inspires, uplifts and blesses you *comes* or is *offered* to you, it *involves* you, calls forth a response from you. You find yourself drawn to it and connecting with it in a profound and personal way. Beautiful music uplifts you; great works of art inspire you. You just *love* it! Even in composing music or in creating works of art or writing poetry or literature, something "spoke" to you, moved you; was awakened in you. You are giving expression to something you have *experienced* or grasped; something that was *there* with which to compose music, create an art work or write a poem or book about! We create from something that was *already there,* already created, already in existence. That is why the magnificence and awesome beauty of creation fills us with such awe.

Our creativity is a *response* to the awe and magnificence of creation, of meaning that is *there* to be found!

Not only things beautiful, but also every act of goodness means something to us. Witnessing the goodness of humane acts of lovingkindness *moves* us. Such things bring tears to our eyes; we appreciate them deeply.

And what about truth, that which has a profound ring of "this is it!" to it? The teaching, study or realization of truth, the deep grasp of the meaning of something, instructs and enlightens us, broadens our vision, deepens our understanding. It inspires and thrills us; moves us to action! How we love and appreciate the truth, how we value *truthfulness* in the world! What a victory over the ugliness of deceit, lies, hypocrisy, vanity and falsehood!

Frankl described all the above experiences of meaning as *experiential values.* In the experiencing of what is **beautiful and good and true**, we receive so much from life, it simply blesses us with a sense of meaning! These values, Frankl explained, are what we *take,* that is, *receive* from life. Taking from life in this way means that we become receptive or open to what is beautiful, good and true in life. We embrace it! We cannot have something we refuse to take. Only if we truly *value* something, see its beauty, its goodness, its truth, does it have meaning for us at all. Without "receiving" these gifts, we will not experience the joy of having them!

How can we have something we refuse to receive?

2. *Creative values*

The *creative values* are experienced when we make any kind of worthwhile contribution to the world around us through the creative things we do. Whereas experiential values refer to what we *take* or receive from life, creative values refer to what we *give* to life. The meaning that emanates from creative values is found in doing what we feel *called upon to do,* for example, doing anything well, whether it is in rendering a service to others or in committing ourselves to a cause in a wholehearted way. The very many devoted acts we perform in seeing to the needs of our loved ones make us feel blessed and needed.

What meaning is there if we have nothing and no-one to love and care for; if we are not *presented* with duties, tasks and responsibilities, causes to commit ourselves to or problems to face and do something constructive about? All these things come from *outside* of ourselves, challenging us to action or response. What we try to force or manipulate to serve our own interests turn out to be mistakes. Running after prestige and a show of success will remain just that: a show. Even building up an empire of success and reputation will remain as mere and collapsible structures without the content of real meaning to it. It does not give us what we were seeking for in the first place. A job, for example, remains just a job, a cumbersome obligation, without the creative element to it. When a job becomes something we are uniquely responsible for, it turns into a vocation, a mission in life!

3. *Attitudinal values*

Lastly, there are what Frankl called: *attitudinal values.* These values are to be found in how we deal with unavoidable suffering, with something we had nothing to do with and could not be blamed for. We may be crippled; we may have been born with some or other constitutional dysfunction and be burdened with some or other physical or mental affliction. We may have grown up in a very impoverished or dysfunctional family and be left with many painful emotional wounds because of it. A tragic accident can happen to us. We can be the victims of a natural disaster, or the victims of crime and injustice, or of a terror attack, or of war, be caught up in a revolution, or suffer the oppression and persecution of tyrannical regimes. We can lose a loved one; even have our entire family wiped out. We may even be faced with our own impending death in the contracting of a deadly disease. We can have a heart attack or a stroke leaving us weakened or even incapacitated. These are all situations we were powerless to prevent or avoid. Even an unhappy or terrible childhood is a matter of fate. We were not responsible for it happening to us. The hurt that others inflict upon us is also a matter of fate. We cannot change others to be what they should be towards us. We also cannot go back into our past and change things, put them right; make the people who inflicted hurt upon us change face. "If only" is a futile lament. The past is past. We can only deal with what it does to us now, in our present lives, in a way different than the way we have dealt with or have things happen to us in the past.

We can change ourselves.

Unavoidable suffering tests us to the uttermost. "Why has this happened to me? How could this happen? Why was I subjected to all this? How can this be just, right or meaningful? It is so unfair!" These kinds of situations call for courage, for a way of dealing with it far beyond just in ordinary ways. Here something *extraordinary* is called for.

If we can make it here, we can make it anywhere!

Ecce Homo!

A heroic dealing with and exemplary attitude towards something painful, tragic or fateful is much more admired and respected than acts of charity and goodness in favorable circumstances. That is why Frankl contended that in situations of unavoidable suffering we can achieve the greatest meaning, take on the greatest human stature possible. How we admire someone who has overcome a terrible life or an awful blow of fate in a heroic, dignified and exemplary way!

What a feat if we can turn a tragedy into a spiritual triumph in the way we deal with what has happened to us and/or to others in the attitude we display towards it! We may be powerless to change what happened or is happening, but how magnificently we can rise above it; have victory over it! Tragic situations have the potential to call out the best in us; call forth hidden spiritual resources and strengths in us; develop strong character traits like tolerance and perseverance; provoke hope that can even turn into resolute faith, patience, inexplicable calm, a peace that passes understanding and an ability to suffer with grace and, how extraordinary: without depression or complaint! We can become more tolerant, accepting of fate, more flexible and open-minded, live with uncertainty in a new and positive way. Our faith in the meaningfulness of life can deepen; we can become more deeply convinced of life's essential goodness. Life holds out an expectation of even greater, more astounding things to come. There is still such a lot to learn from it, to experience about it. We find ourselves pining for what we sense is a World to Come. This faith in an unfathomably wonderful future make us sharply aware of the fact that there is beauty and kindness to be found everywhere, something good to notice in everything and in the people around us.

There is an experience of meaning in life right there where we are, even if in the smallest of ways, in the littlest of things. As we open up to what is forever there to appreciate and enjoy, we can even have moments of feeling overwhelmed by the consoling thought that life is still there and will always be there for us; that we will never be left without it! What can death and the fear of death do to touch these treasures that have become ours through our sufferings? Life becomes incredibly beautiful. It is more intimately ours, more precious to us. We see life as full of surprises, unexpected blessings, as very close and dear to us. We love life, unconditionally, for what it is, always was and promises to be.

In love with life, we surrender to it in awe!

Transported from a worksite back to the camp and crowded around the door of the cattle truck to watch the blaze of red, purple and blue of a magnificent sunset, Frankl heard one of the prisoners sighing:

> How beautiful the world *could* be!

The same sensation that life remains beautiful, despite the pain and ugliness we may have to endure from our fellowmen or the suffering that tragedy may inflict upon us, overwhelmed Frankl upon his release from the camps. Walking through the flowering meadows towards a nearby town, he found himself sinking to his knees as the undisturbed beauty of nature overwhelmed him.

> Larks rose to the sky and I could hear their joyous song. There was no one to be seen for miles around; there was nothing but the wide earth and sky and the larks' jubilation and the freedom of space. I stopped, looked around, and up to the sky – and then I went down on my knees. At that moment there was very little I knew of myself or of the world – I had but one sentence in mind – always the same: 'I called to the Lord from my narrow prison and He answered me in the freedom of space' (Frankl 1968, p. 90).

This is what our suffering has the potential to achieve: We can *prove,* bear witness to the fact that meaning can be found in each and every situation of life, even the worst ones. We can *transcend* our pain, the tragedies that befall us. We can rise *above* the ugly and vicious doings of others. We can triumphantly be what we are as human beings have been commissioned to be!

Way beyond the reach of spoiling by anyone, life's value remains. Life is *always* precious, *always* something to preserve and treasure, experience and live in the best, most receptive and responsible way possible. Seeing it and living it in this way, we become standard bearers, spokespersons for life! We are living testimonies to the fact that life is *unconditionally meaningful.*

"Who Is This Coming Up from the Wilderness, Leaning on the Arm of Her Beloved?" (Song of Solomon 8:5)

Suffering is a watershed experience, a test that refines us. It can bring forth our humanity, strong feelings of compassion and a desire to help; a resolve to do what we can to improve the lot of others - things about ourselves that surprise, even astound us. We lose our indifference, our hardness of heart. We become open to the needs of others, more humane, lovelier in attitude and person than we have ever been before.

We did not know we really had it in us, nor did others know that this is what we were capable of being; that we could be the wonderful people we now prove to be! Our example can bring inspiration and hope, a lifting (awakening) of spirit to countless others. See what a kind word, a loving gesture, can do to bring out the best in others who will respond to you in kind.

Goodness provokes goodness!

Suffering is like a wake-up call; a call to come out of ourselves and into the world that needs us.

Why, therefore, should we be spared suffering? Why should we *not* suffer? We are part of humanity. We share the human lot.

Suffering is another of life's opportunities, yes, and of a truth: its greatest task!

Instead of a lamentable curse, suffering can be seen as a blessing: an opportunity to change things for the better. How much *we* can change for the better in the face of the tragic facts of human existence! Suffering can make us aware of what really matters in life, what is truly precious about life, awaken us to those jewels of experience we do not want to lose and, if we have lost it, provoke a renewed commitment to regain and preserve and foster the very things that make life worth the living.

Life, our lives, the way we live it, can become more important to us than ever before. We can now respond to the situations in our lives in much more sensitive and right, commendable ways. Our attitude towards our suffering can turn our lives around; make it something to behold and admire. We are an inspiration to others, a source of hope and comfort, a reassuring presence in their lives.

The message of worthy suffering is a powerful message of hope: the wrong and evil in the world, the lawlessness that causes so much suffering and despair, *can* be overcome.

It will be defeated.

Good *will* triumph, be proved to be more powerful than evil. This is the faith that the just comfortingly live by.

The Suffering Servant

Human greatness is gained through *compassion*. It is shown forth in the way we serve, assist and care for *the least* or most vulnerable among us.

It is a tragic fact that babies and young children die; that there are hopeless and helpless invalids, the crippled and handicapped, the mentally retarded and the mentally ill - people too restricted by tragic fates to be able to do anything about their lot. But does that make these seemingly miserable and tragic lives meaningless? What about hapless victims of natural disasters like earthquakes, floods, tsunamis, volcanoes and mudslides? What about the starving millions, the homeless, the street children, the victims of terror and war? What tremendous worth is invested in such lives in challenging those who have the capabilities and freedom to do something about their tragic fate! What depth of humanity, what reverence for the preciousness of life, however handicapped, limited or constricted, poverty stricken, diseased, tragically affected and broken, such lives call forth in the lives of more advantaged others! Warped, damaged and powerless lives, lives given over to vulnerability and defenseless helplessness, emit the most powerful call to take meaningful action and change a suffering world.

An answer to the above call, expressed by the Jewish concept *Tikkun Olam* – namely, *to repair the world,* is what makes humanity humane!

The Faith That Sets Us Free

It is therefore absolutely true that meaning is *found,* not only through experiential and creative values but also in the attitude we are to have in our own sufferings, and even more particularly, in the anguished empathy we experience on behalf of a suffering other. This is surely the most precious freedom of all: to not give up on another; to keep on believing in his or her intrinsic worth; to do anything and everything in our power to rescue such a life from whatever misery is holding it captive or to lovingly assist the sufferer in a comforting way.

What a freedom to be able to remain positive, *meaningfully goal-directed;* to retain our faith in the preciousness and meaningfulness of life, to express our belief in the purposefulness of living and to take the stand that we will not give up on life; that life *retains* its meaning and that absolutely *everything* has meaning depending on the way we approach and handle it! The rewards of such a meaning orientation are incalculable.

Life becomes a door of hope into a future we can only dream about!

Do we have this kind of faith in life? This is the kind of faith, Frankl asserted, that floods *all* of life with meaning!

The Call to Meaning

What then is meaning? "*Meaning is what is meant*, be it by a person who asks me a question, or by a situation which, too, implies a question and calls for an answer" (Frankl 1988: 62). Meaning is found in what *confronts or speaks to* us and in how we answer or respond to what we are required or expected (challenged or invited) to experience or do; *what kind of persons we are to be* in each and every situation.

Was the right connection made, did it achieve what it was meant to bring about?

> It is the connection that has meaning. Like an electric plug, designed to be put into an electric socket before the power of the electricity flows through it, our lives, though geared for the experience of meaning, cannot experience the transformative and electrifying power of meaning without connecting to the call made upon it!

Responding in the right way, to what life puts before us, floods our life with meaning. "That was so great: that I did what needed to be done; that I responded the way I should have! I did not miss the mark. How good I feel about this! What an experience that was. How much meaning it has brought into my life! How grateful I am for that opportunity and that I did not turn my back on it by saying no to it. How awed I feel that I had it in me to say yes to what I was called upon to do and actually do it! What a triumph and achievement that was, what an affirmation: I *am* able to be good! There *is* goodness, meaning in life, in each and every situation, I must just know how to perceive and become more aware of it, not close my eyes and ears to it, and be ready to embrace and commit myself to it!"

A Compass for Life

"Meaning is the tension of *direction*", Frankl (1958: 51) stated. It is the tension between what is and what *ought to be*. In every situation, at each moment of time, we are confronted with an awareness of what we are saying or doing and whether we stand approved before our own evaluation of ourselves or not. We even know when we are negligent about, escaping from or trying to avoid dealing with a situation. We also know when we are trying to fool ourselves!

No one can escape the voice of conscience.

It is the task of conscience to disclose to man the unum necesse, the one thing that is required. This one thing, however, is absolutely unique in as much as it is the unique possibility a concrete person has to actualize in a specific situation (Frankl 1977: 34).

We are in *conversation* with life. No two dialogues are ever the same. It is we alone who find ourselves in a particular situation at a specific moment of time under peculiar circumstances. We find ourselves addressed in a very *personal* way. The question is addressed to us and to nobody else. Only we can answer it! Only as *we* respond to the question we are being asked, only as we *answer* it in the right way, that is, in the way it is *meant* to be answered, and do it freely and willingly, do we experience a sense of connection or meaning: "I have done the *right* thing." *Only then* do we experience any real sense of peace or satisfaction; does the whole situation take on meaning or become meaningful to us.

Another famous Logotherapist, Elizabeth Lukas (2000), describes conscience as our ethical sensitivity or "moral compass." She also describes it as our "meaning organ." Meaning is unique to the moment. "What am I to do, now? How am I being *spoken to* in *this* situation?" Our own conscience must be at work! "Conscience could be defined as the intuitive capacity of man to find out the meaning of a situation" (Frankl 1988: 63).

We are constantly being called to be *available* and *there* in each situation, to *be* ourselves in an authentic and very real, open and honest way. *We* must be in everything we experience and do.

We must *meet* life as it comes to us!

The simple point is that we cannot *make* meaning happen. We cannot force ourselves to experience the outflows or consequences of finding meaning. How do you force happiness, joy, spiritual growth, enlightened grasp and profound understanding, a sense of deep fulfillment and truth, treasures hidden in the experience of meaning? Only as we walk in the light of what truly matters in life, does meaning with its consequences or outflows of happiness, joy, spiritual growth, enlightened grasp and profound understanding, a sense of deep fulfillment and truth, "happen" to us!

> If meaning and values were just something emerging from the subject himself – that is to say, if they were not something that stems from a sphere beyond man and above man – they would instantly lose their demand quality. They could no longer be a real challenge to man, they would never be able to summon him up, to call him forth (Frankl 1967: 64).

There is an inspirational take about meaning. It *enlivens* us. It draws out or provokes the best in us to its fullest expression!

The real meanings in life are therefore *given*. We either experience them or we don't, depending on how we respond to the opportunities to experience and realize them.

Before the Court of Conscience

Frankl stated that meaning is not something arbitrary. It emanates from a dimension that *is* and that is *beyond* us. Above our human dimension is the dimension of meaning. Frankl called this the *Transcendent* or *Supra-human* dimension of being.

Not a shadow of contradiction or ambiguity exists on this dimension. It is Absolute: entirely meaningful (filled with meaning alone). Nothing meaningless is transmitted to us from this dimension. It is a dimension of utter clarity and total light. What is transmitted to us from this dimension is, as the Psalmist states, pure, "like silver refined in the finest smelting earth, clarified sevenfold" (Psalm 12:7).

Whatever emanates from the Transcendent or the Divine, *because* it is of divine origin, given by the Divine, is an *imperative*. This is fact, an objective and life-giving truth. We are adjured in the following way: "Do this, the right thing before your own conscience, and you will be sure to experience the meaningfulness (the blessing, the beneficial results or consequences) of what you yourself realize is the only right way to act! What is more, you will discover that other people agree with you. They too realize that there are these unquestionable norms of what is right and good and just, and that what deviates from these norms and in any way nullifies or distorts and falsifies it is *wrong*. Doing what is right holds meaning. Doing what is wrong is a *void;* it holds no meaning at all."

The meanings we commonly experience are *values*, or meanings of universal import. Frankl (1977: 143) contended that "there is hope for survival only if mankind is united by a common will to common meaning – in other words, by an awareness of common tasks." There *are* yardsticks of common import; things we can all agree upon and work towards. These values cannot be twisted around, made out to be something they are not. We cannot say that wrong is right and that right is wrong or give sanction to apathetic, unconcerned or selfishly cruel, lawless, immoral and inhumane behavior. We may try hard to do so, but we will fail. The inevitable end result will prove us wrong. Murder is murder and will always remain murder. There are those who espouse murder in the name of a cause. But however great the effort to justify the malicious plotting and intent to kill off those the murderers hold up as hateful, their acts of murder will always remain just that: murder. They will be judged as murderers and will bring the disastrous consequences of their evil deeds down upon their own heads!

Right will prove to be right and wrong will be shown up as wrong. Our task is to learn to distinguish between the two; to make our choices, one way or the other.

Emerging from the horror of the Holocaust and his own experiences in the hell of the Nazi concentration and death camps, Frankl could clearly testify that there are only two races in the world, the race of the decent and the race of the indecent and that both are found in every nation.

To be a decent human being is to never have malicious intent in wanting to shame or harm others; to prevent and combat suffering in this world, and never to cause it or to stand idly by and see it happen. Frankl saw it as his mission to call the world, every one of us, to this responsibility, even if the race of the decent gets far outnumbered by the race of the indecent.

The question is where we rank ourselves - how we are living *our* lives. We must settle this case ourselves – be our own judge and jury!

A Higher Consciousness

Conscience is an awareness of being *addressed*. Something or someone *other* than ourselves, a situation that faces us, is requiring something from us. A response is demanded from us, but a response of a certain kind. We are to live up to the expectation of how we *should,* or the way we know we *ought to* behave. A *right* action or response is required. Every situation contains a certain *command:* we are called upon to respond in a certain expected way. "Each situation is a call, first to listen, and then to respond" (Frankl 2000: 60). The 'voice' that 'speaks' to us comes to us and resounds within us. It is not our own voice, but a voice that *addresses* us.

> The self cannot be its own lawgiver. It can never issue any autonomous 'categorical imperative' for a categorical imperative can receive its credentials only from transcendence. Its categorical character stands and falls with its transcendent quality (Frankl 1988: 118).

It is our consciousness of being commissioned, that is, our *conscience* that is being addressed.

We cannot just do what we like or act like we feel like acting. We are neither to live by our emotions nor to act out of irrational impulse, or blind instincts. *More* is required of us! We are stopped in our tracks. A *considered* response must be given. There is a norm to live up to – one we know we *can* and, therefore, are expected to live up to. There is a certain and correct response to give in every single situation with which we are confronted.

"Each situation has only *one* answer, the right one," Frankl (1977: 34) maintained. Only the one right way to deal with a situation will work, will have the desired effect. Every other option will fail and not bring about a good or desired outcome. There may be more than one good option. But which one is the right one in any particular moment of time? Choosing a less than best choice will not have the same powerful effect as the one right choice. Even though not a bad choice, it will fall short, effect less than that which could have been.

We realize these truths often only retrospectively: "I should not have said that or behaved that way. I should have known better!" "This is what I should have said or done!" "I missed out; it could have been much better, so much more could have been achieved, had I made the right choice!" Putting this realization into effect will prove the point. Doing the right thing in any situation works - even in admitting a failure or wrongdoing in an attitude of remorse or repentance with the genuine commitment not to make the same mistake the next time round! Mistakes or failures give us a yardstick; make us realize what it is we *should* have done, how we *should* have behaved. That is why Frankl advised that we should live as if we are living a *second* time and as if we are about to make the same mistake we made the first time!

Mistakes and failures have the function to force us to *reconsider*.

We are to be infused with a sense of responsibility, that is, have a considered and aware, discerning and intelligent approach to life, ready to meet each new situation in a way that our conscience dictates. We are not mindless animals but human beings. And being human essentially means to have this higher consciousness, an awareness of the call to master our inclinations and emotions, to direct our thoughts and actions in a responsible way; to constantly bring ourselves and all we are involved with on to a higher level of being; to be the best we can be, to be most fully and most responsibly *ourselves*.

We have to live up to who we are!

The Unconscious God

Frankl (1967: 12) stated that "existence falters unless it is lived in terms of transcendence toward something beyond itself." Only in what can be judged as *lawful*, morally sound and absolutely justifiable and righteous in the way we behave in any particular situation in life, do we find the *guarantee* or *covenant* (absolute and irrevocable *promise*) of meaning in life.

We can thus clearly see and will readily admit that it is not our own whims and fancies or thoughtless, or even stubborn attitudes which are to determine our responses to what we are confronted with in life. To react responsibly is to have a respectful and obedient orientation to *what is required* in each particular instance. We must always remain *open (receptive)* to the demands of the moment. Is it so difficult, therefore, to realize that we are being faced in life with an authority bigger than ourselves? There is something or Someone that can legitimately lay claim to and that has a say in our lives!

"Through the conscience of the human person, a Transhuman agent per-sonats – which literally means, 'is sounding through,'" is how Frankl (2000: 60) described the way our conscience operates.

We are continually being "spoken" to. Are we listening? And are we answering? How are we answering?

Our consciousness of some higher authority with a higher order or code for living may be unprovoked or lie dormant just as much as it can be vigorously *suppressed*. Yet, and however limited or distorted or different and varied our concepts of a higher authority or Transcendent Power may be, a *God-consciousness* is inherent in us as human beings.

> There is a religious sense deeply rooted in each and every man's unconscious depths (Frankl 2000: 14).

Only humans theorize about, worship, deny or set themselves in rebellion against acknowledgment of some higher authority. This opposition is paradoxically manifested in the setting up of a god that suits the particular worshipper and others like him! In creating a "God" that favors you and hates those whom you hate, neatly manoeuvers you out of the awkward position of having to admit that you may be badly in the wrong! The point is that there is in all of us an uncanny awareness of being addressed in whichever way we choose to interpret or distort this fact.

Efforts to fight off this awareness may be the result of a resistance against being personally accountable before any higher authority, especially One Who is Sovereign, a declared One and Only Who solely has a sovereign say over each and every one of our lives. After all, is the Creator not in charge of that which He creates? The thought of a face-to-Face interaction with a Singular Being, One Who continually calls us to a singular account of every once given and singular moment of our unique lives, may be too frightening and awesome for us to bear. We may want to escape the scrutiny of such finalities of judgement. We may want a "sweet" God; one who stands in for us, who offers excuses or justifications on our behalf with the plea that overlooks or covers up our wrongdoings; a God who demands less of us and, in his leniency, lets us off the hook. We are his special, that is, spoilt children that can just run to Him and hide ourselves in his indulgent forgiveness, even if we have proved to be naughty. All that is necessary is just to embrace this sweet oblivion and remove all sense of blame from us.

At the other extreme, resistance against interpreting norms which address and call us to account for our actions as coming from some Divine Being, may be the result of fearing or of objecting to those religions that portray this higher authority or God in His Law-giving capacity as punitive, restrictive and cruel. It is true that rivers of blood have been spilt and are being spilt in the name of religion. "God is on our side!" is the arrogant cry of those who use the name of a supreme deity to elevate themselves above others and even to sanction their hatred and murderous plots in the name of God against those they regard as outside the pale. In the face of this manipulative control over the minds of its indoctrinated followers, often used as weapons or as the means to achieve their inhumane ends, the more benign option is to advocate a humanistic orientation to life in general: "this is what decent people should do". Our responsibility as human beings may then be interpreted as being provoked by our own sense of right and wrong or according to social norms as imperatives if we are to survive as a species and not, in abrogation of these norms, destroy each other with malice, hatred, lawlessness and violence.

However we choose to deal with or interpret the fact of our need to be responsible, there is, as Frankl (2000: 13) stated: "a significant number of people who interpret their own existence not just in terms of being responsible to something" (to some religion or other, or to social and humanistic rules set up by some group or other) "but rather to some*one*, namely, to God" (Frankl 2000: 13).

Frankl (2000: 14) spoke of *the Unconscious God* and explained it in this way: "There is a latent relation to transcendence inherent in man. One might conceive of this relation in terms of a relationship between an immanent self and a transcendent Thou. Man has always stood in an intentional relation to Transcendence, even if only on an unconscious level."

Conscience (an intuitive awareness of right and wrong; what ought to be and what ought not to be) is an uncanny awareness of our existence as sparked by the Divine whether we acknowledge and believe this to be so or not. "Conscience discloses to us the essential transcendence of the spiritual unconscious" (Frankl 2000: 61). We come from somewhere, our existence was intended. We were formed in the womb, given birth to, life entered our lungs. Spirit, a divine spark of peculiar intelligence, unique to us as human beings, was "breathed" into us. It was a potential awareness, inherent to our being, even while we were still in the womb!

Man, in his full consciousness and supremely intelligent awareness of being, may have emerged from a pre-historic image of himself. Pre-historic man is not historic man. He is not Adam. But the point is this: Who gave us this extra or higher form of awareness that began to earmark our existence as distinctly *human*?

Human life, as we now know it, started at a climax point of the evolution of creation. Adam is the crown of creation! He was given the awareness of the Creator. He found himself in a relationship with the Divine. Adam could obey. He could worship! This treasure of human greatness, related as it is to the will of the Divine, is invested in the human breast.

Every single child has an intuitive outreach to a parent-figure. "In the beginning is relation", wrote Martin Buber (1958), in his famous work: *I and Thou*. Without that which the child senses is a life-giving connection to a significant other, the will to live gets seriously injured. Fear and insecurity enter the child's being. Trust and the will to reach out and explore its world are disturbed. An anxious withdrawal and clingy behavior may be the outcome. If not corrected through loving experiences, neurotic states and, in severe cases, mental illness of psychotic proportions can be the result of the thwarting and obstruction of these early stirrings towards meaning in life.

In the deepest of our being we seek our Creator, the reason why we have been given life!

The Irreligiously Religious

As adults, we all uncannily know that we are being called upon to take up our lives in a responsible way and that we are to be held accountable for what we do, especially to innocent others like children, the weak, ill, injured, disabled and elderly, the dependents entrusted to our care. We cannot get away from this inherently provoked awareness, the realizations (reprimand or approval) of our own inner yardstick or conscience.

We cannot really fool ourselves. We know that it is not what we *say* or purport we believe that is a true indication of who we are. It is not in the religious garb we wear or rituals we perform; the front of piety, the outward display of any particular religious persuasion that we hide behind or put up before the world. **It is how we act, what we *do*, that will prove who we really are.** This is the injunction recorded in the books of Law in the Bible, the Torah: "The word is very near you, in your mouth and in your heart, **that you may do it**" (Deuteronomy 30:14). True *confession* (not mere profession) is to put your action where your mouth is. This is *not* to decry certain customs, way of dress or the symbols contained in God-ordained observances such as the donning of prayer phylacteries, practiced by Jews over the ages and still so beautifully manifest among Jews in Israel and elsewhere in the world today. Many religious customs of other faiths also express in an outward form what its followers treasure as meaningful. Such observances can be powerful statements of faith; the outward manifestations of an inner stand. These are ways of showing ourselves to the world; of declaring who we are in the sight of the world. The commission to all of us is to make ourselves *known* in the world but in a way that calls the true magnificence of the human spirit out of hiding!

Frankl (1968: 77) urged us to start thinking of ourselves as those who are being questioned by life – daily and hourly. "Our answer must consist, not in talk and meditation but in right action and in right conduct" (Frankl 1968: 77). This responsibility rests upon all of us, whatever our professed system of belief or unbelief. For even unbelief or atheism is a belief! Therefore, "the question remains whether 'irreligious persons' really exist" (Frankl 2000: 52)!

Even though we cannot see before *Whom* we are living our lives, we somehow know, even in our awareness of ourselves and in the consciousness of how we choose to act, that we are being *watched*. Why do we have the need to present ourselves in a good light and why do we try and convince ourselves of our own worthiness if we did not somehow sense that there is some standard that we are being judged by, some yardstick that our behavior is being held up to? Why do we try to explain, excuse or justify ourselves as if we are under some kind of scrutiny?

Why place ourselves safely behind the walls of belief systems that declare us as being in the right in a very dogmatic (self-righteous) way? There is a great deal of self-defensiveness in the need to rigorously expound, preach or propagate our beliefs and to seek converts to our way of thinking!

Why all these defensive efforts if we do not uneasily and disconcertingly sense that we are under some kind of surveillance? Do we have the uncanny feeling that maybe we are not as right or as truthful as we try and make ourselves out to be?

Are we trying to *prove* ourselves worthy? Or do we want to be declared worthy, uncertain as we are of this fact?

"We are on the stage of life and somehow know that we are seen or being watched even if the audience is hidden by the darkness," Frankl (2000: 147) commented. We are playing out our lives with the inescapable awareness that we are seen, even if only by ourselves before our own consciousness of ourselves. Conscience is such a consciousness, the yardstick by which we measure ourselves in the light of an ideal even if the "audience" (or Onlooker) is hidden from us. We are much like the actor or actress or performers who cannot see the audience before whom they are performing, blinded as they are by footlights and spot lights, yet knowing that they are performing before those who are appraising their performance (Frankl 2000: 14). We all share this awareness, whether we are religious or not and despite the different religious or non-religious views we may hold. This is because we have a common make-up, a common sense that *we were commissioned to become what we were created to be*!

Truth is truth and cannot be denied or lied about. It speaks to all of us!

A Way of Life for Everyone

Frankl (1988: 143) was passionate about his desire that logotherapy should "be available for every patient and usable in the hands of every doctor, whether his *Weltanshauung* (worldview) is theistic or agnostic." Frankl vigorously advocated Logotherapy not as a religion, but as a *therapy,* a way of *healing* available to everyone.

Logotherapy is a human science which proves as fact those fundamentals of human existence that earmark a healthy and meaningful life.

As a therapy, Logotherapy operates on the human plane but is receptive, leaves the door open to truths emanating from a higher or theological plane. "A higher dimension, by definition, is a more inclusive one. The lower dimension is included in the higher one. It is subsumed in it and encompassed by it" (Frankl 2000: 16). That is why faith in the existence of God, or however we choose to interpret and describe our sense of a higher power, is an irrefutable fact of life on the human plane. Faith is an absolute fact, a reality of experience and therefore an inseparable part of human existence. Frankl stated that the search for meaning in life is an expression of man's search for *ultimate* meaning, something that, because of its ultimate nature, if found, floods *all* of life with meaning.

Man is not a closed but an open system. Man has *spirit* (a higher form of intelligence than that of the animal). He is not, like the animal, a two dimensional creature with only a body and soul (or psyche). His whole being is infused with a higher type of awareness. *He is in everything he experiences and does.* He interprets and evaluates, judges and reasons about everything he experiences. He can put body and soul together to work to achieve what he has concluded to be of higher value. He is therefore *open* to be spoken to, and can be addressed. He can be confronted, challenged, called to give an account of himself. He can heed and respond, involve himself and reach out to demands made upon him by something or someone other than himself. He has the power to change himself, to make an impact on his world; to work for a change for good in this world by devoting himself to a higher cause. Because man is therefore not enclosed or patterned within the drives and instincts of lower forms of life, but open to his world and to life and the meaning of it, therapy (or for that matter, any form of belief) must leave the door wide open for a further discovery of meaning on a higher plane of living.

Every fulfillment of meaning leads in an ultimate direction. Growth is a path leading upwards!

The Sovereign Right of Every Person

But, maintained Frankl (2000: 126), "we psychiatrists are neither teachers nor preachers." In Logotherapy, clients are not told what to believe or what they are to do. "The therapist has neither the moral duty nor the right to interfere with the world view of the patient (since any such interference would be a dictate by virtue of the therapist's authority)." Logotherapists do not exercise persuasion to their own committed points of view but lay the facts of the client's search for meaning on the table. Logotherapy seeks to assist people to find their *own* way in life and to respond to the call to become what *they* are meant to be, each in their own unique situation and life.

We each give a singular answer in our unique circumstances to the call that comes *personally* to each one of us. We have to become our optimal best, show forth true humanity, in our own and specific lives. But the call is the same and is the *one and only* call that comes to all of us. It therefore expects the same responses, according to the same yardsticks, from every one irrespective of who we are, where we are, or what our singular and unique role or mission in life may be.

"It is therefore a fact that those who regard themselves as irreligious are no less capable of finding meaning in their lives than those who consider themselves to be religious" (Frankl 2000: 152). This is in no way paradoxical if we understand that all of us, whether religious or not, and whether we hold the same religious views or not, are *well able to be* in tune with our divinely sparked awareness of what we are meant to be like as human beings.

The choice of response is ours. We alone can say a "yes" to this awareness. Nobody can do it for us. We also have a right to say "no" to it. The responsibility of how we answer the call or live our lives is ours, and ours alone! Sometimes what is right can only be proved to be right by what is wrong. What is right works, what is wrong does not! So what if our cynicism, our lack of conviction, needs the space of enquiry and experimentation? Frankl applauded this type of philosophical enquiry. We need to think for ourselves, even in questioning ways, before we can properly arrive at the truth of a matter.

Ignorance is not bliss. It is blind. It is also foolish, naive and lacking. It cannot convince or hold an argument. It has nothing thought-provoking to say. The ignorant can easily be misled and fall trap to irrational, silly, superstitious and even dangerously devious ways of thought. Ignorance can be indoctrinated.

We must all learn; seek knowledge. We all need to be educated to increase our awareness, our intelligent discernment of what is of value and what not. It is a *commission* to mature, to reflect upon and study what life is all about; to come to fully know what is expected of us.

A People of the Book

There is a Book of books, the Bible, with a stamp of Authority that is awesome. Here is its astounding mystery. Its Laws or instructions for meaningful living are spelt out. They are written down and can be read. There are very clear do's and don'ts in life. These truths are *manifest*. They are *real* and can be experienced. But there are great depths of meaning, a myriad of applications behind each statement or commission (law or command) in the Bible. The how to live it is in the context of a relationship that exceeds every dogmatic prescription of how it must operate since this relationship is profoundly personal. The Law becomes lawful and proves to be lawful in *living* it. It is here, in real life, that there is a growing grasp of the intricacies, the delicate nuances, all the rich aspects of godly living.

Truth is *realized*. It does not fall in the lap. Truth can hardly be realized if it is not reflected upon, studied, wholeheartedly searched for and awesomely comprehended. How important, therefore, its exposition! How else can a concrete and naïve reading of the Bible, the misinterpretations and falsification of its facts when seen through the lens of a particular bias or dogmatic persuasion, be confronted and corrected? Who can teach it? Surely only those whose lives can testify to the truth of it; those who have earnestly searched for, found, lived and so verified the laws of godly living as immutable and, therefore, as powerfully *transformative*.

It is incontestably a fact that to search for information, more knowledge; to intensely study many sources of knowledge, to contemplate and reflect on expounded truths; to study its applications in all of life; to sit at the feet of the great masters of thought; to debate matters with one another, enable us to come to more informed opinions. We can speak with greater authority, hold to more valid points of view. But the greater truth is that these more informed views of life help us to more keenly discern how they apply to us in real life. This is where our knowledge becomes truly authoritative. Only then can we truly bear witness to the truth of what we have studied. Only then can we silence belligerent critics, take a sane and rational but also powerful stand against destructive arguments and successfully counteract fanatical viewpoints or misled or distorted opinions.

We are to be truth-seekers, always!

Learning more through reflective thought and life experiences, scaling the heights of wisdom, is an ever continuing process. We must have debate, reason with one another. What is more, different points of view, new perspectives, even contrary opinions that provoke us to more diligently search out the truth for ourselves, serve to more vividly enlighten our minds. So great is Truth that even the most admirable saint or sage or school of thought or religious viewpoint can fall short of it! We need different voices, various points of view, healthy debate. Only the Messiah can claim perfection and can command that we emulate God's ways as they are *manifested* by him. It is this perfection that places all of us under the scrutiny of correction!

The Pursuit of Truth

Irving Charles Krauthammer (2015), a famed American political columnist, Pulitzer prize winner, Harvard-trained psychiatrist and best-selling author, wrote what he called: *A note to readers*, just weeks before his death after a protracted battle with cancer:

> "I believe that the pursuit of truth and right ideas through honest debate and rigorous argument is a noble undertaking. I am grateful to have played a small role in the conversations that have helped guide this extraordinary nation's destiny. I leave this life with no regrets. It was a wonderful life – full and complete with the great loves and great endeavors that made it worth the living. I am sad to leave, but I leave with the knowledge that I lived the life that I intended."

The Truth Made Flesh

Truth has to be realized and, once realized, it has to be made real, lived wholeheartedly with firm commitment and zeal, even if what we have come to know as a truth might yet be far from the whole truth. We serve the truth, rather than have it. The truth has us: has its hold, makes its demands upon us. We can therefore only yield to it!

Frankl (2000: 18) stated: *"Not there is no truth: there is. **And there can be only one truth.** But no one can be absolutely sure it is he who has arrived at this truth. We have to stick to our conscience."*

Conscience, as a consciousness of what is required of us to grow to full human stature and fill out our destined place in life with meaningful content, is something that needs to be developed and refined, sharpened with discernment and wisdom. If left dormant, unprovoked, unenlightened and dull, what is to prevent men from becoming savages, crude and cruel with little sense of decency or grasp of what is right (good towards others) and what is bad, (destructive and evil in its effects upon the lives of others)?

We do not live by bread alone. We live by instruction, but instruction of the right kind! False prophets and teachers abound. Extensive but flawed knowledge can be gained from instructions that are based on devious and twisted forms of thinking or on vain philosophies of life. Not only can such knowledge be misleading, but also intelligence can be *evil*, that is, put to very evil, destructive use. Hitler was a *genius* of deception!

Only one who bears full witness to the truth by bearing the fruit of the truth in real life, by the kind of exemplary person he or she is, has the power to set others free from deception. This is the image of Messiah and of our own messianic commissions in life!

Truths that emanate from the Transcendent must be lived on the human plane. That is where truth manifests. That is where it is made *real,* becomes convincing.

True religion is a godly way of life!

The Certainty of Uncertainty

We are not all-knowing creatures, gods unto ourselves. "Will a man make gods for himself, which are not gods?" (Jeremiah 16:20). We only experience revelations of the truth. And, as Frankl categorically stated, truth is no man's possession. We cannot own truth but only come to grasp and live it from one level to the higher and next level of understanding. We are to become ever more convinced of (persuaded by) what is true.

In its *ultimate* sense, Absolute Truth, truth that is without ambiguity or variation (James 1:17), is ever ahead of us, beckoning. Realizing it in an ever more profound way, we give expression to it, ever more obediently. We *live* it; act according to its injunctions. As we do, we grow in human stature (Luke 2:52).

It is a fact that also the so-called irreligious, the agnostic and the atheist can uncover truths. We can learn from everybody. Our understanding is something that grows. Not knowing everything, our understanding is limited. We can mistake something for the truth or have only a partial understanding of something. We each have a particular point of view, a different perspective on things. We may be seeing the truth from one angle. But there are a myriad of ways of looking at the same thing. We can concur on some things, even strongly agree on basics or fundamentals and share a common viewpoint.

Frankl warned strongly against what he called *reductionism*, our tendency to want to explain everything from just a certain perspective, to make our truth out to be the whole truth. If we do that, we lose out. Only the fearful withdraw within a defensive structure of set boundaries. We may fail to see the incredibly rich and various ways truth can reveal itself, become known to us. We miss out on the whole. We reduce ourselves, come to be little people, pompous and arrogantly sure of ourselves. We cut ourselves off from others who differ from us. In fact, we stop learning. Our spiritual growth, our wonderful leaps of grasp of more and more of more, is stunted.

How displeasing among us are the bigots. How loathsome the fanatics. How sickeningly pretentious the arrogant and high-minded!

Different Levels of Being

There is a *nihilism,* a declaration of "a nothing but-ness" about even brilliant points of view that seek to explain everything from the discovery of truth in just one area of being. Truth is to be discovered everywhere, on every level of being and on every level in a multiplicity of ways. But every truth is only part of a bigger picture. Never can a part encompass the whole. If even all the parts together cannot make up the whole, then what can? Frankl (1988: 22) demonstrated this truth by what he termed *dimensional ontology.*

There are different dimensions of being but each dimension is overarched or taken up in an ever higher dimension of being. Frankl spoke about **the physical, the psychological and spiritual dimensions of being. Man has body, soul and spirit.** On the physical and crudely emotional level we have much in common with the animal and operate according to the laws of nature, laws of cause and effect. But there is also a psychology, an emotional complexity in human behavior that is infused with much greater mental capacities and greater and more complex social structures and behaviors than we observe in the animal world. We can confuse or even manipulate the laws of cause and effect to disastrous effect! When we come to the spiritual dimension, there are capacities of thought and insight, freedom of will and choice, strengths of conviction and a sense of purpose, not found in the animal kingdom at all. The spiritual dimension is the uniquely *human* dimension. It is open to the Transcendent.

There is much to be discovered on every dimension of being, whether on the spiritual plane in seeking meaning and direction in life, and in addressing philosophical, ethical, value and faith issues; or whether in an exploration of the mysteries and wonders of the human psyche; in the discovery of the wonders of our physical beings, the incredibly harmonious way our organs and bodily functions all fit and work together. Research has revealed how our spiritual well-being can release the healing properties of our bodies and emotional or psychological hang-ups and how negative life orientations can damage our physical well-being and can make our emotions go haywire.

Frankl maintained that it is necessary for expertise to be developed in absolutely every field of knowledge. Specialists must specialize but specialists must not *generalize.* One truth, from a limited perspective, cannot hold, be a truth that explains everything everywhere else!

A Little Lower Than the Angels

I am fearfully and wonderfully made (Psalm 139:14).

The very same principle, namely, to not declare any specific dimension of being as an absolute, applies to the uniquely *human* dimension of being as well. We have a physical and psychological way of being, but as humans we are essentially *spiritual.* We seek for the *more* in life. We are not robots, nor are we animals, but we are also not gods. To be human is to reach out to *the more than we are.* We live by the grace of faith and that kind of faith produces decent and moral – godly – behavior. We act on the basis of our faith; give expression to what we deeply believe. Faith, if it is faith, draws ever *closer* but never arrives. The wonders of our being are too magnificent to grasp; their Source forever incomprehensibly great!

We cannot reduce God, pull Him down to a human level; make a religion out of Him. We cannot be dogmatic about what we believe. God, if He is God, is not human. Because He is God and we are human, we cannot fully comprehend Him.

> The dimensional difference between the ultimate being and human beings prevents man from really speaking of God. Speaking of God implies making being into a thing. It implies reification. Personification would be justified. In other words, man cannot speak of God but he may speak to God. He may pray (Frankl 1988: 146).

We do not *have* absolute truth but can only have faith that there *is* ultimate and absolute Truth and, even if not fully sure of it, seek to live by the light we have of it, truthfully.

Conscience, as the capacity whereby we detect truths as these emanate from the Divine dimension of being, is a human phenomenon. However, it can be an all too human phenomenon. "It not only leads us to meaning but may also lead us astray. This is part and parcel of the human condition. *Conscience may err*, and I cannot know for certain whether my conscience is right and another's conscience, which tells him something different, is wrong, or whether the reverse is true" (Frankl 2000: 118). Does the reality of this kind of uncertainty nullify conviction? Of a truth, no! Frankl referred to the beautiful saying of Gordon Allport: "We can be at one and the same time half-sure and whole-hearted."

Humility earmarks the true human condition. It is in humility that human greatness is to be found.

Faith is a risk, the risk of courage; the courage to have my mistaken beliefs corrected in the light of a greater truth!

The Imperative

Here is *the* imperative life gives us: We must raise questions, study, learn about and critically and deeply reflect on life. We must let the truths we are searching for, and the answers that come up in the process, *resonate* with us. That is the nature of our freedom: that we must search out the truth, discover and embrace it. This would hardly be possible if we were not able to put ourselves at a critical distance from what confronts us with a possible answer. It is our *prerogative* to question and to doubt. How else can we reflect or think about anything if there were no alternatives, no possibly different answers, if we did not have the freedom and capacity to weigh up different answers and choose the right one for ourselves? How else do we learn, gain wisdom and understanding, if not through contradictions, perplexities, confusing issues and contrary points of view?

If everything was beyond question, bright and clear as daylight, it would rule out choice! We would be *compelled* to accept the truth. What freedom is there in that, what authentic and personal conviction would there be? We would have no voice. No "Yes!" to a *revealed* truth, to something deeply and comprehensibly and intelligently *grasped*, would be possible. Thought would be extinguished. All praise and gratitude, worship and joy would be silenced!

God is not an autocrat. We are granted the space of a freedom of choice. We are granted the privilege to think for ourselves; to arrive at an ever greater comprehension of the truth through personal conviction. This wondrous capacity is the treasure we carry.

God has faith in *us!*

> Strength from faith is God's faith in us (Sacks 2000).

A Commitment Given in Freedom

We would lose our humanity if we ourselves could not vouch for, embrace and give expression to the truth in our own lives. Commitment is given in freedom! That is why Frankl 2000: 140), far from condemning so-called unbelievers, *commended* those who doubted and questioned whether life has any meaning. "I regard it as a prerogative and *privilege* of man not only to quest for a meaning to his life but also to question whether such a meaning exists at all. No animal asks such a question."

It is therefore even a holy aspect of our humanity that we can say: "No!" to life and disobey its injunctions. Nobody is forcing us to say yes. We therefore have a prerogative to become guilty of resisting what life seeks to teach us. Again, Frankl stressed that it is man's prerogative to become guilty and his task to overcome guilt.

We learn through our mistakes, our misconceptions, our wrongdoings; our incorrect or just partially true view of things that had us act in a less than truly acceptable way. This is a vital and necessary part of our rights as human beings, namely, to establish what life requires and expects of us – to find the "what for?" reason of human existence. And this search, because we are human, can also miss its mark. We are taught, corrected and brought on course through failure and guilt.

We must convince ourselves. Only if we are *convicted* of wrongdoing or of a destructive and distorted worldview, will we repent of it! Even partial blindness, when given full sight, breaks us through to a level of recognition and acknowledgement, to a truth we have never realized before.

Truth humbles us!

A Human Versus a Sub-human Way of Life

The main thrust of our thinking is, therefore, *to make sense of our lives* within the bigger scheme of things. Anything short of this makes us feel restless and dissatisfied in some deep kind of way. "The heart is restless until it has found and realized meaning in life," Frankl stated. The deepest and most profound motivation in the human breast is what Frankl called the will to *meaning*. We are most essentially *meaning-directed*. "It is the meaning of meaning to set the pace of being" (Frankl 1988: 51). We need to move from meaning to meaning, from one level of grasp to the next. It is our spiritual breath of life!

A lack of movement in the direction of grasp and comprehension, of realizing the supreme worth, beauty and goodness of life and living it in ways that make us supremely *humane*, will confine us to what Frankl called the *subhuman* levels of existence. If the human spirit is not provoked to achieve its potential through learning, in being educated to higher levels of grasp and the achievement of ever more humane and godly ways of living, only the concrete and material will present itself to the most tangible of the physical senses: that which you can see, touch and taste. Without *listening* and *hearing,* and *smelling out* the truth (grasping the meaning of it all through a *spiritual* awakening), only the physical instincts and drives and the crudely emotional needs will have the upper hand. Man will then live on an *animalistic* level of being. However, because man is gifted with *spiritual intelligence*, this, our animalistic way of life will be a *fallen* state of being. An animal cannot be conniving, dishonest, decadent and debased. There is no crime in the animal world. All these states are the results of human *choice*. A refusal to obey the injunctions of conscience is a choice! An animal is what it is. As human beings we must become what we *ought to be*. If we *fail* to be what we should and were created to be, our motives can become *corrupt*. Meaning must be infused into all we are and do. For this purpose we have been given *freedom* of being. The choice to live up to what we are commissioned to be, is left up to us. We can obey or disobey. We are *self-determining* creatures. We determine if we will be what we ought to be or not.

The outcome is up to us.

A Personal Experience of the Meaning of Life

If we are downright truthful with ourselves, we will have to admit that we must, are even *compelled*, to make *personal* sense of our lives. Frankl asserted that truth can only be truth to us, that also religious beliefs can only be real, if they have become real to us *personally*. We must feel convinced about it ourselves. It must not be something we hang onto just because we grew up with it; were taught or indoctrinated, passively conditioned to follow suit. That would be to have no mind of our own.

We must feel that we are touched by life in some enlivening way; be drawn to, invigorated and inspired by answers that *address us in a profoundly personal sense.* Nothing else will suffice, also not in the sphere of religion. "If religion is to survive, it will have to be profoundly personalized", Frankl (2000:85) stated.

> Religion is genuine only where it is existential, where man is not somehow driven to it, but commits himself to it by freely choosing to be religious. The existentiality of religiousness has to be matched with its spontaneity. Genuine religiousness must unfold in its own time. Never can anyone be forced to it (Frankl 2000: 71).

Only if we feel personally addressed, personally called, personally destined towards achieving what truly matters to us in our very own lives in the deepest sense of the word, and which we have personally *experienced* as such, will we be at all satisfied. We *know* that we *must* be able to say; "Yes!" to our lives. "This is it! This is for me! This is *life*! This is where I feel fully myself and totally at home! This is *me*!"

Paradoxical as it may seem, we see that a sense of *true* self-satisfaction or fulfillment only comes to us when we are *drawn out of the narrow confines of restrictive thought patterns into an acknowledgement of and obedience to a truth much greater than all of our arguments combined!*

This is what a Job was finally confronted with as he came to clarity about his own life and sufferings beyond all the unsatisfactory answers he was given about his predicaments and about life by those who were trying to explain why he was suffering. We are not to be problem centered, trying to solve the problems of the world, but *meaning* centered.

What is life expecting of us?

> Then the Lord responded to Job from out of the whirlwind, and said: 'Who is this who gives murky counsel with words without knowledge? Gird your loins like a warrior (brace yourself like a man), and **I will question you, and you shall answer Me** (Job 38:1–3).

Life Questions Us!

This then, is the most profound truth that Frankl himself realized and that he formulated as the very heart of Logotherapy in its effort to assist those in search of meaning in their lives.

It is not we who are questioning life for its meaning (and coming up with answers according to our own particular upbringing or communal traditions, or according to our own ideas, theories, needs and fancies) **but life that is questioning us**.

None of us can escape accountability. Life does not have to explain itself to our questioning of it. Instead, it is we who are answerable to life. "It is we ourselves who must answer the questions that life asks of us, and to these questions we can respond only by being responsible for our existence" (Frankl 1997: 56).

Only as we lead fully accountable and responsible lives are we fully ourselves!

> Life's meaning is an unconditional one, at least potentially. That unconditional meaning, however, is paralleled by the unconditional value of each and every person (Frankl 1984: 176).

If we have dispelled the doubts we had about life, we have dispelled the doubts we had about ourselves!

Tragic Optimism

Logotherapy is the most positive of all therapies for the very reason that it addresses the negative and tragic issues of life not as lamentable afflictions we are all doomed to suffer but as tasks we are challenged to embrace, that is, overcome in a spiritually mature and victorious way. In fact, the commission of our lives is to overcome evil with good. We cannot ensure a happy, problem- and pain-free existence for ourselves. We are mortal and very fallible creatures. We all have a part in wrongdoing, failure, suffering and dying; our share of tragedy. But what we do with these negative and tragic actualities of life, how we deal with problems and distresses that come our way, will determine whether we are victims or victors, whether our lives are filled with negativity and despair or full of faith and meaning. In fact, the challenge is to achieve *full human stature* – that which we were created for and commissioned to be!

Logotherapy contends that we are *meant* to be victors, that we have been given the freedom and ability and, therefore, *the responsibility* to overcome evil with good. We are to take a victorious stand against every negative thing in life, whether it be in ourselves (wrong inclinations and negative emotions that we act upon to the detriment of ourselves and to the hurt of others, and that we are challenged to correct and change), or outside ourselves (difficult, hurtful or tragic situations that we are challenged to deal with in a mature and morally exemplary way). The successful performance of these attitudinal tasks clears the air, so to speak.

Freed from the negative and draining emotions of worry, anxiety, fearfulness and uncertainty, we are free to fully appreciate and enjoy every wonderful blessing and preserve and foster and fully commit ourselves to what is good and valuable in life. We grow in human stature. We experience the highest and most optimal state of mental health. We are spiritually vibrant. We have a destiny and are steadily giving it shape. This sense of vibrancy and meaning is sought after by everyone who suffers. Knowing how to attain and experience it, we become powerful instruments of healing and sources of inspiration, encouragement and blessing to others.

Life is ours, waiting for us to live it!

About This Book

As a profound wisdom about life and living, Logotherapy is, above all, *counseling*. Imagine, therefore, the sacred privacy of the office or consulting room of a logotherapist and the encounter with the client that is to take place there. This encounter is illustrated in the most real way possible, namely, as taking place between me and you, the reader. It is basically a deep encounter with ourselves in relation to others, to the life given to us all.

The following is the process we will be going through together:

- **Tender beginnings: the unscathed human spirit.**
- **Who are you sitting opposite me? The person of the client.**
- **Who am I in relation to you? The person of the logotherapist.**
- **What is your real problem? The crisis of meaning.**
- **How am I to address your problems? The methods and techniques of logotherapy.**
- **Why does logotherapy work? The transformational power of meaning.**
- **A new look at psychopathology: this is not you.**
- **The meaning of suffering: you are chosen.**
- **Ultimate meaning: your destiny in life.**
- **The choice is yours: become what you have been created to be!**

In its most profound sense, logotherapy represents the most private and personal *dialogue* that life has with each one of us. That conversation unfolds from birth and continues throughout life. Logotherapy embraces that which is in the first and final instance *a call*. It is a most basic call directed to the first man in human history:

Adam, where are you?

Exercise: The Power of Right Choices

At this point of our reflections on the truth of the tenets of logotherapy, it will be most enlightening to read, once more, the story of Frankl's suffering during the Holocaust in his book *Man's Search for Meaning*. Note every critical choice he made. Using the above title as a guideline, answer the following questions:

- What critical choices did Frankl make at the outset of his journey into suffering?
- How did Frankl come to realize that suffering was another of life's tasks, even its greatest task, one which he did not need to run away from but needed to *embrace?*
- What sustained Frankl, gave him courage, or even inspired him during the time of his suffering?
- Were there times when Frankl experienced a breakthrough into a higher dimension, when he experienced a sense of profound meaning in the midst of his sufferings?
- What would you describe as the outcome or prize of having suffered courageously at the end of Frankl's story of suffering?
- What did Frankl's suffering mean to him? What kind of a person do you imagine he became as a result of all that he went through? Did the kind of

(continued)

choices he made during his suffering influence the kind of person he became?

- Did Frankl's suffering present him with a particular calling or mission in life? How would you describe the particular vocation or life task that he was called upon to follow or perform *after* the time of his sufferings?
- Reflecting on your own sufferings and the costly or crucial choices you had to make in your own life, how did these choices influence you? How did you change or grow as a result of what you went through?
- Do you feel that *you* have a particular vocation or calling in life? What is *your* life's story?

References

Buber, M. (1958). *I and thou*. New York: Scribner.
Frankl, V. D. (1997). *Viktor Frankl recollections: An autobiography*. New York: Plenum Press.
Frankl, V. E. (1958). The will to meaning. *Journal of Pastoral Care, 12*, 82–88.
Frankl, V. E. (1967). *Psychotherapy and existentialism: Selected papers on logotherapy*. New York: Simon and Schuster.
Frankl, V. E. (1968). *Man's search for meaning: An introduction to logotherapy*. London: Hodder and Stoughton.
Frankl, V. E. (1977). *The unconscious god: Psychotherapy and theology*. London: Hodder and Stoughton.
Frankl, V. E. (1984). *Man's search for meaning. (revised and updated)*. New York: Washington Square Press.
Frankl, V. E. (1988). *The will to meaning: Foundations and applications of logotherapy*. New York: New American Library.
Frankl, V. E. (2000). *Man's search for ultimate meaning*. New York: Basic Books.
Krauthammer, C. (2015). *Things that matter: Three decades of passions, pastimes and politics*. New York: Crown Forum.
Lukas, E. (2000). *Logotherapy textbook: Meaning-centered psychotherapy*. Don Mills: Liberty Press.
Sacks, J. (2000). *A letter in the scroll*. New York: Free Press.

Chapter 3
Tender Beginnings: The Unscathed Human Spirit

Abstract The first phase of the logotherapy journey is set out in this chapter: the need to believe in the unconditional worthiness of our person. This is where every therapy should start: to provoke from the clients their will to triumphantly emerge from their suffering and victimized state. No-one can develop and grow if there is a lack of self-esteem and sense of worthiness. The need to experience a "Yes!" from life in an affirming and loving acknowledgement of its person is the first enlivening experience in an infant's life. The chapter challenges readers to consider where their lack of confidence in themselves and in the meaning of their lives came from. In therapy there is a need to find the client at the point where that inherent sense of innocence and the goodness of life became lost. Frankl's view of the unscathed spirit of the person hidden behind the façade of the problems and anxieties the client presents in therapy, is discussed as the potential for healing.

Keywords Unconditional self-worth · Experiencing a "yes!" from life · The unscathed human spirit; resources for healing

The Question

> What does it profit a man if he gains the whole world but loses his own soul? Or what will a man give in exchange for his soul? (Matthew 16: 26)

Who are you at heart? Who do you sense yourself to be in essence, in the innermost and core part of your being?

How is this very essence of your inherent human nature manifested? How does it show itself?

We see that we cannot live without a sense of meaning or connectedness to our world, get anywhere if we do not experience ourselves as a worthy, that is, a needed and wanted, appreciated and acknowledged part of it. We need to love and respect ourselves, experience ourselves as loved and respected, to be able to step into our

© Springer Nature Switzerland AG 2020   51
T. Shantall, *The Life-changing Impact of Viktor Frankl's Logotherapy*,
https://doi.org/10.1007/978-3-030-30770-7_3

lives and live it with purpose and determination. We can hardly live without a sense of dignity and self-esteem!

The Unscathed Human Spirit

And God saw all that He had made, and behold, it was very good (Genesis 1:31)

We must have a purity of soul; there must be something about us that holds promise, something that is totally worthy, good, innocent and unspoiled. We sometimes catch a glimpse of it; have some foundational sense that there is something wonderful about us.

Invested in us *is* the hope of glory! It has to be, otherwise all is lost.

If no-one believed in us, could we believe in ourselves? Only if we are seen in our *worthiness,* could we experience ourselves as worthy. No call can be made upon us if that call is not a call to live up to what we essentially *are!*

Self-respect is *essential* to any and every experience of meaning in life. Without it, we have no ground to stand on; no foundation on which to build a life worth living.

We must be seen as *good* in order to be good. Goodness must have been bestowed upon us. We must have come from goodness and be moving towards it! Without these two essential pillars and poles the in-between is utterly senseless. There must be an Alpha and Omega, an origin and destination in the shaping and design of the lives given to us. This is what gives our lives purpose and direction; what makes the beginning towards the end worth the while.

There must be a divinity of spirit. We must have a spark of the Divine, the potential of perfection, a promise of completion, a sacred space to fill out, to make replete with the achievement of who we essentially are: holy. This is the wholeness of life, its contentment, its joy, its destiny!

"The soul You placed within me is pure. You created it, You formed it, You breathed it into me, and You guard it while it is within me" – from the morning prayer in the Siddur (2010), the Jewish prayer book, with the commentary: "an affirmation of Jewish belief in the freedom and responsibility of each human being."

Perfect Love Casts Out All Fear

Do you believe in yourself? What do you believe about yourself? If you are not convinced of your own dignity and worth, of your singularity, uniqueness, like a pearl of great price, how can you go through life in terms of gaining anything of value? You will *always* question whether what you have succeeded in doing was good enough. You will *always* question your self-worth. You will live in self-doubt, be distrustful of life; you will exist in a semi-state of being. The call upon your life is to come out of this kind of hiding! So what if there are ups and downs in your life, does it detract from your worth as a person? Your best is *always* good enough!

"The salvation of man is in and through love", Frankl came to realize as he longed for and thought about his wife in the utmost misery of the concentration camp. He loved her. She loved him. They loved one another. This was a fact, whether she was still alive or not. Their love transcended and existed beyond the grave. This realization *liberated* him. He is loved, no matter what! He owed it to his wife, to the very memory of her, to rise to the occasion, to believe in himself and not give up – he wanted to prove himself worthy of her love. To give up on himself was to give up on his life; to not believe in its worth and meaning. Whether he would see her again or not, whether he would live or die, that was not the issue. To retain his dignity, his humanity, his self-respect; to retain all that his wife loved about him; to continue to be what others thought and admired about him – that was the issue. He did not want to fail himself; be less than he was in their eyes and his. He would go through his suffering with dignity. If he had to die, he wanted to die with dignity. And if he survived, he wanted to live with dignity.

The thought of his worthiness, the preciousness of the life given to him, saved Frankl from the defeat of despair at the lowest points of his suffering in the concentration camps. It sustained and kept him through the worst.

After his liberation from the camps, he was liberated from fear. So convinced was he of the precious worth of his person and of the ultimate meaning of his life, that he could make this concluding statement:

> The crowning experience of all, for the homecoming man, is the wonderful feeling that, after all he has suffered, there is nothing he need fear any more – except his God (Frankl 1968:93).

Famed columnist, Charles Krauthammer, in an interview when asked about his belief in God, replied: *"There was once a philosopher who said, 'I don't believe in God, but I fear Him greatly.' That's about where I am. I've had a fairly difficult and complicated notion of the Deity."* Krauthammer added that Albert Einstein's concept of God most resonates with him. He said that Einstein's idea was *"a recognition and an awe before the mystery of the order and beauty of the universe which would imply that there is something very mysterious and very awesome – awe-inspiring – about the universe."* (https.//ww.youtube.com/watch?v=pH5yZxCvNOs)

There is something awesomely magnificent about us as well: *"I will praise You, for I am fearfully and wonderfully made; marvelous are Your works, **and that my soul knows very well"*** (Psalm 13,914)

The Saving Grace of Love

Who you potentially are, that is, meant and expected to be, you have the awesomely given capability to become.

It must be so!

You were fashioned in a way that made your life a promise. Your life, waiting for you to live it, would challenge you to action. What was said at your beginning: "behold, this is very good" (Genesis 1:31) was also to be said at the end of your life with the completion of all the good that your life was meant to accomplish: "It is done!"

If you could not become all that you, from the very depths of your being uncannily know you essentially *are* and can be, you may as well give up, give in and give over, and let the blind forces of fate rule and overpower you. Your life will be swallowed up and vanquished; extinguished without a trace. You may as well have never been born.

You cannot become what you are *not*!

The message of hope, the promise of redemption, the messianic mission we must believe we have, is based on the reassurance that we *are* loved; that we *are* worthy; that our lives *do* have purpose and destiny. Only this conviction enables us to get up out of the dust; out of the trash heaps of life where we may have landed ourselves. We get up onto our feet by the very empowering of the divinity of spirit *invested* in us. Repentance is the heartfelt grief and conviction that what we have *lost, rather, failed to realize and embrace,* was ours in the first place. It is a *return* to what could have been and is meant to be.

Repentance is an acknowledgement of what should never have been; a confession of wrong that is to be made right by a *changed* way of life. "Go, and sin no more!" (John 8:11) is an empowering message, the commission to live our lives as it was *willed* (or ordained) to be lived! This is our unique and personal task in life. Nobody can do it for us.

We must do it ourselves.

> A man cannot redeem a brother, he cannot give his ransom to God. Too costly is their soul's redemption and unattainable forever (Psalm 49:8).

Only we can turn our lives around. This is a profoundly personal right. The prerogative to do so or not, is ours and ours alone!

A Right to Life

Here is the cardinal issue: Do you have a right to life or not? If you were born for inevitable failure, you have no birthright! Then your life would be void of meaning, left empty of your responsibility – *your* ability - to live it. Then somebody else would need to take your place, step into your shoes; live your life for you. Then life would become tyrannical and cruel. You would be left in a position of weakness and incapability, a place of humiliation and shame, unable to be what you are expected to be. You would have to be rescued and saved from yourself as a miserable, failing and fallen creature. Your standing would be in the one who stands in for you. Without that intermediary, you would be vile, unacceptable in the eyes of God and man. You would be robbed of your inherent dignity.

Life loses its meaning if it is not yours to live it!

But how great the empowerment if you know you are *loved*, not judged as unwanted or unworthy, but invited to become all that you were given to be in an *unconditional love of and trust in your person!* When you fall, you will rise again; when you stumble, you will find your feet again. Why? A hand is always held out to you, faith in you never wavers. The encouragement is always: you *can* be what those who love you believe you to be!

The Silencing of Foe and Avenger

Out of the mouth of babes and sucklings You have established strength because of Your enemies, to silence foe and avenger (Psalm 8:2)

Have you got a picture of yourself as a baby? Do you have a child, did you really gaze at the face of your child as a newborn baby? If we open our own souls to the soul of a baby, what do we see? What impresses us? What impact is made upon us?

We are looking at pure innocence, something so tenderly beautiful, so awesome, wondrous, of such infinite potential, that we feel like weeping, worshipping. We are touched to the core. Have you looked into the eyes of children? How open their look, how free of suspicion, of any dark and evil thought! You see right into their purity of soul, the sublimity of being.

You are looking into your own soul! How precious it is, how beautiful!

Have you lost that soul or are you busy losing it? Where are you taking it, what are you exposing it to? How are you letting it be spoilt, wrongly influenced, abused, trampled underfoot and spurned?

Have you lost touch with yourself? Have you become someone else, some fake person; a distorted image of yourself, someone you do not recognize as yourself anymore? Are you role-playing an identity that was thrust upon you and that you, out of subservience or out of a false sense of loyalty, took upon yourself? Or are you acting out some kind of identity that you feel will impress others, or gain the respect and admiration that you do not feel towards yourself? Is your sense of genuine self-worth, of being authentically yourself, very dubious or even gone?

Have you thrown your pearls to the swine?

How imperative to find yourself again! And what is healing, what is therapy, if it is not to restore to you what you may have lost or were deprived of? Is it not all about restoration, finding your way back to paradise: your unscathed and pure beginnings?

Are you to take your soul into possession again; take charge of how *you* are living your life? Are you letting your essential self or soul unfold and show itself in the full splendidness it holds within itself?

Let this truth hit home to you: You and you only, are in charge of yourself.

You are commissioned to be!

Paradise Lost: Losing Face

Man is glorious but (if he) understands not, he is likened to the silenced animals (Psalm 49:21).

What changed your image? What made you believe that you are worthless, not quite up to standard, or that you are helpless, the plaything of others? What made you yield to pressures and false promises; forced or lured you away from being who you were created to be? What drove you to self-despair, to painful feelings of inferiority or its opposite: to become arrogant, cynical and hard of heart? What made you give up on life, cynically taking from it what you could, while you could? If you were born to be great, so very wonderfully yourself, where have you lost your sense of self-worth? What happened to you that you no longer believed that your life was something to revere and treasure? When did you start accepting definitions of yourself that were groundless and unreal? Or how did you come to the conclusion that life was cruel and senseless and that it was up to you to carve out your own destiny; that you had to make space for yourself since you believed or were told that no such space was granted to you?

At the basis of all of the above distorted images is a fear to be yourself; a fear that you are unwanted and therefore unworthy, maybe even a bad person. You may try to deny this unsettling fear by becoming overly self-concerned; overly keen to impress others as a good person. Or you may even become enraged, angrily insisting on rights that you felt, or were told by indoctrinating others, you were deprived of,

Have you ever wondered where your fears came from; why you feel so full of doubts about yourself; why you are so plagued with insecurities; or why you are so cynically distrustful of any real meaning in life?

You may sense that the source of these feelings lie deep in memory, ingrained in you, maybe even way back to a time when you still did not know quite how to interpret your world; exactly how to make sense of the hurtful, oppressive and frightening things you may have experienced. Buried deep in the unconscious layers of your mind, these early hurtful and growth-constraining influences formed the basis of the negative way you began to perceive yourself; the false ideas you began to form about yourself.

The Need to Experience a "Yes!" from Life

Let me take you to the possible starting point of your fears, to its deep origins of doubt.

At the same time I also want to take you deeper, even before that to when you were innocently open to the world, like a huge question mark (a totally receptive openness to experience) so characteristic of the totally innocent, yet also frightening vulnerability of a newborn baby. Because that is how you started off your life. You were anticipating that you would be received by that world; be embraced and welcomed into it. You had the inherent urge and need to be seen and heard and given the space to explore and discover your world; to find out things for yourself and grow into full stature; allowed to fulfill your potential as a person of inherent dignity and worth. All along your developmental path, you needed significant others in your life to have taken you by the hand; to have led you into the discovery of wonder upon wonder of a world you had the ingrained urge to be part of. You needed to know that this was your world also.

Life was to be a beautiful thing.

What, oh what, then went wrong? Why, oh why, are you in bondage to fear and frustration?

The origin of your fears may not go back that far. Your fearful and false perceptions of yourself and the world may have started later in your childhood, in your teenage years, or fairly recently, when you experienced something shocking and hurtful, a trauma from which you may not have recovered. The truth of the matter is that your fundamental need to feel embraced by your world got cruelly and painfully frustrated. Even a forceful shaping of your personality by being subjected to what you were being molded to be by dominant and overpowering others in your life, obstructed the need to reach out to life and to experience it in a unique and singular or personal way. The world remained strange to you; you felt alienated even from yourself. You suffered a loss of soul. Finding it again, is to awaken the child in you, to go back to and understand your beginnings.

What promise did life hold out to you then; a promise you believe is now no longer yours or that you feel does not pertain to you?

What do you need to do and experience in order to find yourself again?

Do you need to cry? And do you need to know that your cry is heard?

The Cry of the Abandoned Child

Let me take you into the world of the autistic child. Autistic children can be seen as the most tragic of children, children developmentally thwarted at the very outset of their lives; at the stage when the most basic connection to their worlds needed to be forged. Unable to connect to the significant others in their lives during their 1st weeks of life, no interactive bond with the world around them could be formed.

What is life like when the will to meaningful participation in life remains dormant and unprovoked?

An exploration of the life of the autistic child will reveal to us our own most basic needs in life that, if not met, will thwart our ability to become fully ourselves.

The Normal Versus the Abnormal

Autism is one of the earliest, most devastating pathologies of childhood. It predates the first smile of the four to six-week old infant at the point of coming into its eyes and making face to face eye-contact with a significant other for the first time. This first time event is accompanied by the first social smile; a smile of recognition, the first real person to person interchange. It is the child's first connection to the world.

In the healthy emergence of the person of the infant, a dramatic moment of meaning happens at this more or less six-week stage of life. In place of the unfocused stare of the neonate, there comes some form of recognition of the caregiver, the first eye contact with a caring other and, with it, the first real smile, a kind of: "hello there!" Before that love is *sensed*. There is someone *there*, taking care of it in a sensitive and loving, trustworthy way. Facial expressions of love, being spoken to in loving and approving ways, being kissed, fondled and held, provokes in the infant the yet unshaped feelings of worthy identity. Experiencing enough caring or stability to give it a sense of safety, the infant makes its first own delicate efforts to reach out to its world.

It is a truly awesome moment. It is a moment of *encounter* between caregiver and child. This is but a first moment of a lengthy emergence of the unique person of the child. But, being a first moment, it is unforgettably precious.

Not so with the autistic infant. Not even over years of physical or mental growth is there this moment. No eye-contact is ever made, no smile of recognition ever given. The person of the child is still there but hidden from the world. A sense of intimacy with a loving other, the development of a close attachment bond between child and caregiver, is missing. Its caregivers, others in its world, are but objects among objects. It is striking that soft and cuddly toys are not chosen by the autistic child. Hard and movable objects are preferred. No personal, warm or cuddly connection is made with anyone in any human or personal sense of the word. There is no real interaction other than only with the very surface of things.

The severe form of disconnectedness to their worlds displayed by autistic children is evidenced by the fact that they do not communicate with others. Their use of language is sparse and meaningless. Why learn to speak, or why speak at all, if there is no real personal contact with others? This does not mean that autistic children do not understand language. Their intellectual abilities are mostly intact. They can comprehend the meaning of words but have no need to use them. It is most interesting that in the cases where some language is used, two words are strikingly absent from the vocabulary of autistic children, namely the words **"Yes"** and **"I"**.

The autistic child provides graphic proof that what any child needs in those 1st weeks of life is a welcoming: "Yes!" to its existence. It is much like a delighted mother's response as she holds her newborn baby in her arms: "I am here with you, my baby, and I'm so happy that you're here with me." It is from this cradle of intimacy, from this affirmative response to the fact of its worthy being in the world that the child's perception of his or her personhood or identity develops. By being affectively aroused and drawn into interaction with its caregiver, the child's first meaningful connection to the world it has been born into is made. It is here, in this reassuring and welcoming pattern of early communication between the child and its mother, that "the child's appetite for living is given its most arousing boost, and the infinite expectation he has that the world he has come into belongs to him is given its strongest justification" (DesLauriers & Carlson 1969:362).

So what went wrong? What are the causes of such an autistic disconnectedness from the world?

Shut Away from the World

Bruno Bettelheim (1967) entitled his work on the autistic child: *The Empty Fortress,* and saw autism as an early form of childhood schizophrenia. He interpreted autism as the child's defensive withdrawal from a frightening world by enclosing itself within a protective and impenetrable shell. Severely traumatized children may show signs of autistic behavior or regress to infantile positions. In much the same way that certain insects play dead to ward off attack, such a kind of non-being or non-emergence can be seen as an effort to safeguard their existence. "I am not here, I do not exist", is what they seem to be saying. This defensive warding off of anything outside of themselves is an effort to make themselves unseen and overlooked by what they believe are hostile others. The child's space of being thus remains uninhabited; left empty. The child exists on the fringes of things motor and sensory, on the yet *im*personal parameters of its being. This surface kind of being, so characteristic of autistic children, becomes a fortress, a place of refuge for hiding from a frightening world.

Without some kind of controllable order or walls around their disorder (their inability to connect to their worlds in a meaningful way) autistic children are left vulnerably exposed to what threatens to overwhelm or eradicate them. An obsessive focus on routine can be seen as a way of guarding themselves within some kind of safe or predictable space. It provides a sense of familiarity in an otherwise strange and confusing world; a world without definable, safe and secure boundaries. If the autistic children's obsessive routine is disturbed, they experience not fear, but stark terror. Terror is the cruder and earlier form of fear. When you fear, you have a person or sense of self who fears; you have some conception of what it is that you fear. This is not the case with autistic children. They feel assailed by the indefinable forces of death itself; their very existence is threatened with extinction.

Pathological Slumber

Deslauriers and Carlson (1969) in their work entitled *Your Child is Asleep,* convincingly argue that a neurophysiological and developmental dysfunction is at the base of the mute isolation of a child who does not know how or is *unable* to reach out to the world. They postulated a functional imbalance between two arousal systems in the brainstem of the central nervous system, namely, between the drive-response system and incentive-motivation system. The result is that the autistic child seems emotionally unresponsive. No cues for interaction emanate from the child to which the caregiver can respond to affect a bonding between them. Unable to "arouse" her child, to get any signal of his or her awareness of his or her presence with her, the mother of the autistic child may despair of making personal contact with and may defensively withdraw from her child. In not being able to provoke from its caregiver the responses the child needs, the child is left in isolation from any affirmative acknowledgement of its person from which a sense of self or personal identity can grow.

The Person Behind the Affliction

Frankl (2004), in his great work: *On the Theory and Therapy of Mental Disorders,* made the very perceptive comment that whereas a mental disorder like autism may indeed have a constitutional basis, *it is what the afflicted person makes out of the affliction – how his or her world is interpreted as a result of the organically based disorder – that should be our psychotherapeutic concern.* The important point that Frankl made here is that **there is a person behind the mental affliction who is struggling to make sense of the disorder.** It is the *pathological* interpretation of the disorder that gives rise to the distorted views of self and the world, and that can develop into a full-blown psychosis. A mental illness therefore consists not only of the organically based dysfunction that the person is suffering from but also with the malfunctioning – the distorted views - of the person as a result of the trauma the dysfunction is causing him or her.

Frankl speaks about *the unscathed human spirit* which means that the person who is suffering a mental illness is not ill, but only suffering the illness. It follows that besides whatever medical treatment is required to alleviate the suffering, therapists have the task to assist and provide comfort to the mentally afflicted and, if at all possible, help them to effectively deal with the illness and to so restore their sense of autonomous being. Whether they are able to fully emerge from the affliction or not, the inherent dignity of the mentally ill person remains intact. Without the belief in the inherent worth and dignity of the severely mentally afflicted person, Frankl stated, his profession as a psychiatrist would be meaningless!

Lewis

Very early on in my career I was presented with the task of undertaking therapy with an autistic child. He was a 12 year old boy, diagnosed as having some form of autism. He was the only such a child in a school for cerebral palsied children. He did respond in terms of learning mechanical or person-divested activities by the learning program he was exposed to at the school. But he had no speech; made no eye-contact. Obsessed with his strict routine, he became hyperactive and out of control, even destructively manic, when that routine was disturbed. He was too intense and was projected into his body in a nervously stiff, inflexible and mechanical way. He seemed to experience himself as an object among objects, almost as if living in his fingertips; in the world of his five senses, in the feel and sight, sound, smell and taste of things. Life to him was somehow evoked by twirling objects. He was strangely fascinated by the movements of things and liked objects with hard surfaces.

I had the impression that he was boxed into himself, fenced in, as if he had walls around himself; walls that were hard and unyielding, allowing no penetration. He seemed frozen in time; caught in the senselessness of mechanically repetitive moments, each moment disconnected from the next.

Yet, he knew his name. He understood language even if he just echoed it or just repeated words meaninglessly.

The Challenge

I was a young therapist, just starting out in my career as a clinical psychologist. How was I to get through to him?

I had to! The school committee had decided to transfer him to a school for the mentally retarded. His obsessive and uncooperative behavior became a real problem. In those days in South Africa, there were no schools for autistic children. But there was an occupational therapist, his teacher, in charge of a class in which he was a pupil, who deeply cared about him. She had faith in him. She believed him to be highly intelligent and she vigorously objected to the school committee's decision. Why not refer him to the newly appointed psychotherapist; grant him at least this last chance?

Her passionate plea was accepted and I was assigned the task. It was arranged that we should meet.

The meeting was to take place in her empty classroom during a school break. Colorful pictures hung on the walls. There was a cheerful and happy feel about the room. I very much liked his teacher. And she liked me. We spent time together, talking about Lewis, for that was his name. I felt her compassion. She felt mine.

She brought him into the room. I was waiting in anticipation, ready to meet him. As he hesitated in the doorway, my heart went out to him. Although he looked right past me, I sensed that he was very much aware of my presence. Am I to be trusted, could he venture nearer? He did, yet in a disconnected, unfocused way, as if not seeing me. Was he allowing himself to at least sense what I am like? He stood very still and near me for a few very quiet moments with only his teacher's voice introducing me, telling him that I was going to try and help him and that I wanted to be his friend. He was taking me in, absorbing me. Then a fit of excitement overtook him. He ran to a washbasin in the corner of the room, opened the faucet and drank greedily from the gushing water. His eyes were focused on my breasts. What was he drinking in, thinking about, longing and hoping for?

An Imprisoned Existence

Lewis had developed an obsession for the old fashioned type of film reels, still in use at that time. The school went to a lot of trouble and expense in capturing their treatment methods of the cerebral palsied children of the school on film. These film reels were kept in the steel cabinet of the headmaster's office. Lewis often forced his way in there, banging his head against the steel doors until it bled or until he was taken away by force and returned to his classroom. "No! No! No! You are not allowed in there," he was constantly told. In fact, an angry "No, not allowed!" seemed to earmark his day. He had on occasion succeeded in getting hold of the reels and made a total mess of them in wildly unwinding them from the spools and bringing them to his mouth.

I carefully considered his obsession with film reels. What did it mean to him? Unrolling the tape, he would keenly peer through the negatives as if trying to see what was on the other side of it. Was he trying to see through his yet unfocused stare, the veil that his autism never allowed to lift? Did he want to see the world outside the autistic prison he was hidden in?

I considered the fact that he tried to eat the tapes. Did he want a taste of the world that remained so incomprehensible to him?

I saw his anguish, his terror when these objects were taken from him, his longing to connect to them once more.

Lewis, Where Are You? The "Yes!" Game

It was arranged that we would meet first thing every morning. In preparation, I got hold of a few old film spools. I removed the film reels of the school from the cupboard of the headmaster's office (with the headmaster's somewhat dubious consent), and replaced them with the acquired spools. With our very first meeting I took Lewis by the hand and led him to the headmaster's office. We stood in front of the cupboard. I opened it, pointed to the spools and said: "Yes, you can take them." He looked dumbfounded but then, with a swift movement, grabbed them in his arms and ran off with them as if expecting me to snatch them from him.

I didn't. Instead, I went to where he dropped them and helped him unroll them, encouraging him with a "Yes, you may" all the time. He looked incredulous, but happy, greedily bringing the tapes to his mouth and making eating sounds, smacking his lips.

We attracted quite a bit of attention. Was this therapy? The playground was full of unrolled spools of tapes in wild profusion and, after our time was up, and his teacher came to fetch him, it took me quite some time to roll all the tapes back onto their spools again.

This became our routine, the "Yes!" game. After some weeks of this wild but enthusiastic play, he began to help me roll the tapes back onto the spools again. Soon I was able to tempt him to bring the spools into my office where we could play our "Yes!" game in the privacy and containment of the four walls of my office, away from all the prying and critical looks of others. We needed to form safe boundaries around our sacred togetherness.

Slowly his play became more ordered. He would choose a bigger film spool to represent me and a smaller one to represent him. I told him so. Flat on the table, he loved to unroll the tape from the bigger spool onto the smaller one as if taking from me what I was so willingly giving him. I said this to him. And just sometimes he would roll a little bit of the tape back from the smaller spool onto the bigger one, as if responding to me. I showed him how happy I was about that. At first his response was most tentative. He would stop himself and quickly roll the tape back onto the smaller spool. Could he risk reaching out to me, or would what he had to give me be snatched or taken away from him – could he trust me? I voiced all of this to him, telling him what he must be feeling and what he was trying to convey to me and maybe how this related to how he experienced the world outside of my office and how he was defensively reacting against it in an effort to protect himself.

But more than all of this, I showed him how happy I was to see and be with him; what a special boy I experienced him to be; how clever he was; how very much I liked him.

A Rebirth Experience

And then the moment arrived. He had rolled a tape equally onto both the smaller and bigger spools. Our roles had been equalized. He had found a source of secure trust. He took my scissors from my desk and cut through the tape holding the two spools together, as if cutting the umbilical cord between us. Then he looked up and looked straight into my eyes.

He made eye contact with me, the first eye contact of the twelve years of his life!

He got up and ran out of the office. I hurriedly followed. He rushed into his teacher's classroom, took a piece of white chalk and wrote a row of numbers down on the black board, one number (e.g. 23) under another (e.g.78), then drew a line underneath the numbers and wrote down the answer, the exact number if all of the numbers were added up!

What was he saying to his teacher if not that her faith in the fact that he was intelligent was founded and now vindicated?

Lewis began to speak, although haltingly. He made eye contact with me regularly, also with his teacher.

His mother and father were brought in for counseling by the social worker of the school. His mother was said to be deeply depressed about the fact that, throughout his infancy, she "could not get through to him". Feeling as if she failed in her role as a mother, she despaired of forming a relationship with him and had emotionally withdrawn from him. When he started with strange behavior, like banging his head against the cot and rocking himself, and especially after it became obvious that he had failed to develop speech, the father stepped in and they sought help which eventually led to him being put in the school for cerebral palsied children.

Having to relocate to another city, I handed in my resignation. The process of assisting Lewis was to continue. His teacher took up where I had left off using more intensive and lovingly intrusive programs of teaching and interacting with him in the work with autistic children that became known at that time. His parents participated in the program, continuing it at home. I felt that Lewis was in good hands and that what I was called upon to do in therapy with him had been completed.

Finding the Child in You

Why not take note of children, of their natural fascination with life, their joy in living with spontaneity and unaffectedness, their purity before all of this gets spoilt by the way we treat them or through the afflictions they suffer or frightening things that happen to them?

Alice Miller is a psychoanalyst who came to insights other than those which her Freudian training in psychoanalysis led her to believe, namely, that as human beings we are by nature selfish, lustful and destructive and driven by need-satisfaction. But, says Alice Miller (1988:xi): "All of us have entered the world as innocent infants, with the primary goals of growing, living in peace, and loving – never of destroying life" and describes herself as freeing herself "from the intellectual constraints and concepts of my upbringing and my professional training, which I now recognized to be false, deceptive, and disastrous in their impact" (ibid:x).

How I recalled my therapy with Lewis when I read what Alice Miller in her book: *The Drama of being a child and the search for the true self* (1988), had to say about the primary needs of children and of clients who come for therapy! Referring to the child, she says: "The child has a primary need to be regarded and respected as the person he really is at any given time, and as the centre – the central actor – in his own activity" (ibid: 21). What is needed, not just in parenting, but also in therapy, is "the presence of a person who is completely aware of them and takes them seriously, who admires and follows them" (ibid: 22).

The Purity of Innocence

The essential goodness of human nature is no more starkly revealed to us than in the disabled child. How many countless examples of this we have!

Have you noticed the sweetness of a Down Syndrome child, seen the glimmer of something entirely unspoiled in the retarded or cerebral palsied child? What about a Helen Keller, born deaf and blind? What an inspiration she is to all of us!

Who is disabled, the child with a physical, emotional or mental handicap or those who regard these children as "abnormal"?

A student of mine in Logotherapy wrote up her perceptions as a grandmother of her little granddaughter who was born blind.

It was the child's purity of innocence, her delight in life before she would be made aware of the fact that she was blind, "abnormally" different from other children that broke the heart of this grandmother. How were they to protect this delightful little girl from the stares and pity of and judgmental treatment by others, something she will not see, but deeply sense? But what a gift to the world is the disabled child in drawing out the best in us, she writes! What seemed like such an unhappy tragedy with the birth of a blind little one in their family has turned into a triumph! They have become knitted together as one in the care and protection of this little girl, so full of enthusiasm for life, so receptive and responsive to their love and their care.

The Concealed God

Jacques Lusseyran (2006: 6,7), a blind hero of the French Resistance during the Second World War, wrote his autobiography entitled: *"And There Was Light."* He graphically spoke of "the clear water of childhood" and "the revelation of light", the "cure for blindness" of "the visually blind".

He writes: "My parents were protection, confidence; warmth. When I think of my childhood I still feel the sense of warmth above me, behind me and around me, that marvelous sense of living not yet on one's own, but leaning body and soul on others who accept the charge. My parents were heaven. I knew very early, I am quite sure of it, that through them another Being concerned himself with me and even addressed himself to me. I had no name for him. He was just there and it was better so. Behind my parents there was someone, and my father and mother were simply the people responsible for passing along the gift."

Frankl (2000, p.15) wrote about a student of his that had a mental breakdown and quoted him as follows: "In the mental hospital, I was locked like an animal in a cage, no one came when I called begging to be taken to the bathroom, and I finally had to succumb to the inevitable. Blessedly, I was given daily shock treatment, insulin shock, and sufficient drugs so that I lost most of the next several weeks. But in the darkness I had acquired a sense of my own unique mission in the world. I knew then, as I know now, that I must have been preserved for some reason – however small, it is something that only I can do, and it is vitally important that I do it. And because of the darkest moment of my life, when I lay abandoned as an animal in a cage, when because of the forgetfulness induced by ECT, I *could not* call out to Him, He was there. In the solitary darkness of the "pit" where men had abandoned me, *He was there.* When I did not know His Name, He was there; God was there."

The most liberating truth is this: we are born with the purity of total innocence. Embedded in our being is the need to step into our world and be a needed part of it, however small the parameters of the freedom to do so may be.

Inherent to our very being, is the will, and therefore also the right, to be worthy.

Exercises For You, The Reader: Say "Yes!" to Life

Exercise 1: Recall particularly hurtful experiences in your life

- Thinking about it, why were these experiences hurtful?
- What possible negative impressions have you formed about yourself and about life as a result of these hurtful experiences?
- Contemplating this view of yourself, others, life, is it a view that, if not your own, you would feel attracted to or would endorse? Do you really want to have such a view? How would you rather like to see yourself; what view of life would you rather have?
- How did this negative view of yourself and the world influence the way you started behaving after your hurtful experiences?
- Do you like the way you have started behaving? Do you want to continue to behave in this way?
- How would you like to see yourself behaving? Why? Would you like yourself more if you behaved differently?
- Consider that the hurts that you have experienced may perhaps now, when you think about it, reveal what is really important to you or what you really want in life. Can you describe what that is?
- What can you learn from the hurts you have experienced? Has it benefitted you in any way? Has it made you understand better what we, our world, ought to be like for us to experience our lives as meaningful and good? Write down your thoughts.
- What kind of person, do you believe, were you born to be? Can you perhaps imagine what you may have expected or desired to experience as you entered this world and as you grew up in it?

If you put into action what you believe should be the kind of thing anyone should be doing to make this world a better place to live in, would you begin to experience yourself as someone and life itself as something *of worth?*

(continued)

Consider this:

Are you really at heart, or essentially, a good person in wanting to experience life as something worth living and the world as a good place to live in if people only did what, you believe, they ought to have done or should be doing? Would a change in how you view yourself and the world and what you think about life bring you closer to what, as you have thought about it, is really important to you and that you really value in life? Would it change things for you if you put your beliefs into practice or become more active in making a change for the better in the world? Do you think you can regain what you may feel you have lost or failed to experience in your life?

Exercise 2: Recall good and happy experiences in your life

- Thinking about it, how did it impact on your life?
- Do you think it provided some impetus or courage to keep you going despite the hurtful experiences you have encountered?
- What, do you think, made you still hope that there is some good in the world, something you can trust and reach out to or seek to find?
- What about your future still seems inviting; is there some call, some promise of better things to come? What do you want to see happen or come to pass in the future? Why?
- How would you like to conclude your life? If you looked back on your life one day, what would you like to think of it or see accomplished in it?
- What would give you a sense of consolation or hope on your deathbed?
- What about today? What can you do today; what kind of person can you decide to be today to make progress towards the end goal or ultimate meaning of your life?
- Where can you see yourself serving in some way to change the world, your own circumstances, into what you believe it ought to be?
- What will give you great satisfaction, a sense of self-fulfillment, doing what?
- What is meaningful to you, right now, in your own life and circumstances?

Consider this:

Having contemplated all the above questions, can you really say that you have been totally deserted or let down in life? Are you really the helpless victim of cruel circumstances or do you have the power to change things, make a better life for yourself? What does having free choice and the ability to put your choice into action, say about you? What does it say about the way you were created or about the One Who created you? Is there a benevolent force in your life; a golden thread of meaning that you can see running through it? Can you see your life as an opportunity and as a task and with many enriching and life-

(continued)

changing experiences always open to you; as something up to you, but with a source of support, somewhere always there, to help you achieve what you yourself can see is what you want and, in fact, are meant to achieve?

Can you really deny that you are a part of the bigger picture; that you are a valued and needed part within the greater scheme of things?

References

Bettelheim, B. (1967). *The empty fortress: Infantile autism and the birth of self.* New York: The Free Press.

DesLauriers, A. M., & Carlson, C. F. (1969). *Your child is asleep: Early infantile autism.* Homewood, Illinois: The Dorsey Press.

Frankl, V. E. (1968). *Man's search for meaning: An introduction to logotherapy.* London: Hodder and Stoughton.

Frankl, V. E. (2000). *Man's search for ultimate meaning.* New York: Basic Books.

Frankl, V. E. (2004). *On the theory and therapy of mental disorders: An introduction to logotherapy and existential analysis.* New York: Brunner-Routledge.

Lusseyran, J. (2006). *And there was light.* Sand Point: Morning Light Press.

Miller, A. (1988). *The drama of being a child and the search for the true self.* London: Virago Press.

Siddur, K. (2010). *Koren Sacks Siddur, Hebrew/English, Sepharad Prayerbook.* Jerusalem: Koren Publishers.

YouTube. (2018). *The life and times of Charles Krauthammer.* https.//ww.youtube.com/watch?v=pH5yZxCvNOs

Chapter 4
Who Are You, Sitting Opposite Me?
The Person of the Client

Abstract This chapter explores what healing impact is made on the client by the orientation of the logotherapist who holds the unshakable belief in the inherent worth of the person of the client. The aim is to confidently reconnect the client to his or her world. Each client is seen as a *unique person*, confronted by *a unique task* in the here and now of their lives. Clients are called to step out of hiding by confronting and constructively dealing with the problems that face them. As the resolve to do so grows, the voice of their own conscience begins "to speak" to them more clearly. They are helped to realize that they were brought to this moment in time with every capability to perform what life is inviting them to do. There is a choice to be made and an action to perform that will release a move forward in their lives.

Keywords A logotherapist's orientation · Uniqueness of the client · A unique life task · The voice of conscience · The one right choice · The healing in moving forward

Who Are You?

So who is this person, seeking my help and sitting opposite me?

Who are you, dear reader, if you should be the one to have come to see me? Are you a total stranger, someone alien to me? Have I no sense of connection to you, other than as someone seeking my professional help and expecting to find it?

Even writing that last sentence causes me stress. The onus is on me to somehow solve the problem you will be presenting to me.

I am expected to have to "do" something. My background is supposed to have provided me with all the answers to common and predictable psychological distresses. I am to establish into which diagnostic category your psychological disturbance places you. Then I am also supposed to have a treatment program, the tools with which to rid you of the problem that is causing you stress. You are to leave my office feeling that, on my part, it was a job well done. You will pay me my fees without resentment.

If I am "to deliver the goods"; if this is what you will be demanding of me and if this is the role I will see myself cast in, what pressure I will be placing on myself!

I may feel compelled to take more and more courses on counseling and psychology, become more expert at this and that or the other counseling approach and technique to allay my fears of not quite knowing what to do with a mentally afflicted person like you. The many certificates on the wall of my consulting room will be meant to impress and reassure you of my competence and that I am qualified enough to help you. I may want to develop a calculated "warmth" or *rapport* (the required empathy to "build a relationship of trust") as part of my professional stance. A studded leather chair on which to sit, a shiny desk, a chic outfit and neat hairstyle, the formally polite way you will be received and ushered into my office; all the aforementioned may have to become part of the show of professionalism. Careful notes and files and reports and regular bills will be needed to help ensure that we are in business.

A Logotherapeutic Orientation

But logotherapy has changed all of the above for me. It will also drastically change things for you. Logotherapy is a radical re-orientation to life, a completely new way of looking at things. In logotherapy we are not out to "fix" things, but are invited to relax and be ourselves. The challenge is to find each other in a face to face encounter.

To me, logotherapy was like a homecoming. All that I have personally sensed to be meaningful in life, especially in my interactions with my own children and with those close and important to me, and beyond that, all that I have learnt and could take to heart in my training and practice as a clinical psychologist, hit home to me as truths in my study of Logotherapy.

I recalled Lewis and the real and deep encounters I have had with children, adolescents and adults in therapy. I discerned the golden thread of meaning weaving through all the many and varied experiences. Developmental psychology, a subject I taught for many years at the Department of Psychology at the University of South Africa, became a life's passion.

What does the developing child need; what do we all need to develop to optimal levels of being?

I was trained in psychoanalysis and psychodynamic psychotherapy. As a university senior lecturer in psychology and involved in the training of clinical psychologists, I was familiar with all the different personality theories and schools of psychotherapy. I was acquainted with the various paradigms of thought (different philosophical world views and theories of human behavior and existence) as a teacher and researcher in the field of psychology. But it was in logotherapy that I found a home. It was there where all my observations, insights and realizations; all my own convictions and personal beliefs, came together and began to make perfect sense!

Who then are you, dear reader, as I personally open the door for you to come into what is now my warm and homely living room, the place I use to see my clients, and as I have you sit in a comfortable chair opposite me?

We are alone. It is quiet. We will not be disturbed in the hour I have set aside for you.

This time is ours.

The Beauty and Power of the Human Spirit

I will be somewhat in awe of you, yet excited about getting to know you. You are most interesting to me. I have never met and will never again meet anyone like you. You are a one and only. If from a culture different from my own, I may struggle to remember your name and may not pronounce it quite as you say it, but I will not write it down or make notes while you are speaking to me. That will distract me; put an obstruction between you and me. I am most keen to encounter you, the real person behind perhaps your slight nervousness and awkwardness, and not quite knowing what to say or do.

You may ask me what I am expecting of you; what you are to say, where you are to start. I am utterly relaxed about that, not minding any point of departure at all except perhaps for a cue to get us talking by saying: "What has brought you to me? Why have you come to see me?"

I am aware that you are looking around; you may even remark how pleasant the room is, how beautiful the view. Or you may just be looking at me, trying to size me up, form an impression of me. I do not mind what you think about me at all. I am totally un-self-conscious, utterly forgetful of myself. My whole focus is on you; on what brought us together. I am set on one thing only: to discern the meaning of our encounter; why we are together; what we are expected to discover together; what we are to do.

It is your life we will be speaking about, that we will explore, not mine. Where are you now, what challenges are you facing in what you will present to me as the reason for coming to see me?

What then do I believe about you, dear reader? What do I believe about each and every client that enters through my door? Who are you to me, a logotherapist, assigned the task of helping you to come out of your cares and worries, even your wrongdoings, and to find meaning in your life, deeply and personally?

You

At heart, you are a good person. How else, if you have every potential and capability to be good and to achieve what you were expected to be? If you did not become what was expected of you and what you were capable of becoming, you have failed yourself! And I am here to call you out of such failure. The call, after all, is to step into your own shoes!

I therefore believe in your inherent goodness.

The human spirit is *pure*. It is actually *you*! You are at the heart of and behind everything that you think, feel and do. Your thoughts, feelings and actions are yours. You have an outward appearance, and as I get to know you a bit more, intellectual and psychological capacities. But these are mere givens. They do not define you. What you are trying to do with your life, what you are looking for, your struggles in the process, these are the things that make you known to me. I see your struggle to make sense of your own life.

To find your way in life is no easy matter. So much could have happened to you up to this point. Through your interaction with your world, through your experiences, *you* formed certain impressions, impressions that may not always have been the right ones. You began to react to them in a characteristic way, a way that began to typify you, the kind of person you impressed others as being. You took on a certain type of personality. Your personality is the outward expression of yourself. But your personality is something that is shaped. You have everything to do with its shaping. But that means that you also have everything to do with changing it!

Shy, reserved persons with strong feelings of inferiority, who react in an awkward and clumsy way, are not well-spoken and hate the limelight, may, after some life-changing experiences or therapy, become far more assertive and self-confident. Finding their own voices, they may radically change from the kind of person they impressed others as being. Even a most rebellious and obnoxious person, always seeking to make trouble, is expressing a deep sense of inferiority and feels as if he or she has been pushed out by life, ignored and replaced by others somehow more "worthy" and deserving of attention, love and care. By going to the depth of the origins of these distorted views and experiencing the opposite in the intensive dialogue and close interaction with a loving therapist, such views can undergo radical change. People with these kind of characteristic features can gain the courage to let go of their bravado, to step out of their angry and rebellious reaction to the world and become more receptive and sensitive people who are more tolerant and understanding of others.

Personalities can change; undergo a transformation. Therapy can uncover the real person of clients behind the fronts, the emotional hang-ups and fears that concealed them and assist them to be much more expressive of their authentic or real selves!

The masks would have dropped.

You too can come out into the open, step into your own life, even if it takes time and even if your first emergence out of hiding behind your fears and emotional hang-ups may be somewhat shaky and unsure. Vulnerability and need are true features of your real self. But the point is that you have become genuinely yourself. This is the starting point in your journey towards meaning; towards discovering the unique purpose and destiny of your own life.

How do you come to see the beauty and value of your own life? How do you discover your own worth, experience the dignity of being called to take up the reigns of your life and fulfil its very meaning and purpose? You may protest: "Who me? You mean to say my life has meaning and purpose, that I am somebody worthy enough to live such a life? You mean that I can do it; that I can actually change my life?" You may have difficulty in perceiving yourself in such a good light.

But are you really so out of touch with yourself; do you really believe that the doubts you have about yourself really have the power to rob you of your worth? What was stolen is still yours. It can be claimed back!

Why seek my help if you were satisfied with the kind of perceptions you have formed about yourself?

You have come to see me because you have a case to settle, and the case is that you are deeply *dissatisfied* with the perceptions you have of yourself. Are you really that bad? Is your life really at such a dead-end? You may initially be battling this issue with those you seek to blame for your condition; present them as the problem in your life. But this kind of lament is not what I will be listening to. I will ignore all your complaints about the unfairness of life. What you may initially believe the real issue or problem is, may be totally off the mark. But that does not bother me. That you are restless and questioning, this is what interests me. What are you searching for; what are you hoping to find?

It is your restlessness of heart that I will be focusing on.

And Your Life

Then there is more. There is your life and that life is busy with you. It has not given up on you. It never has. It was always there, every breathing moment of your existence. You may feel that life is out of your reach, that you are forgotten, given over without protection or defense against forces much too strong for you to resist. You may believe that all you have is your misery, your deep disappointment, frustration and dissatisfaction with life.

But here I am, sitting opposite you, looking past all that. I am looking at *you*. And I am *listening*. You are going to give me glimpses into your real person and your own unique life. The more you open up to me, the more I will find *you* in what you are telling me about yourself, and the more I will be able to discern how life has interacted with you, what it gave you, what it taught you, tried to say to you, allowed you to go through and experience, where it brought you and why, and what it is *saying* to you right now.

And it is *you* who will be telling me all that!

One of the first and maybe most significant thing I can immediately say to you is this: How could the negative perceptions of yourself and of your life be true if you have come to see me about them? Is it *because* you cannot tolerate or no longer endure such misperceptions about yourself or of life and that you are, in fact, looking for a way out of such a state of unhappiness and negativity in coming to see me!

What and who else have we got to talk about? Not one of your accusers or abusers is present. It is only you in the room with me! You may be obsessively focusing on someone else, the person you blame for your misery. You may even insist on bringing someone else for therapy, a husband, a wife, a parent or a child, but I will help you see that this is but a front, a defensive strategy, that it is really *you* that you want to bring out into the open. Even if it is your real and healthy concern for any one of your loved ones that has brought you to me, you will be part of the picture, part of the therapy for that loved one if that was the real need, and if the particular person was willing to enter into therapy.

So, if you are in therapy with me, is it really your problems and only your problems that you want to focus on and have solved?

Or is it a question of where *you* are in this picture?

Another Side to the Story

You are here with me to hear another story, a story that happens to be the truth. Life and with it, the purpose of it, has never left you. It was with you all the time. It may have been hidden in the wings, it may have even concealed itself from you as you flew in its face with rage, anger, bitterness and lament, but it never withdrew from you. It came to you again and again with little glimmers of hope, little acts of kindness, with help along your way. This is what I will be looking out for, what I will question you about and search out.

Frankl (1968, 90) related the story of a young woman whose death he witnessed in the concentration camp. This young woman knew that she would die in the next few days. Pointing through the window of the hut, she said, "This tree here is the only friend I have in my loneliness." Through that window she could see just one branch of a chestnut tree, and on the branch were two blossoms. "I often talk to this tree," she said to Frankl. Being a psychiatrist, Frankl was startled. Was she delusional? Did she have occasional hallucinations? Anxiously he asked her if the tree replied. "Yes," she said. What did it say to her? She answered,

It says to me, 'I am here – I am here – I am life, eternal life.

It will be the above realization, if therapy with you had proved successful, that will become a truth for you also.

A One and Only, Once and for All Time

But there is even more that I believe about you and about your life. Essential to the basic goodness of your person and your life is your uniqueness. Life has and is challenging you to step out and show yourself. Life was in the constant process of teaching you about yourself, your unique task and mission in life. Even life's tragedies and hardships were not such disasters. Your suffering had meaning. It had something to say to you, somewhere to take you. It was there to bring you on course or to test you, to bring out your worth, to teach and enlighten you, give you understanding, skills and sensitivity. Like clay in a loving Potter's hands, all that has happened to you in all the good and bad of your life was meant to give shape to you, bring to full manifestation the unique person that you are, that you have the full potential to be.

Hillman (1997), a post-modern psychoanalyst, in his book: *The Soul's Code. In Search of Character and Calling*, calls his theory, the "oak theory". We are like an acorn that eventually grows into a mighty oak tree.

> In the acorn lies not only the completion of life before it is lived but the dissatisfied frustration of unlived life.

This is the restlessness of the heart Frankl spoke about, a restlessness that sets us searching to make sense of our lives and to realize or bring about, give expression to its meaning; that is, to give full expression to the person we were called to be. We will not experience a sense of fulfillment until we have grasped and are giving expression to our unique destinies in life.

> "The essence of the oak is all there at once," Hillman states.

We are constantly being urged to find and become what we deeply sense it is we are *meant to be*. Hillman echoes this saying in his words: "There is a sense of calling, that essential mystery at the heart of each human life. **Each person bears a uniqueness that asks to be lived and that is already present before it can be lived**." Our lives have been preordained but not pre-planned. We have an essential part to play. Like Frankl, Hillman states: "**I am answerable to an innate image, which I am filling out in my biography.**"

Applying the above truths to your life, it means that you are *not* a hapless product of your circumstances, with no say in what happened to you. You had and have *every* say. After all, *you* formed the impressions you hold about yourself and your life; *you* interpreted things in the way you have. *You* reacted the way you did, became what *you* allowed yourself to become.

Your life, in a very real sense, has been and is up to *you*!

What else will we be talking about if not about you, how you see things, how you came to see things. Are those perceptions right or are they wrong? This is a question *you* are going to answer as we contemplate your life together. I may be a questioner, yes, even a challenger as I confront you with your own questions, the deeper lying issues of your own struggle, the answers you are seeking to find even in the kind of negative statements you make and in how you will try and contradict what I feel provoked to say to you on the basis of what you have conveyed to me. "Can I really believe that my life has meaning? But what about this and what about that, surely not!"

You make take issue with me, challenge me with resistance, throwing your own painful doubts back at me. But behind all that, you are listening and *hearing* the hope you want to have, the faith you want to have restored, *the Basic Trust in Being* that you *want* to regain!

Down to the Very Depths of Being

Slowly, even in an imperceptive way, the ancient and ever immediate cry of the Transcendent will filter through to your awareness. This call from the Transcendent comes to the heart of everyone, no matter how this is often and hotly contested! It is particularly refreshing to hear this truth coming to us, not from the channels of religion, but from psychiatrists like Frankl and psychoanalysts like James Hillman, those who are working with people in the down to earth struggles of everyday life.

"Why," asks Hillman, "is it so difficult to imagine that I am cared about, that something takes an interest in what I do, that I am perhaps protected, maybe even kept alive not altogether by my own will and doing? Something saves me every day. Despite this invisible caring, we prefer to imagine ourselves thrown naked into the world, utterly vulnerable and fundamentally alone. It is easier to accept the story of heroic self-made development than the story that you may well be loved by this guiding providence, that you are needed for what you bring, and that you are sometimes fortuitously helped by it in situations of distress. Why not keep within psychology proper what once was called providence – being invisibly watched and watched over?"

Frankl spoke about the Unconscious God. From the very depths of our being, we can at moments be struck with the realization that we are being related to in this *unseen but yet profound way*.

Every situation in life contains a call to respond to that situation in a meaningful way. Life *encounters* us; makes a call upon us to find and realize the meaning and purpose of our lives. Hillman describes this invitational nature of life as **"a call that beckons us to search."** We are being drawn into dialogue with life. Life beckons us. Hillman speaks about "being inherently *ahead* of ourselves." The future that awaits us comes to us *in the present moment*. We are challenged to get on with our lives; to move forward and make progress. The call comes from the Transcendent as a call to us to *transcend* our present circumstances; to make a change for the better. There is an *imperative* embedded in each and every moment of our lives. Frankl emphasized the awesomeness of this moment by moment call upon our lives and expounded it in the following way: Each situation in life comes to us or occurs only once. We can realize the meaning of that moment or miss the opportunity to do so. It is a task either done or left forever undone. We are singled out to answer the call of a singular moment coming to us once and never again! This very singularity, stated Frankl, is what constitutes the *absoluteness* of the task: it is a task wholly consigned to the moment and wholly given to us to perform. The call thus made upon us in each and every situation of our lives bears the stamp of divine authority. It is a call that beckons us to respond!

It is a call that comes to all of us. It is a call that comes to you.

It is from your spiritual unconscious depths that there will come *a receptive awareness*, an ear to the voice of the Divine at any particular crisis or turning point in your life, whether you are conscious of it as the voice of the Divine or not. I will not labor that point. In a sense, it does not matter to me. Why? It is because **the**

meeting place will be your conscience, your consciousness or *realization* of what it is you ought or are required or challenged to do. However, in my own receptivity to the meaning of the moment, I recognize, and very awesomely, that what you are called upon to realize and to do comes from the dimension of meaning, the dimension of the Supra-human, the Transcendent. That is why the required response to the situation is so right, why it is so clearly the one and only *right* thing to do. The answer to the situation is not arbitrary; not some kind of cheap advice I am giving you; some recipe for healing based on this or that theoretical school of thought that you are to follow. Coming from me, any suggestion I make is questionable. It can be corrected, prove to be not altogether right or really helpful. After all, I am only sensing what life is saying to you. **I am the hearer but you are the doer, the one to respond to the call.** For that to happen, the call must come to *you*. What will be right and be a liberation, an "Aha!" realization on your part as a truth that sets you free, is directed to you and to you only.

There will be nobody else in the picture but *you*.

I will be listening and responding to your heart of hearts. "Logos is deeper than logic", Frankl contended. "The heart has reasons that reason cannot understand", he stated. How apt Frankl (2000: 44) was in putting the truth into words when he also said: "Feeling can be much more sensitive than reason can ever be sensible!" Your intuitive knowing, your gut feeling (spiritual grasp) goes deeper than what the so-called facts of the rational mind are trying to set before you as the truth or that suppressed emotions may be raging or lamenting or be in terror about.

Facts can lie if taken out of context. The intellect can be cruel and heartless. Emotions can badly distort the truth.

We need to see the real picture.

The Real You

The dignity and strength of your person and the purpose of your life is where I will put the focus. I will make you aware of your strengths and courage, what you have revealed about your *true* self in how you have struggled against the hurtful effects of the bad experiences in your life. Your struggle is evidence of your *refusal* to accept the impressions that tragic events have left upon you, namely, that you are abandoned and helplessly alone or even worse: that you are worthless, inferior, bad, your life of no real consequence at all.

After all, you are sitting opposite me!

Frankl often startled his clients in the face of all their laments and threats to end their lives by asking: "but why then have you not committed suicide?" Clients are shocked into an awareness that their lives *are* precious to them, that there is a lot about living that they *do* care about! You too, deep down, *know* and *want* to believe that your life is something meaningful, something of supreme and unique worth. That is why you came to see me.

You are challenging *me* to believe in you!

And you *want* to win the argument about your own worth, an argument that you are not having with me since I *do* believe in you. It is an argument you are having with yourself. We both have the same focus, the same end in mind. We are united in what life itself intends to accomplish: for you to find your own worth and the calling and destiny of your unique and beautiful life.

How then, could we *not* succeed?

A Confident Hope in the Outcome

You are unique. To the measure I am able to comprehend this and bring it home to you, to the measure that you are willing to comprehend this truth and take it to heart, to that measure do we, together, give affirmation and power to what our therapeutic encounter has been ordained to accomplish: **your liberation**!.

What, then, does your uniqueness mean to me? Yes, that I have never and will never encounter anyone quite like you. That is why, as a logotherapist, I cannot classify you as typically this or that personality type or as this or that type of neurotic, or place you in this or that category of mental disturbance. And even if you suffer from what can be diagnosed as this or the other type of emotional or mental "illness", *you* suffer that affliction in a totally unique way. Your stamp is on it in terms of how you are dealing with it and in what it means to you.

My focus cannot be on your problems, the afflictions that you suffer, but can only be on *you*. This is my role as a logotherapist since I am not your medical doctor, psychiatrist, physiotherapist or practitioner of whatever other form of therapy and treatment you may also be needing.

My focus has to be on your uniqueness, on what has happened to you in your life and what it has sought to teach and bring home to you.

Why all this preparation if it was not meant to bring you to the realization of your own specific place in the world?

Your calling and election is to be made *sure* (2 Peter 1:10)!

In Dialogue With Life

Life is confronting you in a unique way. Behind every problem you bring into therapy there is a call. You are uniquely involved with your own life and life is uniquely interacting with you. No dialogue between life and the person being addressed and called to response, *no conversation, is ever the same*! I am being brought into a conversation that is unique, profoundly personal and private. It is a conversation between you and your life.

Life, meaning itself, is confronting you. Are you listening, how are you responding? Are you resisting, fighting or seeking to understand the call? What has blocked your ears or to what other voices are you listening?

You may feel dubious and perhaps more than just a bit skeptical about what I have communicated to you up to this point. Can you believe all this about yourself? Can you be sure that all I need to know is all there inside of you, within your own range of knowing; that you are actually the one to come to a process of healing yourself as you react to life in the way it is calling upon you to do? Am I not supposed to be the expert, the one with all the answers to your life? What do clients pay me for?

Then let me share some logotherapeutic encounters with you. In story after story that clients bring into therapy, the same truths emerge! Will that convince you that the same story may be true of you also?

The Heart of the Matter

The first example is from a client that paid a visit to our student, Tanya Rubin, from Johannesburg. Tanya is a qualified social worker and is employed as a counselor in a fertility clinic. I will extract the important portions from the hour long session and give my comments in italics.

• *The power of love*

   Tanya (T = therapist), starts the session with the client (C = client) by saying:

T: We can spend the next while looking at what is important and valuable in your life. We can also look at difficulties or problem areas and hopefully together we can come up with the meaning behind the difficulty and in that way turn it into a growth experience.
C: That's great! It's always good to look at things from a different perspective.
T: Great. So have you thought about a specific topic that we can discuss?
C: I have actually and it's a current situation, so hopefully you can shed some light on it for me.
T: Tell me about it.
C: I have been trying to fall pregnant for the past two years with no success. … It feels like I have been trying to conceive forever. … I have been to so many gynecologists, homeopaths and reflexologists that I just feel it is all pointless. Nothing has worked… I feel so lost, I wish I knew which way to turn and what to do next.

(The client is clearly highlighting the fact that, driven into the corner as she is, the important thing is "what to do next." What, right now, in this moment, is she being asked to consider? A mere discussion of her problems has led nowhere. Logotherapy speaks about "a window of opportunity". It is pointless to keep on knocking at closed doors, the things in the past that have not worked. What freedom is left? What possible other avenues remain open? Elizabeth Lukas, a famous logotherapist, entitled those things in life that can no longer be changed, "areas of fate." Which are the "areas of freedom"?)

T: Well, maybe we can use this opportunity to look at some of the options that you do have?

C: Ya, I guess so, but what are my options really?

T: In my experience in working in the field of fertility for the past seven years, as well as some of my own personal experiences with infertility, there are always options – some are more challenging than others.

C: I know. I often look at my life and wonder if maybe I should give up the notion of trying to conceive because the choices ahead of me seem too daunting.

(A clue to the real issue at stake is given here by the client. The fertility clinic specializes in egg donations. The client will receive the egg of another woman that, if fertilized by the sperm of this mother's husband, will allow her to have a child. The client fears the choice that is put before her. To accept the option of an egg-donation is for her "too daunting". Will that sound a death knell to the dream of being a biological mother?)

T: It's normal to feel overwhelmed in this process especially when looking at the choices in front of you – it's as if you are going through a mourning process. However, the loss that you are mourning is something that is not tangible; it is mourning the loss of a want, a wish, a dream or a desire.

(The therapist brings to light the **real** loss that the client is to face, the area of fate that she can do nothing about: the dream to have her own child as the biological mother. This is the obstacle in the path of a clear choice. The client is still lamenting the past by fruitlessly holding onto something she clearly cannot have or bring about.)

C: I know and that's what makes it so hard because that dream is something I so desperately want.

T: I can understand that and sometimes when you want something so desperately you almost need to explore the options you have in order to see how far you are able to go in order to achieve this dream that you are trying to fulfill.

(The therapist gently urges the client in the direction of the choices she does still have in fulfilling her desire to have a child.)

C: You are so right. The way I see it is that I only really have two options: the one is adoption which my husband is really not keen on. The other is to use an egg donor which I am really not keen on – so where do we go?

(The client looks ahead of her now and considers the options open to her. Which will be the right one? This becomes the focus.)

C: I just wish there was an easy option, I wish someone could tell me what to do!

(There is only one right answer to any situation. Which, in this situation, is the right one?)

T: You're looking for answers and hoping maybe that I or someone else will make the decision for you, take away the pressure and tell you what to do. But I guess no-one can really do that for you, as it is your decision. You have two difficult but wonderful options that both will give you an opportunity to hopefully have a child of your own. What is it about adoption that your husband is not keen on?

(The different options must be explored to discover the right one, the one that will be a decision from the heart on the part of the client.)

C: My husband just feels that if we adopt, we have no idea where the child is from, we have no control. We don't know what the mother did while she was pregnant. I guess I do feel the same way as him but using an egg donor seems like I'm not even involved in the process.

T: So, in a way if you adopt, neither of you are involved in the process but if you use an egg donor, it becomes about your husband being a part of it and you feeling as if you are completely separate.

(The therapist highlights the fact that the decision to have an egg donor has greater weight than the choice to adopt. The question remains around the attitude of the mother which now becomes the focus.)

C: Exactly. It's like with adoption, neither of our genetics are there. With egg donation I have to give up my genetics. I have to exclude myself. What if I never love the child or feel connected because the child is not part of my DNA?

(This is where the challenge comes in and where the meaning of the moment takes shape! Can the mother make a selfless and sacrificial choice? The therapist confronts the client):

T: Do you feel connected to your husband?

C: Of course I do, he's my husband.

T: But you have different genetics yet you still feel connected to him, you still love him.

C: I didn't think about it like that! It just seems so bizarre that I will have someone else's genetics in my body.

T: It is a huge loss for you that you are not able to use your own genetics. You need to mourn that loss, the loss of you in the process. However, as hard as that is, maybe you can view it from a different perspective; maybe you could see that without your body feeding that embryo it actually doesn't exist. Without you, there would be no pregnancy.

C: You are right, I know!

T: But it is so hard to see it from that perspective.

C: I want to try though because I agree, without me there will be no pregnancy. I also know that genetics is not the only thing that makes up a child and that nurture and love is often more important.

T: You're right, it's often the connections we have in relationships, the effort we put into relationships, the love that we give that makes nurture more relevant than "just" genetics.

C: Maybe if I have all the information and I can then make an informed decision, it then becomes an easier choice to make.

T: That is such an important way to look at it, once you have all your questions answered and all the information that you need, then you can move forward in making the right decision for you.

C: You know, just talking about it has put it all into perspective for me. I guess I just need to shift my thinking a little!

T: Yes, because if you do choose to use an egg donor, you will have the opportunity to hopefully fall pregnant and have a child of your own.

The spiritual challenge and the very meaning of the situation facing the client is to give herself to and experience *the power of love*. This is a challenge exactly because she is being asked to transcend the natural process of falling pregnant and having a child with her own DNA by loving a child with a DNA different from her own. But the child will have her husband's DNA, the DNA of someone she deeply loves, someone who wishes for a child as much as she does.

Who Is the Person, Emerging from This Situation? We see a woman with the maturity, the spiritual stature, who could let go of her own needs and wishes and who rose to the occasion, namely, the challenge to accept the egg from another woman in selflessly letting it merge with the seed of her beloved husband. The wonderful goal presented to her was to increase the happiness of her husband in bringing a child, as if waiting to be created, into the safe embrace of a loving home.

- *"In your grief, live!" (Ezekiel 16:6)*

The second example of a shift of focus away from the problem of unresolved grief and onto the challenge of meaning, is given by another student in Logotherapy, Carin Marcus, who today is a most successful bereavement counselor, using Logotherapy. The client was referred to Carin for counseling following the sudden death of his girlfriend. I am using only a short extract from the session.

T: How has your week been since our last session?

C: Well, when I left here last week, I actually felt quite energized, so I went to the office to do some work, and that was good. Then, the day of the anniversary (*of his girlfriend's death*) was shocking. I did not want to get out of bed, so I decided that I would stay there for a while, because that is what I needed to do. Then I went to Jane's house (the home of the sister of the deceased) to be with her family. It just brought back so much for me. But I remember in the last session, we were talking about how each day is hard and each day is a day of missing but also of survival. So it helped to put it in perspective. I am just so tired of coping, I feel as though I just don't have the energy any more. …I just so wish to be with her. It is just so hard. I often think about my life, and about how I am going to live until God decides to take me.

T: What will it take to live until you die?

C: I think about that often, and I have come to realize that there are three options: to merely exist, to exist miserably, or to make something out of life.

T: Sometimes the decision to live is the harder decision to carry out because it requires energy, attitude and courage. I suppose sometimes it would be easier to just exist.

C: I know I cannot just exist, but I also don't know if I have the energy to start living. But I also know that I need to make a decision and then do it, it cannot be a long process.

T: Perhaps you have already made your decision. The decision can be the quick part, but it is living the decision that is the process.

C: As I always say, what choice does one have but to survive?

T: It most certainly is a choice, because one can choose to not survive.

C: True, but I would never do that, so my only option is to go on with life.

T: That is a choice and a very courageous one.

(The therapist then explored what was meaningful in the client's present life: that his suffering gave him a sensitivity that made other people turn to him in their own suffering.)

T: You are a very gentle, caring wise and special person. And sadly through your experience you have come to know human suffering and as such, others will find you a great source of support and compassion.

C: Yes, but then I need to also look after me. In fact, I intend just relaxing this weekend.

T: How are you feeling now?

C: It's funny but last night when I saw I was coming here today I was so pleased! YES! So much has been happening; I just needed to come here today!

In her evaluation of the session, Carin wrote: "I perceive J. as a brave young man, who will, with time, be able to transform his pain into something meaningful. It has been a long slow journey this. However, each session is a journey in itself and one step forward."

Carin's father died when she was but a little girl. She grew up in a house of mourning. Her mother never got to grips with the death of her beloved husband. What her mother could not do, Carin did. She has turned their loss into something meaningful in becoming a bereavement counselor, helping clients out of their unresolved grief!

Who Is the Person, Emerging from This Situation? In the case of this young man, we see a person coming out of his grief and taking up the challenge to live his life, not mindlessly, not in misery, but with the courage to make it serve a higher purpose. It was to be a monument in loving memory of his beloved girlfriend. It was to honor the gift she gave him: to turn the mourning of others into the joy of meaning. Life is precious, always, also beyond grief and anguish!

A Radical Shift in Focus

Both therapists in the above examples shifted the focus of their clients away from being helpless in the face of daunting decisions because of traumatic situations in their lives to the capabilities and strengths their clients have in being able to deal with their problems victoriously and, as a result, grow from it by learning to step into their own shoes courageously.

There is the famous case of Frankl's dealing with an elderly general practitioner who could not overcome the loss of his adored wife. Frankl (1967, p. 24) confronted him with the question, "What would have happened, Doctor, if you had died first and your wife would have had to survive you?" "Oh," he said, "for her this would have been terrible; how she would have suffered!" Whereupon Frankl replied, "You see, Doctor, such a suffering has been spared her, and it is you who have spared her this suffering; but now, you have to pay for it by surviving and mourning her." The client said no word but shook Frankl's hand and calmly left his office. Suffering ceases to be suffering in some way at the moment it finds a meaning, such as the meaning of a sacrifice (ibid, p. 24).

• *A sacred spiritual castle*

The next session was conducted by Andrea Trope of Johannesburg, South Africa, a life coach and now a trained logotherapist. We will not divulge her client's name even though the story of the client can proudly have her name put on it! We will simply call her: "Di." Her initial complaint was of suffering from an eating disorder: bulimia. I will give you just the gist of the hour long session between them and will comment on the process as I see it unfolding.

The process is one where the client comes to ever clearer realizations as she is questioned, led, provoked and challenged by Andrea who keeps the focus unfailingly on the client herself. The story is hers. Her life is her own. But it is up to us who are listening to her story to track its true meaning. What is she *really* trying to say to us? After all, she would hardly have come for help, for a time of reflection with a therapist, if she was not trying to search out what her life was requiring of her right now, that is, what the real *meaning* was of what she was going through, a meaning that somehow and for some reason or other, was escaping her.

What, in fact, is she being called upon to recognize and *do* about what she is experiencing right now?

If we are listening *well* and pick up the cues or logohints (hints of meaning) her story gives us, illuminate it to her with probing questions, challenging statements, possible answers, affirmative responses, the truth she seeks will dawn on her. All that we would have done is to have helped her keep her thoughts on track!

In Session!

T: It's good to meet you, Di.

C: There has been a lot going on, but I am glad that I have taken some time out to talk to you, Andy. There are some things that concern me. My life is really good and everything is on track. Yet I have an anxiety.

(Immediate insight into the client's situation is given to us: her life is good, everything is on track, but there is something in the way: an anxiety. Logotherapy teaches that life is naturally future-directed. If it is not, then something is disturbing this thrust ever forward and onward in our lives. The therapist in this case had this orientation, even though not giving voice to it. She chose to try and find out from the client what it is that the client perceives is holding her back.)

T: Can you identify this anxiety?

C: Yes. It's all about my eating and my weight. Everything is good. My marriage is fine. My kids are good, my work is great. I have finally got a handle on my eating, but I just hope that it's a permanent recovery.

T: Tell me a bit about this recovery?

C: Well, I was bulimic for many years. I call those the lost years actually. I feel like I lost so much in those twenty odd years.

T: What does the word lost mean to you, Di?

C: I could have achieved more; I could have been more honest to friends and family, to my husband. Instead, every time I had some kind of conflict that came up, I threw up. I lacked a voice.

(We are always listening for "meaning cues", also called: logohints in Logotherapy. What is the real issue behind the so-called problem? Logotherapy is not problem-focused but **meaning-focused.** In other words, what does the problem, in this case bulimia, and the fear whether the recovery from it is complete, actually mean? What does it say to us? Therapies with a psychodynamic orientation may want to explore the causes of the bulimia in the client's relationship with the significant others in her life, especially the mother since she is the one most closely identified with eating habits because of her role in the feeding and nurturing of the child. This is legitimate but, whatever the conflict, **it is the suppression of the person of the client, her own freedom to be herself that is the real crisis of meaning!** And this is exactly the cue the client gives us: **"I lacked a voice."** In fact, having pinpointed the real issue, this becomes the focus, not whether the bulimia is totally recovered from or not or whether some suppressed conflict (e.g. with the mother) has not come fully to light and has not been "worked through.")

T: You speak as if all of this is in the past tense. It sounds as if your life has taken on a new direction?

(Another, constant focus of logotherapy is on the strengths, the abilities of the client, the power of the human spirit to overcome problems and reach out to meaning in life. This is what the therapist does here in affirming that the problem is in the past tense, something that the client has already successfully dealt with. Feeling empowered by an illumination of her strengths, the client is inspired to move forward, that is, to the real issue at stake.)

C: It actually is. I am in full recovery. I haven't been bulimic for about two years. And even before that, it was so occasional that it didn't qualify as a disorder. At this moment in my life, no matter what I do, no matter how much I eat, I never ever have an episode.

T: That is something to be proud of, Di.

C: I am proud. It's my greatest achievement. I still feel so anxious though.

(Having put the "problem" of bulimia out of the way which, after all, was but a symptom of the real issue, the therapist pushes towards the client having a full look at the real issue, namely, that she feels she is not giving full expression to herself.)

T: Where does the anxiety reveal itself?

C: It doesn't come when I eat too much, it comes when something happens and *I can't speak my mind (italics mine!).* Like when my husband is irritating me or when I am overwhelmed. I can see the signs coming and I get a mild panic attack coming on. These are the signs of a binge, a purge session. *So it's not about eating. (Italics mine!)*

T: How do you know it's not about eating?

C: It's not about feeling full. If I get full I ignore it. Food isn't a trigger anymore.

T: So it's the stress of life that feels like a trigger?

C: Yes. It is. I watch it all the time. What I really want to be doing is not watching it. I don't want to have to be so vigilant with myself.

(Even though the client acknowledges that food is not the problem anymore, she confesses that this is what she is still watching, namely, her past patterns of dealing with the bulimia. What we seem to be dealing with is the client's reticence, her feelings of uncertainly in venturing out in a new way. She still has her eyes turned on herself instead of the goals ahead of her in her life. The point is that she**knows** that this is what she is doing and must rid herself of!)

T: What would it mean to you to not be so vigilant?

C: Every day I say to myself – today I am not going to binge and purge. *And it's so stupid because I never do it. (Italics mine!)* I have this dialogue in my head that seems stuck there. *I don't think I need it anymore. (Italics mine!)*

(The challenge in logotherapy to the client and to all of us is to step out of self-absorption. A problem was a problem because it made us focus on ourselves and obstructed our reaching out and getting involved in our lives in a real and meaningful way. The call is to come out of ourselves and to step bravely into our lives! The call is to move **forward**, that is why life seems to be **calling** us, like a voice coming from the future or from somewhere **ahead of us.** A therapy that keeps the focus on the problem, namely, as something from the past, still haunting us, in a sense stalls movement by turning us back into a position of focusing on ourselves in a negative way: "something is wrong with me." **Undue importance is then given to the problem.** A focus on the problem as the all-important issue in fact increases the client's sense of helplessness, of being no more than a poor victim needing someone else to expertly take the problem out of the way! This kind of focus and conversation between client and therapist shuts the door to meaning, to the call that is being made on the client by the very problem itself. The problem is there exactly because the client has allowed it to be there by misperceiving who he or she is in relation to life that is continually beckoning the client to become his or her authentic self, to in fact **grow** into what he or she is **meant to become**.

Frankl spoke about shutting the door to meaning in a problem-focused type of therapy as engaging in two monologues. Only with reference to something outside of both the client and the therapist: on life that is calling the client to live it, is there a real dialogue, a dialogue that illuminates meaning: what it is the problem is challenging the client to do! The "dialogue in her head" is getting the client nowhere and she is realizing this. The therapist turns (dereflects) the gaze of her client away from herself and on to what might be out there in the world waiting for her to step into):

T: Di, how would you feel if you had a day off from this dialogue in your head? Or even an hour. What would be there if there wasn't this dialogue?
C: Well, this dialogue is taking up a lot of valuable space in my head. It is occupying space that other lovely healthy things could take up in my head. Thoughts and movies. Maybe just nothing. There is this constant chatter. I am sick and tired of this chatter. I don't think it is serving me anymore. At what point do I say, I don't need you anymore. I am actually healthy. I will never throw up again. My weight is constant. The thing is, I am not thin, and I think that this drives me a bit nuts. I am normal.

(The client is able to highlight what she perceives as holding her back. The bulimia – which was her secret for many years – provided a safe and familiar place for her, a secret place that kept all that she was unwilling to face away from her. Her problem was made a friend. But this relationship with escapism was very costly. It was actually harming her. It also harmed relationships she really cared about. Instead of accepting herself, the "normal" thing to do, she turned what may have been a lack of acceptance of her person by significant others in her life into a punitive yardstick of perfection: being thin. The battle was to find her own boundaries. The threat was, as she said later in the session: "I was so afraid that I would get 'humungously' huge and fat", that is, that she would totally lose herself in being totally absorbed and taken over, almost engulfed or eaten up or swallowed by an overpowering figure or force that exercised an oppressive and jealous hold over her. She was not allowed to be her normal or real self and was being forced to take on the identity forced upon her. The thin or more perfect version of herself was, paradoxically, also a way to defensively withdraw into very narrow and tight boundaries. This did not remove the threat, however. She was still at the mercy of the oppressive figure in the form of an overwhelming compulsion to somehow appease or make peace with the problem. The boundaries of "thinness" – of perfection, of being "pleasing" in the sight of critical others – became taut. It was squeezing the life out of her: "I have suffered right through it", she confessed. But then she also confessed what she now came to realize):

C: The problem is that I inflicted it on myself, so I have guilt about the suffering. **I actually chose it to a large degree.** Eventually I couldn't blame my parents anymore. It became a habit.

T: It's an amazing thing that you take ownership of this, Di, that you were responsible for this habit.

C: Yes. I do think I was ultimately responsible for this habit.

(The client makes the most significant statement of truth: that what we have negatively experienced in our lives and from which we have formed wrong impressions – distorted perceptions of our own worth and the meaning of our lives and that we consequently accept as the truth about ourselves – becomes an ingrained part or a habitual way of response subsequent to the hurtful experiences. The reasoning can be as follows: "I am treated like a slave; it must be true that I am a slave; I therefore act like a slave; I perpetuate my own slavery." We can fall into these habitual ways of behaving for a very long time until the realization hits homes that the habitual way of going about our lives is destructive to us. It spoils what we value. It keeps us from what we really want to discover about ourselves: our inherent goodness and capability to overcome bad with good, that is, to break free of our bondages and receive a new way of living through the sheer impulse to find more satisfying answers to our lives. We need a Mount Sinai – a revelatory or life-changing – experience to come out of bondage! To remain with the habit is to stay in a state of not being released to fulfill the true purpose of our lives. What thinking or reflective person can remain satisfied with this stalled state of affairs? It is nothing but a living death! Taking responsibility for our lives, taking up the reigns of living our lives in an authentic way, is the thrust that the therapist spells out as a challenge to the client, based on the client's own deep and dawning desire for this to happen.)

T: Taking responsibility has certainly helped you in your recovery. That is such a brave thing to do to own your habit.

C: Well, maybe it did. Eventually it's not anyone's fault, *and it comes to me as an adult to find my voice, (italics mine!)* and to stop my self-abuse, and to be aware of the triggers.

(Here the client, in her own words, expresses what she is realizing is the call upon her life right now: to find her own voice. She has been holding back in doing this, still holding onto old familiarities, her old way of doing things, a bit fearful and uncertain about this new life ahead of her. The therapist gently encourages her):

T: It's as if you have come through a crisis, and now you are on the other side.

C: I am on the other side of the chaos. It's very calm here.

T: It seems as if you are trying to define yourself again.

C: It's hard to define myself without this disorder. I am holding so tightly on to this disorder. *Who am I without this disorder? (italics mine!)*

T: Di, to face an eating disorder; to overcome it; to stop the triggers and to stop the actions of the eating disorder, means that you really have faced your fears.

C: Yes, I did. ... I stopped purging before I stopped binging. Then I stopped binging because it's a really uncomfortable place to put myself. And my weight has stabilized. It was quite an amazing discovery that.

T: It sound like so much has emerged: new habits, new patterns.

C: Yes. A new me has emerged from the ruins.

T: How would you describe this new you?

C: Well, I am clearer. I can see things more clearly. I have more of a voice and at times when I can't say what I wish and my anxiety escalates, I don't resort to harming myself. I will not inflict harm on myself. I have more self-respect.

T: This new life – how would you describe it?

C: It means I am healthier, that I not playing with the death force. I have a future. I won't die a young death.

T: What else does it hold for you, this new life?

C: *It makes me more present* with my family *(italics mine!)*. I am not thinking what I am going to put in my mouth next, or when I am going to purge. *I am in the room with them, and I remain in the room with them emotionally and spiritually. (Italics mine!)*

(The client perceives where she has come to, that she has indeed emerged from her state of pathological hiddenness. She is emboldened by this realization to even more clearly answer the call: "Adam, where are you?" Her state of shame and withdrawal from the world had served to evoke her real desires, her dormant will to meaning that James Hillman graphically describes as "a condition of want **beyond** personal needs". The suffering her withdrawal had inflicted upon her had made her receptive to the call in her life to emerge from her self-made prison. After discussing that her struggle has brought her to where she is now, that it had meaning and she responded: **"I don't think I ever lost anything,"** the therapist could affirm):

T: It sounds as if you found something wonderful after the struggle.

C: Yes. My life, myself. ... My life now is so full and rich and I am not tied to my food or my starving or my binging. It's like an amazing house that I have built that has deep foundations as opposed to a tented village that I created on sand. I feel stable.

T: Di, what gives you this anchorage, what holds you?

C: Well, what anchors me are my children. I also can believe in myself. I know that I can do anything because if I can give up this addiction, I can do anything!

(The client now spells out some amazing truths, truths that heal and free us:

- *She realizes that she is called to **responsibility**: to be there for her family, to be present in their lives.*
- *She now believes that she has also been given the capability to do what life is requiring of her.*

- *In fact, the suffering she went through was to challenge her or to put her to the test. What was invested in her will bear dividends: she will not only be shown what it is that life is expecting of her but also come to see that she has the ability to overcome adversity triumphantly!)*

C: You know I never accepted the suffering. I felt I brought it upon myself. I was obviously a symptom carrier for my family, but *I held onto it. (italics mine!)* I knew that I needed to do the work. I never accepted that this was going to be the rest of my life.

(Another amazing truth emerged, namely, that the client now felt that she had a mission. A pathology may have been handed down to her from her parents, something she had taken on and suffered. But she was the one to break the chain and to retrospectively release her own parents from bondage by her forgiving attitude towards them and by relieving them of the heaviness of the burden of pathology in seeing her freed and healthily transmitting her new found values to the next generation).

C: It has given me something for my children. I am much more available and much more of a mother. I know that I wasn't really there with them for a long time. **Now I don't go through the motions. I am really available**.

(The past, its problems, everything associated with the bulimia, must be put away, moved away from. It no longer features!)

C: I need to put this box down. It's getting heavy. … You know, Andy, it's not the burden of an eating disorder that I have anymore; it's the burden of my memories and regrets of this eating disorder that I carry around. … Maybe we should do something with the box on the floor?
T: What do you suggest? Put it in the cupboard?
C: No, I would like to tie some helium balloons to it and watch that box float away. Blue and white balloons actually.

(The client is Jewish. The blue and white balloons correspond to the blue and white flag of Israel, symbol of a homecoming of the nation of Israel to their own promised land. It is a symbol of a release from bondage from a painfully long dispersion among the nations of the world as aliens in hostile and foreign lands. The client had suffered a victimized state for over twenty years of her life in a place that was foreign to her. She felt an alien, not in her own and promised space. She was not herself in what had held her back for so many years!)

T: What would that mean to you to watch your box float away?
C: I would feel so much lighter, so relieved to see my past issues and my suffering be taken away. … Those memories are part of me. … I can remind myself where I came from. And that my suffering brought me here. … But I need that heavy box to drift off. There is too much pain there.
T: And without that box of pain, what would there be?

C: A new life. A new beginning. Not so weighed down. I can focus on other things. I can jump in the pool with my kids; I can read a book at night. It's amazing.

T: This addiction has called you to action, and you have risen so wonderfully to the challenge. You have answered this call.

C: I did answer this call.

T: What was asked of you, Di?

C: *I was asked to overcome it. (italics mine!)* I am being asked to speak up a bit more. I am asked to reinvest in my future. And have a bit more faith in myself.

T: You have been called to action, Di. You have been called to another life for yourself.

C: I have been called to another life. I am glad I have dealt with this now, because I believe addiction is passed on from generation to generation, and I needed to heal myself. I needed to fix this.

T: You have spoken about a new life. What does this new life look like?

C: It's cleaner, not so messy. My marriage is in a much better space. I am more direct with my husband, although it's not always easy. But I have much more integrity, I am much more congruent. *I am who I am. (Italics mine!)*

T: A new life, Di. It's almost like a monument that you have created out of what has gone before and what is to come.

C: Yes, I like that. It's like I have built this beautiful palace. *A spiritual palace. (Italics mine!)*

T: What else does this palace hold for you?

C: It's built on strong foundations of healing. It honors me, and it honors my past.

T: You don't have to give up your past and memories of your past. Your past holds meaning.

C: Yes, my past is meaningful. It defines me, who I am right now, and who I am to become.

T: Out of your suffering, you chose a new way, Di. What is this new way?

C: To live more honestly, to say what I need to say, and not be so hard on myself.

T: Can you imagine that there is a part of you that is untouched by this illness, this diagnosis? It's been there throughout the addiction. And this part of you has remained intact.

(The therapist now challenges the client with the most important truth: that she is at heart innocent and pure, inherently good. This is what Frankl meant when he stated that the human spirit remains **unscathed**. This is a liberating freedom from guilt and oppression that remains for us at all times, no matter how awful our circumstances or how dark the pit we have fallen into. Frankl called it the "last of our freedoms", namely the freedom (the ability) to take a stand, to choose our own way. No force, however evil, can rob us of this freedom. It is the kind of freedom that allowed the horrifically victimized and terrorized camp inmates to enter the gas chambers with a prayer on their lips, the faith, the expression of human goodness that can overcome the fear, even of death! This truth hit home to the client in a powerful and empowering way):

C: That's a nice way of looking at it, Andy!

T: How would you describe this part of you, Di?

C: Well, I suppose this part would be ok with myself, and *it's innocent. That is what I value in myself. Being innocent. Yes, I like that word! (Italics mine!)*

T: So throughout all the suffering, and all that has gone before, there is a part of you that has remained innocent, pure and ok with yourself.

C: Yes, there is *that innocence that sits alongside the wisdom (italics mine!).* I like this concept a lot!

T: And being ok with yourself is something that you are proud of.

C: I am proud of myself. I like being ok with myself. I may not be perfect, but am probably the most perfect version of myself right now.

T: That's a wonderful way to end the session. Thank you, Di.

C: Thank you, Andy.

The most amazing truth became the possession of this client: that our inherent innocence has to become responsibly informed! It has to become *wise: it must gain the discernment of what life constantly requires of us.* Responsibly informed innocence makes us *whole.* It is holy! Becoming what we can be potentially, we give full expression to ourselves. We become completely ourselves!

Who Is the Person, Emerging from This Situation?   What a story we have here of a woman who, in her own words, rose to a new life: "a new me has emerged from the ruins". From the ruins of her conflict-laden past emerged her own unscathed, pure and innocent spirit! It was a true rebirth experience. All her past problems, and how she struggled to be free of them, had brought her to this point: to let the heavy burden of struggle lift. She reclaimed herself. She found her own voice, began to give greater expression to herself. She became fully available; there for the others in her life, free to embrace all that life has to give her!

Let's Summarize!

Who then, are you, sitting opposite me? What will I, as a logotherapist, have to say about you, about every client that comes to me for therapy? Let me state it clearly, point by point.

You are and every client is:

- A unique person,
- confronted by a unique task,
- called to responsibility through the voice of conscience
- brought to this moment with every capability to perform what life is requiring in the situation.
- There is a choice to be made
- and an action to be performed
- that will release a move forward towards
- greater spiritual vitality, mental health and mature human stature.

- There is a destiny to fulfill.
- The past has led to it.
- The future awaits it.
- The moment is now!

Life is always immediate! All of the past is right here in the present moment. All of your life has brought you to **this moment** and seeks to meet you right now. "Adam, where are you?" echoes throughout life!

Listening with a Third Ear

A greater presence, the presence of meaning, is in the room. Am I as the therapist discerning it? You too, like the clients in the sessions above, are being called out of yourself by the very awareness of meaning, of what life is calling upon you to be. Paradoxically as it may seem, stepping out of yourself, you become yourself!

And as for me, the therapist, do I sense that call, am I aligning myself with it? It is *your* life that I am focused on. Can I discern what you are meant to be in an astute enough way?

Do I have faith in you?

Frankl warned: "If we are to bring out the human potential at its best, we must first believe in its existence and presence. Otherwise man too, will drift, he will deteriorate."

In my encounter with you, life is addressing *me!*

Exercise for You, the Reader: The Unconscious God

Answer the following questions thoughtfully:

What do you really enjoy doing? What gives you a feeling of happiness and pleasure, a sense of satisfaction in doing it? What really interests you, captures your full attention? When do you feel fully and happily *yourself*, doing what? What excites you or inspires you when you contemplate what you really want to do with your life, where you want to be, with whom, doing what?

An answer to the above questions may point out to you where it is that you are being called to be; the place you were ordained to fill in giving full expression to yourself and embracing all that life is holding out to you.

(continued)

Now consider the full facts of your life, what situation you are in and the people you are involved with now. What are your commitments, duties and responsibilities right now? Does what you have written in answer to the questions above fit the present picture of your life? Does it bring out the very essence of what life is asking of you at the moment? Does what you have written affirm what you can treasure about your life right now; does it point to how you can change things for the better? Can you describe what you have written as a move forward; does it take all of your life up to this point meaningfully into the future?

These questions are important to answer to determine **the authentic and true destiny of your life**, which is NEVER at the expense of others in seeking any selfish or need-gratifying wish or dream of yours. A wish or dream disconnected from the reality, the givens of your life, may be no more than just an escape from where you are meant to be: right there where you are even if where you are, is calling for change, for a move in a different direction.

The meaning is in the moment. True joy, authentic being, triumphant selfhood – the true well springs of deep satisfaction and fulfillment – is to be found in a full grasp of the treasure that is right there for you, right now, in the present circumstances of your life.

References

Frankl, V. E. (1967). *Psychotherapy and existentialism: Selected papers on logotherapy.* New York: Simon and Schuster.
Frankl, V. E. (1968). *Man's search for meaning: An introduction to logotherapy.* London: Hodder and Stoughton.
Frankl, V. E. (2000). *Man's search for ultimate meaning.* Basic Books: New York.
Hillman, J. (1997). *The Soul's code: In search of character and calling.* London: Bantam Books.

Chapter 5
Who Am I, in Relation to You? The Person of the Logotherapist

Abstract A summons of unique responsibility is issued to logotherapists. They must heed the call to listen with a third ear: an ear to the hidden meanings in the client's life. They must see beneath the surface to hidden matters of the heart. Frankl warned: "If we are to bring out the human potential at its best, we must first believe in its existence and presence. Otherwise man too, will drift, he will deteriorate." The ability on the part of the therapist to see the hidden potentials of meaning in the client's life is to a very large degree dependent on the therapist's own experience of meaning. There is no transference or countertransference or any such emotional interference in the person to person interaction between the logotherapist and the client. Frankl strongly stated that logotherapy is more than a mere I and thou interaction. If reference is not made to meaning addressing both therapist and client, their conversation will simply be two monologues.

Keywords Logotherapists are summoned · Listening with a third ear · Grasping hidden meanings · No transference or countertransference · A dialogue of meaning

Who Am I?

I am most reticent to talk about myself. Why? Because when I am out of the picture I am best focused on you. I do not find myself getting in the way. How true Frankl's saying that we are most ourselves when we are not conscious of ourselves. When we are focused on something or someone other than ourselves, we forget ourselves and we lose a discomforting sense of self-consciousness. And I want to be myself, very much so! Why should I self-consciously think about what you think of me, what best to say to impress you? Why should I lose sight of you as I think of what method or technique to use, what procedure to follow, as I anxiously scramble through my own mind in trying to find an answer to your problems?

© Springer Nature Switzerland AG 2020
T. Shantall, *The Life-changing Impact of Viktor Frankl's Logotherapy*,
https://doi.org/10.1007/978-3-030-30770-7_5

The Summons

Feeling summoned by you, the fact that you have come to see me to "get things right" for you and, even worse: that you are *paying* me and therefore can *demand* that I do what I'm paid for, lands me in a state of anxiety. I have to put on a face of confidence, give you the assurance that I am perfectly able to do what you are expecting me to do for you. In this process, I am already thinking of who I can refer you to, who can better help you if I fail to live up to your expectations! What is more, you may be thinking of going to someone else yourself as you size me up as I awkwardly sit there, immobilized by the tension that is there between us!

But, yes, you are right. The onus *is* on me. I *am* being summoned! I *am* the professional. But what is the real summons? It will certainly *not* be what I think you are expecting from me. It will also *not* be something just between the two of us. It will be more, much more. And it will be something we will *both* have to give an ear to. We are *both* involved with something that will call *both of us* out of ourselves.

Both of us will be faced with an awesome responsibility.

A summons must be *read* to know what it is about. Why we are brought together is a question that must be carefully *listened* to in order to know how to answer it correctly. We must understand what is *meant*, what exactly it is we are required to do before we can respond appropriately. We must understand what is meant by the question if we are to answer the questioner correctly.

Yes, there is a questioner, one who wrote out the summons, the reason we were brought together!

Listen and Heed!

I must start this process, yes, but by *listening*. A lot of careful listening will be involved. I must encourage you to talk, to open up the subject. If you can do that easily, I will let it pour out of you, without interruption. If you find it hard to talk, I will encourage you by promptings and questions. I may spell this out to you, namely, that I need to hear what you have to say. Only if you will allow me into your world, can I possibly grasp it. I am not to remain a stranger to you, but someone who will accompany you on *your* journey, one that will follow all that you have to say, absorb all that you feel, soak myself in *your* impressions of your world.

I will reach out my hand for you to take it. The onus will be on you to do so!

You must allow me to listen by telling me about yourself. The so-called issue or problem that you present is only part of the picture. It is *you*, the one experiencing the problem or facing the issue that I will be looking at. You must allow me to *see* you and nothing and nobody else but you!

You have a responsibility too: to release me out of all my own self-consciousness as you take me along with you. I become more and more involved in the process. As

I succeed in doing this, I will be released from all tension. Every obstacle in the way of our having a true encounter will be removed.

And what, in effect, will we be doing? We will be moving further and further away from the so-called presenting problem, from the appearance of things, from the shallow grasp, the rash conclusion. We will *both* be taken along in the process leading *both* of us to the meanings that are beckoning you in your life, waiting for us both to grasp them.

Look and See!

The meanings that we are to discover in your life are not only out there in the world but right here with us in the room. They are to be found in what you will be telling me and in what will be transpiring between us. As I listen to you and comment on what you are impressing upon me, I am helping *you* to listen. We are therefore *both* listening to what is being said to us, what truth is busy unfolding before our very eyes.

But can I, the therapist, really listen and hear, look into your life and see what it is *I* am being called upon to grasp and illuminate to you if I am hard of hearing and blinded in ways that will keep me as an outsider or even worse: as an intruder into the sanctity of your life and person?

How open to truth am I? How far along life's journey towards an embrace of the meaning of my own life have I come?

Have I a voice to speak to you? Do I have an ear that can hear what you are trying to tell me?

What kind of life, what kind of person am I bringing into the therapy with you?

Let me tell you about myself.

My Own Experience of Meaning

I was studying psychoanalysis in London.

The training in psychoanalysis also included a personal analysis during which I had begun to feel increasingly restless about the fact that, in focusing solely on the problems of childhood and the influence of past experiences on present behavior, I was missing out on my present life that I felt was somehow passing me by. The training of prospective psychoanalysts is need-focused. With my analyst, I was delving into frustrations and unsatisfied needs in seeking ways to resolve conflicts and to reach a greater feeling of happiness and satisfaction. The origins of these conflicts could invariably be traced to repressed childhood experiences.

Getting the past "sorted out" was one thing. But the opportunities presented by each new day seemed to come from the future. I was somehow missing to fully live my present life with an eye to a future that was "waiting" to be reached out to. My life seemed to lack vision – a dream to realize or ideals to be inspired by. I was being absorbed by my own needs and fantasies and could not escape the uncanny feeling that life was passing me by, that time was running out – and when would I have time to catch up with what I was now missing out on?

I had bought only one book when I left South Africa for London. Browsing through a bookshop, the title of the book caught my eye: "Jesus and Logotherapy" (Leslie 1965). I had studied the works of Frankl in my pre-graduate courses in Philosophy and remember being very drawn yet also challenged by it. But what had Jesus to do with Logotherapy? But the question became: What has Logotherapy to do with *me*?

Frankl was living in Vienna at the time and was teaching only in German, a language I was not familiar with. I nevertheless took the plunge and in my desperation wrote to him, explaining my disillusionment with the psychoanalytic training that I was receiving. He wrote back and invited me to his first training school in English that would open that coming summer at the United States International University in San Diego! What synchronicity!

Was it life calling out to me to heed its call and follow its direction?

I had no sooner joined Frankl in America when I was shocked by the news of the death of my beloved father back in South Africa. A spell of intense grief followed during which I was particularly plagued with the remorse over lost opportunities. In many ways my past had been wasted since the kind of life I had been living was a trial-and-error and a type of haphazard way of being. Needs and dissatisfactions, painful self-consciousness and a looking for love, a very self-focused and aimless kind of wandering, earmarked my life. I had to find some purpose and direction for living or life was not worth the living.

I had to know where I was going and go there! Nothing else would do.

As much as it was a point of utter determination, it was also a point of surrender. I had given up on myself, on the self-centered way of living my life. I was aching for something different, for something beyond the narrow confines of mere day-to-day existence.

I fell into an exhausted sleep and dreamt that I had written a loving letter to my father which I was about to mail. I woke up with a painful start, agonizingly realizing that I would never be able to communicate with him again.

Just then, I remembered the Diary he had given me as a parting gift.

That very morning Frankl had spoken about embracing each new day as a precious opportunity, the events of which we had to write up in our book of life and file away in memory. "Having been is the surest form of being", he told us. What we have experienced and with whom, what we have learnt, how we have dealt with difficulties, all of that could be stored away out of reach of anything that could spoil it or take it away from us.

Looking at the empty pages of my Diary, I heard my father's voice, challenging me: "Fill up your Diary!"

With crystal clear clarity, I felt that my father was expecting me to fill the yet empty pages of the Diary he had given me with the events of my life that I would now undertake to live fully and with care. I had an awed sensation that he was instructing me to take up my life in a new way. I felt his presence with me. He was there, for those few awesome moments, like a strong witness for life, waiting for me to accept the commission before he would take his place on the grandstand of time to watch me winning the race that I too had to run, yet a race, strangely, set out only for me.

It was *my* race which could only be run by me!

The pain that I had felt a moment before, changed to a surge of inspiration which seemed to have sprung up from a deep and innermost region, like some core experience, which permeated my whole being, filling, what I only then realized, was an all-pervading emptiness. I felt brim-full with joy – such a paradoxical feeling in a situation of grief!

The dawn was breaking outside. As I stepped out into the new day, I was struck by the clarity with which I was seeing everything. It was as if the scales of an inward-looking type of living had fallen off my eyes and that I was now, perhaps for the first time, able to see life clearly.

An Essay on Meaning

The section above was written in the foreword of my book: "Life's Meaning in the Face of Suffering", a book prescribed for students in the advanced course in logotherapy. A question given to the students to answer was based on the sentence: "as much as it was a point of utter determination, it was also a point of surrender." They had to write a short essay about their own experience of meaning, especially in terms of the balance between exercising responsibility on the one hand, and dependence on something other than themselves on the other.

The following was one of the answers to the assignment:

"The key to Frankl's theories is the concept of meaning. It is the heartbeat of his work, and for me, it is the key which opens the door to higher consciousness. In every book I read on Logotherapy, Frankl and his colleagues invite me, the reader, to experience my life in the most powerful and profound way possible. He reminds me over and over again that I am unique and exceptional, and that I have the world at my feet. He calls me to discover the meaning in my life, no matter what suffering or joy I am experiencing."

Frankl writes that the prerequisite for finding meaning in our lives is when we engage with life's challenges. This resonates with me on a profound level. I have found that the suffering that I have endured over the past few years has shaped me in a totally different person to what I was in my twenties. I could never have known then that the loss of both my father and brother to cancer would define me as a person going into her mature years. The personal agony of years has been the greatest gift I could have ever received. For it has been in my suffering that my life has found true meaning.

Death reveals life in its most exquisite beauty. Death shows us the way to living each day as if it were our last. Death teaches us that life is fragile and when life is over, it is over. Death calls us to live and dance and eat and play and cry and love. Death calls us to live our lives completely.

Today is 2 years since my brother Leigh passed away. He suffered his brain cancer with the courage of a warrior stepping out into battle. He endured his creeping paralysis with bravery and valor. With every capability that was taken away from him, he replaced it with a silent dignity that only suffering can create. Leigh surrendered to a spiritual dimension. He connected to the G-d-like consciousness that resided within him. This speaks to the ultimate meaning in life. Being witness to this level of suffering, and being able to witness Leigh's ability to step out of himself and reach another dimension greater than himself, has to be the most potent lesson I have ever learnt.

There was very little distinction between my brother's suffering and my own. His daily struggle just to keep alive for one more day became enmeshed in my own daily struggle to bear witness to his dying. And yet, when I look back to those terrible few months before his death, they were significant and meaningful. I took away all my life's lessons from the greatest teacher of all – my brother Leigh.

My brother chose to die with honor and dignity. This showed me that we are always faced with choice even if it appears that choice has been taken away from us. It taught me that we need to take the gift of free choice and become accountable for the decisions we make. These choices give us access to morality and spirituality. This access brings with it a responsibility to make more of ourselves and our lives than ever before. Responsibility is about finding our own true north. It's about making decisions or engaging in deeds that have at their root the best intention for our souls.

Responsibility is about responsibleness. We owe it to ourselves not only to do the right thing but to be the right things. In the months leading up to Leigh's death, I took immense comfort in small acts of love, such as rubbing his feet or massaging his back. I made every effort to keep flying to Cape Town to be with him. Doing these small actions provided the platform through which I could express my love for my brother and connect with him. This connection allowed me to bear my pain with dignity and gave meaning to an agonizing time. I also hold close to me the thought that my being there for him gave his anguished passing some meaning too.

The paradoxical equation in logotherapy is seen when Frankl asks us to take responsibility for our choices, which means going inside ourselves and owning our lives and yet, at the same time, he asks us to surrender to another dimension outside ourselves. Logotherapy commissions us to embrace both the profoundly intimate dimension of meaning, as well as taking a view outside of ourselves. Consciousness points to something outside itself. Meaning is this kind of consciousness. Leigh's passing has commissioned me to a higher consciousness, a deeper sense of meaning in my life. Consciousness is not only about meditating or self-reflection. For me consciousness is found in simple pleasures or in meeting the challenges that come to us in seemingly ordinary ways. Meaning is found in doing something. I made sense of my brother's death by studying logotherapy. My liberation from the pain was found in doing assignments. Meaning in my life is found in the love I have for my husband and children, for my family. Meaning is therefore found outside myself and can be quantified. When I count my blessings, I literally count the way my life holds meaning.

Frankl contends that when we experience meaning, we feel directed towards the future. I am filled with hope and faith. I truly believe that the future holds love and light, meaning and endless possibility."

Written by our logotherapist, Andrea Trope, when she was busy completing her advanced course in Logotherapy in South Africa in 2012.

This Is My Moment Too!

Who am I and where am I in this encounter between us in therapy? How does the meaning of our moment speak to me? For surely, this is my moment too! Our therapy means something to *me*. *I* have been brought into this process of interaction with you. If my own life has convinced me of its meaning, and I believe that things no longer happen in a haphazard way for me, that I have found purpose and direction in my own life, then you are not just a client to me. Our therapy is not just another job outside of the very thrust of my own meaning-directed life. It is very much part of it, and more: it is a *destined* part of it! In other words, however awesome and a bit frightening this may sound, *we were ordained to meet*! This boggles the mind a bit, does it not?

Are we not making something too serious of our meeting? Can't we engage with it more lightly?

No!

Here is something paradoxical: To believe that our meeting was not accidental or just another exchange among many other exchanges that you and I have had in our lives – that you are not just another one among my many other clients – does not bring something heavy or the pressure of expectation into it. If I believe that our meeting is not for nothing, that there is more to it than meets the eye, I can begin to feel quite excited about it. All of what is to happen between us is not all up to me or up to you. If I truly believe that we are to find meaning together, that we are accompanied and led by life itself towards what it wants to reveal to us, the burden lifts! I can lose all tenseness; relax into the process.

We will be shown the way!

Believing, as I am, that I am open to being addressed; convinced as I have become in my own life that I can detect the meaning of the moment: what I am being asked to do, how I am expected to be in every situation of my life; if the door to meaning in my life is wide open, as open as Andrea described herself, as open to and directed towards a beckoning future, full of possibilities, love and light, why then should I be afraid that nothing of much consequence will happen between us or, at the opposite end-point of this fear: that what will happen will be too much or too difficult for me to handle?

I have to only declare myself *ready*, that is, *available* in this moment. The rest, in a sense, will happen by itself!

Does this mean I have no real confidence in myself? On the contrary! If your life led you to me for this moment then my life too has led me to this moment! *I am fully prepared for this moment.* Whatever experience I have gained, grasp I have achieved, the kind of person I am, will be sufficient for this moment.

I am *infinitely* capable!

Is this arrogance? Indeed, no! It is *faith*, the faith that life will not fail me as it will prove not to have failed you. I am fully equipped with the right kind of attitude, an attitude of inspired hope!

Frankl spoke about *anticipatory anxiety*, the kind of fear and obsessive worry that trips up everything and that actually brings about that which we so dreaded. We fall victim to our fears. We predict that we are going to fail and then, to prove the point, we fail! Faith in the unconditional meaningfulness of life: that life is not cruel and spiteful, just waiting to pounce on us with dashed hopes, rude disappointments, failure and despair, but that we can trust life to be what it is: wonderful, beautiful, awesome and great, *liberates* us. We are free to be ourselves fully in the moment of every situation in our lives! What I have, therefore, is an *anticipatory hope: an unconditional expectation of sure meaning!*

I am, therefore, wide open to you, ready to fully receive you. Without fear and trepidation, I am fully available for what life will show us it is intending for you. And what it intends is *always* for the good! How that blesses me, time and again!

I must illustrate this to you.

The Unquenchable Thirst for Meaning

Thirst is the surest sign of water, the Austrian novelist, Franz Werfel (1890–1945), is contended as saying. I had this experience with an Israeli client during his short stay in South Africa while visiting his family and where I was living at the time. He had serious marital problems and had come to see his family to inform them about it. The family was shocked and worried. Everything was going so well for him! He had made a life for himself in Israel. He had a successful career as a medical doctor. He had married a lovely girl. They had such a good marriage. What went wrong? His family referred him to me.

We managed only three sessions.

But three sessions proved to be enough. I had been put in a position of readiness to meet him.

I knew the story that preceded his visit.

He was the third generation son of a most remarkable family that I had become involved with as their family therapist. His mother was undergoing therapy with me, so were her brothers, his uncles. I also had a number of sessions with his grandmother and had been the therapist of some of the other grandchildren. The dysfunction in the family seemed to have started with the client's grandfather, the one person in the family that I did not have the privilege to meet.

The client's uncle heard me speak on Logotherapy at a public meeting and after the talk came up to me and asked whether he could come and see me. His mother was with him. This started an unfolding relationship with almost the entire family as member after member came for therapy.

Unto the Third and Fourth Generation

The breakthrough moment came during the last and final session. The grasp of this momentous meaning moment did not at first come to him, *but to me.*

He was an observant Jew. But we did not talk about religion. The discussion was around his present crisis. The relationship between him and his wife had become very strained. They were quarreling most of the time. He could not tell me what the quarrels were really about, except that he felt full of forebodings about the relationship. Why? When did he start feeling all his forebodings; what started the quarreling between them? It eventually became clear that the trouble between them began at a point when his wife expected them to start a family of their own.

Verses from the book of Deutoronomy (5:9,10) came sharply to my mind, namely that the "sins" of the fathers are "visited" upon the children unto the third and fourth generation. "You know," I said to him, "you made me realize the truth of a portion of Scripture I have never understood." I quoted the verses. "I always thought it extremely unfair that children should suffer for what went wrong in the lives of their parents, even up to the third and fourth generation! I now understand. You are in the third generation from the time of your grandfather. I was told that your grandfather was a very successful businessman in Iraq. But when the State of Israel was declared, the Jews in Iraq became singled out for persecution. He had to flee the country, leaving everything behind. Was South Africa to be a haven to him? I was told that he was a difficult man, not easy to relate to, but who is to know what problems he himself had to face? Speaking to your uncles and mother, members of the second generation, it became clear to me that they all suffered, in various and different ways, from the problems that had been passed onto them because of the way your grandfather related to them. I have witnessed the effects of that hurt as it was carried over to your siblings, nieces and nephews – the third generation down the line. Tell me, do you think that the conflicts that started developing between you and your wife had anything to do with your fear that, if you had children, you would be passing the burden of suffering in your family on to your own children as well?"

He looked at me somewhat stunned.

I continued: "But do you realize what this means? And thank you so much for helping me to at last understand the meaning of that Scripture! So strong is the will to meaning implanted in our hearts that whereas the second generation suffer the ill effects of the so-called 'sins of the fathers', the third and fourth generation are further removed from the original source of the problem. You took up from where the second generation left off in their own search for meaning in their lives. You moved to Israel and made a great success of your life. You also married a wonderful woman and had a good marriage. How far you have come! How strong the will to meaning is! You can break the chain of family hurt. You can sever the link to your family past, start a new family, have a new beginning without the fear that you will be passing on anything emotionally harmful to your children. You can release the power of love on to the following generations to do its wonderful work far beyond what we can possibly imagine! Such a triumph of love also works retroactively. It can bring healing and comfort to your entire family."

His face lit up. His eyes were sparkling. He could hardly wait to leave my office! Just over 3 months later I received a telegram to say that his wife was pregnant. Then a most astounding thing happened. Life itself witnessed its meaning to him. The baby boy was born on Rosh Hashanah, the Jewish New Year. At the climax festival of the Jewish New year called *Simchat Torah* (the rejoicing in the Law), Jews start the rereading of the Torah (the five books of Moses) from the beginning again. "Breishit" (Genesis) is the Hebrew word for "beginning". Genesis is a book of new beginnings. Was a new era ushered in for his entire family?

Then I got another telegram: they named the little boy: "Adam"!

"Comfort, Comfort My People" (Isaiah 40:1)

As Logotherapists we are commissioned. A student said to Frankl concerning Frankl's life: "The meaning of your life is that you are to bring meaning to the lives of others."

The following case history was told to the most famous disciple of Frankl, Dr. Elizabeth Lukas by Dr. Robert Barnes, President of the Viktor Frankl Institute of Logotherapy in the United States, and was recorded in the International Forum for Logotherapy (1993, 16, 51–54).

Two families, both with little girls, living next to each other, were close friends. One morning one of the mothers, on her way to the supermarket, stopped at her friend's house, jumped out of the car, leaving the car door open and, without even turning off the motor, asked her friend, as she often did, if she could do any shopping for her. The other mother was pleased because she was preparing her 4-year-old daughter's birthday party and needed some party snacks and decorations. The two women quickly made a shopping list.

Meanwhile, the little girl, Mary, saw the neighbor's car in front of her house. She had often been taken along in the neighbor's car, and she climbed through the left-open door. What happened next can only be presumed. The child probably released the parking brake and the car, standing on a slight uphill, started slowly rolling back. The little girl fell out of the open door and rolled under the car. The front wheels of the car rolled over her and crushed her.

The mother came out of the house at that moment. Terrified, she rushed to the child and scooped her up in her arms. Mary, who was still conscious, looked directly into her mother's eyes while blood flowed from her nose, mouth, and ears. Then she died.

Time, in this case, was not a healer. The severe shock of the trauma was ever-present. Night after night the mother awakened, tortured by dream images in which she saw the girl's blood-drenched face, her breaking eyes focused on her mother. A therapist brought no comfort – on the contrary, searching questions into the past (for instance, if Mary had been wanted) upset the mother to such a degree that she became hysterical in the therapist's office. The therapist quickly guided her out the back door, not wanting other patients in the waiting room to see the "scene". Well-meaning, but not exactly tactfully, the therapist gave the woman the address of a suicide-prevention clinic and then returned to the office.

After this disappointing attempt at finding help, many wretched weeks passed. During the day the woman remained passive, paralyzed by the fear of the night-mares that tortured her body and soul. Then her sister, on a visit, suggested she see Dr. Barnes. "He is also a psychotherapist, but working with a different method. Perhaps he can help."

Dr. Barnes told Dr. Lukas the following, recapturing what in essence transpired between him and this anguished mother.

"The patient seemed numb, suffering from an inner conflict. What was it that stood between her and her ability to master her fate? One sentence which she repeated over and over again gave me a clue. 'Why did I have to watch my girl's dying? Why did I have to witness this horrible moment that I can never forget?'

Here was the core of the tragedy, the opening through which logotherapy could enter. 'My dear Mrs. X.,' I told her. 'You have suffered unspeakable pain. But I am so glad that you took your daughter into your arms; that you didn't stop, half-way to your child, frozen with terror, covering your eyes at this unbearable sight. By hugging your little one, you enabled her to truly say good-bye to you. Otherwise the last thing she saw would have been the dirty tire that rolled over her. Your action allowed her to face the eyes of her mother and read in them the love that had sur-rounded her all of her short life. We can be sure that the child didn't feel pain at that moment because such severe injury deadens all sensation of the nervous system. She felt safe and secure. There is no greater security on earth, especially for a child, than in the mother's arms. Your action enabled your little girl, surrounded by moth-erly love, to slip from the safest shelter life has to offer to still another shelter – what a beautiful good-bye! But you do have a price to pay for the gift you gave your child – the price of your memory of that terrible moment of parting.'

While I spoke, the woman listened attentively and seemed to find an inner peace.'You mean it was good what I did; good for Mary?' she asked, and I saw the dawn of a meaning behind the darkness of her pain. 'It was the best you could do in your situation,' I assured her. 'No pain, and secure in my arms,' she murmured. Then she straightened up. 'If this is so, then I can live with the memory of little Mary's blood-covered face.'

'When you see her in your dreams again, take her in your arms and cradle her once more,' I told her when she left my office. My hopes were fulfilled when I learned in a subsequent follow-up session that she was able to sleep undisturbed by nightmares."

Dr. Lukas concluded: "The grief was not gone, nor was it supposed to be, for grieving over a person we have loved and lost keeps that person somehow alive. But those who can grieve without rebelling are regenerated in their sleep with its fluid borders between this and another world, where the living and the dead may visit each other."

Grief as a Gift

The next account is of a qualified Logotherapist and appointed trainer in logotherapy as she encapsulates her own experience of grief within the framework of Frankl's exposition of experiential values and the ways we find meaning in life. She is also a trained physiotherapist and uses a logotherapy as a powerful orientation in her physiotherapy. She writes:

"According to Logotherapy there are three ways to find meaning in life:

1. What we give to life through creativity
2. What we receive from life through experiences
3. What stance we take towards life through our attitude

Experiential values, according to Frankl, are what we experience, what life gives us and what we receive from it. We receive things that we have not earned, deserved, merited, worked for or achieved. These are the blessings, the free gifts, we receive from life. In the experience of LOVE, BEAUTY, NATURE, GOODNESS or TRUTH, we can find meaning. True experiential values impact greatly upon us and change us. We connect to someone or something outside or higher than ourselves.

While it is true that such experiences come to us as free gifts, and are ours for the taking, it depends on us whether we take them. All too often life offers us gifts and we do not take them due to insensitivity or unawareness or being wrapped up in ourselves and we miss 'the meaning of the moment.' To quote Frankl:

> For though only a single moment is in question – the greatness of life can be measured by the greatness of the moment: the height of a mountain range is not given by the height of some valley, but by that of the tallest peak. In life too, the peaks decide the meaningfulness of life, and a single moment can retroactively flood an entire life with meaning.

Love

In *Man's Search for Meaning* Frankl stated: 'Love is the highest goal to which man can aspire. Love is the only way to grasp another human being in the innermost core of his or her personality. No one can become fully aware of the very essence of another human being unless he loves him.'

In *Doctor and the Soul* Frankl stated: 'Love is not deserved, is unmerited. It is simply grace. In addition to the grace of being loved and the enchantment of loving, a third factor enters into love: the miracle of love.'

How miraculously sustaining were the loving thoughts of his wife, his inner communion with her that Frankl experienced amidst the debilitating influences of camp life! How powerful the love they had for each other! 'My mind clung to the image of my wife. A thought crossed my mind. I did not even know if she was still alive. I knew only one thing – which I have learned well by now: Love goes far beyond the physical person of the beloved. It finds its deepest meaning in his spiritual being, his inner self. Whether or not he is actually present whether or not he is still alive ceases somehow to be of importance.'

Beauty and Nature

In *Doctor and the Soul* Frankl wrote: 'Imagine a music-lover sitting in a concert hall while the most noble measure of his favorite symphony resounds in his ears. He feels that shiver of emotion which we experience in the presence of the power of beauty. Suppose now that at such a moment we should ask this person whether his life has meaning. He would have to reply that it had been worth while living if only to experience this ecstatic moment.'

I would like to share something about music and consciousness from *Communing with Music* by Matthew Cantello (2004): 'As human beings, we possess a unique ability to respond to beauty when it reveals itself to us. Over the course of our lives, if we are lucky, we may find ourselves becoming increasingly drawn to beauty of all kinds, catching on that the recognition of beauty can offer some of the most meaningful experiences available to us. When beauty reveals itself through music, however, the sound becomes much more than simply a transient object to admire and move on from. The experience of beautiful sound opens to a much more extensive internal experience. In lighter, more sanguine expressions, the beauty in music can be pleasurable or comforting to the spirit. But in more intense articulations, the warmth of melodious themes can have a profound humanizing effect on the soul. When experienced deeply, beautiful music can serve to open the heart of the listener. At its height, the beauty and tenderness of music becomes a powerful stimulator of our propensity for love, compassion and forgiveness.

On certain occasions, when the time is right, an encounter with music can become so exquisite, the expression so exalted, we can encounter peak experiences. The peak experience occurs when the music offers a glimpse of the sacred, evoking an overwhelming sense of wholeness. Tears, or some other release, are a common reaction to this intense state of being, as the music becomes a doorway to the Divine. When opportunity presents itself, these are profoundly spiritual experiences.'

In *Man's Search for Meaning* Frankl (1968) wrote that as the inner life of the prisoner tended to become more intense, he also experienced the beauty of art and nature as never before. Under their influence he sometimes even forgot his own frightful circumstances.

Frankl recalled what it meant to him to suddenly see the sunset through the barbed wire in the concentration camp. It was an exquisite experience of beauty. Coming home, exhausted and hungry and crowded into a cattle car, the train moved through the beautiful Bavarian countryside. An inmate at the door called them to come and look at a magnificent sunset of a stack of clouds of bright purple, orange and blue. As they stared at the incredible sight, someone sighed: 'How beautiful the world *could* be!'

An extract from *Three Days to See* by Keller (1933), reminds us of the beauty which the world reveals to us: 'Use your eyes as if tomorrow you would be stricken blind. Hear the music of voices, the song of a bird, the mighty strain of an orchestra, as if you would be stricken deaf tomorrow. Touch each object as if tomorrow your tactile sense would fail. Smell the perfume of the flowers, taste with relish each morsel, as if tomorrow you could never smell and taste again. Make the most of every sense; glory in all the facets of pleasure and beauty which the world reveals to you.'

Goodness

About goodness Frankl wrote that in the worst days they who lived in concentration camps can remember the man who walked through the huts comforting others, giving away his last piece of bread.

He also wrote that it was found after the liberation – only the camp doctor, a prisoner himself, had known of it previously, that the commander of the camp paid no small sum of money from his own pocket in order to purchase medicines for his prisoners. Frankl remembered how one day a foreman had secretly given him a piece of bread which Frankl knew he must have saved from his breakfast ration. It was far more than this piece of bread which moved Frankl to tears at that time. It was the human 'something' which this man gave him – the word and look which accompanied the gift.

To quote Shantall (2003:35): 'The deep or profound truth of something inspires us, makes us come alive with excitement, wonder, awe and reverence.'

My Experience of Finding Meaning in Suffering Through Experiential Values

I would like to share my own experiential values of *love, beauty, nature, goodness* and *truth* while I spent 2 months in Sydney, Australia, a few years ago.

My husband had died 8 months previously and my grief and suffering were unbearable. My husband and I had been married for 45 years and loved each other very deeply and unconditionally. We had spent 17 wonderful days in Sydney 8 months previously. He died less than a week after our return home. How was I now going to be able to manage my deep grief on returning to Sydney again?

Love

For me the greatest experiential value is *love*. I have always had a very special loving relationship with my son and three daughters. One loving daughter and little granddaughter escorted me to Sydney and delivered me into the arms of another loving daughter and her family. The joy on the faces of my 10 and 7 year old grandsons when they saw me at the airport almost stopped my heart. It is difficult to begin to describe the almost overwhelming love and care that I received from my daughter and her family. I was treated like royalty and nothing was too much trouble for them during my entire stay there.

My daughter lives in a lovely three storied home which has a breathtaking view of the sea and coast line from every window of the house. I had an entire floor to myself and I could lie in bed and watch the occasional ships and yachts sail by. It felt like living in a 5 star holiday resort. The beautiful coastal walk of about 20 kilometers began just down the road from the house.

Beauty and Nature

I started walking almost every day for many kilometers along the beautiful coastline, feeling the awesome beauty entering my soul.

I walked into my grief wailing and lamenting as if my heart would break. I just walked and walked. I listened to the pounding of the waves breaking on the beaches and rocks and then receding again.

Then slowly and almost imperceptibly, I started hearing the mantras of the sea.

As the waves broke I heard: "I AM WITH YOU" and as they receded: "IN YOUR GRIEF." This continued for many, many days.

Then slowly the mantra changed, as the waves crashed, into: "WHAT IS LIFE "and as the waves receded: "ASKING OF YOU?"

I just walked and walked and after many, many days, again the mantra changed into: "TRUST" as the waves crashed, and as they receded again: "THAT THE ANSWERS WILL COME TO YOU."

All this time I felt the very presence of the Divine enveloping me and guiding me through my grief.

Goodness

I experienced such wonderful care and goodness from my extended family and friends who came from all over to see me. A family member of my husband came all the way from Canberra so that he could spend a few days with me. And then there was the most wonderful gift of Sue (my co-trainer in logotherapy) spending a week in Sydney. She had come for a friend's son's wedding. We spent a glorious day on a harbor cruise and having lunch outside the famous Sydney Opera House and then walking through the quaint shops at the Rocks which is the oldest part of Sydney. We also spent a lovely afternoon together with my family clambering over large rocks while my son-in–law and grandsons were fishing. When we are with dear friends our lives are flooded with meaning.

While I was in Sydney I conducted a Stress Reduction Group for my daughter and some of her friends. They were all successful, stressed out professional women. For me to experience the very evident positive effect that this had on them was very gratifying and meaningful for me. Their beautiful letters and gifts touched my heart.

Truth

The Sydney Harbor Bridge is a huge bridge which spans over the sea connecting the central part of the city to the northern area of Sydney. My husband always wanted to climb the bridge but somehow we never got around to doing it. It is an expensive organized climb which takes three and a half hours.

My daughter had wanted to give it to him as a gift for his birthday when we were last in Sydney but he was certainly in no condition to even consider it.

Even before I left South Africa I had decided to do the bridge climb for him.

My daughter and I climbed the bridge with great purpose and meaning. I could feel my husband's presence every step of the way. The bridge is 134 meters high and there are 1439 steps. The beginning of the climb was the most difficult because there were about four stories of sheer perpendicular steps. It was a most beautiful day and the view over the whole of Sydney was absolutely breathtaking.

We had taken a little gemstone up with us which we placed right at the top of the bridge in a safe place where it could not be blown away. I said a prayer and blessing for my husband. It was a most awesome spiritual experience.

It was there that I experienced my most profound truth and that is:

> Love never dies. When you lose someone who has loved you and whom you have loved, a part of you dies but also some of that person's spirit and energy is left with you and gives you greater strength and courage.

I stood on top of the bridge filled with the greatest awe, wonder and reverence.

When I climbed down the bridge I was not the same person I was before I had climbed it. A change had taken place in me as a result of this totally meaningful experience.

My heart will always remain broken and I will always suffer from a sense of loss and grief but I feel that I have received an energy which has now given me the strength and courage to face the challenges that life is asking of me.

Where Am I Now?

On 31st July it is some 3 years since my beloved husband died. My heart will always remain broken and there are times when I think I will die of a broken heart.

I will share with you what has helped me survive these last three painful years:

Gratitude

I live in very deep gratitude:

For having had the most amazing husband who loved me beyond words and whom I absolutely adored.

For my four very special caring and loving children.

For my five adorable grandchildren.

For the wonderful and exciting life I did have.

For my friends.

For everything in my life.

Treasure Chest

I have a very large mental treasure chest filled with the most wonderful memories which I open whenever I feel the need to sustain myself.

Journal

Since his death I have written to my husband every night for about half an hour before I go to sleep. I discuss my day with him, give him news and even ask his advice. I have found this very healing. After he died, a Rabbi said to me: "The person who died will always be connected to you but it is your responsibility to remain connected to him." I feel that my writing is keeping this connection very strong.

Logotherapy Values

I try to embrace the logotherapy values in my life.

I try to live with greater awareness of the responsibilities, tasks and experiences which life offers me every day.

Creative Values

I have moved from my home of 43 years in Pretoria to Johannesburg where I have two children and three grandchildren. I have established a little home for myself which I am hoping will be a place of peace and healing. Here I facilitate groups called "Meaning Centered Stress Reduction and Creating Well-being". I believe in the mind/body/spirit connection. The workshops include Body work, Relaxation techniques, Meditation and Logotherapy. Money donated by the groups is used for the benefit of the Tswane Home of Hope, a home of safety for abused street girls in Pretoria. This is a very positive way for members of the group to transcend themselves for the benefit of others.

I am also trying to help others who have lost their life mates.

Experiential Values

I am living very much in the present moment and I am open to all the experiences that life offers me every day.

Attitudinal Values

I have chosen not to feel sorry for myself and become a victim of my circumstances, but to honor the memory of my husband by using this precious gift of life in a positive way.

Often I recall the Mantras of the sea from my time in Sydney:

I AM WITH YOU............IN YOUR GRIEF.
WHAT IS LIFE................ASKING OF YOU?
TRUST..........AND THE ANSWERS WILL COME TO YOU.

I still feel the Divine presence guiding me through my grief and suffering and the challenges of my new life."

Restoring a Lost Past

Sometimes what transpires between the logotherapist and the client (or between the trainer or supervisor and the student who is being supervised) has ramifications far beyond imagining. Representing life as unconditionally meaningful, no matter how great the tragedies that may befall you as the client, I, as your logotherapist, am more to you than meets the eye. Not only as a witness to the unconditional meaningfulness of life but fine-tuning myself to the meaning of what life is trying to convey to you, I may be instrumental in opening the flood-gates of stored up, hidden and unreleased meanings in your life.

I have moved from South Africa to Israel. Along with my Jewish colleague in Israel, Batya Yaniger, I was supervising what is called the Diplomate project of a student of ours, living in Europe. Her project was to set up a web-site that offered logotherapy via the internet to clients unable to visit or living out of reach of logotherapists willing to assist them. Her name is Marylyn Hodkinson. She wrote the following in the introduction of her project:

"It is only a matter of time before one comes to the realization that logotherapy is about a chosen way of life. It will not be compartmentalized. It demands to be included in all aspects of life, professionally and privately. We do our clients the greatest disservice should we not live logotherapy fully.

We find that once we open up our lives to logotherapy, we are kept active and busy not only with learning from our clients but growing ourselves spiritually and evoking meaning in ways never before contemplated. My personal challenge has come about in truly understanding the powerful impact of linking the thread of meaning through all aspects of my life."

Our student related a most riveting happening in her life during the course of our supervision of her work. She wrote that her mother and her mother's brother suffered a conflict-laden relationship with their mother (her grandmother). Her grandmother always kept herself secretly aloof from her children, never allowing them to come too close to her. Marylyn's mother and uncle often wondered why they did not have any extended family members on their mother's side. But they could never get any satisfactory answer from the grandmother. But when her uncle was searching through his mother's papers, he came across her birth certificate that showed where she was born. The certificate showed a different surname than the one the mother claimed was her own. It was a Jewish surname.

At that very time a historian on the Holocaust was gathering information about what had happened to the Jewish population of the German town mentioned on Marylyn's grandmother's birth certificate! Meaning is so often to be found through synchronicity: the flowing together of events that "speak" to us in most revealing ways.

Almost the entire Jewish population of the town were rounded up and sent to the Nazi concentration camps where they all perished. There was also the story that some parents, before they were carted away, succeeded in hiding their children. The historian was keen to see if any of these children did find their way to safety and did survive.

Marylyn's mother and uncle confronted Marylyn's grandmother with these revealed facts about her life as a child. She was furious and chased her son out of her house. But she did break down eventually and confessed that she wanted to hide her horrible past after being left by her parents and all the struggles and hurt that entailed. The knowledge of what happened to her parents and so many other millions of Jews, terrified her. She wanted to shut out those thoughts. She married a non-Jew and brought up her children as Christians.

The Jewish line passes through the mother. Marylyn was shocked to discover that she was in fact Jewish!

Upon her shoulders, she felt, there rested the task to bring reconciliation to her family, to restore to them what a tragic past had snatched away from them.

The process of the healing of a broken and lost past was set in motion. The following loose pieces of the puzzle of her own life began falling into place for her:

The first was the uncannily deep impact Frankl's book on his Holocaust experiences had on her. She relates: "My first experience with logotherapy was reading Man's Search for Meaning. The result for me was a feeling of 'coming home'. It was an 'AHA' moment, of simply feeling that Viktor Frankl's logotherapy connected with me at a very deep level. It is this sense of 'coming home' in hindsight, that would have the greatest impact on me.'

She was struck by the synchronicity of studying with Jewish supervisors, living in Israel. She understood why she felt so strangely at home in Israel when she met with Batya in Jerusalem. All of this was like a preparation for the news she was to receive about being Jewish herself. She writes:

> In our studies of logotherapy, we learn how vital it is to find a meaning for suffering. Here I was learning and empathizing about others' experience of suffering when I was completely blind to the suffering of our family for generations. How was that possible? How could it be that I did not see what is now so very obvious? What I have learnt after considering this last question, is the gift of logotherapeutic mentoring in one's professional and personal life. To be able to be guided gently and yet challenged when appropriate, adds the dimension of being able to live logotherapy experientially. Only when you are immersed in the experiencing of challenges put to you by life, creating new possibilities or visions and shifting of attitudes, does the active searching for meaning amidst confusion and suffering reveal rewards. Then the true magnificence of logotherapy is revealed. The confrontation of logotherapy will not allow you to wallow in misery and self-pity. Arise, you are greater than you think! You shall realize your full self-worth. And, it will amaze you!

Who Then, in Conclusion, Am I in Relation to You?

In all that I have related above to illustrate who I am as a logotherapist in relation to you if you were a client of mine, the following points have emerged as truths:

As a logotherapist

- I am called to responsibility
- of a real encounter with you, the client;

- an encounter for which I have been prepared and that
- I am competent enough or have the ability to deal with effectively.
- After all, our encounter is my moment too!

Upon me rests the following responsibilities:

- I have to be fully available for the task and unique process ahead of me.
- I have to be ready for anything in the role I will be expected to play in every shade of our unfolding relationship.
- It will be a relationship that will contain every element of a full interaction and involvement of any really meaningful face to face, person to person relationship with this one and unique exception: As the logotherapist I will be in the role of a *giver.* However much I am involved and am personally blessed in sharing your life with you, it is not my life that is the focus of our attention. You are not there for me but I am there for you! Involved with you on this professional level, I will be in the role of facilitator, affirmer, comforter, encourager, admonisher, guide and teacher.

Yes, logotherapy is teaching but of a very specific kind:

- I teach you about yourself. I help you to see and experience your own uniqueness, the preciousness of your singular, once and for all irreplaceable life. I make you aware of your strengths, coping skills and talents. I help you to see that you are in everything you experience and respond to and, in effect, that *you* are the one in charge of your own life. The responsibility to live it, is yours and yours alone.
- I help you to explore your present situation in terms of its meaning – what does it ask of you? You are in dialogue with your own life. It is your dialogue with life that I am listening to, and responding to. It is not about the dialogue between you and me. Our dialogue only has sense if it focuses on your interaction with the meaning of your own life! In this dialogue that I encourage you to have with your own life, I will point out to you what life has to offer or what logotherapy teaches about the experience of meaning in whatever situation life may present to you.
- I will help you to see your past as meaningful. I will explore with you what led up to the situation you find yourself in. Why are you experiencing the problems you are having now? What is the core crisis behind all that you had to go through? Where is it leading? What is it pointing to – what is it challenging you to do? What promise does it hold?
- I will help you perceive your own destiny; to discover the golden thread of meaning running through your life. In that, I may present you with what Frankl taught about human nature and the task quality of life. What are you being commissioned to accomplish? What is your calling in life? Your calling may be something very particular like a certain profession that your whole background prepared you for but it will inevitably include other very important tasks as well. In fact, it includes every moment of your life. Every moment has invitational value. Just as no day is the same, life tasks also vary and change, get completed

or emerge as you journey through your life. A calling is not just one thing. *You are your calling!* It is what you are called to be and do, also how you are destined to grow and mature throughout your life in every one of its facets and phases. Your calling is therefore only complete at the very end of your life!

What happens in this process?

- You may come to trust me and co-operate with me. You may come to feel that we are in this together; that our paths were meant to cross;
- You may come to realize that the process is directed, that our meeting has been ordained. There is a greater purpose involved. Life itself is calling you!
- You may come to see that through the process of therapy, you are being called to the responsibility of stepping out into your own life in a singular and much more personally accountable way. You are being challenged to say: "Yes!" to life, not half-heartedly, but fully.

Who am I then, in this process of therapy?

- I am a messenger, a servant of the truth in your particular life.
- I am accountable to more than myself as I search out the meaning as it seeks to manifest itself to you.
- I am therefore not a friend or a partner. The focus is on your life, not mine. My private life remains private, however fully committed I am to you in terms of fulfilling the task given to me to be of assistance to you.
- The relationship between us thus transcends personal involvement. It is fully and awesomely *professional.* I am exercising my profession!
- The relationship therefore has distinct boundaries which neither I am nor you are to overstep in becoming personally or emotionally involved with one another. In logotherapy there is no transference or countertransference, no emotional interference of this kind. I do not become a mother you; you do not become a son or daughter to me. I do not project my problems onto you or allow your problems to impact on my personal and private life outside of therapy. We do not fall in love with one another or have any kind of emotional or sexual attraction to each other! The boundaries of logotherapy are sacred. Therapy in the presence of Transcendent meaning takes place on holy ground!
- This does not exclude an intense interest in your welfare nor cancel out an awed love for your person. It is your supreme worth, uniqueness and dignity that has brought me to the position of wanting to be nothing other than to be of service to you. Logotherapy is my life's commission!

The conclusion therefore, dear reader, if you were to be my client, is simply this: *We are both* are under obligation before a Greater Presence to whom we are *both* accountable.

Exercise for You, the Reader: "The Dissatisfied Frustration of Unlived Life" (James Hillman)

Consider the Following
- The logotherapist believes that central to the motivations of clients who come for therapy, is a search for meaning. Restlessness, dissatisfaction, feeling at odds with others, out of sorts with themselves and out of love with life, may mask what Frankl called "the existential vacuum" – The emptiness and frustration of a life void of meaning.
- The task of logotherapists is to help clients come on course: To find the golden thread of meaning in their lives and have to find meaning in everything they do and experience.
- Centrally connected to their lives in this way, living from the very core of their beings, in vital touch with what enlivens or gives full impetus to their unique persons, they will have the clarity, perspective, sense of purpose and will to give full expression to themselves in every area of their lives.

References

Cantello, M. (2004). *Communing with music*. Los Angeles: Devorss and Company.

Frankl, V. E. (1968). *Man's search for meaning: An introduction to logotherapy*. London: Hodder & Stroughton.

Keller, H. (1933). Three days to see. *The Atlantic Monthly, 151*(1), 35–42.

Leslie, R. C. (1965). *Jesus and logotherapy*. New York: Abingdon Press.

Lukas, E. (1993). Case study by Dr Robert Barnes. *The International Forum for Logotherapy, 16*(1), 1–7.

Shantall, T. (2003). *The quest for destiny: A logotherapeutic guide to meaning-centered living, therapy and counselling*. Pretoria: University of South Africa Press.

Chapter 6
What Is your Real Problem? The Crisis of Meaning

Abstract What is at the very basis of every hurt; the real crisis behind whatever problems the client may have to deal with? The chapter sets out to prove that *every* distress, whatever its nature is, in essence, a disturbance of the sense and experience of meaning in life. The real issue that is to be dealt with in therapy, over and above whatever other treatment may be required, is *a crisis of meaning*. When we suffer, *we* suffer. What lies behind what Frankl called the tragic triad of human existence, the inescapable negatives or tragedies in life? Why the **pain**, why do we suffer **guilt**, what scares us about **death**? The pain of any kind of suffering makes us feel discarded by life, out of the normal, healthy and blessed flow of things; guilt makes us feel bad and under judgement, no longer loved and accepted and part of it all; and death ends our life and perhaps its purpose in the eternal scheme of things. Suffering in itself is senseless, unwanted and wrong. It is not something to be desired or wished on anyone. It is something that is to be combatted, overcome and removed. It is to no longer be! Suffering, Frankl contended, makes us aware of what ought NOT to be.

Keywords A crisis of meaning · Pain, guilt and death · Suffering is senseless · Overcoming suffering · Suffering ought not to be

The Unheard Cry for Meaning

So what is your real problem? What is at the very basis of every hurt; the real crisis behind whatever problems you may have to deal with?

As a logotherapist I have come to see *every* distress, whatever its nature, as a disturbance of our sense and experience of meaning in life. The real issue that is to be dealt with in therapy, over and above whatever other treatment may be required, is *a crisis of meaning*.

When we suffer, we suffer. *We* suffer! When we are in physical pain and have to bear physical hardship, like being disabled or crippled, or when we fall mortally ill or suffer material and financial disasters and loss (physical or material hardships); when we suffer emotional anguish and are afflicted by whatever kind of mental illness or emotional disturbance, or when we are faced with difficult, hurtful, embarrassing or humiliating situations (psychological distress); when we are plagued with overwhelming feelings of meaninglessness and despair (spiritual problems and anguish) —*we* suffer the pain, the distress, the anguish. It is not the pain that is the pain; it is not the distress that is the distress; it is not the problem that is the problem. It is that we distressingly feel disconnected or severed from, or outside the normal flow of things.

Life is going on without us. The sentence of exile from what others still enjoy, has been passed on us.

We suffer alone. *Nobody can suffer in our stead.* We may find hope and comfort, encouragement and renewed faith when others share our pain out of a sense of compassion for us; when they suffer grief and anguish for our sakes. They may carry the burden of our sufferings with us; devote their lives in trying to help and save us from our pain, troubles and hardships. They may be interceding for and even standing in for us, take our suffering situation or blame upon themselves, but that does not remove us out of the picture. *We* bear the brunt of our sufferings and *we* have to come to terms with it. It remains *our* pain, *our* distress, *our* problem. And the *true* pain, distress or problem is *our* struggle to make sense of what is happening to us. It is a *spiritual* pain, distress and crisis that is at the basis of or behind the pain, distress and problem. We are struggling with the *meaning* of the "why" of what happened to us. Even when we lose our minds, are driven insane, the tragedy is that *we* have lost our minds, that *we* have gone insane.

We have to make things out for ourselves, even in the darkest depths of despair. As we do, we will find ourselves moving away from the many accepted theories about human nature and human existence. The many arguments, given as reasons for his suffering, did not convince a Job. He had to make it out for himself, find the answer to the: "why me?", "what for?" questions that his sufferings tore from his anguished heart. He had to be faced with the truth as it addressed *him* and nobody else.

It is in the uncovering of layer after superficial layer of the explanations commonly offered and so readily accepted by a less than perceptive analysis of the nature of human existence that we come to the more real answers as to why we suffer. Some even deeply indoctrinated beliefs, or seemingly solid theories about human existence, holding sway for decades or even centuries, will simply not hold up when exposed to the light of what we, ever more, deeply discover are the true reasons for our sufferings.

Our deeply provoked reflections will lead us down to the solid rock of truth. Our rationality will become profoundly *spiritual*; our spirituality profoundly *rational*!

What is more real than reality itself; more true than truth itself?

The Suffering of Suffering

What lies behind what Frankl called the tragic triad of human existence, the inescapable negatives or tragedies in life? Why the **pain**, why do we suffer **guilt**, what scares us about **death**? The pain of any kind of suffering makes us feel discarded by life, out of the normal, healthy and blessed flow of things; guilt makes us feel bad and under judgement, no longer loved and accepted and part of it all; and death ends our life and perhaps its purpose in the eternal scheme of things.

We lose connection with what really matters!

Suffering *throws* us. Things are not what they *should* be. Things are not sane or normal. They are *insane* and *abnormal*. Something very *bad* has happened or is happening to us. In the sea of emotional turmoil and conflict, the distress and anguish of it, can totally mask or temporarily submerge the essence of who we are as spiritual, free-willed human beings.

Here is the truth: **We are not meant to suffer!** Suffering in itself is senseless, unwanted and wrong. It is not something to be desired or wished on anyone. It is something that is to be combatted, overcome and removed. It is to no longer be! All our yearnings, our efforts, our searching, will be aimed at coming *out* of situations of suffering. We want an end to it, be rid of it forever!

Suffering, Frankl contended, makes us aware of what ought NOT to be. We are not meant to be in such a place. Our place is opposite to it, very much elsewhere!

The World as It Should Be

We are *open vessels,* Frankl maintained. We reach out and need to make connection with what is out there, beyond ourselves. Our need for this connection is based on the faith that the world needs us; that the love we seek is there to be found. On yet a deeper level of faith, we believe that we are being searched for, that the love that exists outside of ourselves is seeking to find us also.

The connection is to be made!

James Hillman spoke about "a call that beckons us to search" for it. Human consciousness, Frankl pointed out, is *intentionally* directed. It is inherent in our human nature to *seek connection with that which is seeking to find us*! We belong to it, we have been created for this connection, this sense of deep and sublime union! None of us can really live without some sense of connection to something other than ourselves.

The truth of the matter is that we have been put together, created and designed to find this vital connection with the more than ourselves.

It is also fundamentally true that it would be the height of injustice for a call to be made upon us if we do not have the capacity and more than that, the deep need to respond to that call! Why call if there is no interest in the call, no need and desire to hear it; if the call is to fall upon ears that *cannot* hear it?

Life *is* a calling, this is fact!

Open to the world as we are, we can be *addressed, challenged, invited, interacted with.* We can be found! We have a place in this world! Someone, and the others in our lives, can get through to *us*, make us aware of *them*.

We have been designed with a keen consciousness of the other; our very being is geared for connection!

Interaction, sharing, communion, at oneness with each other and with the world out there, with life itself, is meant to move from its innermost and most intimate circle: the intimacy of a face to face or a one on one relationship and close bond between parent and child, and progressing to the sense of belonging in a family. This is *my* family, *my* father and *my* mother; *my* brother and *my* sister. We are a family unit, given to each other to love and care for. We will *always* belong together! From this home or haven of foundational togetherness, many other relationships are meant to get forged in an intimate face to face, respectful, appreciative and loving way.

Having our own background and family base, we are meant to become fully individual, our unique (affirmed and loved) selves. We are to become ready for love in a more mature way. We will experience the need to love someone special, someone outside our family circle, a true mate from out there in the world. We will want to find our *soul*-mate, someone meant for us and with whom we can form a special bond of unique togetherness. Our togetherness can birth a new family. How deep and fundamental the desire for children!

Love is found in intimacy, in a sense of complete oneness with another. This is the kind of bond found between partners, between husband and wife, two people who forge their commitment to each other in the sacred bond of marriage. Their intimacy is sealed through a physical union, in the sacred space of sexual intimacy, an intimacy that not only expresses their committed love for one another as a one and only in their lives, but that produces offspring, with an added strengthening of the unbreakable bond between parents and children.

"God sets the lonely in families" (Psalm 68:6). Even if we remain single or childless all our lives, others are given to us as families, as children close to our hearts.

Family life extends and is awesomely *meant* to extend into the group, community, language, culture and nation we are part of. There is the commission of national unity as well. The brotherhood of man is a brotherhood of nations, of nation interacting with nation in the bond of a family of nations.

Loving your neighbor as yourself means that nations relate to each other as they would to their own. Your brother is my brother; your concerns mine also. There is therefore a further outreach to issues on the international scene; involvement with situations calling for intervention and help elsewhere than in our own countries.

Together, and finally, the process is meant to move towards the ultimate destiny of humankind; to what our shared world was meant and is intended to be.

There is a golden thread of meaning woven into the very fabric of human existence as a whole, and it is discernible in our own lives as well. It is in lived experience where truth births itself.

It is a between you and me.

Who We Were Meant to Be

Our lives are *not* meant to spiral inwards in a vicious circle of self-absorption, but outwards towards the fulfillment of the purpose and destiny of our lives within the greater scheme of things.

We belong somewhere *specific*. We have our own part to play in the greater story. Like a small piece of a jig-saw puzzle, we fit in a specific somewhere. Our unique place in the unfolding story, the bigger picture, can only be filled by us. Try and squeeze another part of the picture (someone else) in there and it will not fit. It will distort the bigger picture, be out of place; not be in harmony with the rest. Or leave me out of the bigger picture and this one missing piece will spoil the whole, draw attention to what is missing from the meaning and message, the beauty of the whole.

Life without me, without my participation, is incomplete!

This link with the more than just ourselves, with a whole we are part of, is vital to us. It is life-giving, exhilarating; purposeful. It gives meaning to our existence.

A Broken Vessel

What happens if this link is broken or was never properly forged? What if we are trapped in ourselves, in the suffocating space of a fearful retreat from the world? What happens to us when, instead of being met, being called out of ourselves into invigorating and loving relationships, we find ourselves threatened, our freedom to be ourselves encroached upon, the sacred space of worthy selfhood rudely invaded and occupied, when our voices are silenced and we lose our say in the world; if we are dictated to and ruled over, victimized and oppressed? What if we go bent under the fact that our persons are unloved, rejected, abused and discarded? What if we live only at the behest of others, ruling the roost over us, exercising a vicious hold on us, dictating what we can and cannot be?

What then will be the kind of ideas we have of ourselves and of the world?

The Prisoner of Our Thoughts

Then he showed me Joshua the high priest standing before the angel of the Lord, and Satan standing at his right hand to be his adversary and to accuse him (Zechariah 3:1).

Harsh and insensitive criticisms, accusations and abuse directed against and hurled at us, can stick, be like the "soiled garments" Joshua, the high priest, found himself clothed with in the story above. Joshua stood before the angel of God (before the angelic image of man as he was created and ordained to be) in a state of shame and humiliation!

How torturous when we accuse ourselves, hold ourselves somehow responsbible for being the victims of accusation; when the pain we have suffered at the hand of others is internalized as a self-critical feeling of unworthiness!

A well-known logotherapist, Alex Pattakos, wrote a book entitled: *Prisoners of our thoughts* (2010). There is no greater torture than the torture we suffer under the yoke of our own assailed and imprisoned minds. The painful and horrible thoughts that plague us, the images that haunt us, the disapproving jeering and critical voices, the doubts, insecurities, and self-loathing we feel as we pass judgment on ourselves—*this* is the fountainhead of suffering. It can haunt us throughout our lives.

This anguished state of affairs is captured in the following story of a remarkable woman. I want us to see our faces in hers, our pain in hers, follow the plot of our own stories through hers. Suffering is not something to theorize about. It is not abstract, nor speculative, but real. It can be seen in the lives of people all around us. Suffering is inflicted upon us; it *happens* to us. We *experience* it. We are to therefore *know* it, come to terms with it; *overcome* it with the right attitude and grasp. We are to step right out of it, exonerated, our characters refined, rid of the dross, the ugly dirt that was slung at us; dirt that has somehow become part of who we deemed ourselves to be.

We are to be given a change of clothing in a renewed confidence in who we were created and destined to be: "You are altogether lovely, my love, there is no blemish in you" (Song of Solomon 4:7). Restored to the image we are meant to have, we can take our rightful place in life!

We are, therefore, to *combat* suffering, put it in its rightful place.

Let us begin her story with a statement of its plot:

The Need to Matter

As a child who was being abused in a world where no one seemed to be there to help me, where I was neglected and hurt by those who should have loved me, I began to feel invisible, as if no one could see me, or hear my cries for help. This feeling of being invisible has been with me throughout my life. It has often threatened my feelings of belonging, and even of existing, as if I had become a "nonentity" in this world. There is often a sense of being close to death… maybe a wishing for death… even a fantasizing over death… (I believe that I have true friends in heaven)… if the "winds of hurt" blow just one more time in this world, I somehow imagine that "my flame" might finally be completely extinguished and nobody would even know or remember that it burned in the first place!

Her story, unique to her own life and circumstances, has a ring of truth to it for all of us. It settles in our own hearts, in our own areas of suffering and its effects: the scars upon our thinking that it left and leaves upon us.

Her name is Panayiota Ryall, a name she wants me to mention since she wants the world to know that she has stepped into that name. She is now a person with a right to life and with a place of worth in this world. She has scaled many painful heights, and is still scaling some intimidating peaks of suffering, but her life has become one of *overcoming* as she is *becoming* what she was meant to be.

The following is her story:

She was the older of two girls, two sisters, who together went through years of the most terrible suffering. She remembers them clinging to each other after their stepfather had raped one or both of them and left them on the bed, whimpering, very scared and vulnerably helpless.

Their biological father had divorced their epileptic and emotionally disturbed mother and married another. The two girls were given into the custody of their mother who married their depraved and abusive stepfather. Their younger brother mercifully escaped their lot. He went to stay with his father and loving and gentle stepmother. Their father's home, in which the girls spent holidays, was their saving grace, all the more so because of the lovely nature of their father's new wife whom they called their Greek mother.

Life with their biological mother was sheer hell. Not only was the mother given to violent outbursts accompanied by severe beatings of the girls, but she subjected them to obscenities (like making them watch her defecating on the floor). She made them suffer emotional and sexual abuse (like standing naked before them, masturbating and forcing them to partake in the act). Panayiota recalled an occasion when, after her mother had violently assaulted her to a point of unconsciousness, she regained consciousness only to be subjected to a new horror: the lewd and sexual play and caresses of her mother as if, in a sick and psychotic way, coaxing her back to life.

The mother, herself sexually abused as a child, knew of the sexual abuse by the stepfather but did nothing about it. If Panayiota cried that her vagina was painful when having to get dressed in the morning to go to school, the mother would coldly tell her to put on some cream and stop her whining or else. As a nurse, the mother was often on night duty, which was the time when the stepfather would abuse the girls. Panayiota was always the first choice. Put in a bath by the stepfather "to clean her up", Panayiota was terrified as to what was being done to her younger sister. Panayiota captured aspects of her childhood experiences in her many writings.

The Mournful Wailing of a Child
Throughout my life, I could hear in my mind and even in my sleeping-dreams, a child crying somewhere in the far distant corners of a large building. In my dreams, I'd always be searching for the source of the haunting, echoing voice of the child who cried so mournfully. I'd open door after door along the dark corridors of the massive building I was in, but I could never find her to save her from her bitter tears. I have always wondered who that poor sad child was. I have two theories, either that child's mournful wails came from my own

(continued)

inner-child and sub-personality, Patty, the name my mother called me, (hearing or remembering myself crying whilst in a dissociative state… after the rape) or, I think that maybe there is another more chilling possibility.

After my stepfather had had his way with me, he'd put me in a bath to wash away all the evidence of what he had done to me. I know from flashbacks, that whilst still sobbing in there after the rapes, I would be in a deeply dissociative state… (I still struggle with dissociating from time to time, especially when I bath, and therefore, I have trouble just getting my bath time over and done with. I long for the day I can live in a house with a shower, because then I would not have to have this time-wasting problem anymore).

I believe that it is possible that after he'd washed all his disgusting evidence off of me and out of me, and while I was still sitting in the bath in a numb and dissociative state, he'd then leave me there and go to spend "his time" with my little sister! I think that it might be "her crying" that I have heard all these years, and there was and still is nothing I can do to help her… I am too far away, and no matter how much I search for the wailing child in that large and scary building with all its long dark corridors, or how many of those tall dark doors I struggle to open, because their handles are too high up for me to reach easily, I just can't seem to find her… I can't reach her to save her from her misery!

A drawing Panayiota drew in a flashback to this time, vividly depicts her anguished state at the time.

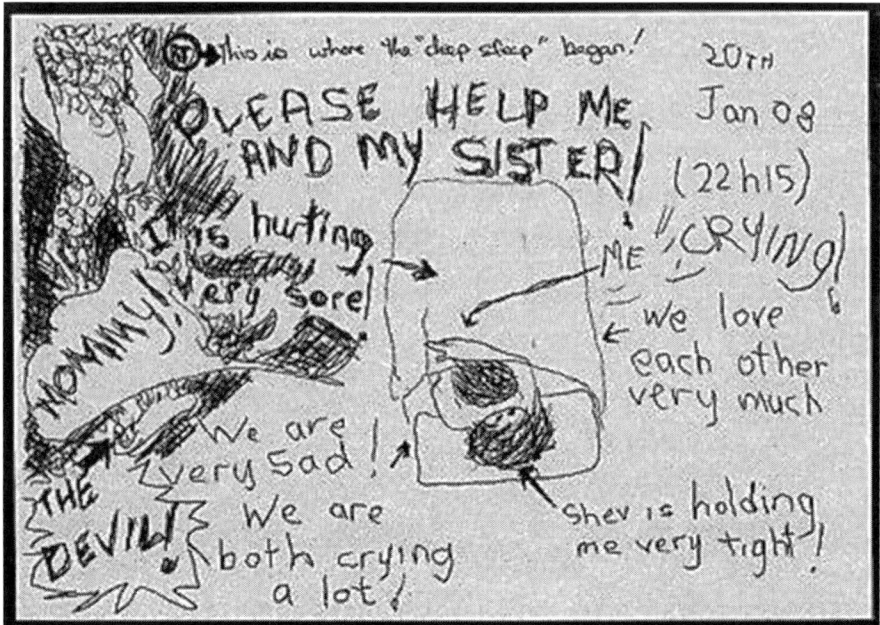

Her world was a nightmare and, as she later described it, a terrible daydream. In adulthood she re-enacted the trauma she had suffered as a child in marrying and divorcing two abusive husbands who not only sexually abused her but also sexually molested their children. Only at age 50, after failed attempts at therapy, did she find her way into a training course in logotherapy.

Her therapist had told her about courses in logotherapy that were being offered at the University of South Africa. After a traumatic end to therapy with that therapist because of emotional embroilment between them and in an effort to stay sane, Panayiota scraped together what money she had, and enrolled at the University of South Africa for the logotherapy courses. The sensitive tutorage of the trainers and her interaction with the other students, began a long and arduous path to healing. The courses helped her to get on her feet, and she successfully passed them all. She has recently completed a book she hopes will help other adult survivors of childhood abuse. It is entitled: *The Silent Scream – the Loudest Shout: the Cry of the Sexually Abused Child.*

The Will to Meaning

Her book is an exposure of the full face of suffering, but through it runs an unmistakable thread of hope. She recalled her efforts to protect her little sister. She described her keen awareness of the beauty of life outside of her own home: how she loved nature and horses; how deeply she loved her loving stepmother, her father and her brother. She described her love of her three children and how she sought to protect them. She wrote down some of her poems. She had written over a 1000 of them! She wrote about how her love of writing sustained her. She described her love of gardening and cooking; mentioned her readiness to help others, her love for the stray and lost. All the above counteracted her fears, her insecurities, her deep doubts about her own worth and the value of her own life; the terrible memories and flashbacks of what had happened to her in her childhood, the abuses she and her children suffered at the hands of her abusive husbands. Through it all, like a strong and sustaining and life-giving umbilical cord or sense of connection to something outside of herself, was her relentless efforts to find, experience and maintain a sense of meaning in her life; her bid to victoriously survive and overcome her sufferings.

Panayiota's following drawing graphically portrays her search for meaning (the light at the end of the tunnel) during her dark years of suffering. The little girl is appealing to the owl, a symbol of wisdom in the owl's ability to see in the dark. Caught in the entanglement of the roots of the trees in the dark and threatening forest, underneath her hand, is a rock-like figure, totally helpless to escape its imprisoned existence. The little girl raises her eyes to the owl, appealing for help, for hope in a seemingly hopeless situation.

This heroic struggle is captured in her writing about the daily onslaught of the impressions her suffering had left upon her and her unrelenting urge and efforts to counteract them. What powerful proof of the deepest motivation embedded in the human breast: *the will to meaning!*

The Lies the Terrible Daydream Was Telling Me:
I am stupid; I'm weak; I'm an idiot; I am useless; I cannot succeed; I may not succeed; I should not succeed; It's no use trying; I'm a loser.
I am not important; I have no rights; my opinion doesn't count; my efforts will never be enough; I'm not good enough; I'm good for nothing.
I am causing problems for others; I'm guilty; I am always being watched and judged; I must always listen to others; I must not fight back; I must comply; I must stay silent; I must be and do good; I must keep the peace.
I'm invisible to the world; I have no voice; I don't deserve respect; I am not worthy; no-one cares about me.

(continued)

*No-one will ever love me; I'm dirty and ugly; I deserve to suffer; I deserve
     pain; I deserve to be beaten; I deserve to be punished; I'm terribly bad; I
     don't deserve to live; I should not live; I should be dead.*
There is no peace; there is no rest; there's no escape; I'm trapped.
My real crime is THAT I WAS BORN!

**What 'Positives,' I Was Saying to Myself as I Fought for My Life in
There!**
*I must fight to survive; my life must have a reason; I must be worth more than
     this.*
I must believe in myself; I must endure; I must be strong; I must stay strong.
I am strong! It is all up to me.
There is always hope; I'm not the only one.
I must survive the loneliness, pain and fear; I must have courage.
I am courageous!
I must choose the right way; I must keep trying.
I am not stupid! There is some goodness in the world.
There must be an end to this. I will NEVER, EVER GIVE UP!

A Jacob's Struggle

Panayiota's struggle was to retain a sense of meaning in her life, and all her desperate efforts were to somehow get out of the entanglement and imprisonment of overwhelming feelings of terror and anguish. Her struggle, for a name that she could
worthily be called by, bears striking resemblance to a similar struggle by a man
called Jacob.

Why is it that Jacob, in the story recorded in the Bible, fought a battle that lasted
through the night and that only ceased with the first light of day? Who was he fighting with or what was he fighting against, and the more important question: *what was
he fighting for?*

Jacob was fighting his fears in his desperate desire to be liberated from what
trapped and ensnared him. He wanted to free himself from his life-long battle and
emotional embroilment with his brother, Esau. He no longer wanted to plot and con-
nive, and through deceitful means safeguard his own place in this world. He wanted
much more. He wanted to be a person in his own right; become the man he was *meant*
and was given the full potential to be. He fought to find the right image of himself, to
break through to the stature of an *only begotten*, a unique person, someone *intended*
with an *assigned* place in this world. He faced his fears, his fear of man, his victim-
hood under the powerful emotional oppression of his brother, Esau. He wanted to find
his own worth, the godly image of himself, something he was desperate enough to at
last *demand:* "I will *not* let you go unless you bless me!" (Genesis 32:26).

The light dawned, his mind cleared, and he could demand the meaning and worthiness that was always meant to be his. Triumphantly transcending his fears, in fact, breaking through to the image God meant him to have, he became a commanding power before God and men. He was called by a new name, a name that combined the words: *isra* and *el*, which in Hebrew means: *to prevail* and *Divine*. In response to his courageous and unrelenting struggle to find the meaning of his life, the Transcendent answered him: "No longer will it be said that your name is Jacob, but Israel, for you have striven with the Divine and with man and have overcome" (Gen 32:29).

Jacob came out of the battle limping. Who can "see" God and live; realize the awesome commission entrusted to man and not feel humbled under the magnificence of it? In what need he was of God's blessing upon him! He was dependent on a power greater than himself; a power that would *empower* him! He would rely, moment by moment, in each and every situation he would encounter, on the prompting to take the right action, the word of wisdom that would come to his open and receptive, always *enquiring* mind. His actions would have effect. He would be granted the strength to see things through. His life would impact his world for the good!

In Panayiota's struggles against what became a severe psychogenic neurosis (a psychological or emotional illness) as a result of the devastatingly hurtful experiences she had suffered as a vulnerably innocent and helpless child, and beyond that at the abusive hands of her husbands, she demonstrates what Frankl called *the defiant power of the human spirit.*

Our fundamental human need is to not only survive but to battle our way through our own areas of darkness into the light of healing through meaning.

Height Psychology

Logotherapy places the focus on our fundamental will to meaning and on our efforts to struggle through to the light, to breathe the free air of meaning, free from what is so torturously and viciously holding us back.

But, ask the critics of logotherapy, is this outreach to meaning not just a defensive denial and futile effort to evade looking at and analyzing the hidden conflicts and dark recesses of our being? Should these dark fears and hidden sources of conflict not be brought to the light of consciousness and "worked through" if we are ever to rid ourselves of a sense of displeasure and dissatisfaction with life and find some sense of peace for our tortured souls?

Is the path of psychoanalyses and all other problem-focused therapies not rather the path to follow?

Panayiota's therapist used the psychoanalytic path to delve into and bring Panayiota's hidden traumas to light. However, in missing to go even deeper into the crisis of meaning behind these traumatic and repressed events, and finding the self-transcendent perspective that would allow Panayiota to constructively and triumphantly deal with them, a situation of emotional embroilment took place between them. In psychoanalytic terms, this process is called *transference,* which is a transfer by the client of unfulfilled needs or aggressive impulses as a result of repressed childhood experiences onto the therapist, and *counter-transference,* which is when the therapist, due to unsolved problems or areas of weaknesses of his or her own, gets emotionally involved with the client in overly identifying with the client.

The distance and perspective of *meaning* was lost between this otherwise excellent therapist and Panayiota. Their relationship lost its otherwise great therapeutic value and impact.

But what if, in contradiction to the premises of psychoanalysis, there was a bigger picture, a more holistic and yes, more positive and inspiring view of human existence? What if this is the truer face of human nature? If we went deeper, that is, to the *spiritual* depths of our beings, and also higher, to the uniquely human and *spiritually transcendent* aspects of being, the picture changes face!

We are *not* what we are made out to be, namely, a sorry victim of dark forces of conflict, forebodings, twisted thoughts and feelings, desperately living in denial or fatalistically capitulating to forces we feel helpless to resist. We are trying to make sense of these hurtful happenings, find a way out of them to the true light of meaning.

What is the truth that we seek to realize?

It is a realization so deep and awesome that is like a born again experience! We find ourselves *unconditionally loved*, not just now, but all along. *Everything* worked out for our good; brought us to this breakthrough point in our lives. With our minds *renewed*, everything changes face. We feel very differently about ourselves. Suddenly the world looks amazing with this new gaze of wonder, gratitude and appreciation.

We have crossed over to the other side, away from seeing ourselves as helpless victims to a realization that we are called upon to overcome every negative, bad, ugly and evil thing in life with this new victorious faith that our lives have a purpose. We have a destiny to fulfill, day in and day out, as we move from one point of victory and overcoming to the next and on towards a clear point of a glorious destination.

We worship!

Even though Panayiota carries the wounds of her past and often has to force herself to go on with her life *despite* bouts of depression and the strong urge to defensively withdraw from the world, she has turned the tables on her past: she is now a sought-after and very successful counselor, especially of adult survivors of childhood sexual abuse. She has also come to occupy the post of the secretarial administrator of the Viktor Frankl Institute of Logotherapy of South Africa!

She wrote the following poem which graphically portrays her persistence in not giving up but to triumph in the faith that her life has meaning and worth and that, in fact, her terrible past could be defiantly turned around to serve instead of haunt her.

BORN TO BE
How lovely this sweet spirit who lives within,
How beautiful is she,
She's true and wise and full of love
As she was born to be.
Her nature truly is divine,
For she was created so,
God the Father's Love for her,
He wants her to always know.
So He sent her to this world to live
And has given her tests and trials,
And though she's struggled very hard,
He's blessed her with His Smiles.
No trial could ever destroy her,
No one's cruelty,
Because her spirit who lives within
Is strong enough, you see.
And all those who've never believed in her,
Will not cause her to give in,
For her spirit who lives upon this earth,
Never forgets where she has been.
She keeps Heaven in her memory
And has carried it throughout her life,
It's been the strength she's held onto,
Through all her toils and strife.
How lovely this sweet spirit who lives within,
How beautiful is she,
She's true and wise and full of love,
As she was born to be.

From the Periphery to the Center of Being

How strong is the will to meaning in the human breast? How persistent the call to find meaning in life?

A whole revolution of thought may be called for in seeing a struggle to find some sense of meaning, however futile and senseless, behind wayward, pathological and emotionally disturbed behavior.

Panayiota found a strange "comfort" when her mother sexually fondled her. She was, at least, being "held" or embraced by her mother. She loved hugging her mother and hugs meant a great deal to her throughout her life. Every effort was made to somehow hold onto the idea of a "good" mother, someone who should have been "there" for her and should have "loved" her. This was projected onto her therapist who became "mother" to her and their hugs became part of their over-involvement with each other.

How often emotionally disturbed women find "comfort" in the dangerous arms of fake lovers, like Panayiota found in the false embrace of her mother and her abusive husbands! How such women seek to hold on to the "romance" of such destructive involvements, try and make it the "real thing", fear to see it for what it really is and desperately try to somehow make it out as something "good"!

The motivation to resurrect a "good" mother was behind Panayiota's efforts to exonerate her mother, find excuses for her behavior as someone who herself was abused as a child. As a grown woman, Panayiota even tried to bring her into the therapy she was undergoing. It was a mournful day when she, at last, symbolically "buried" her mother, breaking off all continuing contact with her, just as she had to painfully extricate herself out of a therapy that had gone wrong.

Apart from this pathological need for "love", emotionally abused and traumatized persons often seek comfort, some sense of meaning, through alcohol and drugs, or try to experience themselves as loved through sexual promiscuity. Flight is taken from the intolerable feeling of self-doubt and worthlessness, of being a nothing and nobody, often in the most devious of ways. Living on the outskirts of themselves, in their bodies and not in themselves, and by indulging in what *feels* pleasurable and comforting, these anguished souls seek to escape from an unbearable sense of emptiness. Frankl calls it an *existential vacuum,* a depressive and mournful state of feeling deprived of love in a world that seems robbed of all value.

Do we recognize the struggling person and their continued, even if twisted, search for some sense of meaning in their lives behind their emotionally disturbed behavior?

The following quotations come from the mouth of one of my most outstanding students of logotherapy. She cast new light on the other side of the shock and condemnation evoked by sexual promiscuity, drug taking, and alcohol abuse:

> Drinking eased my pain, helped me to talk to other people and pass the time rather than killing myself. It gave me something to look forward to. Drugs helped me see into spiritual vistas. Partying was a spiritual experience, where I could find people to philosophize with me and have deep conversations with—impossible for me in a sober state of mind as I was too self-conscious and had zero self-esteem.

Was I, in responding to her writing this in an assignment submitted to me, to put the focus on her drinking, drugging, sexual promiscuity as a result of this or that emotional problem in a subtly disapproving and "corrective" way? No! The focus was on what she sought and tried to find in these deviations from healthy behavior, namely, to have a non-threatening "contact" with people; to have something "to look forward to"; to "reflect" on the meaning of life; to "find" herself where she had lost herself.

There was a thwarting of her *will to meaning,* of her ability to reach out to others in a real and genuine, authentic way and to experience the meaning that was there, out in the world. She failed to find some sense of goodness within herself, affirmed as it would be if someone would take the time and make the effort to make her aware of her own worth. Her drinking, partying and sexual promiscuity provided immediate, if delusional, sensations akin to the pleasurable, happy and self-affirming outflows of experiencing real meaning in life. The only problem was that it was fake and that it did not last, that it had to be sought, even if fruitlessly, time and again, for the sensation of love and meaning, thrill and excitement it did provide, be it for just that moment.

Knowing her story, one of my comments on her assignment that she afterwards told me had a great impact on her, was this:

> Could all the humiliating experiences of your childhood which caused such self-loathing touch who you really were, concealed within an inner space that no outer violence could penetrate? Kept for its emergence when the shaping was done, like a diamond unearthed but cut to perfection in the underground hiddenness of being, was the defiant power of the human spirit. What will prevail, those simulations of meaning you were running after or the far more powerful motivation to become yourself when what is unreal will at last prove to be just that: delusional?

Her response, after further e-mail exchanges with me was:

> Now my journey is to wrap myself in the cocoon of self-love and kindness, and take whatever time it takes to transform into a butterfly who loves and values itself. I trust that my inner angel is reminding me and awakening me to who I really am while I 'sleep' in safety.

From Shame to Conviction

If we but give sufficient ear to what is so graphically brought to light in so many accounts of clients and others, the truth that will hit home to us is this: Deeper than what was perceived as the *psychological unconscious* where, according to the genius of Freud, traumatic and threatening childhood experiences are *repressed,* that is, hidden from or self-protectively *denied* access to the conscious mind, there is a deeper unconscious still, namely, *the spiritual unconscious.*

This deepest part of our being is what Frankl called the Unconscious God. It is a profound grasp of more than we can consciously know or comprehend, an uncanny intuition of destiny, a sensing that our lives are given to us for a reason and that we are *called* to come out of ourselves and find our purpose. Our births were not arbitrary. We were *meant*, that is, *ordained* to exist.

Who can deny that we are all placed in situations, each unique in character, that somehow make a call upon us? There are problems to face, challenges to overcome, experiences to be had, all of which somehow "commission" us. We uncannily, even discomfortingly, realize that we are in this world not just to sit back and enjoy it or to run away from facing up to what it is trying to tell us.

What is more, and we will all confess to this: we *actually want to* reach out for and experience "more" in our lives. We want to be on the move to somewhere much better, much further along the road than where we are right now. We do not always exactly know what that more is, but we yearn for it and, in an ultimate sense, cannot do without it!

We do not all agree that this call comes from a Transcendent God whose will for our lives has been embedded in us as a yearning to fulfill it. But this we *can* all agree on: in the deepest part or core of our being is an inescapable and undeniable *will to find meaning* in our lives.

Without a sense of meaning, or a meaningful *connectedness* to our worlds, we can hardly breathe. It is a *despair of meaning* that drives us to suicide or to desperate and deviant forms of behavior.

This deep sense of a need for or will to meaning emerges into consciousness as *conscience*: an awareness of what is right or wrong for us, what will be life-giving or life-destructive. We cannot seek and find good in bad places, do what we cannot deny is unworthy of this sense of divine commission embedded in us. The consequences of being "out of line" with what we are *meant* to be, "out of touch" with this deeper will or call to live a meaningful and accountable life, come back to us in a bad way. We *scar* our inner image of what we ought to be. We feel saddled with guilt, uneasiness, fear and shame. We hide from open scrutiny. We put up fronts; wear masks. We become *deceitful* and *false*. We are no longer truthfully ourselves!

Conscience is *an awareness of the call to come back to ourselves, to what we were **intended** to be: Worthy!*

Listen to what yet another client is seeking to teach us in a statement she made about her life: **"I am ashamed. I have let myself down."** Her story illustrates the premise that, caught in the pangs of psychological conflict, we become disconnected and lost to meaning in our lives. The angel in us turns into a demon. Our search for ourselves, through the maze of psychological confusion, takes us into areas of darkness and despair, right down to rock bottom, that hellish anguish of being caught in the snares of self-destruction. But that rock-bottom also means there is nothing left, no alternative other than *up* and out of it!

Our client had, at first, a good-enough relationship with a father onto whose lap she climbed as a little girl. Even then, she sought a sense of comfort in being in bodily contact with him because she knew that he only wanted boys, not a girl. She was even given a boy's name! When, in her teens, she began developing breasts and started to menstruate, her father rejected any physical contact with her. She felt she somehow disgusted him, even to the point that he would not allow her to use his shower cubicle. She sensed that her naked sexuality became a real problem for him. It turned out later that he had a promiscuous mother whom he despised; and that he had sexual problems of his own, repressed as they may have been. Our client felt the brunt of it, describing herself as some kind of alien creature, not wanted in the ordinary world of warm relationships.

Her first sexual encounter at 14 was a disaster. *"A part of me shut down at that time"*, she confessed. She lost her sense of freedom, of feeling love-worthy. She felt she had lost herself and that she was given over to frustrated needs and desires. Her effort to still these raging emotions resulted in the development of sexual promiscuity. In all her consequent sexual encounters she never experienced orgasm. She felt her body was separate from herself, something she used as a tool or medium for what she was searching for: to be loved and needed.

Her first orgasm occurred when she actually felt some sense of friendship between herself and a much older partner. However, it did not last. The situation deteriorated until she started waitressing in a brothel and became a prostitute herself. In this free-fall into the subterranean seas of a fully developed psychogenic neurosis, there was another awareness; one that made her cry bitterly in confessing it:

I have dishonored myself. At the time it didn't feel like sex but just about body parts, but there was something more, something possibly more sacred than I had ever allowed: the realization that I had possibly not loved myself, showed myself no respect, that **I just gave myself away.** **"That was my sadness really"**

She had given away her freedom of choice. *"I never saw that I could say no or yes; I never saw that I had that power."* That was until she tried to get herself into another job and fell in love with her much older employer. She experienced it as a real friendship. Was this the father figure with whom she could at last come to love herself? But he was a married man and only kept her on as a mistress. The relationship dragged on for years until she at last came for therapy.

In therapy, she kept trying to understand the voices coming from her **psychological unconscious** where all the anguish of her conflict with her father was deeply buried. *"I have to ask myself"*, she said, *"what is the script running beneath?"* She experienced a healing and restoring relationship with her therapist who was one of my logotherapy students, Rain Aronson. In therapy with Rain, moments of deep insight and meaning miraculously surfaced from this client's **spiritual unconscious** along with psychological flashbacks emerging from her psychological unconscious. She expressed it as *"a particular journey from the dance that I had with my father around sexuality. Somehow this has been a journey for me. The fact that I can feel (sexual) pleasure feels like there is still potential for something healthy."* Real contact, sexual intimacy, in a real and loving relationship, was an emerging possibility.

Even though she had given herself over to sexual depravity, it never had her sanction. *"**It has always been a NO. It is wrong!**"* That kind of sexuality was abnormal, off course and deviant; not within sacred boundaries. This conviction became so strong that towards the end of the therapy she was able to say the following about the relationship with her employer that still dragged on:

Now I must go. Now it's about getting out. It interferes with my relationship with God. I'm now prepared to lose the relationship, the friendship and everything. It feels like I can't anymore. I'm a hypocrite, I can't. My relationship with God is stronger and bigger.

Her own emerging sanctity of spirit brought a breakthrough in conviction:

I have kept myself locked up. Not anymore. I have a desire to not have any secrets, so I can't be in a secret relationship. There are many things that have made me want to get out, also because I want to have an opportunity to have a loving partnership, and I don't think that's available whilst I'm still in something like this.

Most amazing was her confession of having found herself again:

There's a deep sense of self that is not broken that I have not realized before. There is hope, it still feels intact. I feel that there is a lot intact. I feel quite optimistic, particularly where I am right now, and I think that it was there always: **What's intact is change and the ability to change.**

Coming Out into the Light

Healing is the spiritually fresh air that clients breathe when the connection to meaning is made. Let us listen to what another client describes as a loss and, thereafter, as a finding of herself again.

Her dramatically successful therapy was undertaken by my South African colleague and friend, Prof. Cora Moore (1998) who wrote up this case study after a very successful presentation of it at a Logotherapy World Congress in Dallas. After a course of therapy over a period of 4 months, this teenage girl looked back on what was a depression of psychotic proportions, a state where she preferred to lie curled up in a fetus position, resisting all efforts by her family to get her out of bed. Near the completion of therapy, the client was presented with a variety of plant materials from a garden and asked to make an "arrangement" which would represent herself both at the time she entered therapy and at the present time.

The session provides a graphic description of mental illness in vivid contrast to mental health. The client chose to describe this contrast in terms of "the old" and "the new". Her descriptions, based on her very real experience of both, provide us with important insights into the essence and nature of mental health and what is needed, therefore, to combat the factors leading to mental ill health.

Let us close this chapter with a thoughtful reflection on the wisdom given to us out of the mouth of this lovely young girl.

For You, the Reader: Coming Out into the Light

"The Old"
The client seen by Prof Cora Moore, described what she termed "the old" as "the depression that has died and things that go hand in hand with the depression." These were:

- Uninvolvement
- Involvement totally with yourself and negativity
- Insecurity and worry
- Emotionality
- Basically anything connected with the self that was of a negative nature
- Like a dying plant, scorched by the sun, losing its green colour and turning yellow, or lacking a sufficient amount of potassium in the soil
- Pain, sorrow, doubt, fear
- A sense of non-existence like the colour white—a neutral colour—neutral in the sense that you feel insecure, too scared to venture out, too scared to do things for yourself
- Docile, someone who was not prepared to take too many risks

(continued)

Impressions: The metaphor of a dying plant seems to form the theme of the above description. Note also the sense of non-existence as if life, and all that gave it vitality and meaning, was slipping away. A sense of a lack of involvement is described as being thrown back on only herself with nothing and no-one to reach out to that left her the victim of insecurity, worry, fear and doubt. Everything turned negative: Emotionality replaced spirituality. Harsh factors were operating in her life, like the scorching sun. she could draw no nourishment even from within herself. A sense of connection was lost to her. She felt cut-off and left or abandoned by her world. She had only herself in a much diminished sense of the word. The world had turned hostile and she felt too afraid to venture out.

Coming out of her depression is described, by contrast, as **coming alive again**.

"The New"
- The developing of new interests
- Better interaction with people
- A change in the inclination to withdraw into yourself and only to be concerned with yourself
- There is growth, there is colour, an ultimate goal
- A lot of thoughts about and plans for the future

  – What you would like to become
  – Something special that you would like to work towards
  – Dreams and aspirations
  – Hope, green representing hope
  – Like if you stood on a beach, watching the sunset
  – You dream, you think towards a future
  – You move away from the pain, the sorrow, the doubt, the fear

- Every day hope develops a bit more
- Belief in yourself develops
- You slowly become more confident
- You let go, relax, not as paranoid as before
- Close ones. family, people you encounter, that you have known for years, will notice the change
- Ability to love and be loved in a close and intimate sense
- Ability to love other people in your environment and the world
- Someone full of surprises, the unexpected may arise
- You can rise to the occasion and meet whatever is required of you
- That which looked dead, is ironically enough, very much alive

(continued)

- Feeling quite comfortable, not afraid, unique: everyone has colour about him or herself, everyone has his or her own character, own abilities
- Feeling that you have a lot to give to your environment, to your home, your family and everything else
- And then the creative self—the ability to make new
- Revising a lot of things you did before, especially your behaviour
- You can actually see what is happening: there is development, there is growth, there is something positive happening
- Lastly, there is a part of you that has regrets, sorrow and surprise at what was done in the past, often asking: but how could that have happened? I was like this before and I was doing this and I was doing that....

Impressions:
She described herself as opening up to and tuning into life again. She found life leaping up from inside herself again. In being able to reach out to the world with restored trust and confidence, she could move forward and further away from the depression. Instead of being able to diminish her to the point of her slipping out of life, the depression became a thing of the past, the thing that had died. The negative effect of that depression and which caused a fearful withdrawal from life was diminishing. She felt lifted out of emotionality to a higher level, the spiritual level of being. Out of chaos and fragmentation there came harmony and wholeness. On the uniquely human or spiritual level of being, there was the experience of full personhood. Being who she felt she really was, she became inspired with a sense of worthiness and love, full of surprises, with bursts of creativity and thoughts towards a future, an ultimate goal in life.

What looked dead, was so deprived and withered away, was alive again and growing. Fear had gone. She could relax comfortably into being a young woman, feminine, her beautiful and worthy self, hoping for the self-affirming intimacy of being loved and giving expression to herself in loving. She was fully in life, ready to realize and experience its unconditional meaning. Fully herself without doubt, insecurity or worry, that is, in the joy of a sense of unconditional worthiness and uniqueness, she could rise to the occasion and meet whatever life was requiring of her.

She felt filled with a sense of revitalized life, an awakened will to meaning. She experienced a restored sense of liberation, freedom of choice, the ability to view the past depressed and angry state of being with regret and surprise. How could she have acted or behaved in the way she did? It made no sense! What lies were operating against the truth that she was so liberated to experience now?

The dead stem in her vase of flowers, served as a reminder of where she came from. It bore testimony to how far she has moved away from that past into the future that was always there, always waiting; always hers.

Life is a colourful display of flowers!

Synopsis and Conclusion

The following are the words with which the client concluded her last session:

"The one thing that is true of depression is that there is more chaos than calm. There is more worry than peace and there is no harmony.

Each person needs to have a sanctuary in their lives—somewhere you can flee to. Somewhere you can find yourself again.

In depression all you have is yourself, and it's your inner self. It is your inner emotional being that is the only thing you are confronted with. Your thoughts are your primary interest.

But when you move away from that state, you begin to grow into a person again, because **when you are there you are not a person**. You can't give, you can't love and you can't live, because you are always anxious, you're always worried and you're always in a state of turmoil."

References

Moore, C. (1998). The use of visible metaphor in logotherapy. *The International Forum for Logotherapy, 21*(2), 85–90.

Pattakos, A. (2010). *Prisoners of our thoughts*. San Francisco: Berrett-Koehler Publishers.

Chapter 7
How Am I to Address Your Problems?
The Methods and Techniques
of Logotherapy

Abstract Logotherapy embodies the call to step out of our problems and into our lives. Life questions us. We are expected to answer. The meaning is in every moment. The call to be in the moment in a responsive way is at the very heart of the three main methods and techniques used in logotherapy. The **Socratic dialogue** challenges us to step into our lives that are uniquely ours to live; **dereflection** moves us out a state of being consumed with negativity, worry and lament, and directs our attention to what there is, right now, waiting for us to do or to be, while **paradoxical intention** assists us in defeating our fears by defiantly facing them so as to be able to get on with our lives in a real, confident and courageous way. Logotherapy is all about *overcoming*. Frankl maintained that as human beings we are challenged to turn a tragedy into a triumph by transcending the situation. Gaining an objective view of it, we can judge it for what it is, then deal with it in a way that will change things for the better. In doing so, we grow in human stature. The fight/flight syndrome described by Frankl is discussed. Through the various logotherapeutic methods and techniques, the unique human capacities of *self-transcendence* and *self-distancing* are evoked to powerfully break the stranglehold and victimization of fear that causes clients to run away from or to fruitlessly fight their problems.

Keywords Life questions us · The Socratic dialogue · Dereflection · Paradoxical intention · The fight/flight syndrome · Self-transcendence · Self-distancing · Turning a tragedy into a triumph · Growing in human stature

"Adam, Where Are You?"

Logotherapy embodies this call. It is invitational, questioning, provocative and confrontational. Where are you, what are you doing, are you on or off course? What do you really want and treasure in your life? Where is your focus?

Life's call has a negative to it; the negative of warning you not to neglect or spurn it. Life is a precious commodity. Why waste it?

© Springer Nature Switzerland AG 2020   141
T. Shantall, *The Life-changing Impact of Viktor Frankl's Logotherapy*,
https://doi.org/10.1007/978-3-030-30770-7_7

"I Will Question You, and You Shall Answer Me" (Job 38:3)

This is the provocative stance that is at the heart of the logotherapeutic encounter. Life questions us. We are expected to answer. The meaning is in every moment. The call to be in the moment in a responsive way is at the very heart of the three main methods and techniques used in logotherapy.

The **Socratic dialogue** challenges us to step into our lives that are uniquely ours to live; **dereflection** moves us out a state of being consumed with negativity, worry and lament, and directs our attention to what there is, right now, waiting for us to do or be, while **paradoxical intention** assists us in defeating our fears by defiantly facing them so as to be able to get on with our lives in a real, confident and courageous way.

The Arsenal of Logotherapy

1. The Socratic dialogue: the release of the will to meaning

At the very heart of logotherapy is what Frankl called: **the Socratic dialogue**, the question and answer type of dialogue between therapist and client around the call life makes upon the client. The famous Greek philosopher, Socrates, believed that instead of pouring information into the passive minds of his students and subjecting them to the views they are pressurized to accept, their dignity as human beings can only be served by provoking their own critical thinking, their own intuitive realizations of what really matters in life.

The main thrust of the Socratic dialogue in logotherapy is to awaken a sense of *personal responsibility.*

The logotherapist does not tell clients what they must do in dealing with a particular problem or stress situation but, through provocative questioning and statements, evoke an awareness of what the situation is asking of *them.* Their evoked self-determination to accomplish what the situation puts before them as the specific course of action to follow, releases their dormant capabilities to do so!

A Case in Point

A meaningful life is offered as a possibility to all of us. No-one is excluded. It is a free gift, available to whosoever, wherever, whenever and despite whatsoever. That is one of the strongest statements made by Viktor Frankl.

No great standing in life, no great intelligence, no impressive reputation or social position, no stamp of approval because of our gender or religion is required for us to be able to play a meaningful and significant role in this world. We all qualify for the job!

Since the deepest motivation in the human breast is a will to meaning, finding and realizing meaning in life should be *natural* to us. It is what distinguishes us as humans! Our release from what entangles and confuses us frees our *natural* tendencies towards what is good and right and just in this world. *Naturally ourselves*, the veil is removed. We easily, simply and accurately discern what is meaningful in life and what is not. With the blockages of defensive self-consciousness out of the way, we find ourselves *naturally gifted* to help others find their unique place in this world.

Nowhere did I experience this simple yet profound truth more clearly than with one of my African students, Caroline Mamabolo.

Caroline's love and concern for people, her deep desire to serve her own community in their impoverished and disadvantaged state in a remote area in South Africa where the disease, HIV and Aids, has taken on epidemic proportions, made her a most suitable candidate for a training in logotherapy. Though she did not finish her own schooling due to dire circumstances, she got a governmental position in a department offering educational programs to deal with and combat the disease, a job at which she excelled.

Caroline took to logotherapy like a duck to water. All she needed was a clarification of what she intuitively knew. She literally blossomed under the training. Her natural gift for counselling, her ability to empower those who sought her assistance, emerged all the more strongly. She had a sharp sense of what is for the good and what is for the bad in the lives of those she worked with, a distinction she had no fear in holding out to them in a provocative and challenging manner.

Her ability to almost immediately get through to the heart of the matter in dialogue with her clients during her training, proved rather disconcerting to her fellow students, some of whom included qualified clinical psychologists and other mental health professionals. Despite their academic backgrounds, degrees and training in psychology, they were no match for Caroline. Her success with clients in eliciting their will to meaning was almost unparalleled!

The following is one of her remarkable sessions, translated by herself from her own language into a somewhat broken English.

"LOGOTHERAPY SESSION WITH ALINA AT THE HOUSE IN LEBOWAKGOMO TOWNSHIP: POLOKWANE.

I met Alina in town after not seeing her for a long time. We were attending the same church at Lebowa before I moved to Westenburg (Polokwane Suburb). She requested me to come and see her as she is having so many problems and needed to share with me. We secured the appointment of Saturday morning at 11h00.

I honoured the appointment with Alina on Saturday at 11h00 and the session went on as follows:

Caroline: Alina I am here this morning per our appointment.
Alina: Sister Caroline I am happy that you came and I think you are the best person to share my problems with.

C: Please feel free to share your problems as you call them, I call them challenges because they are there to challenge your life. I am here for you.

A: In June 1995 I lost both my parents, following one another in March and June. In June 1998 September my husband met an accident and died the same time. I was living in pain and couldn't sleep. In 1999 September my child died, she was sickly from birth. The pain continued and I was even more frustrated. In 2002 I was pregnant and I got a premature baby of 7 months, and the child died. After the doctor's examination I was diagnosed HIV positive. Since then my life deteriorated, I lost weight, I was confused and frustrated. I thought there was no need for me to live any more.

C: You said all painful stories that followed one another. What do you think when you look back at all the things that happened to you, are you saying that your life was not worth living?

A: No. What I am saying is that the way I had painful experiences in my life, I felt I don't want to continue with life anymore. I felt that my life is just useless.

C: At this moment what are you doing to try and see the value of your life?

A: At the moment I am staying with my younger brothers and sisters as our parents left us when they were still young because I am the eldest daughter.

C: What did you gain from deaths following one another?

A: How can I gain from the pain I suffered so much? I am going to Church and come back. I am still the same even then.

C: It is good that you are going to Church. What are you saying when you hear about the story of Job who suffered, lost all his wealth and children, worst part of them was that he got sick, developed rash all over his body? When his wife told him to insult his God and die, do you remember what his answer was?

A: Yes. Job said to her she is speaking like a fool talking to other fools.

C: Does this give you a meaning of something in your life?

A: Yes! I suffered like Job, I lost my parents, husband, and children and now I am sick. So that means I must be like Job! God tested him to see if Job will turn away from Him and he didn't. He still loved his God irrespective of all the pain he went through. Oh, that means God tested me too!

C: It is good that you now see the example of people who suffered like you and how they reacted to their challenges.

A: I was confused, I didn't even understand anything in the Bible even when the Pastor is preaching. They get in through one ear and out in another ear.

C: Everything that happened to a person has got a meaning and that happened to you. Do you think there is a meaning out of what happened to you?

A: Yes. A lot!

C: Now check in your life what you have achieved out of your suffering.

A: You mean the pain I went through is an achievement when you say I have achieved?

C: Yes. Because you have achieved them through suffering and nobody can take them from you, they are your experience in your life and they will help you and your generation.

A: I did not realize that, I have achieved a lot through my sufferings! When my parents died I have experienced the pain and responsibility of looking after my brothers and sisters. I was married. It was an experience and achievement of marriage and losing a husband. I had children. I experienced the pain of birth and the love of children and their deaths. I am sick. It is also an experience and achievement of sickness which I can even share with others.

C: You have experienced death, are you scared of death now?

A: No. I am like Job, now I am prepared to face all challenges and I understand now why you call them challenges. I can challenge everything that comes my way including death, pain and HIV!

C: What is the meaning of deaths of people who are living with HIV to you?

A: Most of them, they give up, lose hope, they think HIV is a death sentence.

C: How are you going to live from now on with HIV because it is the challenge you are facing?

A: I will eat healthy foods, drink vitamin tablets. I am going to live positive life because I have got the responsibility of looking after my sisters and brothers.

C: If you compare the experience of joy and pain in your life, which one do you think had a meaning in your life or had challenged your life?

A: My painful experience, because I can always help other people who are also in the same problems, and my brothers and sisters. It is the history of my life and I thank God for that.

C: Alina, I want to thank you very much for the time we spent together and for showing interest and dedication to your life and seeing the importance of the responsibility ahead of you, and for changing painful situation in your life into challenges.

A: Sister Caroline, the way you let me look into my problem in a different eye made me a complete new person. After a long period I experienced the joy that comes from inside again. I was a moving corpse but now I am a David that needs Goliaths to fight with! I am going to challenge life. My life is not gonna be the same again."

The above kind of dialogue, one used so skilfully by Caroline, effects a radical change in attitude on the part of the client. Life is seen in a new way. Negative events are viewed in a positive light. Life changes face. Elizabeth Lukas (2000: 86) called the Socratic dialogue **"attitude modulation".** It is the lifting of the head!

Logohints

Logotherapy is an art. There are no defined steps to follow, no set-out theory on how to practise it. There are principles and guidelines, yes, but no more. When you are employing logotherapy, you have to find your own way. You will be questioning yourself: How do I find the person of my client; what is at stake in his or her life? How do we find our way together out of the ensnaring traps holding my client captive? What am I to say or do?

The challenge is to get to the heart of the matter.

But there are guideposts, indications of how you are to proceed right there in the unfolding of the story of the client's life. There are hints of meaning along the way of where to put the focus; of how to bring the real issues out into the open. There is a struggle taking place. Your clients are searching through the rubble of their lives for the treasure that is buried there. It is in the face of the problems that are assailing them that they are to find the meaning of their suffering, to come to a realization of what life is calling upon them to do and to become.

We were inspired by the story of Panayiota Ryall, captured in the last chapter. Out of the broken pieces of her past of childhood sexual abuse, there arose a powerful ministry of help to others who suffered similar fates. She has become a logotherapist in her own full right. The following is what she wrote about those precious hints of meaning in counselling clients coming from a background of child abuse:

THE GLOW OF A LOGOHINT
My client sat before me
Surrounded by a dark bubble of despair
Pouring out her sorrows
Of those who hurt and did not care

I listened very carefully
But not to each angry, pain filled word
I would not allow her bubble
To become all that I had heard

Looking deeply through the darkness
I was searching only for a light
A little glowing ember
A spark buried deep inside

I knew it might be very small
Glowing weakly for a while
But when I chanced to spot it
I'd feel a certain smile

I looked for "a glow of meaning"
Escaping my client's gloom
Though she may not have even noticed
While she shared her woe filled doom

I focused not on the darkness
But on that little ray of light
And helped my client to realise
It was her personal insight

I helped her to discover
The meaning that was there
And slowly drew it from her
Until to her it became quite clear

That's when I saw her eyes light up
As if she finally knew
The course she had to take
And just what she should do

The Gist of The Matter

Frankl said that for the will to meaning to be elicited meaning has to be elucidated. When it is seen or realized, the will to heed it comes alive.

Let us follow this process of increased illumination, of being led from one logo- or meaning moment to the next until the enlivened will to move ahead emerges in full strength.

I had conducted a session with Lorna, a young mother, caught in a struggle resembling a post-partum depression. What was the actual nature of her struggle, what truths did she want to clarify and break through to; what course of action would set her on the path of living the kind of life she was longing to lead?

Lorna was a student of mine. During one of the classes, students asked whether the techniques of logotherapy could be demonstrated and practiced through role-play. I objected. In role-play a problem is imagined which gives the dialogue between those acting the roles of therapist and client false overtones. I did say, however, that if someone had a real problem that they were willing to share, we could try and address it through role-play. Was there someone who was willing to be the client in this way? Lorna shot up her hand. In asking who will be willing to act as counsellor, Lorna pointed to the only male in the class. "I want him to be the counsellor," she insisted. With some trepidation—this was just the introductory phase of the 3 year program in logotherapy—he agreed. My colleague and I decided to video-tape the session.

Watching their interaction from behind a two-way mirror, we became increasingly worried. Our male student, acting as counsellor, wasn't handling the session well. His way of conducting the session was problem-focused. In the process of focusing on all that was wrong in Lorna's experiences and giving advice as to how to correct it, he completely missed to see her and her desire to reach out and have a real encounter with him. At moments Lorna even curled up her entire body away from him. It was clear that she felt let down and disappointed. She became angry and even depressed as if whatever hope she had in having a session with him, collapsed. She even voiced it: "Is there something wrong with me?" Asked if she was satisfied with her husband's role, she answered: "He's distant. He does all the right things. He goes through the motions but he doesn't support me. I almost feel desperate. There's nobody to tell. He's as distant as my father was. Why should I bother?" Was this how she was experiencing her fellow student in his role as logotherapist?

We eventually stopped the session with the excuse that enough had been said. We approached her privately after the class, offering her a session with me to try and restore the damage we fear may have been done to her. She accepted the offered opportunity and came to see me at a time that suited us both.

We set ourselves up in a way she originally wanted, namely to "roleplay" her problem. In "roleplaying" and videotaping the new session, all sense of heaviness left after the failed session with her fellow-student could be removed. We could use both sessions as "experimental" or learning sessions. That would make the mistakes in the learning process perfectly acceptable, even desirable. Mistakes are there to be learnt from! Understanding this, both our male student, a clinical psychologist with a typical problem-centred approach and new to logotherapy, and also Lorna, graciously agreed that we could use these video-taped sessions for instructional purposes to demonstrate the difference between problem- and meaning-centred psychotherapy.

Lorna and Teria

T: "Can you perhaps tell me why you came to see me?
L: I think one of the main reasons is I've been suffering from depression for a while. I think my life changed significantly after my daughter was born. Everything was fine before then.
T: Did you feel there was a change?
L: Yes, there was a change. It was something that I wasn't prepared for at all.
T: It came as a kind of shock, something you didn't feel quite prepared for?
L: Yes, I wasn't prepared. I was enjoying the pregnancy. I felt it puzzling that women felt as if they were losing their figure as the pregnancy proceeded. I just enjoyed getting bigger and bigger.
T: In other words, there was a feeling of expectation. You enjoyed the pregnancy.
L: I think I was living in a fool's paradise. It was ridiculous not to think of the reality of having this child, looking after it, that it was going to wake me up at night as much as she did and I couldn't cope. And my husband had to look after his own business, so there were *two babies*. He had his own baby to look after.
T: Well it seems you highlight the lack of support after your baby was born?
L: From exactly after she was born I wanted to breast-feed her. It was difficult at first but I persevered. The birth was fine, although there was a slight complication but it wasn't really that problematic. So for 4 weeks I struggled with pain, breast-feeding... and there was just me and her. Then and still now, she doesn't sleep during the night. Every 2 h she wakes up and she cries. To try to study

with her... it's just like my world was like this (motions with hands a world collapsing in on her). As for my husband, I could be dead on the on the floor, and he'd just step over me. It's like I don't exist.

T: Well, it seems that those words, "It was just me and her" are significant. You were feeling the lack of support, a lack of being undergirded. You felt not affirmed in your role as a mother; not assisted in the task. All of these things you felt were missing.

L: My friends also, especially in the church, when I became depressed they became angry as well. They didn't understand what was happening and they pushed me aside. So yes, it was only me and my child, and a few others who supported me. I can't forget them but.....

T: I want to just highlight the contrast between your pregnancy and then the after birth experience, because it seems that during your pregnancy there were so many positive feelings, a great sense of wanting this baby. You didn't mind how the baby changed your body. So it was like you wanted to receive her in that kind of way. You wanted to have a strong, nurturing context. And when you felt it was missing, you were overwhelmed in your task of looking after her. That is when you started feeling the depression. But let's look at that depression. What do you feel when you say you suffer from depression?

L: I feel angry, angry with people who didn't support me, angry with the things that have come up for me. I'm no longer important. There's this child, and I just have to carry on.

T: Your existence was a bit extinguished.

L: I feel angry at my past, at my mother for not preparing me for that, and what that was all about. Something was missing.

T: In other words you felt a great responsibility towards this baby. Your depression was a sense that this was a task that was almost too big for you. Where is that extra energy, or inspiration or guidance that should have come from your mother into a preparation for this role? And then somewhere also there is your husband, feeling he's not in the picture either in terms of support.

L: Yes, I feel very lonely, extremely lonely, and I have no time to really just stop and think, to be by myself. There's no time for me.

T: *This* time is for you. And *this* time between you and me is a time that you use to think and meditate about things.

L: But it's easy for you because I walk in here as the client and the next one's waiting for you and I'm just another client.

T: You know, it's so wonderful to be able to contradict you. When you are in here, it is only you in here with me. Nobody else. And there's nobody like you. To share your world with you is for me a unique experience. There is only you, Lorna, nobody else. Nobody's waiting. I'm not thinking about anyone else. I'm here, just for you... (She starts crying). (After a long silence, I broke it gently): You feel those longings, those yearnings of wanting someone to hold you in that kind of secure way that would make you enjoy this kind of responsibility instead of being overwhelmed by it.

L: My husband would remind me very much of my father, the distance. I thought he was so different when I married him, but then this came along and I thought, they're just the same. I didn't have a father that held me, and did that, what you're saying. So it was unfamiliar to me and perhaps, I don't know, maybe I push people away.

T: He was an important figure, your father, when you speak of the need for nurturance. Perhaps there's a specific kind of nurturance for your femininity, your womanhood, which was such a thrilling thing while you were pregnant because you felt there was something real happening, something affirming your womanhood. And this was such a comedown after the birth. Because where was this appreciative male who unleashed all these creative things in you while you were still pregnant? And now all of a sudden it's just dead. But you have a yearning for a father who could have affirmed you and said, you are a uniquely special woman in my life. I affirm your femininity; it's something beautiful and gracious.

L: I want to tell my father about all the times he should have just been there for me and not pushed me aside. I must achieve, I must look nice, and I must do so many things. I must always achieve. It matters what the other people say. And now I'm angry about that.

T: In your pregnancy things were so different from what you're describing now, because there you could relax into being a woman. Something was happening, something real, something was growing inside you. It was so different from having to achieve, having to perform. There you could just relax back into your femininity. It was real and it was growing.

L: Why couldn't I have that again? It's gone. It's stupid to even go there, to think about that. There must be something wrong with me that I can't cope.

T: You know it's wonderful that your problems can often bring you into a corner that forces you to think and make certain decisions. And who's to say that you cannot find something very meaningful, something that would restore you in your personhood, in your femininity like nothing else can, by finding your baby, by establishing the link you had. And it's there! The link is there. You're the mother of this baby. Nobody else is. The baby is so to speak waiting for you to reach out and *be* that mother, be that full feminine person. Just that contact can begin something that can be growth-producing for you.

L: I remember that feeling. I haven't forgotten it, that feeling of peacefulness and the anticipation of this birth. But she restricts me. How can I express myself to her when I have no energy to express to her how I feel? And she doesn't understand, and she cries a lot.

T: I think you feel forced back into the role which you so hated, in having to perform so many responsibilities and now with your baby. And that makes you feel alienated from yourself. And you resent it. And you feel she's asking you to do things that you don't want to do.

L: There are so many restrictions on me that I don't even know what I want to be but can't be, whatever.

T: Perhaps you can just try having moments, even if they are only moments with your baby where you relax back into just being what you felt you were in such a real sense during the pregnancy. You know what? A bond with a baby is an unspoken one. It's beyond understanding. It's a feeling almost like you had when you were carrying her in your womb. She was just part of you. And to have quiet moments with her, where you almost push away all those restrictions, all those responsibilities, all those having to perform, and just be with her.

L: Sounds like a feeling I used to have some time ago. I used to be a ballet dancer for the ballet company down in Cape Town. I remember times like that. That's the feeling which was similar to the pregnancy. But that's gone. My husband always says to me that I try to hang on to that identity. I am longer that person. Anyway, that's in the past. But I'm saying it was that same type of feeling - that wonderful freedom to express myself. And even when people were watching me, I forgot that they were there. Not all the time, but sometimes.

T: You know, I've got goose pimples because I think you've really touched upon and opened up who you really are, and that you experienced when you were a ballet dancer.

L: Yes, but it's over.

T: It's something that can never be over, Lorna. Who you are is always with you. It's there. It's just been pushed aside, it's been thwarted, and it's not been acknowledged. But it's there. And we're going to find it."

She cradled her head in her arms, her knees pulled up to her chin. Then she lifted her head and looked at me with tears in her eyes.

Lorna left me with the arrangement that she would phone me to set up a next appointment if and when she felt the need for it. How surprised I was when, contrary to my expectation that this would happen, she phoned me some weeks later, a changed person! She had gone to visit her father. She had invited him to join her for a visit to a famous historical site, the home of the deceased artist, Helen Martins, in the little Karoo village of Nieu Bethesda.

This Is My World!

Helen Martins' story was studied and written up in a doctorate research by Sue Ross, later published as a pamphlet entitled: *This is my World!* Helen had a very conflict laden relationship with her father who never really accepted her. After his death she started sculpting. Her work became known as outsiders' art. Collecting discarded pieces of wire, bottles and tins, she wired and cemented them together into beautiful works of art. Out of the rubble and discarded pieces of her own life she was making something beautiful. She was freeing herself from the captive hold that an unhappy relationship with her father had exercised upon her. Her garden became filled with these figures, all facing east, towards Mecca, to Helen a place of hope and splendour. Helen's home was turned into a historical monument after her death. Entering it, the visitor is bathed in a cascade of light. She had plastered her walls with glass pieces of different colours. Everywhere she had hung mirrors, reflecting the light of lamps and candles that she had arranged everywhere.

"I have banished darkness!" she was recorded to have exclaimed upon reflection of what she had achieved, "yet halfway on my road of dreams."

I had shown a film, *The Road to Mecca,* portraying Helen's story based on a play by the South African playwright and actor Athol Fugard (1984), to the introductory students in logotherapy during the course that Lorna attended. The initial cause of her problems, being the disturbed relationship with her father, made it obvious why Lorna had at first chosen a male and not a female figure to do the role-play with her. It was therefore so significant that Helen Martins' home was the place she chose for a little holiday with her father!

Lorna and her father had a most meaningful time together. He told her that he had such high expectations of her because he loved her and wanted the best for her and asked her forgiveness for the strain it had inadvertently placed upon her. This acknowledgement of her real person by a father whose approval and affection she so much needed, helped Lorna to relax into a role of natural and spontaneous motherhood as well.

She had no further need to see me!

Hands on Exercises

Let us see just how astute your own grasp of logotherapy has become after all you have read and considered up to this point. After all, the book has been written for you; for you to become more sharply focused on how to discern and realize meaning in your own life and, in so doing, how to impact on the lives of others in a meaningful way.

We are here to serve each other!

Carefully read the following two accounts of clients in logotherapy. What are the logohints or meanings that slipped through in their responses to the therapist? What is the core issue at stake in each case?

How would you, as a logotherapist, have brought these hidden meanings to the awareness of these clients?

> **Hannah** is a young mother of three small children. She impressed as a sensitive, loving and caring person. What happened to her was something she experienced as strange and foreign to her nature. She felt she had a happy marriage. She was therefore very shocked and unnerved when she began to suspect, and was later told by her repentant husband, that he had been involved in an affair with his secretary. She went to share her distress with her parents who, being very protective of her, were infuriated. They advised her to get

(continued)

divorced from her husband even though he had broken off the relationship with his secretary who had left his employ and had since become involved with somebody else. Feeling that something sacred had been spoilt forever, our client pressed for a divorce. Her husband felt he deserved what was coming to him and, although very sad at her request for a divorce, agreed to it. He moved out of the house, agreeing that the children could stay with her. Our client is still a young and attractive woman, and was advised by her parents and friends to put it all behind her and to get on with her life. However, she felt she needed help and came to see me.

H: "I have gone on with my life. I mean, I see to the children. I try to make things as happy for them as I can. I allow them to see their father whenever they want to. I have gone on teaching. I go out with friends. I've made a renewed effort in my faith. I've tried to put it all behind me. Of course I'm hurt and all that. I question my stupidity for not knowing something was wrong with our marriage. Why did he have a need to get involved with someone else? There must have been something wrong! I must tell you, though, that I've met this woman. She's a manipulator. She gets what she wants. My husband, I mean my ex-husband, is such a softie. He listened to her sob stories. Oh, I don't even want to tell you how she spread her nets for him! But point is he gave in to the temptation. He got involved and then didn't know how to get out of it, he said. I began to suspect that something was wrong when he got so moody, short-tempered, also depressed. His nerves were on edge. He wasn't himself any more. He stopped making love to me and couldn't tell me why, until one day he snapped and confessed it all to me. He cried and begged me to forgive him. He told me that he did not know what got into him. He loved me. But I was so shocked, and so very angry. And I felt soiled. I felt he allowed our marriage, to me something sacred, to be invaded by this foreign, ugly thing. I felt wounded and hurt. I went to my parents and cried my heart out. They were very angry with him. They still do not speak to him or want to have anything to do with him. But it has been dragging on, all these feelings of mine. I can't get closure. I can't put it behind me, however much I try."

Now, the question for you, dear reader.

What is a give-away statement, almost like a Freudian slip but this time from the client's intuitive or unconscious spiritual will to meaning in this particular situation? What gives us an immediate indication of what it is she really wants, over and above her emotional hurts, needs and resentments and the influences exercised upon her by her parents and friends? Why can she not get "closure", any true happiness in trying to make a new life for herself? What does the situation require of her?

Did you identify the give-away statement?

(continued)

The slip of the tongue, a main meaning cue was: "My husband, I mean my ex-husband.." Does this not indicate the need to still have her husband as her husband; that she still loves him? Is this not the reason why she could not get "closure", succeed in putting it all behind her and go on with her life without him? If so, what then does the situation require of her? Is it not to have the grace of self-transcendence, to be more spiritually mature in rising above her hurt feelings in viewing the situation more objectively? What does she **really** want? She wants her husband, now her ex-husband, back in her life! How can she do that? What is necessary, what is required, to allow that to happen?

She must forgive him; restore their marriage!

That the above is the right perception was borne out in practice. After listening to the above account, I simply said:

"Are you **meant** to get closure?"

The statement immediately hit home to her: No, she was not meant to get closure! She was to forgive her husband, become reconciled to him! She asked whether she could invite him into therapy with her. He came. He begged her forgiveness once more and she forgave him, also asking his forgiveness for being such a child in their marriage; for not being more sensitive, more maturely aware of his needs. They were remarried, had two more children together and became prominent and exemplary members of their community!

Anneke is a 28 year old single woman. She became a client of one of our students who is also a trauma counsellor. Our student met her when she was called by the police to the site of the suicide of Anneke's cousin, Riana.

Riana had committed suicide by gassing herself in her car at home. She left an ex-husband and two daughters aged 10 and 7 years. Anneke arrived at the scene after the ex-husband had left. Her cousin's body was still lying on the paving in the driveway while the policemen were waiting for the mortuary van to arrive.

Anneke was extremely upset. She was very close to her cousin and two children. Our student spent about 30 minutes with her and gave Riana her name and phone number and told her that she could contact her if she wished to, which Anneke did after the funeral 2 weeks later. The extract comes from a session sometime after the funeral.

Besides the above traumatic experience Anneke had also experienced the following traumatic events:

She had an unpleasant divorce a few years before. The marriage was childless. She came from a dysfunctional family: her father was an alcoholic and her mother was abusive and neglected her. She was sexually abused by another

(continued)

family member from the age of 6 until she was 16 years old. She related the following:

"I learnt that my cousin's ex-husband is seeing someone. The person that he is seeing used to be one of our friends for about 4 or 5 months before Riana died. We broke off contact with this woman. She had an affair. That's why there was a divorce. She had a fully blown affair with her best friend's husband! She had weekends away leaving her two kids with her husband and lied about it all the time. Then he found out about it and sued for a divorce. And now I found out that she is seeing Riana's ex-husband. I was very shocked when I phoned Riana's sister-in-law to find out how the kids were doing and she told me about it and that this woman has gone out and bought a packet of sanitary pads and was going to tell the elder daughter the facts of life this weekend. And I thought: Who are you? You are not family or anything, how can you do this for her? I am really worried because she is quite sordid and does not have any values and now she is going to tell Riana's daughter all about sex. I am very worried about the way she will do it. Her values and morals are very, very grey. I was also told that they (the father and this woman) were holding hands and everything in front of the children. I just can't believe it, because it is not even 2 months since Riana's death! Apparently the children get very upset by it. The younger one will start shaking and cry, asking for mommy. I was really upset when I heard that. I feel very hurt and protective towards the children. I can identify with the children and them not having a mother now, because my mother was never there for me. So I feel for the children. I am not coping with this at all! I am devastated and I am so cross, I can't explain to you how cross I am. I am repulsed by what she has done. But the fact that she and Riana's ex won't put the children's emotional needs in front of their own make them like, to me, two animals that are just reacting on their instincts, like two animals that just want sex. The husband has always been like that. I think that was what drove Riana to end her life. I just don't know. I am so worried about these children. The one is only seven, I mean they are babies still, they are young children and the borders have been crossed. I just can't tell you how repulsive I find it. When I heard what was happening I just lost it. I got so emotional and I just cried and cried."

At this point she broke down and cried, hardly able to stop.

"Sorry about that but you know what, that is the first time since Riana's death that I have cried like this. I just miss her so much and when I think of those children left without a mother now. You know, I just can't stop thinking about the children and that they must now go through life without their mother. You know what I just thought of, maybe one of the reason that I am so angry and so upset, is that I know what it is like being in a house without a mother being there for you."

Now the question for you, dear reader.

(continued)

How would you have responded to this client? What were the meaning cues pointing to the heart of the matter? *"I can identify with the children." "I feel for the children."* It was a situation that, because it so distressed her, was addressing her; a situation which called upon her to do something about it. Would you agree?

Our student, new to logotherapy, followed the typical psychodynamic approach in focusing on the client's past: That this whole issue brought unsolved childhood conflicts of the client to the fore, conflicts that they were "to work through".

Would that have been what you thought about the related situation? Was the children's distress but a trigger to discuss this client's childhood hurts; to take the focus off the children and onto her?

The client's past can be discussed, indeed, but from a logotherapeutic point of view, namely, that she is *angry* about what was done to her as a child; that she is in *protest* about it; that she is turning her back on it in a considered stance that judged what was done to her as *wrong*. This is the anger she is feeling now about what is being done to Riana's children. All of this indicates that she *is* a most moral person. She is certainly NOT a languishing victim of her childhood traumas! To take her back to her childhood in terms of the feelings she suffered then, would be counterproductive, it would deny what she has *already achieved*!

A typically Freudian or psychodynamic approach focuses only on the psyche, on the client's hidden or denied and repressed feelings, without reference to the client as a person with spirituality: Freedom of thought, choice and conviction in a *present* situation, a situation calling for action!

What makes this Freudian kind of approach ineffective and wrong, only half and therefore a *distorted* part of the story? In this particular case, an obvious reason is that the Freudian approach humiliates the client; disavows her dignity and assails her sense of integrity. Can she be so self-absorbed that the children's anguish should be but a means to discuss *her* needs or unsolved problems?

Several meaning cues would also be lost: **the high sense of morality the client revealed** *in her denunciation of the immoral and callous behaviour of that ex-friend of theirs. This was not the stance of a woman in emotional need and conflict! The strongest meaning cue, however, was* **her great distress, her anger about what was being done to Riana's children**. *It deeply grieved her.* Yes, she remembered her own past but in terms of how it served her: to have compassion for children who suffered the same fate she had experienced. She identified with the children, felt great empathy for them. What maturity this showed, what achieved victory over her own past problems!

What then, did the situation require of her? It called her to do something, to take some responsible action to assist the children in their plight.

(continued)

After the student's initial and failed approach, which angered rather than helped the client, our supervision set a new and logotherapeutic approach in action. The following is what happened:

Follow-up sessions with Anneke reported by her logotherapist

"In the previous session with Anneke" (recorded above), "she revealed overwhelming feelings of responsibility towards Riana's two daughters. Realizing this, after the supervision of this session by my trainers, I took up the challenge and suggested to her that these overriding feelings of responsibility were calling on her to act—to do something. I said that this may be a unique task that has been put before her. She could take up the challenge and the opportunity before her or not. She could fulfill this unique task and that the freedom and choice was hers and hers alone.

I said to her that she was in the unique position to carry out this task as her own childhood has given her a depth of understanding and empathy that only she could bring into her relationship with Riana's children. The fact that she had grown up to all intents and purposes without a mother, without someone who would protect her, step in and prevent the sexual abuse she was being subjected to, placed her in this unique position to be of help to these children facing, in so many ways, the same situation.

In the following session she told me that she has thought about what I had said. She had taken up the challenge and organised for the children to go for counselling. She had spoken to the grandfather in Namibia and he had offered to pay for their sessions. Anneke was going to take them once a week. She told me that she felt incredibly relieved because, although she had taken on this responsibility, it had, in actual fact, relieved her of the overwhelming feelings of responsibility she had felt before. She said that by acting on those feelings and choosing to take up the task before her, it had made her realise, for the first time, that there was a unique role for her to play in life and in the children's lives and that she herself had the freedom to decide what that role could be.

Anneke told me in a following session that she sees the children once a week. She takes them out for a burger or to the movies and tries to entertain them for a few hours. She was finding this time very upsetting and difficult and was unsure about how to cope with these feelings.

I put it to her that her memories of Riana and love for her also placed her in a very unique and special position with the children. Her memories are unique and she can pass them on to the children. That although their father, grandfather and aunts also have memories of Riana, no-one else will be able to give to the children the unique memories she has of their mother, having been so very close to her. This was a very special gift that she could give to the children.

(continued)

I suggested that the next time she was with them she should share one of her special memories of Riana with them.

In our next session she was like a different person. Her face was alight and she could not wait to tell me what had occurred. She had taken the children for a milkshake and while they were sitting looking very subdued drinking their milkshakes, she told them a very funny story about herself and Riana involving milkshakes at the Spur (a well-known restaurant in South Africa).

She said that the children just laughed and laughed and that after that they could not stop talking about their mother. They asked her all sorts of questions about their Mom, her likes, dislikes etc.

Anneke said that it was the most incredible afternoon and it made her realize that her memories were unique and just what a role she could play in the children's lives. She said that she now understands what I meant and that her relationship with the children was truly unique—there was no-one else that had the same memories of Riana that she had and could give to the children. What a special and beautiful gift she could give to them! She also said that she was sure Riana was looking down on her and the children and laughing and sharing the special memories with them and that Riana would be so very happy to know that Anneke was sharing these precious moments with her children."

*A further meaning cue that was not that evident at first and that emerged subsequently, was her own unsolved grief about Riana's tragic death. The situation required further action, namely, that **she was to be the link between Riana and her children**. It was as if Riana, incapable as she felt to continue her miserable life with her husband, was passing on the torch to Anneke. This completed the picture for Anneke who ended the counselling in a happy and contented mood!*

The Analysis of Happiness

The above account of Anneke clearly shows that the accent in logotherapy is on *meaning*. Logotherapy is not problem-centred but meaning-centred. To the mind of the logotherapist, every problem contains a meaning. To resolve the problem is to find its meaning and respond to the particular task embodied in the problem. The problem, therefore, is presented as a *crisis of meaning*. The client's sense of meaning in life is under assault. What, therefore, must be done about the *wrong* of the situation? A focus on the problem as a problem is to miss the mark. Undue attention is given to the problem. This makes the problem more ominous, the client more a victim of it! The problem is not the problem, the task is to find the meaning of the problem! **What, in essence, is the client challenged to do about the problem situation?** *That* **is the issue!** It is not a question of removing (solving) the problem but of doing something about it! Every situation requires *right action*.

Life is a moral issue!

Homeostasis, a state of undisturbed, trouble-free and happy equilibrium is not the focus of human existence, Frankl contended, but a state of *tension* is necessary, namely, the tension between what is and what *ought to be.* The client must be *challenged* to be happy. What must the client *do* in order to be happy? Happiness must have a *reason!* Happiness is the *result* of doing something that makes you happy. You cannot make the result of something the aim! Happiness is an *outflow* of meaning, of an experience of something most meaningful, of having performed the one right and required action; of having been the kind of person you could be proud and happy about; the person, in fact, you were being challenged to be!

A focus on the meaning of a problematic situation; on what the situation is requiring in terms of responsible action, *liberates* the client. The truth of the matter sets the client free from being caught in and victimized by the problem. That is how Frankl described the essential nature of human freedom: it is a freedom *from* something (from being victimized by a problem) *towards* something (towards the exercise of our freedom of choice, our ability to choose and victoriously enact the required or *right* response in any particular situation).

Human freedom is the freedom of *responsibility*!

A Life of Overcoming

Logotherapy is all about *overcoming.* Frankl maintained that as human beings we are challenged to turn a tragedy into a triumph by transcending the situation. Gaining an objective view of it, we can judge it for what it is, then deal with it in a way that will change things for the better. In doing so, we grow in human stature. **In doing what we should or ought to do, we become more of what we should or ought to be.** We release our dormant spiritual capacities, the ability to do what the situation is requiring of us.

In logotherapy the client is challenged to overcome what is *wrong* (what is painful, distressing, victimizing, morally twisted and misleading) with what is *right* (actions that will *defeat* the victimizing effects of what is painful, distressing and morally twisted and misleading).

Two other logotherapeutic techniques, based on these principles and both used in the Socratic dialogue between therapist and client, are *dereflection* and *paradoxical intention.* Both are employed to assist clients to triumphantly deal with the incapacitating fears evoked by a fear-provoking situation in order not to retreat from, that is, fear the feared situation, but to become free to properly *deal* with the situation in question.

Clients exhibit a **fight/flight syndrome** in trying to combat or flee from the fears that a traumatic situation evokes and can leave in its wake. Both are futile efforts leading nowhere. Both entangle the client even tighter in the grip of his or her fears since **the more you try and escape from your fears, the more they haunt you; the more you fight them, the stronger their hold.**

Dereflection is used as a specific technique when the client is obsessed with a problem, mulling over it, **hyper-reflecting** on it, hardly able to move away from it. In deliberately, and even persistently, taking attention *away* from the problem and shifting the focus onto something that is meaningful to the client, the problem loses its exaggerated importance and is put in proper perspective. The uniquely human capacity of *self-transcendence* is evoked by this technique. The client transcends the problem situation by moving their attention away from their fears and by focussing on what meaningful things there are in their lives that call for their commitment and involvement. Their focus is where it should be; their attention is on what matters!

Paradoxical intention is used especially in cases of paranoid fears (phobias), panic states and obsessive efforts to ward off or control the terrorising thoughts and feelings associated with a much feared situation. The typical state of **hyper-intention,** that is, excessive and compulsory efforts to ward off all the fears provoked by the original stress situation, is addressed by the technique of paradoxical intention. By encouraging the client to paradoxically *intend* exactly that which they fear to happen instead of fighting or trying to get away from it, the wind is taken out of the sails of the threat. A stand *vis-à-vis* the fears is taken. Instead of gnawing inside the mind of the person, the fears are placed in opposition to the defiant stand of the person. The human capacity of *self-distancing* is evoked. You cannot wish for that which you fear! That is surely ridiculous! But this is where laughter and ridicule come in. Imagining the threat and actually commanding it to show itself in the most preposterous and ridiculous or funny way possible, the client is enabled to laugh about it. Laughter snaps the cord of tension tying the person to the fear. **Humor** is a most powerful tool to deal with the immobilizing effects of fear. Nowhere are you more distanced from and *freed* from your fears than when you can laugh at them!

2. Dereflection: putting the focus where it matters

Frankl has left us with many powerful examples of the use of paradoxical intention and dereflection. What follows is a demonstration of dereflection with a schizophrenic girl under treatment at the psychiatric unit of the hospital where Frankl was the director. She was obsessing about the inner turmoil caused by her mental illness.

Most psychotic disorders have a constitutional basis. A dysfunction of the brain is involved. That is why logotherapy in such cases is not the primary but a supplementary form of treatment. Psychiatric intervention through drugs and other forms of therapy, aiming to relieve or deal with the symptoms of the disorder, is indicated. Frankl (1988: 125–131) called logotherapy in this regard: **medical ministry.** However, the mental disturbance *disturbs* the sense of meaning in the life of the mentally ill and makes their fear of the illness take on threatening proportions. Mental illness is, therefore, also a crisis of meaning, calling for *more* than just medical treatment.

Anna

Frankl: You are in a crisis. Strange thoughts and feelings beset you, I know; but we have made an attempt to tranquilize the rough sea of emotion. Through the quieting effects of modern drug treatment we have tried to have you slowly regain your emotional balance. Now you are in a stage where reconstruction of your life is the task awaiting you. But one cannot reconstruct one's life without a life's goal, without anything challenging one.

Girl: I understand what you mean, Doctor, but what intrigues me is the question: What is going on within me?

Frankl: Don't brood over yourself. Don't inquire about the source of your trouble. Leave this to us doctors. We will pilot you through the crisis. Well, isn't there a goal beckoning you – say, an artistic accomplishment? (She was an art student). Are there not many things fermenting in you – unformed artistic works, undrawn drawings which wait for their creation, as it were, waiting to be produced by you? Think about *these* things.

Girl: But this inner turmoil…

Frankl: Don't watch your inner turmoil. But turn your gaze to what is waiting for you. What counts is not what lurks in the shadows, but what waits in the future, waits to be actualized by you. I know, there is some nervous crisis which troubles you; but let us pour oil on the troubled waters. That is our job as doctors. Leave the problem to the psychiatrists. Anyway, don't watch yourself, don't ask what is going on within yourself, but rather ask what is waiting to be achieved by you. So let's not discuss what we have to deal with in your case: the anxiety neurosis or neurotic obsessions, whatever it may be, let's think of the fact that you are Anna, for whom something is in store. Don't think of yourself, but give yourself to that unborn work which you have to create. And only after you have created it will you come to know what you are like. Anna will be identified as the artist who has accomplished this work. Identity doesn't result from concentration on one's self, but rather from dedication to some cause, from finding one's self through the fulfilment of one's specific work.

Girl: But what is the origin of my trouble?

Frankl: Don't focus on questions like this. Whatever the pathological process underlying your psychological affliction may be, we will cure you. Therefore, don't be concerned with the strange feelings haunting you. Ignore them until we make you get rid of them. Don't watch them. Don't fight them. Imagine there are about a dozen great things, works which wait to be created by Anna, and there is no one who could achieve and accomplish it but Anna. No-one can replace her in this endeavour. They will be your creations, and if you don't create them they will remain uncreated forever. If you create them however, even the devil will be powerless to annihilate them. Then you have rescued them by bringing them to

reality. And even if your works were smashed to pieces, in the museum of the past, as I should like to call it, they will remain forever. From this museum, nothing can be stolen since nothing we have done in the past can be undone.
Girl: Doctor, I believe in what you say. It is a message which makes me happy.
(And with a bright expression on her face, she got up and left Frankl's office.)

The severity of an affliction or tragic event necessitates placing a *distance* between the client and the affliction or tragedy. The client is, in effect, *loosened* from the stranglehold of the malady or fateful event. This gives the client the freedom of perspective: the ability to let the tragedy or illness be; to no longer fight or run away from it. The illness is to be treated, yes. It is there but there are also other realities, a life to live outside of it. Many other things in life have remained intact: there are still good experiences to be had, tasks to complete, causes to serve, people to love.

The Ecce Homo Technique: A Special Case of Dereflection

James Crumbaugh and Rosemary Henrion (1994), two well-known logotherapists, have given special attention to shifting the focus of a client who has suffered some or other tragic fate onto the magnificence of the courage to bear it in an exemplary way. The following is an extract from their writings in their reference to another of Frankl's famous recorded cases.

"The technique's basic framework starts with exploration of the client's suffering, including the history behind it plus the client's feelings associated with it. Next, a clear picture of the client's assets and liabilities are formulated, with emphasis upon not only the uniqueness of the suffering but also the uniqueness of the opportunity to use assets to respond to such suffering as an "exemplary sufferer." The potential attitudes, (attitudinal values,) toward the suffering are explored, including avenues of behaviour through which attitudinal values may be expressed toward the suffering. Finally, the client is reinforced by encouragement for emitting behaviours fulfilling the attitudinal values. The key to the Ecce Home technique lies in building self-esteem by demonstrating that the individual has achieved unique personal meaning as somebody through becoming an exemplary sufferer."

Frankl's Prototypical Case: Frau Anastasia

"The procedure can best be made clear by a short recapitulation of Frankl's case of Frau Anastasia. At a class for medical students, Frankl had invited her to join him in conducting a session with her in front of a most interested audience of medical trainees. This lonely, old woman had been stricken with a terminal illness, and she was angry and depressed. She told Professor Frankl in effect, 'Why shouldn't I be depressed? Here I am in my 80's with nothing to show for my life. I was always going to amount to something, but I never got around to getting married. All I ever did was domestic work, and now I am about to die. How can my life now have any meaning?'

Frankl expressed understanding of her feelings, and he explored with her the jobs she had held. She had occupied important positions of trust as a domestic for several leading families who had treated her almost as one of them. She travelled with them; gone to special events with them, met many famous people around them. So it was clear she hadn't failed as badly as she thought—which she now admitted with a smile. But then she added gloomily: 'I have no future—nothing to look forward to.'

Here Frankl explored her attitudinal values—medical science could not change her situation and she had only two ways to go: either down the drain in despair, or out with a bang instead of a whimper. Would it make a difference which way? Yes, because with a positive attitude there was still something important that she could accomplish, something that she had overlooked. The hospital staff had noticed that she was a leader among the terminal patients, and that in spite of her own desperation she always found time and strength to comfort others. 'Frau Anastasia,' Frankl told her, 'you have already achieved a remarkable feat. You have made the best of an otherwise impossible situation by making your time count in the helping of others. Perhaps the purpose for which you were put on this earth in the first place was just so you could do what you are now doing in the ward.'

She was surprised, but fascinated by this thought. Frankl followed it up: 'You are now achieving something which few people ever get a chance to do. I congratulate you and commend your example to this class of medical students. Ecce Homo! (Behold the human being)!' The medical students burst into applause, and the episode so motivated Frau Anastasia that she faced her final days without depression or anger. Her last words were, 'Yes, my life has meaning, which Professor Frankl showed me.'

This special case of dereflection had worked well for her. The arousal of a sense of meaning and purpose in an otherwise hopeless situation produced exemplary suffering and made this suffering more tolerable and worthwhile."

Comments About the Ecce Homo Technique

The writers of this paper, Crumbaugh and Henrion (1994), considered some of their most successful cases to have been those in which the clients were helped to become aware of the meaning of their suffering and of their role as exemplary sufferers. This created an awareness of new meaning and purpose in the clients' unique situations. The writers continued:

"One key to success, embedded throughout the technique, is getting the clients to feel good about themselves through pointing out assets and thus building self-confidence and self-esteem. This enables the dereflection to occur in spite of whatever limitations the clients have suffered. It enables them to utilize potentialities, and to recognize success in themselves even if the world does not.

The Ecce Homo technique accomplishes this by stimulating new insight into old habits of escape and defence. That leads to reframing the total situation and yields a new perception of the self in relation to the situation. New action results from the new perception.

The overall picture as applied in logotherapy is one of utilizing attitudinal values to deflect; to determine action that circumvents individual limitations and magnifies remaining assets. This elucidates new meanings in an otherwise hopeless-seeming existence, and enables the clients to go on courageously and hopefully in a life that has become seemingly meaningless."

3. Paradoxical intention: calling fear's bluff

Exaggerated and irrational fears, evoked by a traumatic experience, are put in their place by the technique of paradoxical intention. Paradoxical intention is a mind-game. A distressing event conjures up all sorts of horrible outcomes in a future similar situation in the agitated mind of the person. The more the client fears to fall trap to the same distress again, the more this fear makes what is feared happen! Through a vicious circle effect, the fears are reinforced. The client becomes trapped, a victim of his or her fears with a consequent defensive withdrawal from the world.

Paradoxical intention is designed to counteract **anticipatory anxiety** ("the world is a frightening place and something bad is bound to befall me"). Paradoxical intention is a most powerful way to challenge a client out of the captivity of fear. The client is encouraged not only to step out of his or her fears but also to actually turn around and face them, challenging them to their face in the most preposterous way possible. Instead of threatening, the fears become laughable. Instead of being terrorized by these fears and trying to hide from them or run away from them, this about turn to actually face and confront them, releases **the defiant power of the human spirit.** The person steps into the space occupied by the fears. The strongest weapon against fear is the ability to laugh at it. What seemed so ominous and serious before looks ridiculously laughable now! Who is the boss: the person whose space and life this is, or the fears that seek to invade and possess it?

Paradoxical intention is the exact opposite of persuading. Clients are not advised to suppress or overcome their fears through rationalization but, through a deliberate exaggeration of their fears, to free themselves from their fears. Are the fears really that big? Let it be put to the test!

Immobilizing fears are actually provoked to show themselves for what they are: bullies. And like with a bully, when he is confronted, his big show of bravado collapses and is shown to be exactly what it is: a show. Underneath the parade of a terrorizing show of power, lurks a coward, an already defeated foe! Instead of being oppressed by his or her fears, the client is challenged to say to them:

"Come on, show yourself. Blow yourself up as big as you can. Just a prick of real courage on my part, will deflate you like a balloon!"

A person who has developed a phobia of blushing, having blushed excessively in a most embarrassing situation, is encouraged to *intend* the blushing in a next and similar situation. Paradoxically intending it, in fact wishing that it should happen, it actually does not. The wind is taken out of the sails of the fears when the person courageously takes a confrontational stand towards the anticipated and feared situation of embarrassment and claims the space it has taken up in his mind as his or her own. The fears illegitimately lurking there are cast out!

Unfounded as the fears basically are in suggesting to the terrorized person that they are powerless, helpless and weak, poor and sorry specimens of human beings without a real standing in the world, the truth of the opposite unmasks the invalidity of these fears. With the lies exposed, the fears, pricked like a balloon, evaporate into thin air!

What occurs is an existential turnabout from fear (self-castigation) to faith (self-liberation). The person is called out of hiding; liberated from a sense of shame and withdrawal from the world and challenged to stand his or her ground with dignity.

A Case Study

A student of logotherapy presented the following interlude with a friend of hers where the use of paradoxical intention helped her friend to face her incapacitating fears head-on. Our student acted in the role of the logotherapist and related what happened as follows:

"It was with a measure of hope and apprehension that my client, W., told me of her opportunity to sit and do portraits at a crafts market venue. To put it in context, W. Is divorced and has not been earning an income for the past 6 months. She is a fine artist but has not completed any projects or fulfilled any orders despite plenty of encouragement from family and friends. She has displayed a tendency to get everything ready, but then find something else more "pressing" to do, such as tidying or filing things. What follows is a reconstruction of a portion of the counselling session.

T: 'What can get in the way of your taking hold of this opportunity?

W: Well, I haven't phoned my ex to see if he can have the kids...

T: No problem. I can take them off your hands and take the whole crew for a nice outing.

W: Thanks. That's a great help. But I've never drawn from live models before. I don't know if I will cope with people sitting while I draw them.

T: Well, why not work from photographs rather? You know you can do that. Take a couple of the kids or even a magazine picture. Do a couple on display.

W: That's a good idea! I could even do a famous person from a magazine! And people sometimes carry pictures with them.

T: Perfect! That way you can set yourself up to succeed rather than fail. Now what about getting there? So often you make plans and then things happen to prevent them from going as planned.

W: You know, you are so right. Look at the time R. and I planned to celebrate our birthdays together! I was supposed to meet her in the afternoon and we were going to go out for coffee. I was so late that she had gone without me when I arrived, and my present was waiting for me on her doorstep with a note attached. And so many times I have planned things to do with the kids, and I have really looked forward to them and then things happen and we never have our outing. I just don't know what to do.

T: I want you to plan to fail - plan how you are NOT going to get to your destination. Something like this: plan to sleep late, then, because you have overslept; wake up in a really bad mood. Have a fight with M. (her boyfriend), and then have a fight with the kids, especially T. (a particularly difficult child).

W: You know that's exactly what happens!

T: Good. Only this time you are going to plan it! You could also have a bad hair day so that you can't possibly go anywhere until your hair's right.

W: Ok, and what about a pimple?

T: Brilliant! Then you will have to have a facial!

W: (laughing). But I don't see how this will work....

T: I bet that if you plan to have a fight you'll find it difficult to actually have that fight!

W: But what will M. (her boyfriend, living with them) say if I tell him? He'll think I'm mad!!

T: Get him to help you. Maybe he has some ideas to prevent you getting there as well.

W: And the children. I'll ask them for ideas too!

T: Wonderful! Get them all involved! You'll probably all be laughing so much you'll never be able to make it work - have a fight and not get there, I mean. This time, instead of chopping a hole in your boat to sink it just any old way, you'll plan the hole, and maybe you'll find instead of sinking the boat you'll have a place to fit a mast, so you can turn your rowing boat into a sailing boat! Dash it all!! For all the chopping you've done so far, your boat still hasn't sunk! Isn't that marvellous?

W: Yes it is. (Giggling) Ok, I'll try it.'

I gave W. a couple of examples of how it had worked for other people. This eased her slight anxiety at the bizarreness of my suggestion.

When I arrived to collect the children on the Saturday morning, I found W. almost ready to go and well on time. She told me she had asked the children to have a fight with her and that they had said, "Mommy, we don't think it's a good idea!" Unfortunately this particular time did not generate any immediate income for her, but it was a major step in the right direction and a breakthrough point for W. just to be where she planned to be on time."

Elfrieda G.

Another of Frankl's famous cases to illustrate the use of the technique of paradoxical intention is the case of a patient suffering from *obsessive compulsive neurosis*, a mental affliction earmarked by *hyper-intention*, compulsive efforts at controlling fears associated with impending doom.

Robert Leslie (1994), another well-known logotherapist and pastorial counsellor, one of Frankl's students at the time, described the patient as follows:

"When Elfrieda was brought into the amphitheatre, she had the typical appearance of a deeply depressed person. Every aspect of her body conveyed despondence. She barely moved her legs as she shuffled across the floor. There was no animation on her face, only a blank, worried expression. Her hair was uncombed, her whole manner was one of careless indifference. When she reached the chair beside Frankl's table, she slumped into it with an air of resignation. She presented the classic picture of depression (Leslie 1994: 115–116)."

Frankl reported his interview with her under the following headings:

Arousing hope
"In the lecture hall of the hospital, in the presence of a class of students, I spoke to the patient for the first time. I asked her (on the basis of the clinical notes about her): 'Are you accustomed to check the door many times before leaving home, or to check whether a letter has really fallen into the mailbox or not, or to check several times whether the gas valve is really closed before going to bed?' 'Yes, that is my cause,' she said anxiously. I then proceeded by pointing out that this meant she belonged to a certain type of character structure which in traditional European psychiatry was conceived of as 'anankastic' and that this meant immunity to psychoses. A sigh of relief was her response, relief after long years of suffering from the fear of becoming psychotic. Because of her fear that the obsessions had been psychotic symptoms, the patient had fought them. By this very counter pressure, however, she had increased the pressure within herself. I then remarked: 'You have no reason for such a fear. Any normal person can become psychotic, with the single exception of people who are anankastic character types. I cannot help but tell you this and destroy all your illusions in this respect. Therefore you need not fight your obsessive ideas. You may as well joke with them.'"

Changing perspective
"Then I started paradoxical intention. I invited the patient to imitate what I did. I scrubbed the floor of the lecture hall with my hands and said: 'After all, for the sake of a change now, instead of fearing infestation, let's invite it.' Stooping and rubbing my hands on the floor, I continued: 'See, I cannot get dirty enough; I can't get enough bacteria!' Under my encouragement, the patient followed my example. She hesitatingly got up from her chair, got down slowly on her knees, and began to rub

her hands on the floor. I encouraged her to 'rub harder' and then to rub the germs off her hands on to her face. As she did so, a strange expression came over her face. I noticed it, and turned to the students in the amphitheatre seats, and said: 'Do you see, she's smiling. She's getting well already.' It was true. Through her fingers on her face the students could see that her face, which up to that moments had shown only indifference and despair, was now breaking out in a smile."

Dereflection and centring on meaning
Robert Leslie (1994) described the next phase:
"Frankl invited her to be seated again and talked with her at some length, not about her anxieties about germs but about her love for her family and especially for her children. As she talked with him, her manner radically changed. There was animation in her voice and on her face. She spoke clearly and confidently. It was obvious to all that she was a changed person. When she got up to go out, her actions were completely different. She marched confidently from the amphitheatre with her head held high, a transformed person!"

Changing for responsibility
Frankl continued the story: "On the sixth day after the onset of logotherapy, Elfrieda G. left the hospital to buy wool to knit a pullover for her youngest child, a child she could never get herself to fondle or embrace for fear of infecting him with some or other horrible disease. She wanted to knit the pullover 'here in an environment full of bacteria.' 'On each loop of the sweater', she said humorously, she wanted 'one bacterium sitting.' She was beaming with joy and felt completely healthy. When she went home for Christmas her behaviour was, for the first time, as normal as it had been before the onset of her neurosis 3 years before. There was no longer any need to apply paradoxical intention. She embraced her children, caressed them without the slightest fear of infecting them. She was able to devote herself to her youngest child for the first time in his life!"

In a follow-up visit, Frankl asked her about her washing compulsion. She replied: "I have to laugh at that now. It seems quite unreal to me that I ever had to suffer from anything like that. Now at ten o'clock in the morning my housework is finished. Before, I got up at three in the morning and even by night my housework was not completed.'

As she left the hospital, Frankl challenged her: 'Regard yourself as cured.'"

A Possible Cause of the Illness?

What was the cause of this woman's phobia about germs? What underlying emotional conflict, what traumatic event, one too dreadful or unacceptable for her to face in conscious terms, caused her obsessive compulsive neurosis?

She may have picked up an infection after the birth of her youngest child that may have been passed onto the child. The baby may have nearly died. The anguish of this situation may have caused her to blame herself. Was she a bad mother? Look what she did to her baby! Dare she touch any of her children again? How can she protect them? She must fight all the germs everywhere and keep them at bay! Not this realization may have been in the mind of the mother—the whole traumatic incident may have been pushed into unconsciousness. All that she was left with was her obsessive fear about germs. It was this present situation that Frankl addressed.

The fact that is so often overlooked in psychoanalytic or psychodynamic type therapies is that it is not the suppressed emotional trauma that is the important factor, but *the suppressing of it out of guilt and concern for what damage it may cause in a valued and present situation.* Even if this pathology was brought into focus during therapy, something which Frankl did not care to do, a logotherapeutic understanding of it would go deeper than only to her psychological unconscious. It would lead her to her *spiritual unconscious,* that is, to what *truly* mattered to her in her life. She very much needed to see herself for what she in fact was: a good and *caring* mother. Any other and dark thought or suspicion about her basic goodness was *intolerable* to her, so much so, that she *suppressed* whatever negative, angry and resentful, dark and foreboding fears she may have harboured. Her fruitless efforts to keep these anxiety-provoking thoughts at bay led to the development of a fully blown obsessive compulsive neurosis.

Exposing the delusional nature of her fears through the powerful confrontation of such fears by way of paradoxical intention, Frankl helped her see the reality for what it really is, namely, that she cared deeply for her children and loved her family. The truth of the matter *released* her from the entanglements of her fears that she was a bad mother, wife and person. In fact, looking back on her pathology, the result of distorted, delusional, morbid perceptions and tumultuous feelings, it felt to her like a bad dream!

Frankl commented: "I was not concerned with all this when starting therapy. I did not delve into the background of complexes and conflicts.' Why? Not that these factor were not legitimate data in her case, but because **recovery into health required finding and being centred on the real meanings in her life.** Disentangled from her fears, she took up the reigns of her own life again."

She found healing through meaning!

Exercise for You, the Reader: A Radical Shift in Focus

Having read this chapter, how can you see yourself being shifted out of your problems to finding meaning in your own life? How would this process unfold? How were you seen, your problems looked at by the logotherapist in the effort and commitment to have this shift take place? How could you have an about-turn; face and deal with your problems in a new way?

The Logotherapeutic Creed

The First Stage

On the Way to Meaning
- The logotherapist believes in the logo-assumption that good (that which is meaningful and life-enhancing) has the power to overcome evil (that which is meaningless and life-destructive).
- Through logotherapy, the logotherapist will seek to free you from the stranglehold of self-destructive behavior, thoughts and fears, by tapping into your spiritual resources: your ability to self-transcend, to distance yourself from your problems, gain perspective on and constructively deal with them. There will be a distinct move away from the trap of obsessive self-preoccupation.
- Instead of an exclusive focus on the self, you will be made aware of the responsibilities waiting to be fulfilled by you, especially in terms of those close to you and who have been entrusted to your care; the opportunities that are offered to you in your life in rendering a service, in making a difference for the better in the world.
- You will be made aware of having a calling, a unique destiny to fulfill, that your life is endowed with the dignity of a purpose and that the reasons for your existence are to be found right there in the immediate moments and situations of your life—the opportunities and duties staring you in the face, as it were.
- You will be made aware that the dreams, the future goals, the prospects to strive towards, all have their starting point right there where you have been placed, in the kinds of experiences you have had, the lessons you have learnt, the kind of person you are—the peculiar gifts you have to give to the world.
- There is only one space to fill, your own space; only one life to live: your own.

The Second Stage

The point of crossing over into a life of meaning
- A concentration on what is meaningful in your life will bring you onto the uniquely human dimension of meaning. You will no longer be caught in the entanglements of a sub-human level of existence where your person is submerged in emotional strife and turmoil and dictated to by the conflicting demands of unsatisfied needs and wants leading you hopelessly astray. Meaning is the foundation from where you will now have to launch forth into life in an entirely new way.
- You will make an about-turn. Instead of being weighed down by your problems, you will step out of those problems and face them head-on.

The Third Stage

Leading a meaningful life
- You will have a new commission: to no longer be the passive or helpless victim of evil (the things that cause distress, suffering and pain), but to take on the task of overcoming evil. How is the negative, the destructive, the bad or evil overcome? It is done by turning evil on itself. Evil loses its sting, its hold when you will wrest meaning out of every situation. Evil will not be given prominence, the right to exist, when you will always have meaning (the good, the beautiful and true) in mind, when you will preserve what is precious and valuable in life, when you will encourage and affirm justice and goodness wherever it is found and, above all, when you will resolutely exercise it yourself.
- A concentration on the good will not only elevate your spirits, uplift and encourage you and make you feel good about yourself, but your right attitudes and actions, will also return to you in terms of reward, namely, the love, admiration and respect of others. Doors of greater opportunity will open. Your sensitivities will deepen; your understanding will grow. You will gain in human stature; become irreplaceably you! Your life will become something beautiful, something intensely worthwhile—a precious and wondrous gift shown forth in ever greater splendor.
- You will become aware of an added dimension in your life, as if living your life has taken on greater meaning. There will be an extra presence of blessing, care and protection, as if you are being protected and sheltered. You will become aware of an extra dimension of strength that will be able to take you through the worst and that will imbue you with uncanny wisdom and understanding. You will become a blessing; your life something of supreme significance. You will be filling your space in life.
- Evil will back away from you!

References

Crumbaugh, J. C., & Henrion, R. (1994). The Ecce Homo Technique: A special case of dereflection. *International Forum for Logotherapy, 17*, 1.

Frankl, V. E. (1988). *The will to meaning*. Penguin Books: New York.

Fugard, A. (1984). *The road to Mecca*. South Africa: Fugard Theatre Production.

Leslie, R. C. (1994). Frankl's case of Elfriede G. *International Forum for Logotherapyy, 17*, 2.

Lukas, E. (2000). *Logotherapy textbook: Meaning-centered psychotherapy*. Toronto: Liberty Press.

Chapter 8
Why Does Logotherapy Work?
The Transformational Power of Meaning

Abstract Readers are asked how they would have responded if, in therapy with me, I have used the kind of methods and techniques discussed in the previous chapter. Would it have had a transformational effect on them; have been a life-changing experience for them? If we are being plugged into what really matters in our lives, the invigorating power of meaning can be expected to flow through us! Readers who are psychotherapists or counselors, would be very much aware that, throughout this book, two orientations are in question: the purely psychological approach of psychotherapy and the essentially spiritual approach of logotherapy. Psychotherapy, as the name indicates, deals with the psyche, the effort to restore psychological equilibrium through emotional need-satisfaction. Logotherapy, as the name indicates, seeks to evoke and illuminate the spiritual, the tension and will to find meaning in life. Frankl warns against placing the focus on psychological or emotional needs only. The approach in logotherapy is radically different. Not emotionality, but rather spirituality is the focus in logotherapy. The transformational power of meaning: a stepping out into life in an inspired and goal-directed way, is what is effected in Logotherapy.

Keywords Life-changing experience of meaning · Plugged into life · Illumination of the spiritual · Beyond need-satisfaction · The tension of direction · The transformational power of meaning

Life Changing Encounters

If you were in therapy with me and I had approached you in the way set out in the previous chapter; if I used the kind of methods and techniques discussed in that chapter, how would you have responded? Would it have had a transformational effect on you? Would the encounter with me, as I sought to reconnect you to what holds true meaning in your life, have been a life-changing experience for you?

© Springer Nature Switzerland AG 2020   173
T. Shantall, *The Life-changing Impact of Viktor Frankl's Logotherapy*,
https://doi.org/10.1007/978-3-030-30770-7_8

If we are plugged into what really matters in our lives, the invigorating power of meaning can be expected to flow through us!

Logotherapy, if it is logotherapy at all, is an encounter not only between logotherapist and client, trainer and student, you and me, but a very real encounter with life itself, so real and vibrant, invitational and beckoning.

Life's meaning is that it calls us to be what we are being called upon to be, and to do what we are being called upon to do, in each and every situation in our lives.

Encountering Life

> Whether you turn to the right or to the left, your ears will hear a voice behind you, saying, "This is the way; walk in it" (Isaiah 30:21).

If you, dear reader, are a psychotherapist or counselor, you would be very much aware that, throughout this book, two orientations are in question: the purely psychological approach of psychotherapy and the essentially spiritual approach of logotherapy.

Psychotherapy, as the name indicates, deals with the psyche, the effort to restore psychological equilibrium through need-satisfaction. Logotherapy, as the name indicates, seeks to evoke and illuminate the spiritual, the tension and will to find meaning in life. It deals with what James Hillman (1996) described as "a condition of want *beyond personal needs*."

In so many ways we see the same distinction in the world around us: those bent on experiencing happiness and success, attaining an impressive position of self-satisfaction in life whatever the cost, contrasting with the much smaller number of those who seek the meaning of their own lives. In giving shape to it, these rather exceptional people are often in the position of having to make decisions and take courses of action at great cost to themselves.

Let us explore the difference.

The Empathy of Pity

The typical problem-centered approach of traditional psychotherapy "sides" itself with the client in his or her distress. A supportive stand is taken with the client against the "unfair" nature of events or circumstances that have caused the state of distress. This is the empathy of pity. The client is seen as a victim of unfair circumstances, circumstances that, in some instances, the psychotherapist seeks to alter or improve ("why not get this or that kind of help, do this or that, say this or that"). Clients are typically "helped" by strengthening their "self-esteem" by advising them to do things that will boost their self-confidence and make them "feel much better". Advice, homework projects or a treatment program that will exercise clients in strengthening their coping abilities form a significant part of the latter kind of approach. Not that these kind of suggestions are not helpful. They can be.

But do they get to the heart of the matter? Do they go far enough?

The Empathy of Empowerment

Frankl warns against placing the focus on psychological needs only. Often the aim with a purely psychological approach amounts to no more than establishing a kind of happy or satisfied relief by offering an experience of a boost in self-confidence for the client who then feels vindicated in scoring points over the resented other or situation that caused the distress.

Frankl referred to that kind of outcome of psychotherapy as a state of equilibrium or homeostasis. It is a state of restored balance, of being on an even keel. Oil was poured on the troubled waters of the client's emotional turmoil. But is this the answer? Has the so-called problem been dealt with? Has the client been truly freed to go on with his or her life in a better, more meaning directed way? Where is the tension of direction in life, the ever ongoing challenge to put the call of the client's unique destiny in life into effect, situation after situation? Where is spiritual growth, the increase in human stature, the client becoming what he or she is being called to be? Or will the same old issues crop up again, sometime or other, in one way or another?

Has the case been cleared?

The more intensive psychoanalytical approach (the analysis of the psyche, of going to the hidden roots of emotional hurts and the repressed feelings towards the original "oppressors" in the client's early life) is based on the medical model which regards the person as "ill" and in need of "treatment," and the "problems" that the patient "presents" as something that needs "solving" and "fixing". Underlying that kind of approach is a mechanistic view of man. It fails to elicit the spiritual strengths and abilities that, in logotherapy, the client is challenged to employ. What is more, far from securing the vitality of optimal being, feelings of self-pity and anger on the part of the client at his or her state of helplessness in the world, and in the face of life that is perceived as cruel and unjust, are being reinforced.

In place of the two fundamental principles of Logotherapy, namely,

- the unconditional worth of the person (who has the capacity to turn a tragedy into a triumph by learning from it, becoming wiser through it, gaining character and greater feelings of self-respect as a result of it, and taking constructive action in the face of it) and.
- the unconditional meaningfulness of life (that holds meaning in all, even the worst situations that are presented as challenges and opportunities for growth in human stature and wisdom and as effecting change for the better in the world because of it),

most traditional approaches or psychotherapies, the detrimentally opposite is in evidence:

- The "confidence" gained by the client is a self-defensive type of rebellion or aggressive self-assertiveness.
- against life that is seen as basically "unfair."

Self and world remain in opposition!

The outcome of the latter type of therapy is infused more by a will to pleasure (self-satisfaction) and a will to power (self-elevation) than by a will to meaning. A song made famous by Frank Sinatra: "I did it my way" encapsulates this type of self-righteous defiance towards the world and life in general. "What I wanted and succeeding in getting"" is the focus rather than "what life wanted and expected from me".

Feelings of a Different Kind

How radically different the approach in logotherapy! Not emotionality, but rather spirituality is the focus in logotherapy. Frankl refers to Max Scheler's distinction between feeling as a mere "emotional state" (*Gefulszustand)* and feeling as an "intentional feeling" (*intentionales Gefuhl),* a feeling or intuitive sense of being called upon by or drawn into interaction with something or someone other than oneself. "As a matter of fact, such intentional feelings may well have their roots in the spiritual unconscious, but the mere emotional states have little to do with spiritual existence as do any states caused by instinctual drives" (Frankl 2000: 44).

The distress suffered by the client is seen in a totally different context. It is a *spiritual distress,* not merely an emotional state of arousal or upheaval. The accent in logotherapy is not on the client's feelings ("what do you feel?") but on the client's *intentions* ("why are you feeling this way?").

What is it that the client is truly wanting, reaching out to, missing in his of her life? It is the frustration of these fundamentally *spiritual* needs that causes the distress and is behind the protest that clients bring into therapy. To get to the heart of the matter is to explore what it is that the client, out of love and conscience, intuitively senses or feels the situation is requiring of him or her.

In logotherapy we are dealing with feelings of a different kind! Here we are not dealing with free-floating or anchorless feelings that are the haphazard results or mere abreactions to the problem or distress situation the client is experiencing, but with *gut-like or intuitive feelings* that originate from the client's spiritual unconscious. These "I know that I know that I know" kind of feelings act as guidelines, indicators as to what any particular situation is really about and act as promptings as to what the right response to that situation should be. Frankl (2000: 44) described the clarity that these kind of gut-feelings engender: "To say that the concept of feeling is vague in no way implies that feeling itself is vague. At least as far as 'intentional feeling' is concerned, it is rather the contrary: Feeling can be much more sensitive than reason can ever be sensible" (Frankl 2000: 44).

The Spiritual Unconscious

What is really at the heart of the problem the client brings into therapy? What spiritual hurts, what frustrated spiritual yearnings, are hidden **behind** the problem? A focus on the essentially *spiritual* needs of the person evokes the will to meaning out of dormancy. The client is enabled to perceive or clearly sense the meaning that is beckoning **beyond** the problem. With a revelation of the true reason for the problem, real healing is effected, real ground gained.

The focus in logotherapy is on *the spiritual unconscious.*

The truth which You desire is in the concealed parts, and in the covered part is the wisdom which You teach me. (Psalm 51:8).

> **Statements by Frankl (1986):**
> *Hitherto psychotherapy has given too little attention to **the spiritual reality of man**.*
> *What is missing is a form of psychotherapy which gets **underneath** affect-dynamics.*
> *Logotherapy goes a step further, past the affect-dynamics of neuroses in order the see **beyond** this, **the distress of the human spirit** and to try to alleviate this distress.*
> ***Only when the emotions work in terms of values can the individual feel pure 'joy'.***

Psychodynamics Versus Noodynamics

To me, as a logotherapist, there is no more amazing a person than one who is striving, struggling and longing for meaning in his or her life. Such active seekers are more beautiful, more inspiring, than those who have found safety and satisfaction through a defined purpose in their lives and live on the more upper floors of meaning. **Without the foundations of our deep and ineradicable search for meaning: the strongest, most enduring and most authentic motivation in the human breast, where will the finding of meaning be?**

The will to meaning from within is meant to be met by the meaning of the moment from without!

This *from within* and *from without* dynamic of meaningful living is called: **noodynamics**, a fundamentally deeper, higher and more holistic approach in therapy, as opposed to psychodynamics which confines itself only to the psychological and psychophysical dimensions of being.

We cannot be beheld in part; we must be seen as a whole. "It is a violation of man to project him out of the real, of the genuinely human dimension into the plane of either soma or psyche" (Frankl 1986: 138). A partial picture of ourselves will distort the picture. If we function as a part—where drives and needs predominate—and not as a whole person, we will fall victim to *mental ill-being.*

We need and fundamentally *want* to find the fountains of well-being within ourselves!

"Where the spiritual self steeps itself in its unconscious depths, there occurs the phenomena of conscience, love, and art. Where it happens the other way around, however—that is to say, where the somatopsychic id" (physical drives and emotional needs) "intrudes into consciousness—there we have to deal with a neurosis or a psychosis, depending on whether the case is psychogenic or somatogenic" (Frankl 2000: 45).

Life is only meaningful when we are the master of our fate, when drives and needs are not driving us, but where we have our full being at our fingertips!

The Tension of Direction

"What man needs, first of all, is that tension which is created by direction," Frankl (1988: 47) stated. For mental health and well-being, that deep contentment, joy in living and peacefulness of being, we need to be drawn, inspired towards what is forever beckoning us. When driven by drives, unsatisfied needs and instinctual urges which push and throw us into a state of frustration, dissatisfaction, worry and strain, we lose footing, fall captive to or collapse into a state of *lesser* being. We lose perspective.

"Mental health is based on a certain degree of tension, the tension between what one has already achieved and what one still ought to accomplish, or the gap between what one is and what one should become" (Frankl 1988: 48).

Need-Satisfaction Is Not Our Goal, But Meaning Fulfillment!

A psychodynamic approach seeks to dissipate or resolve tension; a logotherapeutic approach seeks to provoke it!

A focus on the client's problems in an effort to relieve the client of stress, turns the gaze of the client inwards. Tension is reduced, yes, but at what cost? The client becomes self-absorbed and self-focused. A focus on the meanings waiting to be realized in the client's life provokes tension, turns the gaze of the client *outward,* away from him- or herself in committed devotion to the calls made upon his or her life.

Is tension always a bad thing? What if it contains a call, a restlessness of heart to change course and be on course in living life in the way it is meant to be lived?

A 2012 student in logotherapy, Elvira Holz, an autogenic trainer, pointed out that tension reduction on the somatic and psychic levels does play a role in logotherapy. De-stressing from unhealthy stress is part of the logotherapeutic process and exercises in relaxation are used by many logotherapists to help the client reach the quiet of calm so that the meaningful aspects of the client's life can come under consideration. However, in logotherapy tension is not seen as pathological but, in a healthy context, as providing an opportunity for growth. After studying Frankl's book *The Will to Meaning,* she expressed her thoughts as follows, starting with a statement by Frankl:

"'Man does not need homeostasis or a tensionless state. He needs the longing, striving and struggling for something worth longing, striving and struggling for. For this he needs the appropriate tension that holds him oriented towards the world, the values to be actualized; the meaning of his personal existence to be fulfilled.' This would promote and sustain mental health, whereas denying or escaping from tension-filled or challenging situations by indulging in the immediate pleasures of sex, drugs, alcohol or in giving vent to frustration through aggression and violence, could lead to an existential vacuum: the experience of meaninglessness and emptiness, a lack of purpose and direction in life."

For the Sake of the Other

No greater love has a man than this, that he lays down his life for his friends (John 15:13).

Prof Alexander Batthyany (2018), the President of the Viktor Frankl Institute of Logotherapy and Existential Analyses in Vienna, captured the following riveting story of a client that lost such a sense of meaning and purpose in life after being urged to free himself from the tension of looking after his paralyzed wife. He became severely depressed and received psychiatric treatment for months. No medication worked.

The story captures the difference in therapeutic approach between a focus on homeostasis and a psychodynamic interpretation of the client's condition versus a logotherapeutic or noodynamic understanding of his plight. Fifteen years before Prof Batthyany met and counselled him, this man's wife was paralyzed as a result of a motor accident. For 14 years he cared for her at home. He took her to the toilet, fed her, helped her, read books to her, was there for her and loved her, despite the hardships. He did not have any holidays; never left her side. He had sacrificed everything, and yet, for 14 years he seemed to remain healthy and happy, despite his difficult situation. But friends and relatives tried to persuade him that he was wasting his time and throwing his life away, that neither his wife nor he were profiting much from this and that she should be placed in a nursing home. He should enjoy his life and that wasn't possible with the additional baggage of his ill wife who would be better off where she could receive professional care. After 14 years he finally gave in and followed their advice.

Paradoxically, it was then that his depression set in. Instead of being happy and enjoying his life, he was finally brought into a psychiatric clinic because of severe depression. Many therapists tried their best, but he was not interested at all and didn't work with them. Finally, it was concluded that because of these 14 years of being sexually abstinent, devoid of so many pleasures in life and with no breaks from the tension of having to look after his wife, he was so deformed psychologically that there was little more to be done to change his pitiful state.

"He gave his wife away far too late" was the diagnosis.

"I visited this man," Prof Batthyany (2018) wrote, "actually he was not my patient but I met him when he was having a day out and friends had invited him along. We talked in the garden, and I had a very different impression than his well-meaning friends who told him to give his wife over to professional care. He only wanted to talk about his wife and the 14 years they had spent together. He was not bitter despite the hardships it involved, rather, I had the impression that there was an immense value conflict when he told me about their parting moment. Although his wife could not talk, he caught a glimpse in her eyes that expressed what she would have wanted to say: 'Yes, I release you, if you want your freedom—I understand and I thank you for caring for me during all these years. We had a good marriage despite of my being paralyzed. Thank you.' How brave she was when she tried to hide her tears from him when she was carried out of their home after so many years! He said his own conscience was telling him that it was not yet time to give her away, that it was like a parting not only from her, but also from their love for each other. And then he said: 'In good and in bad—that was our marriage vow.'

I visited him once in the psychiatric clinic. He was still depressed and the doctors came to the conclusion that he was a chronic case with little hope of full recovery from his major depression. But after leaving his room, I wandered about for half an hour, debating with myself. Could I, was I entitled, to tell him what I thought, that he should correct his decision, that he should follow what he so obviously knew was the right thing to do?

I was not his therapist but, sometimes, you are asked not by anyone but by life itself what the meaning of a particular moment is. What was I to do? What did this situation require of me? I returned to his room and said: 'Mr. Myers, stand up from your bed and leave, check out of the clinic and drive home; take your wife home again. You are not mentally ill, you are only not in tune with your conscience, and unless you come into tune with yourself, I honestly believe, you will never become happy again. No medication can silence your

(continued)

conscience. Take your wife home, care for her as you used to do it. And if it is getting too much, get professional help to support you in taking care of her. But take her home.'

He looked at me in astonishment. But, at that very moment, life returned into his eyes. He did what I urged him to do shortly afterwards, despite the very grim prognosis of his supervising psychiatrist who—at the same time—admitted that there was little else he could do for the patient.

His depression was gone within a week!

I visited him a few weeks after he took his wife home. He was running between the kitchen and the living room, getting cookies and coffee and tea for me and his wife and some friends who were with us. He was fully alive, and peaceful.

The last time I saw him, he was wearing a black suit. His wife had died. He came to see me because he wanted to thank me. He said: 'If you hadn't been there, my life would be over now. The feeling of having left my wife alone, of having forsaken her, would have been too much for me to bear. It would have haunted me. Her lonely death in the care of the home would have killed me too. But you know, she died in my arms. I was there, held her hand, and now my task is done. I have fulfilled my task. We said farewell and it was good. Now I can live with her death and I even look forward to moving on with my life. So many things are awaiting me, but first of all, I am thankful and glad that I did my best. That phase of my life is over. I did what I had to do. I mourn her, and at the same time, I am deeply grateful.'"

Coupling with Life

Logotherapy releases you into relationships, an interaction with others where your personal growth, thwarted in so many incapacitating ways before, now flourishes. You can only become fully yourself in the loving embrace of another. Where you freely and committedly give of yourself, there you receive yourself. There you are affirmed, see yourself reflected in the gaze of love, respect and admiration in the eyes of the other. An intimate union with life, of feeling connected and part of life, is experienced in the harmony of true togetherness with a beloved other.

This is the particular prize in doing logotherapy with couples. How is a true bond of love forged between couples? How are they called out of the inevitable conflict that results if both of them are looking out only for themselves, if their own needs are made central and more insistent and urgent than the needs of their partner?

Logotherapy shifts the focus from the self to the other. Here follows a couple-therapy with a newly engaged but struggling couple conducted by one of our Turkish students. Her name is Nur Meric. She has a practice as a marriage counselor in Istanbul.

Hello. I am Nur Meric (the marriage counselor).
I am Kubra (the female partner).
And I am Ugur (the male partner).
Nur: I want to thank you, first of all, for seeking professional help in order to achieve a more quality relationship. What would you like to talk about?
Ugur: Let us talk about our problems and what annoys us about each other.
Nur: Actually, no, I would rather have us play a guessing game.
Kubra: What do you mean?
Nur: We can start by looking at an instance that creates a crisis for both of you. Each one is then to guess what upsets the other one. What annoys your partner and what makes your partner angry? What does your partner feel? What is your partner thinking? It is like a guessing game.
Kubra looks to Ugur.
Ugur: Why not?
Nur: Who wants to start?
Kubra: I want to start.
Nur: Go ahead.
Kubra: He thinks I do not care about his opinions, that I do not take what he believes is right into consideration. He is upset that I am not setting limits; that it is wrong for me to be spending so much time with my friends. My relationships with male friends annoy him. Once I did go out with my friends a couple of times in a row. When he called me, I thought he was going to be angry. When he asked: 'Where are you', I lied and said: 'I am at home'. When he realized that I had lied to him, he got really upset. He is not trusting me because of that. He thinks that I am not doing anything about cutting down my relationships with my male friends while he is cutting down his relationships with his female friends. He thinks that I am not caring about his feelings. (There is silence for a while)
Nur: Ugur, do you agree with what Kubra said?
Ugur: More or less.
Nur: From her perspective, what are the things that you think that upset her?
Ugur: She may be regretting that she got engaged to me. She may feel that this is limiting her freedom and it makes her feel under pressure. She is annoyed because I do not get on well with her friends, that I am sometimes bored with them. For that reason she wants to meet with her friends without me. I think the reason that she lied to me is because she felt guilty about seeing her friends instead of being with me. Now she thinks I will not trust her again.
Nur: Do you agree with what Ugur guessed about you?

(continued)

Kubra: Yes. I do feel frustrated when I feel obligated to fit into a pattern. But I am not regretful for getting engaged to him. Maybe I am a bit frightened at the thought of losing my freedom after marriage.

Nur: So, Ugur; what do you think you can do to make Kubra feel different? What would make her happy?

Ugur: For sure I want to make her happy. But marriage also brings some responsibilities.

Nur: Are the two of you clear about the point of responsibilities in a marriage?

Ugur: We should talk more about that, become clearer about how she sees those responsibilities and about what I mean when I talk about responsibilities.

Nur: Yes, in understanding about how each feels about responsibilities in a marriage, you can become more relaxed about it.

Ugur: Yes, I think that I should make an effort about that. (And he continues): I can try to be more active while I am with her friends. She can feel better if I am willing to accompany her when she meets up with friends that she wants to see. I do not know if I could do it or not, but if I try to accept her as she is, that can make her happy. She is now aware that she did a wrong thing to lie to me. I hope she will not do that again. Even if I get upset about her seeing a friend without me, it is better to tell the truth than to lie to me.

Nur: What can you do to win back Ugur's trust and make him more relaxed about the situation with your friends that he feels uneasy about?

Kubra: I can promise that I would not hide anything from him. I would not tell lies even if he gets angry and annoyed. In time, he would rely on me for telling the truth. I can notice that he feels alone sometimes among my friends and I should be more sensitive about that. I can be more devoted to him in spending time with his friends also. Maybe I can make him feel that he is precious to me by considering his opinions much more. I can also try to adapt myself to a changed situation, be more realistic and responsible, rather than still wanting things to be as they were before I got engaged.

Nur (after exploring their new attitudes towards each other more): So, what does marriage mean to both of you?

Ugur: Marriage is an important value for individuals and society. Without it, you can feel alone. When you get married to someone you love, spending time with her brings you peace, confidence, happiness and harmony. In essence: when the woman you love opens the door when you come home from work and when you see her face, this is enough to make you happy, marriage means this to me.

Kubra: Even if I sometimes think that marriage should just be about romance with no strings attached, I think that marriage should be like this: It should be like a game, like playing house when we were children. The only difference

(continued)

> in real marriage is that you cannot determine the rules of the game by your-
> self. We should create mutual scenarios rather than selfish scenarios. If both
> parties play the game in accordance to these rules and accept the process, an
> enjoyable married life can be created. Marriage is a sacred concept for me.
> Nur: Well done! Both of you talked about positive things. You have both con-
> sidered the other and are both agreed that you should strive to help and under-
> stand each other. As time goes by, these guidelines, which you have both spelt
> out as important to both of you and that you are both striving to abide by, will
> achieve what you both want: a happy marriage!

Elizabeth Lukas (1991), at the eighth World Congress of Logotherapy at the University of Santa Clara, California, had this to say in her presentation on marriage and couple counseling:

"Meaning-centered marriage counseling strengthens in each partner the ability to self-transcend. The marriage partner is not asked what hurts him or her but what hurts *the other*. The partner is directed to see the wounds of *the other*, and at this moment understanding and compassion naturally arise. This supports the renewal of good will (the will to meaning) and the readiness to take the right action. At the center of meaning-oriented marriage counselling are not the demands on the other but the vision of improved behavior *demanded of oneself*—demands for no other purpose but to save the partnership, which is of high value".

Transformed into Being Ourselves!

Logotherapy reconnects us to what we are *fundamentally geared* to be. It highlights who we *essentially* are and what we are challenged to be. The masks drop. False images of ourselves and of others, of life itself, vanish. The proof that we really want to be connected to others in loving ways, that it makes us happy to serve them, to make a meaningful contribution to our world is that, when we in fact do so, we feel fully and happily ourselves! We get transformed into being much more power-fully and effectively, more *wholly ourselves*.

We come out of hiding!

We come back to our roots, to the promise of our beginnings. We clear the air, banish those misperceptions of ourselves that made us feel so much less than we are.

Were we born warped as selfish, sly and conniving little creatures or were we warped by the hurtful and *inhumane* things that happened to us?

Has our childhood been stolen from us?

A client who had suffered many wasted years of emotional turmoil and anguish due the life-long abuse by an older sibling, showed me a picture of herself as a little girl. "Look!" she said, "I have always felt that I was empty inside, that I had noth-ing, no creativity inside of me. But look at that smile, those shining eyes! You can see the creativity in her, her reaching out to the world, her eagerness to get involved. I like to see what I see in this little girl! That is the truth, not the lies that I began to believe about myself as I was put down, again and again, by the abuse I was made to suffer."

Logotherapy helps us to regain our inner compass, the ability to steer our lives in creative ways. We regain a lost childhood! A joy in living, the ability to be spontaneously and un-self-consciously ourselves is restored to us.

Jane Landsberg, another of our top logotherapy students in South Africa, is the principal of a Montessori pre-primary school. She incorporated the principles of logotherapy into the Montessori method of education, noting the close correlation between the two schools of thought.

An Experiment with Children

Maria Montessori (1870–1952), an Italian physician and famous educator, noting the inherent creative intelligence of all children, no matter their background or social class, founded a method of educating young children with astounding success. Thousands of schools all over the globe have been established using her pioneering methods of eliciting the naturally given creative abilities of children. Our student opened one such school.

Bonding with the children in her charge and encouraging them to bond with each other, an atmosphere of connectedness was created that allowed them to give full expressions to themselves. The results were astounding. What emerged as fact was the transformative power of meaning.

The children became what they were naturally gifted to be!

Jane wrote up her work with a focus on how the natural and un-thwarted behavior of children substantiated the premises of logotherapy.

The creative values and the child:

> The child's spirit needs nurturing to be able to create. Montessori (1974: 67–69, 1972: 71–73, 1992: 178, 145) saw the hand as the instrument of man's creative energies: 'The hand is the direct connection with man's soul. **When a free spirit exists, it has to materialize itself in some form of work,** and for this the hands are needed. Everywhere we find traces of men's handiwork, and through these we catch a glimpse of his spirit. **Guided by an inner teacher indicating the activities he or she needs for his or her development at each developmental stage, the child needs the freedom to choose his or her own activities. When the child executes purposeful freely chosen work, accompanied by deep concentration, it almost always results in the child's whole being becoming filled with pleasure and a calm happiness**. As a result behaviors such as uncooperativeness, passiveness, disruptiveness, inattention, destructiveness, greed for possession, selfishness, disorderliness of mind, and flights of fantasy, disappear.' Montessori referred to this as the phenomena of **normalization** through work. In this sense normalization can be viewed as an educational readiness of the child to develop to his or her physical, emotional, social, cognitive and spiritual full potential.

An individual is led to his or her cosmic task by an allurement, by an authentic passion or interest that emanates from the true self. **The child will awake to his or her own set of attractions when his or her freedom of choice is not restricted** by the powerful influence of parents, teachers, peer groups, cultural trends, the media or perceived obligations and **when encouraged to act from his or her inner core.** When a child unconsciously obeys his inner directives to do the work necessary for him or her to develop and grow, he or she subsequently fulfils meaning.

The experiential values and the child:

When children come into contact with a beautiful work of art it is a deep experience for them, because in fine art they meet an expression of the artist's spirit. When they listen to good music something is triggered in their being and a harmony arises in them. Meaning can be found in nature in the unutterable beauty of a blossom, the grace of a high-flying bird, the roar of the wind in the trees. **At one time or another nature touches them in some personal, special way.** Nature's immense mystery opens the child to its stunning purity, an intuitive union with a Life greater than the little affairs of man. **The greatest existential meaning for the child is found in experiencing love. The child obtains fulfillment in the realization of his or her uniqueness and singularity.** The child becomes indispensable and irreplaceable for the one who loves him or her. **The child has an incredible potential to love.** A child learns to love through the experience of affection, love, patience, understanding, intimacy and belonging. **The child cannot develop without a social life** and actualizes meaning in self-transcendence towards friends, grandparents or other extended family members. Children can experience meaning in a relationship with a caring, attentive, understanding and inspiring teacher that may have a lasting impact on their lives (Montessori 1992: 73).

Ultimate and attitudinal values and the child:

Children can also fulfil meaning in their developing faith. **Religious acts tends toward the completion of being.** To experience religion is to experience love. Children actualize meaning in being made aware of the experience of God's love. Such an experience in childhood has been captured by Cavalletti (1992: 34–35), author of the book entitled *The Religious Potential of the Child.* The description of his experience captures an embrace with the wonder of life itself!

'That embrace that I was experiencing was transformed in my heart into an absolute plentitude of joy. An astonishing joy, a kind of enthusiasm of joy invaded me. I was all aflame in the luminosity of a happiness so intense and complete that I was immobilized by that feeling, in a state that remains in my memory as one of perfect satisfaction and absolute union'.

A Success Story

Jane, with the assistance of her trained teachers, as her writings above illustrate, followed each of the children in her school as they sought out their own areas of interest and met it with providing affirmative appreciation and insightful development of the children's own unfolding talents and interests through the children's self-chosen activities. An atmosphere of love, art, music, of the beauty and a sense of the worthiness of life also by trips into nature was created. A sense of responsibility in the child was actively reinforced by letting everyone pack away their own things and by everyone helping to put the classrooms in order. Sharing was actively encouraged in prompting one child to help another and to show interest in one another's work and take delight in it. Harmonious and loving togetherness was made the theme of their schooling. Doing things together, of playing and having fun together, were inherent parts of the educational program. The children were also helped to face difficulties and heartaches in their little lives, like when a child was exposed to the death in the family or when some or other distressful event happened to one of them. They were helped to give expression to their grief and unhappiness and to deal with it in creative and expressive ways (like sending up balloons of love to a departed in heaven, or creating a project in memory of the deceased). Ways to express comfort to other family members or friends were explored by the children just as much as the children were encouraged to comfort one another; to discuss things together and think of creative and liberating ways to deal with grief and unhappiness. The children were supported and encouraged to be together in all that happened to them.

A little community of meaning, a haven of comfort and of renewed courage and an ongoing zest for life was thus triumphantly established by putting the accent where it truly mattered to the child. The children's self-transcendent and self-distancing capacities released their potential in every area of their lives.

Jane is a true logotherapist in her lived motto: What we are we are from our very beginnings!

Exercise for You, the Reader: You Have Always Known

Some of us, at the back of our minds, have always known what we most wanted to have in our lives, what we most wanted to do with our time. As children we certainly knew what kind of experiences made us feel happy, contented, and full of the joys of life. Children are more readily aware of "knowing" because they have yet to inculcate either the limiting beliefs or the sense of defeat that often cloud the issue for adults.

Recall the happiest memories of childhood. What did you love to do? What were you good at? Where did you feel wholly involved, happily yourself, doing what? Do you look longingly back at this, feeling that you did not really go in the direction you wanted to go, that in a way, you are not what you then sensed yourself to be or saw yourself becoming one day; that you are not fully and creatively yourself in the work you are doing and the kind of life you are leading now? Do you long to make changes, go in a direction in life that excites you more? What is it that you really want to do, that somehow will release or use again what you loved being and doing when you were younger?

What has life in store for you? What did it have in store for you from the start?

References

Batthyany, A. (2018). *Paper at First World Congress of Logotherapy*. Haifa, Israel.

Cavalletti, S. (1992). *The religious potential of the child*. Chicago: Cathechesis of the Good Shepherd Publications.

Frankl, V. E. (1986). *The doctor and the soul. From psychotherapy to Logotherapy*. New York: Vintage Books.

Frankl, V. E. (1988). *The will to meaning. Foundations and applications of Logotherapy*. New York: Penguin Books.

Frankl, V. E. (2000). *Man's search for ultimate meaning*. New York: Basic Books.

Lukas. (1991). *Marriage and couple counseling. Eighth world congress of Logothersapy*. California: University of Santa Clara.

Montessori, M. (1964). *The Montessori method*. New York: Schoken Books.

Montessori, M. (1996). *The discovery of the child*. Madras: Kalakshetra Press.

Montessori, M. (1974). *Education for a new world*. Madras: Kalakshetra Press.

Montessori, M. (1992). *The secret of childhood*. Mumbai: Orient Longman Ltd.

Montessori, M. (2006). *The child, society and the world: Unpublished speeches and writings*. Oxford: Cleo Press.

Chapter 9
A New Look at Psychopathology: This Is Not You

Abstract Psychopathology is discussed as a pathology, the result of a normal or healthy development of potential being thwarted. Abnormality and mental illness results. Frankl held steadfastly to the view that the person who is afflicted retains the capacity for change; the ability to address and transcend the mental disorder, whether of a constitutional nature or as result of traumatic and painful experiences in life. This is a freedom that remains and is elicited in the process of logotherapy. In fact, Frankl contended, in cases of endogenous mental illnesses the person so afflicted *becomes* mentally ill in their inability to make sense of what they are afflicted with! It follows, therefore, that psychopathology represents a *lie*, a distortion of the perception of a person about their own capabilities or worthiness. Evoking the defiant power of the human spirit, clients can distance themselves from their illness in taking up the reigns of their lives thereby *disproving* the torturous ideas of themselves us unworthy and incapable. Their worthiness and capability, once released, *prove* who they potentially are and are, therefore, capable of becoming.

Keywords The pathology of psychopathology · Transcending a mental disorder · False perceptions causes mental illness · The defiant power of the human spirit · Becoming what we are

The Potential You

If you have come to realize who you essentially are, that is, have the potential and therefore the capability to be, then you will no longer continue to be the miserable victim of circumstances; nor will you be flung about and driven by ever nagging needs exercising an oppressive and obsessive hold on your every thought and action. Nor will you continue to be in a state of unhappiness and frustration about unfulfilled dreams and elusive fantasies, chasing after the realization of some

© Springer Nature Switzerland AG 2020
T. Shantall, *The Life-changing Impact of Viktor Frankl's Logotherapy*,
https://doi.org/10.1007/978-3-030-30770-7_9

romantic notion of yourself and your life anywhere but where you happen to be. You will no longer be held captive by injurious and negative views about your own worth or the meaning of your life. You will not be searching here, there and everywhere and never finding what you do not even clearly know you want. Nor will you be stuck in a situation you stubbornly insist must hold promise although nothing about it is working or going right. No. You would have come to a full stop, a dead end, a "this is enough and no more;" or at least: "I have to stop this, or else" point in your life.

What brings about the resolution to come out from these pitfalls of being? And where to from then on?

What has your misery shown you?

Rock-Bottom Realizations

Have you ever been at the point of wanting to commit suicide; when things looked so desperate, so beyond solving or correcting; when you were filled with such shame and humiliation, felt so torn apart and conflicted, so overcome with a sense of helplessness, that you could not take another breath; when obliteration seemed the only escape? The following is a description of someone who had been at this rock-bottom point in life:

> "I am cornered. There is nowhere to turn. I cannot find my way out of this.
>
> Guilt is pointing a finger at me. The scales of judgment condemn me.
>
> Am I, being weighed, found forever wanting?"

How incredible, therefore, that this very person could write the following, not very long afterwards:

> "What is this thing called 'hope'? I have been pushed over the brink of despair but find myself lifted again, believing!"

Moved by testimonies like the one above, I wrote the following piece:

Hope Never Fades

Without hope despair sets in. In its wake, in the pit of despair, comes depression. And when depression becomes morbid, the will to live dies. But even suicide, or a surrender to the deadly effects of hopelessness that can end in death, cannot extinguish a last breath of protest.

Hope remains.

In losing all hope and, with that, any reason for living, then the drastic end to the process before it has run full course, is a last snatch at hope. Maybe it can be found somewhere else, in a life hereafter. There must be another chance.

Life will go on, if not here; there. If not now; then.

What gives substance and life to hope if not life itself, its preciousness, its beauty, its awesomeness; taking a walk, going shopping, having a bite to eat or enjoying a cup of coffee with someone, spending time with friends, getting up in the morning and looking out of the window and seeing a new day and to be awakened to the very promise it holds?

We cannot bear to lose life. We love it too much. Even on the altar of death, the resurrection and renewal of life holds promise.

Hope survives!

What is hope but the love of life? Frankl speaks about the tragic triad: pain, guilt and death. We experience pain at the prospect of losing life, all that we hoped for in life, all that we found precious about it. We experience guilt when we have damaged life, when we have failed to hold it dear.

Death spells the end of life. But is it?

In the face of the tragic triad Frankl placed another triad, *the triad of faith, hope and love:* faith in the unconditional and indestructible meaning of life, its unsullied beauty; the hope that we will remain part of it. It is the love of life that sustains us!

Our lives are meant to tip the scales in our favor: death is to be swallowed up in victory!

"Therefore, Choose Life!" (Deuteronomy 30:19)

Running for our lives, so many of us are running away from our lives!

There are so many stories of anguish, of suffering the pangs of hell, a dread from which there seems no release; stories of abandonment, abject loneliness, desperations; the despair and hopelessness of depression, of everything collapsing around you, with nowhere to go, no-one to turn to; the cruel imprisonment with thoughts that will not go away, feelings that will not dissipate, anguish that just goes on and on; guilt and shame from which there is no escape; states of turmoil and confusion, of things too much to hear; stories of flight from what is perceived as an unpalatable reality, somewhere away from it all even if that place is a senseless place, a place of no sane rhyme nor reason. Yes, even mental disorders and illnesses, even a psychotic break from reality, can act as a place of hiding from all the finger-pointing, from what is perceived as a heartless, judgmental and unforgiving world. Even if such a perception in the disordered mind of the mentally ill is unreal, only a delusion of persecution, it still acts as a torturous feeling of despair, even of unpardonable guilt.

Who can bear to have fallen from grace if grace is no longer there to appeal to?

What are your thoughts on this matter? Do you agree with the opinion that there are, unfortunately, some people whose fate is sealed; that their struggle with what plagues and imprisons them in their mentally disturbed state is greater than their ability to help themselves or to let themselves be helped out of it?

Do you believe that we must accept that there are helpless misfits, people so mentally retarded, so physically disabled, so dysfunctional, that there cannot be any hope for them other than to just be kept alive till they at last die? The death of these "misfits of society" is seen as "merciful". What is merciful about their deaths? Is it a "mercy" extended to us when, upon their deaths, the burden that their care imposes on us is finally lifted?

Or do such thoughts disturb, unnerve and upset you? Why? Does it put you under the spotlight in a discomforting way? Can you be sure that you will always be counted among the "more fortunate"? What if you found yourself in the shoes of the *unfortunate?* Would you then like the more fortunate to look at your sorry state dispassionately?

There is something very distasteful about self-contentment and complacency!

How can you or I feel good about the fact that we have escaped such a lot as we see others suffering, that we were, "thank God", more fortunate or perhaps more blessed, perhaps even "chosen" to not suffer the doom that seems to be the sealed fate of those whom society discards, has to jail and institutionalize, take out of disturbing view?

I do not know about you, but if I had to look at myself in this way I would be disgusted with such a state of injustice. Why must they suffer and I be spared? How can I "write off" a strayed or mentally sick or disabled loved-one, *anyone,* and feel "happy" about my more "fortunate" lot?

"There, but by the grace of God, go I"? What kind of a "grace" is this?

No, my soul is in torment at such a thought. I hate it. It makes no sense to me. Either there *is* meaning in life, there for *everyone,* or there is no meaning, not for anyone! And there can only be meaning for anyone if *everyone* has the capacity within themselves to find and experience meaning in their lives, however far off the mark or lost they may be. And if that capacity has been severely disabled, the person behind the incapacity is *all the more* precious and lovable! How such scarred, damaged and crippled lives bring out the best in us! How it provokes our humanity, our selfless devotion, a love that seeks no reward since it is reciprocated by the very act of loving itself. Freely given and committed service to the weak, disabled, the stricken among us, affords us the privilege to love selflessly. What can compare to what is bestowed upon us in terms of our evoked humanity, decency, goodness and gain in human stature? How such selfless service lifts us way above the cruelty, indifference and arrogance, the inhumanity and evil of the fallen and decadent section of mankind, those doings in the world that we so hate and despise and wish to be forever rid of!

Either life is unconditionally meaningful, held out to everyone at anytime, anywhere and in whatever circumstances and for however long, or life is meaningless! Meaning must be *there* to be found and experienced, even by the weakest in the act of being loved *despite* their ability to respond to it in any expressive way. Meaning cannot be held out only for a limited and trial time and then be withdrawn if the erring or afflicted person fails to comprehend or embrace it. Even death cannot be the end of the matter. Who knows what awaits babies and children who died and so many others who were not wicked people but died in a state of mental incapacity or lack of grasp about what ultimately mattered in their lives? Are they to be condemned along with those who trampled their own souls under foot in a life that was willfully destructive, selfish and wicked?

If grace is limited, is it grace? Grace is grace exactly because it is bestowed upon those who need it most!

Where there is life, there is hope, the saying goes. Frankl insisted that we are only fully ourselves, and pass sentence on what kind of people we were, on the last day of our lives. A visit by Frankl to San Quentin prison in America verified this truth. He treated the prisoners he spoke to not as poor victims of whatever caused them to do wrong, but as human beings who have *retained the dignity of responsibility.* They could look at the wrong they have committed and denounce it as wrong. The option to acknowledge wrong and change, to repent of wrong, even at the very last minute of their lives, was still theirs!

Speaking on a microphone to a prisoner who was to die in the gas chamber in a couple of days, he said:

> Mr. Mitchell, believe me, I understand your situation. I myself had to live for some time in the shadow of a gas chamber. But also believe me that even then I did not give up my conviction of the unconditional meaningfulness of life, because either life has meaning—and then it retains this meaning even if the life is short lived—or it has no meaning—and then adding ever more years just perpetuates this meaninglessness. And believe me, a life that has been wasted may—even in the last moment—still be bestowed with meaning by the very way in which we tackle this situation (Frankl 2000:128/9).

By the insight this prisoner could gain, and from the realization that he had wasted his life, he could still grow beyond himself and, retroactively, flood his life with infinite meaning! He could accept the death-sentence passed upon him and die with dignity!

Arguments for Life

If every life, therefore, is of *unconditional worth*, the following arguments hold true:

- **What is wrong** is whatever causes people to believe that their lives are meaningless; that they are a lost cause, and if people are *treated in a hurtful or disparaging way* as if their lives are of no value. **What is right** is that which makes people realize or experience that life, so full of meaning, is there for them also. Meaning is to be withheld from no-one!
- From this follows that those who *cause* others to believe their lives are meaningless or who treat others as if they are of no worth, are **in the wrong,** and that those who seek to help others to realize that their lives have meaning or help them experience their own worth, are **in the right.**
- If **we are in the right**, it follows that we have to oppose, no, even hate what is wrong! We will *love* what is right and, therefore, **do it**, and *hate* what is wrong and, therefore, **not do it!** And we base our actions on this one unquestionable and fundamental truth as a statement of fact: that we all have inherent worth. This places upon us the injunction to protect the innocent, the children, the weak and disabled and to take a defiant stand against those who harm or seek to harm them.
- **We are in the wrong**, if we do not exercise our freedom as a freedom to be responsible and if we callously set out to take out of life what best suits and serves us, no matter if that is at the expense of others whom, more often that not, we envy and blame for our lot in life.
- It makes sense, in the final analysis, to believe that we are enjoined to choose life, **primarily in the way we treat others**. Why lose out, be so self-absorbed that we fail to fulfill our mission, fall far short of what we could have been had we lived differently? The door to life is open and closed to no-one. **The only door that closes, is the door we slam shut in our own faces.**

I am reminded of the following piece written by and handed to me by one of my logotherapy students:

"If God exists and I believe in Him, that's wonderful.

If God exists and I do not believe in Him, that is also all right because He will still love me.

If God does not exist but I believe that He does, that will also be all right because I will try and live a decent life.

But if God does not exist and I do not believe in Him, then what in the hell is going on?"

Unmasking the Face of Meaninglessness

To me there are two sides, but not of the same coin, for us to consider in terms of our views towards the disabled, the emotionally ill and also towards the ones who have lost their way in life.

1 *The wrong side: A heartless heart*

I totally reject and resist the attitudes and actions of those who write off others. If human life can be despised, rejected, even abused, manipulated and destroyed based on some or other arrogant, self-righteous and fanatical belief system or cause or state of total indifference, then such doings are *evil*, beyond sanction or tolerance. Such stances demand a stand from me, from anyone who has heart. Perpetrators must be confronted, warned and called to book in an effort to bring them to their senses.

Even the wrongdoer is our responsibility! But why; only to help the wrongdoers to repent of their wrongs? What about those who suffer the consequences of their wrongdoing? Are they to suffer without anyone doing anything about it?

Consider this: How can those who perform blatant acts of inhumanity with ruthlessly heartless attitudes towards others do it if they did not regard their intended victims as of little worth, *as unwanted, some kind of mistake, not meant to exist, a threat to them, even a scourge on the rest of humanity?* Only with such cruel and fanatically misled reasoning does it make "sense" to think that it is quite all right or "who cares?" for such people to be hated, slandered, violently attacked with the intended aim to annihilate all of them, wipe their undesirable existence off the face of the earth!

What, therefore, should be our attitude about those not only singled out in this prejudiced way because of their race, color or religion, but also those lost in the darkness of physical and mental or emotional affliction that are also heartlessly judged as unwanted and as not a worthy part of humanity?

Suffering, Frankl stated, makes us aware of what ought *not* to be. The responsibility of working towards what *ought* to be rests upon our shoulders. Suffering ought not to be! In resisting what is callous and wrong, our primary commitment is to those who suffer. Since the focus in this book is on therapy, our focus is particularly on those who suffer under the burden of what is, was or went wrong in their lives.

It is clear, from all our discussions, that experiences of hurt during the vulnerable stages or phases of our lives can gravely affect emotional well-being. Any traumatic experience later in life can have the same effect. Under the blows of what we have or are suffering, we can begin to be plagued by feelings of insecurity and self-doubt and be overwhelmed by dark fears of a world that we believe was or has turned cruel and unfriendly. Our perceptions of ourselves and of the world become pathologically distorted and unreal.

Our psychopathology *lies* to us!

2 *The right side: Unconditional love*

What then is the truth of the matter? Are we helplessly ill, a slave to our torturous beliefs about ourselves, others and the world? Or is it a case of failing to see who we really are and what we can be in a world full of opportunities and loving experiences that can bring about our healing?

Here follow the writings of one of the South African students in logotherapy whose name I did not record. I am hoping that maybe he or she will, in reading this book, recognize who I wrote about and let me know. Such names are worthy of mention!

Reflecting on my own suffering revealed to me that my early years of suffering lacked the constructive shaping experiences that Frankl mentioned about those who found meaning in their suffering. My early experiences of suffering did not change me for the better because I was too busy blaming other people, like my parents, for the tough times I was experiencing as an adolescent and young adult. While I was blaming others, and feeling angry towards God, I was wallowing in self-pity and became more and more self-consumed. I even contemplated suicide as I felt useless and thought that my life was pointless. I felt out of control, the victim of my own life, and doomed to endless cycles of struggle. I was a martyr of life and thought that the point of my existence was just to survive this life; just to make it through this wasteland, and die in the end and hopefully go to heaven where I can be free from all the struggles.

The outcome of these wrong choices was costly. I was like a pendulum that swung from the one extreme to the other. At times, I was rebellious which led to wrong life decisions. At other times, I acted with apathy, just went with the flow, which conflicted with my inner compass and caused confusion and hopelessness. I disliked myself with a passion and other people in general. Yet I was looking for someone or something to "fix" my life.

When I hit "rock bottom" in my adulthood, my experience regarding suffering began to change. Due to the nature of the problem that I faced, I found myself, like a leper, isolated from friends and family and cut-off from society. I had nowhere to turn and no-one to help or "save" me. This experience of profound suffering forced me to "dig deep" within myself and discover my own personal values and self-worth. The emptiness in me slowly gave way to a sense of inner contentment as I began to understand, in the midst of the suffering, that I am unconditionally loved by God. There is no doubt in my mind that I have grown and developed from my "rock bottom" suffering. For example, I've discovered my spiritual strength, I've become more compassionate and caring, and I've learned that I'm more resilient than I thought that I could ever be.

(continued)

> During the sufferings in my early years I felt that "poor me" was being hamstrung by a shameful life, as if life itself had an agenda to sabotage me. From the "rock bottom" experience I gained a sense of feeling proud of myself, which freed me up to reach out further and strive towards realizing my full potential.
>
> It was when I thought I had lost everything that my eyes opened to the fullness of life.

The Greatest Freedom

Another student in Logotherapy, one whom I also hope will recognize her story and make herself known to me, made a most perceptive remark: "To accept past hurts and humiliations is the greatest freedom." Suffering a traumatic incidence of sexual abuse as a child, a marriage to an emotionally abusive husband who flagrantly flaunted his affair with a colleague of hers, not only ended the marriage with a divorce but brought her to the lowest point of shame and humiliation ever. But aflame in her heart was the desire to experience the opposite. This thirst for meaning opened the door to healing. Into her life came a man who loved her, flooding all her past life with feelings of consolation. All was not in vain.

> "I realized I would not have appreciated what I have now if it was not for what I went through, for what they did to me. I think I would have taken what I had now for granted, not realizing how rare and special it was. I would not have known that although love makes you vulnerable, it also makes you strong. One night, I was standing there looking at a magnificent full moon, wishing my ex-husband and his new partner both the best the world has to offer them. To many people it sounds strange, but I view the whole experience as a blessing now—it was a painful period that has brought me to the most beautiful and special time of my life.
>
> Things happen to all of us. We cannot change it or prevent it. It is what it means to be alive. But we have the freedom to choose how we allow these events to impact our lives. It is not easy, and sometimes it is nearly impossible, but like the flower blooming between concrete slabs—it shows there is beauty, or meaning, in everything, you just sometimes have to look very, very hard! Because of the abuse I suffered as a child, it made me more aware of other's pain. Again, it will sound strange to many other people, but I had to go through the abuse again, in order to help me become who I am today."

The above was an assignment question and in its feedback, I answered her:

"Wow, what a thought and what a truth: to accept all that has happened to you, the hurt and the pain, as the greatest freedom! This is what is meant by forgiveness and yet it is more than that. **There is a forgiveness that reconciles and a forgiveness of letting go**. To have wished your husband and his new partner all the best in the world was the freedom of release. You let them go and move out of your life forever. You felt freed from the burden of hurt and humiliation that you had carried with you from childhood. Your adult experience of abuse and humiliation opened the door. How starkly different, how beautiful real love is; how beauty in the world, in bird song, in a little flower growing through the cracks, cannot and will not be obliterated, turned to nothingness or remain out of grasp and experience. It is still there. It has always been there. It always will be there. IT IS. Who can therefore destroy it? Whoever misses to see it and experience it is simply missing out. Life's meaning and beauty is beyond the reach of those who fail to grasp it. You found it. You appreciate it. You know it, deeply! How blessed, therefore, you are!

And it is yours now, within full grasp!'"

Dis-ease

I had an amazing experience with a logotherapy student from Ghana during a teaching session in Dallas just before a Logotherapy World Congress of the Viktor Frankl Institute of Logotherapy of the United States of America. His name is Tony Mensah. In the class of logotherapy students he related the following:

Behold, the Human Being!
The Akan-speaking people of Ghana refer to the human being as "onipa". The word is formed from two syllables: "onim" which means "he/she knows", and "papa" which means "good or right". To know the good or to know the right is an inalienable attribute of a human being who, as a result, is naturally drawn to goodness and righteousness. For the Akan people, the fundamental human search is to actualize the truth of who you are!

The Akan people have no word for disease. If they look upon an ill person, they see someone who is "dis-eased", not diseased. The person, inherently healthy or good, is being subjected to pain, to something *bad* that should not be, or to something that is *wrong*. It causes them *unease*.

The word in the Akan language for that which *causes* the affliction, namely, "yadea", is formed from two syllables, namely, "ya", or "pain" and "adea", something that is "painful". It is used to describe not only mental affliction but anything that is *undesirable, wrong or bad* like poverty, unrest in the community, war, death and the like.

The compassionate attitude towards the ill, the weak, the impoverished, the victimized, anyone who is suffering, coming from the loving heart of an African people, is earmarked by a pronounced *lack of blame* for the physically or mentally afflicted person. There is no censure of the person. The illness, or that which causes the suffering, is seen as a source of blame. These afflictions were *not* meant to be! It is an *unnatural* situation, something that needs remedial or redemptive intervention.

A Therapy of Restitution

Logotherapy is a therapy of restitution, the healing that comes through righting a wrong. It is a therapy of love. This attitude is reflected in Frankl's orientation to suffering humanity, especially those in dire need of our care. This orientation is captured in the following statements from his work: *On the Theory and Therapy of Mental Disorders (2004).*

> The phrase 'lives not worthy of living' was frequently used by the Nazis when speaking of those who were targeted for extermination, above all, the mentally ill.
>
> Now, even if the prognostically most unfortunate psychotically ill person has lost all value of usefulness, he or she maintains his or her dignity, for the value rank of the suffering person (Homo patients) is higher than that of the skilled person (Homo faber). **The suffering person stands higher than the efficient person**. And if this was not so, then it would not be worthwhile to be a psychiatrist.
>
> I don't want to be a psychiatrist for the sake of a ruined mental 'apparatus', nor for a broken machine, but rather only for the human who is ill, **who lies behind and stands above everything else**.
>
> There is a person behind the mental illness or affliction. It is the person who is suffering and even shaping the mental illness. Psychosis is always already shaped, for the person was always at work, the person was always in the game, has always contributed to the shape of the illness.
>
> We are satisfied with lightening the load of our patients, not even permanently, but—depending on the severity of the illness—for a few days or even hours. For the true and ultimate value of such a supportive psychotherapy is to keep patients' heads above water for the duration of their illness, to help them to navigate through the psychotic phase.

The Hurt of Blame

The pathology of psychopathology is to be caught or dragged down and confined to subhuman levels of existence. Frankl contends that we are only fully ourselves when we live on the uniquely *human* dimension of being. Here we are who we are, freely, transparently, accountably, genuinely. This is a dimension of being where we can live with ourselves, where we have feelings of integrity, goodness, worth and dignity. We are neither ashamed of ourselves, nor are we self-consciously awkward about ourselves. We are not plagued nor beleaguered by feelings of inferiority, insecurity and fears. But nor we are cocksure of ourselves. Feelings of self-importance is but the flipside of the same coin. Feelings of arrogance, superiority, prejudice, a looking down upon others, putting up a brazen show of supreme confidence, even if we are pretty good at it, is but an effort to convince ourselves that we are what we make ourselves out to be: someone of importance. Unsettling doubts about ourselves lurk behind this outward show of self-adulation (self-deception). We are role-playing and not ourselves in a genuine way!

Logotherapy seeks to make us see ourselves and others in proper perspective, that is, *in a good light*. A negative or judgmental view of the person can have disastrous effects, especially if it comes from a place of authority or is voiced by someone that the person looks up to. Frankl spoke in this regard of **iatrogenic neurosis**, that is, a neurosis caused by diagnostic categories or suggestions of pathology transmitted to a patient in a dehumanizing way by a person who is regarded as an authority, as someone in the know. The term refers to the psychological harm caused by the psychiatrist—**psychiat**rogenic or psychologist—**psych**iatrogenic—in his or her position of authority in relation to the client. Elizabeth Lukas (2000:139) listed six most frequent professional errors:

- More interest is shown in dysfunctions or the pathological aspects of the client's behavior than in the more intact and healthy areas of the client's life.
- Fateful events in the client's life are viewed too seriously.
- Negative prognosis is given which does not serve a positive purpose.
- Diagnosis is conveyed without explaining its practical implications.
- Silence at a wrong moment.
- Careless interpretations and uncertain hypotheses are expressed.

All of these professional mishaps make you, as the client, believe something negative about yourself. It arouses worry about the fact that there is something "wrong" with you, that you are "mentally ill", lost to the world and "abnormal." It spells some kind of doom for your life that is regarded as something tragic or pitiful, most unfortunate. You are the helpless victim of fate. Not much hope is held out for you.

Frankl (1986:xxvii) warned against such attitudes (intended or not) by authority figures in their treatment of others. What is transmitted is a view of the person that is all but encouraging or hopeful and one that can cause untold harm and make the person believe that his or her life has lost or is devoid of meaning:

If we present man with a concept of man which is not true, we may well corrupt him. When we present man as an automaton of reflexes, as a mind-machine, as a bundle of instincts, as a pawn of drives and reactions, as a mere product of instinct, heredity and environment, we feed the nihilism to which modern man is, in any case, prone.

The Sickness of Shame

Stephen Pattison (2000), in his riveting book on shame, defines shame as the experience of defilement, pollution and *"toxic unwantedness"*. He explores the devastating effects that views of human nature as being inherently shameful, especially if it comes in the form of religious condemnation, can have on those cruelly exposed to it. It condemns them into a state of *chronic guilt*, not because of wrongdoing, but because of *wrong being*. **It is not their actions, but their very existence that is regarded as suspect.**

Life as unconditionally and lovingly meaningful is an experience that is out of the reach of those who believe that they are inherently sinful. Their only hope is to "convert", become someone "new" or other than themselves. They are to take on a prescribed identity, conform to a pattern. This obliterates any real sense of self-worth and condemns the person to a life-long battle against the ravages of their "sinful nature." Life is a continuous effort to find "atonement"; to be given an absolution for their sins. Such views, offshoots of **the doctrine of original sin**, have a demonic hold on man.

> Atrophy of the religious sense in man results in a distortion of his religious concepts. Once the angel in us is repressed, he turns into a demon (Frankl 2000:75).

Under the heavy yoke of shame there is neither an experience of the sanctity nor of the preciousness of the human spirit. Here the affirmation: "You are altogether lovely, my love, there is no flaw in you" (Song of Songs 4:7) cannot be heard.

"I have called you by name, you are Mine" (Isaiah 43:1–3), is the irrevocable statement of the Divine that calls us *out of shame* and to step into our true station as the crown of all creation!

Conscience, as Frankl conceived of it, is birthed in the Transcendent. It is open and receptive, not closed and confined. It is earmarked, not by guilt, but by *responsiveness*. In a conscientious way of living, body, mind and spirit are in divine harmony, not in perpetual conflict!

> Like iron filings in a magnetic field, man's life is put in order through his orientation to meaning (Frankl 1985:35).

We need to be called out of a state of shameful self-consciousness. We need the guidance of correction, not blame, if we are not to lose sight of being loved and sought out for loving companionship. Not a sin-consciousness but a conscientious awareness of what we *ought be and do* is what keeps us on course. To exercise responsibility, do what we know is right and to correct the wrong we have done, is to regain and retain our dignity.

The Sword of Condemnation

Pattison's intensive research into the phenomena of shame in theory, therapy and particularly in theology, clearly highlights the difference, as Frankl clarified it, between true conscience and a guilt-consciousness that is the result of shame.

Guilt as a sense of *conviction* is part of the dignity of having responsibility. We have the capability to discern right from wrong in terms of a required response in any particular situation. We have freedom of will, choice and action. But the guilt of shame is based on the deception that we are incapable; that we are helplessly beset by a nature that is contrary to what is good and acceptable in the sight of God and man.

Our very persons are under censure!

In the light of the above, let us more closely consider this huge and fundamental source of stress and affliction, namely, parental, societal and religious censure. Why accept the exercise of restrictive and condemnatory standards that wield a sword of threat and intimidation and cause such anguish in the world?

The fundamental attitude of the vigilant critic is one of suspicion. The motives of especially the young or the un-submissive are seen as suspect. Disciplinary action is the only means to mold them into the required shape. In fanatical regimes, anyone who is suspect, seen as refusing to submit to the rigorously indoctrinated belief system and failing to pay allegiance to the set authority, is apprehended and jailed. If seen as traitorous enough, the perceived guilty one is executed. Such, and most often, highly ingrained (rigorously indoctrinated) social and fanatical or dogmatic religious norms have an oppressive hold on the developing person who submits to these norms out of fear of punitive retaliation. This kind of system rules by threat and terror. Its authority is manipulative and controlling and is, of a truth, a *fake* or *false, illegitimate* or *unlawful* authority, no matter how prevalent this pattern of governance may be. Let us call it by its name: *despotism* and *tyranny*. It *enforces* its laws with cruelty.

Why tolerate such authoritarian control over others if its consequences are so disastrous, if it is so damaging to the inherent dignity and spiritual growth of those subjected to it?

There are extreme and lesser forms of these societal and religious systems of punitive control over the free will of those born into and brought up under the influence of it.

We have amply illustrated what the real crisis of mental illness is; how feelings of *unworthiness* torture, warp and disfigure the inherent dignity and worth of a person. Let us recap it in the following account by another logotherapy student whose parents may have fallen trap to the restrictive societal and religiously influenced demands they themselves were subjected to by "dutifully" exercising them upon their own children. I decline to mention her name in order to protect her parents from blame.

Circus Elephants

"As a child I thought that life was something over which I had very little control. Adult decisions seemed arbitrary and not usually in my favor. Life felt like a series of traps set for me by my parents. If I fell into one, I ended up being physically punished. My parents did not appear to be on my side and their expectations of me were poor. I realize that my self-esteem was poor and the idea of having a good life appeared as a glimmer of hope that could only be a possibility after leaving home.

I read a story about circus elephants used in heavy lifting work when setting up the 'big top' (circus tent). They were chained to wooden stakes which they could have easily removed. The reason they did not pull out the wooden stakes and run away was because as babies they were chained to metal stakes and no amount of pulling would lift them. The adult elephants were still living in the world they understood as babies and so did not even try to be free. I am still trying to find the 'metal rods' that held me back as a child, and in so doing, I am slowly unravelling my life as it would have been if I had been free from the beginning.

I am questioning the values which were drummed into me as I child. I am trying to understand what my own values are and also the role of guilt in directing what is good or bad in life. I am trying to be guided by a conscience based on values which I have worked out as part of my own life experience. I realize that some of the guilt felt at times has been imposed on me by others. I am looking for what is 'true to me'. I hope to understand the role of guilt more fully and use it in a positive way. I hope that logotherapy will help me gain a fuller understanding of this."

Under the Yoke of Bondage

Teaching in Turkey, my colleague Batya Yaniger and I, both Israelis who come from a culture of tolerance and freedom, found the same precious jewels of people, with the same values of love and family life as in our own community among our Turkish logotherapy students. But there was a difference. Our Turkish students were far more subjected to the strict rules and much more demanding expectations of their culture than our Israeli students with their much freer and independent, and in many respects, much more opinionated, self-assured, freely dissenting and critical, less accepting and respectful attitudes towards authority figures!

To some of the questions in an exercise we gave our Turkish students, there is a striking answer by one of them who negatively experienced the restrictions of the culture he grew up in. The accent on having to achieve and the respect for learning, the positive aspects of his upbringing, were made his own. Nevertheless, he felt a need and had the courage to take the reins of his life in his own hands, and became a clinical psychologist with a flourishing practice. Strong family values also assisted him to find his place in Turkish society, a society he loves and serves.

Recall particularly oppressive or hurtful experiences in your life. Thinking about it, why were these experiences hurtful?

Why? There is no concrete reason for this. For example, it is not like my arm was broken and I felt pain. It was a situation that turned into pain over time because I became afraid, I felt guilty about myself; I felt that others did not like me, that I was not accepted by others; that I was judged, criticized and unfavorably compared to others. Eventually the feeling of insignificance was the result.

What possible negative impressions have you formed about yourself and about life as a result of these hurtful and oppressive experiences?

These are the impressions left on me:
- You are inadequate
- It is futile for you to try anything because you will not be successful
- You are not worthy to be loved, nobody wants to be friends with you
- You should do what others want you to do; whatever you do is wrong
- You have no right to protest, voice your opinions or decide freely. If you do not live up to what is expected of you, you will lose your family and be cut off and alone
- You shouldn't be a burden on anybody
- You have no power to direct your life; everything is determined for you

Contemplating this view of yourself, others, life, is it a view that, if not your own, you would feel attracted to or endorse? Do you really want to have such a view?

No. This view about myself is negative. This kind of life fills me with pain. It causes me to hate myself. I do not want to feel this way.

How would you rather like to see yourself; what view of life would you rather have?

I want to be
- Self-aware
- Have self-love
- And self-confidence
- Feel self-satisfaction
- I want to be a person who does not give up easily, that can be successful; that can have goals in life.
- I want to be a person who can say "No".

(continued)

Actually, all of the above can be summarized as wanting to be "a real individual" who can proceed on the way of self-fulfillment. I want my life to be worth living, discover new things; improve myself until the very end of it.

How did this negative view of yourself and the world influence the way you started behaving after your hurtful experiences?

I became shy, staying away from people, submitting to what others wanted from me too easily and becoming open to abuse. I maintained a low profile; suppressed my thoughts, not daring to voice my opinions. I felt under the control of others and I let them dominate me. I was afraid to be myself, to start anything, do anything that would have my stamp on it.

Do you like the way you have started behaving? Do you want to continue to behave in this way?

I do not like these behaviors. I do not want to hate myself any longer. I do not want to continue in this way.

How would you like to see yourself behaving? Why? Would you like yourself more if you behaved differently?

I want to see myself determining goals, making decisions, believing in and relying on myself. Why? Because my life was the other way round until this day. Changing course will make me like myself more.

Our Turkish student's story, one that took on real meaning despite the restrictions he felt imposed upon him during his upbringing, can be summarized by another student's observations about our inherent will to meaning: "Although not always activated, the will to meaning lies dormant in the human spirit and has the potential for activation in all circumstances, even the most dire" (Julie Povall).

The Shame of Being Blamed

Societal and religious norms that are oppressive provoke an *unhealthy* sense of guilt, the guilt of "not being good enough". That kind of guilt *shames* the "erring" party. The person is viewed as *suspect*. Under punitive scrutiny, faults and failings are identified. The person is "caught out"; his or her "true colors shown." The possibility of innocence is not considered. Hidden motives of evil are exposed and put on public display.

From the moment they are apprehended and charged, they are under the suspicion of "guilty until proven guilty." A prejudiced jury is provoked to pronounce the verdict: "The jury finds the defendant: *guilty as charged*."

Serving their sentence, their release is dependent upon their being able to convince their interrogators that they have been "rehabilitated". They "have seen the light" and will henceforth travel "the straight and narrow". Even given the stamp of "approved" on their release papers, that "pardon" is conditional. They are out on "parole" and must regularly report to the assigned authorities. They must prove that they are "converted"; that they are now conforming members of society. However, they have a criminal record and are blacklisted for life.

Guilt still haunts them.

Original Sin?

The above miserable picture of the shame of blame is based on the Freudian view of man. Freud saw the human personality as split into warring factions. At the very core of our personalities we are, he believed, essentially *driven creatures, lustful and war-like.* He called this hidden essence of our being the *id.* It houses or contains, at the unconscious psychophysical depths of our being, instinctual needs of an extremely self-centered and also sexual and self-defensive or aggressive nature. He distinguished between what he called the life drives: *eros or libido;* and the aggressive or death drives: *Thanatos.* Both drives are animalistic and brutally selfish, that is, geared to satisfy survival needs even if force is necessary to secure them.

Life, in this view of human nature, is a deadly battle!

The full exposure and unleashing of these drives underlying all human behavior, will make society unworkable. Yardsticks need to be imposed to curb and channel and eventually transform these drives into socially acceptable forms of behavior. This is done by way of reward and punishment. It is a heaven or hell option; a choice between acceptance or rejection. An indoctrination of these norms into the consciousness of the developing members of that society until subservience has been accomplished, ensures the survival of the human species.

This internalized consciousness of socially acceptable and unacceptable forms of behavior, Freud called *the superego.* The self or *ego* of the person is assigned the role of *negotiating an acceptable compromise* between id drives and superego censure by way of *the reality principle* (what will work and what will not work in coming to terms with societal norms). The ego is assigned the task to assuage intolerable feelings of guilt. In the light of its own need for acceptance (that its behavior will meet with the approval or *reward* of society) and fear of disapproval (that its behavior will meet with *punishment* and ostracism), the ego submits to superego censure through the cover-up and suppression of forbidden drives and wishes. Such secret wishes are even kept from being consciously realized and are kept hidden in the unconscious mind of the person. However, unresolved and unsatisfied, these hidden wishes and demands build up steam and cause intolerable feelings of pressure and tension. The only way out of this type of intolerable tension in trying to keep censured drives hidden behind a life of abstinence or outward piety, is to transform or express and clothe forbidden drives in ways that will make them "acceptable" and "allowed". This will allow some form of release or satisfaction in real life.

Essentially "guilty", the guilt-laden person seeks to exonerate him- of herself in developing an acceptable front of "not guilty."

Defense mechanisms are strategies which the ego uses to defend itself against the conflict between forbidden drives and moral codes, the taboos which cause neurotic and moral anxiety. The many and varied ways these defenses are employed, are to somehow keep the person out of critical light by covering up what the person fears will lead to disapproval, punishment and rejection. *Repression* makes forbidden desires pressing. Banished into the unconscious, their satisfactions are sought in fantasies and dreams—he workplace of psychoanalysis! Placed *outside,* that is, as not part of the person who cannot, therefore, be accused of having them, forbidden desires are *projected* onto others who are blamed for what the person guiltily desires to do. The defense of *reaction formation* is employed by those who vehemently oppose a so-called societal wrong in turning such opposition into a fanatical cause or campaign to cover up the fact that they themselves harbor such illicit leanings. *Rationalization* is used to make what will be disapproved of seem right, justified and excusable.

The fear of being "found out" and disapproved of is behind all these and other efforts of the guilt-ridden person to present an acceptable front and to make their way in society.

It is interesting to consider that those who are more aggressively inclined, succeed more "admirably" in assuaging feelings of guilt by gaining reputable positions in society where *they* are the ones dishing out blame!

The missed truth of the matter is that when natural human needs are viewed as suspect, and therefore as forbidden, their repression (abstinence) make them take on *exaggerated* importance. Damned up, denied natural outlet in lawful, safely contained and securing contexts, these needs become *unnatural*. Inflamed with desire, these needs clamor for satisfaction. Pressurized by the need for satisfaction, the person driven by these passions falls victim to them.

***Pathology* ensues!**

Civilization and Its Discontents

Freud was a genius. What he in fact uncovered in the sexually repressive and prim and proper Victorian norms of his day, was the *malfunctioning* or *neurotic* personality. It is also a stark exposure of the disastrous effects of viewing human nature as essentially animalistic or basically evil and sinful.

An exegesis of his view of man vividly portrays the pathology of sick societies and oppressive religions and the oppressive hold they exercise over their members and blind followers.

This kind of "civilization", as Freud so brilliantly exposed it, has its discontents. When the socially enforced veneer fails to hold in particularly stressful times and circumstances, rebellion in forms of revolution, mass protests and war will ensue, giving reign to the free expression of violence, rape and plunder. At the other extreme, indulgence in a lawless quest for pleasure and power, erodes the very fabric of society and causes its collapse. All efforts have therefore to be made to maintain peace, to bring warring parties in line and negotiate some kind of satisfactory (win-win) settlement. "The rule of law" is the exercised societal control, even on a world-wide scale in organizations, set up for this purpose over those who are seen as stepping out of line.

Homage to Sigmund Freud

> The heart is deceitful above all things, and desperately sick; who can know it? (Jeremiah 17:9).

Brilliance is the only word to describe Freud's keen perceptiveness of fallen human nature. His exposure of the hypocritical nature both of a society that subjects its members under set-up rigorous standards of behavior, and also of the deceitfulness and conniving nature of those who have fallen victim to it, shocked the world.

Freud himself took recourse to his own little island of happiness in being passionately devoted and faithful to his adored Jewish wife, Martha. He said of himself: "Of few men can it be said that they go through the whole of life without being erotically moved in any serious fashion by any woman beyond the one and only one" (in Jones, 1967:474). In a letter to Martha, his one and only, he wrote: "We will hold together through this life, so easily apprehensible in its immediate aims but so incomprehensible in its final purpose" (in Jones, 1967:123). His mother said she always knew she brought a genius into the world. So close was their relationship that, upon her death in her 90s, Freud missed but never mourned her in any guilt-ridden way. Freud greatly respected his father as a Jewish patriarch. His biographer, Ernest Jones (1967:47), in his monumental work of the life and work of Freud, related the story of Freud's father witnessing a scene where a young acquaintance was argumentatively opposing his own father. Freud's father reprimanded the young man: "What, are you contradicting your father? My Sigmund's little toe is cleverer than my head, but he would never dare to contradict me!"

Freud felt that the task fell on him to expose the human psyche and to illuminate, truthfully, without hypocrisy or shame, also the baser side of human functioning. What he uncovered in the analysis of his patients' communications were often disgusting, or morally repellent, and even personally affronting. This did not deter Freud.

> I understand that from now onward I belonged to those who have "troubled the sleep of the world", and that I could not reckon upon objectivity and tolerance. Since, however, my conviction of the general accuracy of my observations and conclusions grew and grew, and as my confidence in my own judgment was by no means slight, any more than my *moral courage*, there could be no doubt about the outcome of the situation. I made up my mind that it had been my fortune to discover particularly important connections, and I was prepared to accept the fate that sometimes accompanies such discoveries (Freud in Jones, 1967:238).

Frankl (1967:11) stated that he was not willing to live for the sake of his "defense mechanisms", much less to die for the sake of his "reaction formations." Freud was! He was prepared to give an open and honest account before God Himself of the way he lived (and died). He was, after all, a most gifted, morally upright and committed person. He felt that he had fulfilled his appointed task in life in opening the Pandora's box of man's devious and complex psychological waywardness.

> I have no dread at all of the Almighty. If we ever were to meet, I should have more reproaches to make to Him than He could to me. I should ask Him why He had not given me a better intellectual equipment, and He could not complain that I had not made the best of my supposed freedom (Freud in Jones 1967:472–473).

Freud's focus was on the emotionally *ill* or neurotic personality and the mass neurosis of moral restrictiveness of his time. Unfortunate about the Freudian view, however, is that he sees no essential difference between healthy and psychologically disturbed people since both, according to him, are grappling with the same psychic problems, namely: the handling of continual conflict between their suppressed but pressing drives and sense of moral guilt. The difference between the two is simply one of degree—the healthy are better at conflict resolution than the disturbed. A completely conflict-free existence is not possible! Freud saw life as "a grim, irrational, humiliating business—nothing softens this judgment" (Freud in Jones, 1967:19).

The ideal, according to Freud, is to have a strong ego and a superego that is not overly strict. The ego in a healthy person is rational and is more skilled at reality testing. This kind of person use the most effective defense mechanism, namely, *sublimation*. This implies that such a person is able to satisfy his or her sexual and aggressive urges in socially acceptable and appreciated ways which, in turn, implies that such a person will have a satisfactory sexually sublimated relationship with someone and will find fulfilment in work (successfully transferring otherwise unacceptable desires into constructive activities). The ability to love and to work in these sublimated ways is, to Freud's mind, the only kind of "mental health" we can achieve. Compromise, negotiation, bargaining, "making painful sacrifices" in order to achieve "peace" is the only way to prevent the destructive consequences of

unchecked lust (pleasure) and the full venting of aggressive impulses (power). We need to establish this kind of workable society if we are not to eat each other alive!
Psychodynamics within Freudian context consists of the dynamic to

- ensure the survival of the individual
- allow the individual to experience as much pleasure and sense of power as possible
- minimize the individual's experience of guilt

The id is thus seen as the innate, primitive component of the psyche, an *it*, and is in direct contact with the body from which it derives all its energies. Energy drive has the goal of satisfaction. We are therefore *driven* by need. Human nature is basically *animalistic*. Like the animal, we have to adapt to environmental pressures to survive. In order to live in some or other cohesive or harmonious way with others; to maintain human society, our physical or bodily drives must be intelligently transformed by the ego to stand approved before and be protected against the policing and censure of the superego. "Conscience", according to Freud, is a super-ego. It imposes itself upon the ego as its lawgiver. It is punitive, dictating to the ego to keep lawless behavior in check. Morals are societal taboos.

"He Shall Be Like a Tree Planted by the Waters" (Jeremiah 17:7, 8)

How refreshingly different to the Freudian view is Frankl's depiction of man! How profound the grasp that it is a *deviation* from the norm of an unconditional faith in man's natural and inherent potential for *goodness* that causes so much human suffering in the world! Those who fall victim to the *deception* that they are misshapen and inherently abominable, their lives a life-long sentence of serving out their guilt unless they become converted and conformed to specific societal and religious dictates, fall *ill* or become dysfunctional. Their spirits swoon as they go bent under or collapse due to a lack of spiritual sustenance, rootedness and growth!

In a stark contrast to the Freudian view of inherent human "sinfulness" and internalized guilt, Frankl (2000:115) asserted that "true conscience has nothing to do with the fearful expectation of punishment. As long a person is still motivated by either the fear of punishment or the hope of reward—or, for that matter, by the wish to appease the superego—conscience has not yet had its say."

There is a radical difference between the guilt of feeling blamed and in the wrong and the guilt of conviction. The one condemns; the other instructs. The one forces us to bend the knee; the other provokes worship. We submit to the one out of fear; we embrace the other out of love. We pay feigned and lip service to the one; we are heartily convinced by the other!

True conscience acts as a guide, a protector, a comforter and a sustainer. We seek it, and need to live by it. Within its safe and securing boundaries, we grow and prosper, become all that we can and are meant to be. Conscience, as an intuitive perceiver of the voice of the Transcendent, the loving will of the Divine, liberates and frees us! We become at one with ourselves and the world; at one with all that is good and true and beautiful in life.

The tragic opposite is true of prohibitive guilt. It is a superego type of unpleasant and disconcerting censure that condemns us. Such guilt, the guilt that places blame on our person and makes us feel bad about ourselves, is intolerable. No-one can live with such a view of oneself. No wonder that if such a distorted concept of our person begins to operate, we make every effort to somehow change this perception. We try our level best to present ourselves in an acceptable way, not only to the world but, above all, to ourselves. But how the fear lurks! How a sense of self-condemnation refuses to give way! We remain under a painful yoke of bondage, our spirit, our real self, our sense of inherent goodness, is trampled underfoot and enslaved!

How the darkness of depression overcomes us when the angel in us is driven underground! How true Frankl's saying that, when this happens, the angel in us turns into a demon! We remain maimed and persecuted by an unrelenting sense of shame and guilt!

The Truth, the Whole Truth and Nothing But the Truth?

Freud (1971:472) admitted to the fact that he may have been one-sided in his exclusive focus on the psyche and, in doing that, he may have limited his vision. Missing to see what lay beyond his specialized area of study, made him subject to "limiting the scope" of what could become evident if his vision was less limited.

> I recognize that this is my case. I am certainly incompetent to judge the other side of the matter. I must have used this one-sidedness to be able to see what is hidden, from which other people knew how to keep away. That is the justification of my defensive reaction. The one-sidedness had after all its own usefulness.

Freud was too much of a genius not to be aware of the fact that he had limited his research to the lower dimensions of human existence. In a letter to Ludwig Binswanger he said of himself: "I have always confined myself to the ground floor and basement of the edifice" called man (in Frankl, 1988:10). The ground floor is the front man puts up in society. The basement is the dark cellar where all the junk, the broken and discarded items of human depravity are stored and kept out of view. But are we essentially base creatures? Are we sex-driven and aggression-prone? Of a truth, no! Love makes sex human; a firm stand against what is destructive, makes anger righteous. **It is the condemnation and suppression of what is natural that turns it into something pathological**.

Frankl's views put pathology in rightful perspective. The basement is cleared. Light is shone into the darkness of this distorted view of our humanness. "It is a violation of man to project him out of the realm of the genuinely human into the plane of either soma or psyche", Frankl (1968, p.11) stated. We are not a slave to our instincts nor the plaything of our emotions. This does not detract from the genius of

Freud who revealed just how wayward and off course human behavior can become if the spiritual person, the master of his or her fate, is not given his or her proper due.

Poignantly, in one of his last works: *Civilization and its Discontents*, Freud (1930:76) wrote:

> The program of becoming happy, which the pleasure principle imposes on us, cannot be fulfilled; yet we must not—indeed, we cannot—give up our efforts to bring it nearer to fulfillment by some means or other.

What Freud did not foresee was that his genius opened up avenues of understanding *beyond* the human psyche. Daring to plumb the depths of also his own psyche, Freud came to glimpse what he expressed as doubt: there may be *more* to man than what even the psychoanalyst could dream of! In lifting the lid off the psyche, and casting light into the dark and deep workings of the human psyche, a third dimension of being: *the human spirit* came into view. Freud confessed that we may be more moral than we think!

Frankl (1986:3) refers to Freud as a giant in his enormous intellectual impact not only on psychology but on every field of thought relating to man. Freud's discoveries opened vistas which would have remained obscure and hidden from the understanding of future psychologists in their study of the human psyche. Frankl graphically portrayed the indebtedness to Freud by psychologists who followed in his wake and who made their own important contributions to our understanding of man, with the apt saying that a dwarf standing on the shoulders of a giant can see farther than the giant himself.

The Whole Picture

The following statements from Frankl's work: Man's Search for Ultimate Meaning (2000), lift the distortions and makes us see ourselves in true light.

> "Human existence is **spiritual** existence."
>
> "Psychoanalysis **depersonalizes** man. The ego in the psychoanalytic view is ultimately a plaything of the drives. Or as Freud himself once said, the ego is not the master in its own house. Psychoanalysis sees man in the final analysis as the automaton of a psychic apparatus. Logotherapy pits a different concept of man against the psychoanalytic one. It is not focused on the automaton of a psychic apparatus but rather on the autonomy of spiritual existence. **Being human is not being driven but deciding what one is going to be.**"
>
> "The line between the spiritual and the instinctual cannot be drawn sharply enough."

Conscience Versus the Superego

The following account by a logotherapy student of her experience of her own conscience stands in graphic contrast to the punitive super-ego type of conscience of a person who has internalized punitive yardsticks of acceptable versus objectionable behavior. We have also noted that a false or pathological sense of guilt, along with painful feelings of self-doubt and unworthiness, are suffered by those who have experienced the trauma of rejection or emotional abuse during the youthful and impressionable years of their lives.

In the above account, our student highlighted the spiritual experience of conscience as a guide on a higher and, at the same time, a deeper and more profound

---

The Still Small Voice (1 Kings 19:12)

"Unlike the loud and judgmental voice of the superego, the voice of conscience is very quiet and acts by inviting rather than demanding. I experience my own conscience in a number of ways. When my conscience invites me to do something, I am aware that a very important choice is being put before me. I know immediately that I am being faced with something that would be a better way of approaching a given situation. I am also aware that it requires my agreement that this way is right and that I must act on it. I know when I respond positively to the invitation and when I don't. I know when I have gained or lost out, depending on my response. My conscience does not only prompt me to better ways, it also helps me to see when I have spoken or acted in a way that has not been in line with the deeper values I wish to hold. It is gentle with me and provides other opportunities. Not listening to it does not fill me with a sense of guilt or anxiety such as not listening to the superego does, but rather it fills me with a sense of sadness, a sense of loss.

For me, feelings of guilt and anxiety are a good way to gauge whether I am responding to the demands of the superego rather than according to an inner conviction. The superego's demands leave me feeling trapped, de-energized and resentful. When the superego is in charge, I find myself acting without reflecting and am usually more concerned about what other people think. I fear their disapproval. When I am acting out of an inner conviction, I respond rather than react. In this way I move into a task from a peaceful center and am more able to do things lovingly. I am not as concerned about what other people think.

When I look back at my life, the times I allowed my superego to rule are the times I stopped living with joy. The times I followed an inner conviction are the times I felt the richness of living."

level of being. And that is where the voice of conscience, even in the provoked struggle with feelings of condemnation and anguish, will eventually lead us.

We are left defenseless and vulnerable, with the doors open to torturous guilt and self-condemnation, when we are subjected or confined to the unspiritual and subhuman levels of being. Here guilt shouts and accuses, as our student testified. But Frankl has urged us to *humanize* the inhuman torture of feelings of unpardonable guilt suffered by those still under the heavy yoke of a super-ego type of guilt. We must also recognize that, because the finger-pointing and accusatory nature of that guilt is so unbearable, efforts to escape, deny, project or drown out the voice of condemnation in their own heads, will be made by those victimized by it. Since our clients or those we know and work with will present with these types of feelings of guilt, it is important for us to put the punitive experience of guilt in spiritual context. And since this chapter seeks to make you aware of your true self, who you are in essence, we need to focus on the experience of guilt more deeply.

The Release From Internalized Blame

How do we encounter and assist those saddled with the guilt of wrongdoing?

Careful analyses will show that even through no fault of our own, unavoidable suffering carries the challenge of reprimand. How did we live before tragedy struck us? For example, the death of our loved ones can leave us with the pain of regret for not having been all that we could have been towards them during their lifetimes. We can no longer put things right. It is too late. Our very imperfection under the scrutiny of events that we did not bring upon ourselves, is a call to change for the better and to make better use of the time we have with the people we love. *Life seems to be a matter of correction for all of us, all of the time!* But we can still kiss the hand that disciplines us in such situations of unavoidable suffering. We can even pat ourselves on the back for becoming even better human beings. After all, we have an even more likeable face staring back at us in the mirror!

But is good to be found in the sin of wrongdoing? The natural reaction in the face of shame is to hide, to cover up our guilt, to even try to find excuses to justify our actions. It is the old Adam and Eve story. We can try and live in self-denial, begin to blame, feel hostile towards, and even hate those that saddle us with guilt because we failed them, were disloyal to them, or caused them harm. Why? Is it because we cannot stand to feel ugly and shameful?

Who likes to stand in the dock of the accused?

We like to feel good about ourselves, to feel at home with ourselves. Guilt and self-condemnation drive us out of a peaceful and comfortable place. We feel disconnected, alienated; an outsider. The most dreadful feeling is to feel out of touch with ourselves. How can we live with ourselves if we cannot stomach ourselves?

But what does all of this say? "This is all wrong!" "I do not want to feel this way!" "This is not what I want to be!" "I am not myself!" "I have disgraced myself!"

What if guilt is the most powerful factor to provoke real, genuine, and heartfelt change? What if repentance, a heart-rending anguish and sorrow over wrongdoing, is the greatest cleansing, the most liberating way to really live life as it is meant to be lived?

Who can have greater freedom from the hateful character traits of insensitivity, callousness, indifference, pride and arrogance: that snobbish and better-than-thou attitude of superiority, than the one humiliated with guilt?

In recognizing our own faults and weaknesses, we are freed from all those hurtful and devastating attitudes of prejudice, bigotry, rejection on the basis of race, gender, sexual orientation, religion, and a hostility towards anyone who dares to be different from us or holds viewpoints opposing our own. And when freed from the above, we can compassionately make room for the mistakes and failures of others; give the right to others to have their voices of dissent be heard. We are more prepared to listen to the other side of the story. We have greater tolerance, patience, mercy and lovingkindness towards others, more readiness to forgive, encourage and uplift those who have fallen from grace or those who have been brought under the torturous yoke of unfair blame and condemnation.

Who can be as clean as someone who is forced to come clean if they are to go on breathing? Who can really live with unconfessed and un-acquitted guilt? True repentance is the greatest turnabout in our lives, the most powerful change we can make. It is met with the greatest gift that can be bestowed on us: forgiveness, a restoration of all things as they should have been right from the start! This is a new life of joy, happiness, freedom from strain, stress, fret and worry.

We have changed face!

What pure water there is to be drawn from the wellsprings of abject self-despair and disillusionment! Who can be lovelier, have more of the sweet grace of humility, than the one who emerges from the very depths and rock-bottom of brutally honest self-scrutiny?

Who has a more purified heart than the one who asks for forgiveness and asks for nothing more than just to be given the chance to make restitution? Whose dedication to a new life can be more genuine or sincere?

Who can better live than in the way Frankl has encouraged us to live, namely to "live as if you are living a second time and are about to make the same mistake you did the first time"?

Indeed, here is the greatest treasure to be found in life: the courage to confess guilt and the determination to henceforth live before your own conscience, shamelessly!

What a release into being authentic, transparently honest and real!

A Moral Rebirth: the Noodynamics of Repentance

For the inner biography of a man, grief and repentance do have meaning. (Frankl, 1969:87)

Frankl speaks about an *existential turnabout* in our lives. It is a heart-stricken moment of realization of what is badly wrong in our lives. Defenseless in the face of a stark sense of conscience, we find ourselves without excuse or justification. Wrong is simply wrong and very wrong, and right is simply right and very right. The choice is clear and before us. Which way to turn? Away from this point of breakdown before a confrontation we can no longer deny? Yet an escape from this moment of painful scrutiny, of a self-examination that brings the full facts to light, is impossible. We are cornered. Grief, shock and pain overwhelm us. Conviction of wrongdoing cuts deep and accurately. We are in the throes of remorse that sees and acknowledges; that confesses and weeps. Repentance is, in effect, a process of deep cleansing. As it happens, from the well-springs of our innermost being, there begins to flow the purifying waters of healing.

We are born again!

None of our past acts, of the wrong we did and the right we did not do can be wiped off the slate as if they had never been, Frankl stated. Nevertheless, he contended that "in repenting man may inwardly break with an act, and in living out this repentance—which is an inner event—he can undo the outer event on a spiritual, moral plane." Frankl quoted Max Scheler, who said that repentance has the power to wipe out a wrong; though the wrong cannot be undone, the culprit himself undergoes a *moral rebirth*.

Sharpened to a point of focus, this turnabout in our lives is in fact a climax of a struggling process that earmarks all our efforts throughout our lives to find our true place in life; to come fully to terms with ourselves. What is it that we really want and need to be able to live a life worth living? What is it that spoils and harms and destroys life's meaning? It has to come to a point of clarity; some kind of final decision. Full weight must be given to choices that move us forward. Only in placing ourselves on the side of what is good for us, is it possible to counteract, refute, stand against and victoriously overcome what is bad for us.

The past is past. What is done is done. It is a *fait accompli*. Fate cannot be changed, Frankl (1969:73) contended, otherwise it would not be fate. "Man, however, may well change himself; otherwise he would not be man. It is a prerogative of being human and a constituent of human existence, to be capable of shaping and reshaping oneself. In other words, it is a privilege of man to become guilty and his responsibility to overcome it."

Throughout this whole process and up to its point of climax in a decisive turnabout in our lives and climbing to the heights of meaning that follow, is the *tension between what is and what is held out to us*. It is the tightrope that bridges the gap, the rope that helps us climb to the top. There is someone on the other side holding the rope, assisting and drawing us upwards!

"Come Now, Let Us Reason Together" (Isaiah 1:18)

How do we react towards the wrong done by someone we care about and love, the kind of reprimand also required in therapy with a client in the illumination of the harm they cause to themselves in harming others?

What is a true reprimand?

After all we have discussed and considered in this chapter, we have to conclude the following:

A true reprimand is an admonition that does not have a trace of condemnation about it! It can only be given in the sacred privacy of a personal, face-to-face encounter. No-one, no outsider, is privy to it. In this private and intimate space no accuser is allowed to enter. The reviler, the judgmental and arrogant bigot, is firmly shut out. No prying eye can peep through the key-hole.

In the Bible it is recorded that Joseph, when he made himself known to his guilty brothers, did not do so until every outsider, upon his instruction, had left the room. His disclosure of who he really was, their brother whom they had harmed, was wise and loving. He deeply loved his brothers and sought reconciliation with them. He sought no revenge and he bore no grudge against them. The case that had to be settled was not something dividing them. It was a case that needed to establish what was good and right and in the face of what was bad and wrong. The wrong needed to be repented of and the right was to be celebrated in their restored relationships, one to the other! Their father's broken heart was to be healed!

Likewise, we are never to correct loved ones or our children in public. Correction and reprimand are to be given in private. We are *never* to shame anyone! In the case of therapy, and when there is a need to warn our clients, the warning is an exhortation: "Do not do what is wrong and hurtful to anyone. What is wrong will harm *you*. You will lose your sense of integrity and dignity. You will have to go into hiding from your own conscience. You will have to start convincing yourself of your own goodness, deny that it has been spoilt. You may even start to justify what is wrong and be forced to put up a good front. You will have to hide your wrongdoing from view, lie about it. You will no longer be real but become unreal, hypocritical and false. Do you want to live a lie? Do not do that to yourself! Look at the consequences of wrongdoing in your own life and in the lives of others. Do you want that?" And, if the wrong has already been done: "Do you want to be in such a place of misery and unrest? Why stay there?"

(continued)

The only appeal that can have any helpful or positive effect is to point out to those in the wrong what injury the wrong will cause their person and their lives. The harm they are or will be inflicting on others, will boomerang on them. Their own lives can or will lose its meaning. They will no longer experience the blessed effects of meaning-fulfillment in their lives. They will be haunted by guilt that will overshadow everything and shut anything meaningful from view. What kind of choice is that? Who wants to have a life with the blame of "in the wrong" written all over it?

The reprimand is invitational: "you can choose to put an end to this."

A judgmental attitude towards anyone is based on self-righteousness. It makes the ones we seek to correct feel bad in comparison with ourselves or with standards outside of themselves that they are failing to live up to. It is a wrap over the knuckles. We will be disliked and perceived as being prudish and self-opinionated. They will blame us for not understanding them; that we think we are better than they are; and who are we to tell them what to do?

We can only reprimand others if we have removed from ourselves every last trace of moralistic disapproval, The call we make upon them to change is for their sake. It is not because we judge them but because we care about them.

We are calling those who have strayed, back to themselves, to that which is right for *them*.

The Homecoming

Repentance is an utterly private matter, away from the finger pointing of shame and humiliation. Our wrongs are our own. They do not need to be advertised, put out there where those who dislike us can shame us. We do not need to be accused of it. It is *our* prerogative to deal with our guilt, to make up for it,

If we are dealing with someone who has caused us hurt or personal harm, and if such a person seeks to put things right with us, we must make that totally possible. We must bury their wrongdoings, their past behavior, put it out of our minds as if it never happened. We must vigorously deal with our own hurt and anger in what they have done to us and others.

Are we so small that we cannot forgive them for the hurt they have inflicted upon us?

Oh, to be able to carry the hurt inflicted upon us as an agony on behalf of others in what they, in their waywardness, are doing to themselves!

Love has the grace of forgiveness.

How miraculous, therefore, how wonderful, their homecoming! What a feast of joy! Will we even think to mention their past sins when our hurt was for them and not for ourselves?

No, not in a million years.

We will love them all the more!

For You, the Reader: Forgiveness

I wrote the following piece in my book: *Life's Meaning in the Face of Suffering* (2000:43, 44).

> **Mankind with a Mission: A Post-paradise State of Being**
>
> Frankl's views may inspire us to believe that our Adamic forebears were sent out of paradise with a mission. Clothed by God (see Genesis 3:21), that is, not in shame or disgrace, but under the covering of the grace of God's forgiveness, those first representatives of mankind were sent out of paradise with the dignity of a purpose!
>
> In the paradise story God engaged the guilty Adam in conversation (Genesis 9–19). Adam and Eve were called out of hiding and confronted with the issue of evil and its suffering consequences and their own part in it. They may have lost their state of sublime innocence and with it, their unperturbed sense of meaningfulness. This banishment from their paradise state of being can be seen, however, not as a curse, but as a charge.
>
> The curse of suffering and death was not to last forever. Life on this side of the grave was to last, on average, three score years and ten. Placed within the confines of a certain lifetime, the first human family was sent out of paradise to face suffering and combat the causes of it. They were to fully comprehend their human condition and embrace it as a *task*.
>
> Frankl (1967):30) described this mission quality of the human condition as follows:
>
> > *Man is confronted with the human condition in terms of fallibility and mortality. Properly understood, it is, however, precisely the acceptance of this twofold human finiteness which adds to life's worthwhileness, since only in the face of guilt does it make sense to improve, and only in the face of death is it meaningful to act.*
>
> It is the very transitory nature of human existence which constitutes our responsibility. Only under the urge and pressure of the transitory nature of life is it vital to make use of the passing time and to use it well; to store into the past not as opportunities irrecoverably lost, but as achievements irrevocably stored. "Once an actuality, it is one forever" (Frankl, 1967, p. 30).

(continued)

The human story is to be a story of triumph. We have the task to overcome evil with good. We have to exercise our power of choice in doing what we *know* is right, and in resisting, refusing to do, what we *know* is wrong. The confusion of doubt and distrust is to be overcome. No longer ignorant of evil, we must attain a heightened understanding of good (in the face of evil and in vivid contrast to it).

The human commission since the banishment from paradise is to achieve the triumph of a Job: "I have heard of You by the hearing of the ear, but now my eyes sees You" (Job 42:5). "Things too wonderful for me, which I did not know" (Job 42:3), finally broke through to his heightened understanding.

"Human life can be fulfilled not only in creating and enjoying, but also in suffering!" This was the triumphant conclusion of Frankl (1969:85) as he himself could, at last, confirm the unconditional meaningfulness of *all* of life. As he emerged from his own great suffering on the day of his liberation from the Nazi concentration camp, he could testify:

"The crowing experience of all, for the homecoming man, is the wonderful feeling that, after all he has suffered, there is nothing he need fear any more—except his God" (Frankl, 1968:93).

We were sent out of paradise with the commission to regain it. We make our way home through the grace of the unconditional love of forgiveness!

References

Frankl, V. E. (1967). *Psychotherapy and existentialism. Selected papers on logotherapy.* New York: Simon and Schuster.

Frankl, V. E. (1968). *Man's search for meaning: An introduction to logotherapy.* London: Hodder & Stroughton.

Frankl, V. E. (1985). *The unheard cry for meaning: Psychotherapy and theology.* New York: Simon and Schuster.

Frankl, V. E. (1986). *The doctor and the soul. From psychotherapy to logotherapy.* New York: Vintage Books.

Frankl, V. E. (2000). *Man's search for ultimate meaning.* New York: Basic Books.

Frankl, V. E. (2004). *On the theory and therapy of mental disorders: An introduction to logotherapy and existential analysis.* New York: Brunnner-Routledge.

Freud, S. (1930). *Civilization and its discontents: The standard edition* (Vol. Vol. XX1). London: Hogarth Press.

Freud, S. (1971). *Introductory lectures on psychoanalysis: The complete introductory lectures on psychoanalysis.* Oxford: Alden Press.

Jones, E. (1967). *The life and work of Sigmund Freud.* London: Penguin Books.

Lukas, E. (2000). *Logotherapy textbook: Meaning-centered psychotherapy.* Toronto: Liberty Press.

Pattison, S. (2000). *Shame: Theory, therapy, theology.* Cambridge: Cambridge University Press.

Chapter 10
The Meaning of Suffering: You Are Chosen!

Abstract Suffering can be made to serve us. Suffering instructs us, we can learn from it; suffering humbles us, we realize how futile it is to try and manipulate life to get out of it what we want, no matter what it does to others; suffering confronts us, it is not what we expect from life but what life expects from us; suffering shapes us, we lose our hardness of heart, we become caring and compassionate; suffering commissions us, commands us to take up our cross and live life the way it is meant to be lived; suffering inspires us, we begin to have a zeal for life; suffering empowers us, we more courageously take a stand against what is wrong in the world as we reach out to all those who suffer; suffering leads us to our destinies in life, in the area in which we suffered, we have gained an expertise, an in-depth understanding of the kind of suffering we suffered and a desire to help those in similar need: suffering frees us, we are no longer victimized by tragic events but have risen to a position where we can face and overcome those events triumphantly; suffering makes us witnesses for life, we bear powerful and inspiring witness to the fact that suffering can be triumphantly overcome, that life is and remains precious and is to be lived appreciatively and to the full.

Keywords Suffering serves us · Suffering instructs us · Suffering humbles us · Suffering confronts us · Suffering shapes us · Suffering commissions us · Suffering inspires us · Suffering empowers us · Suffering reveals our destinies in life · Suffering frees us · Enduring suffering bravely · Becoming witnesses for life

"I Have Chosen You in the Fire of Affliction" (Isaiah 48:10)

What a thought that we are able to deal with suffering in a triumphant way; that suffering can bring out the best in us; that suffering can be made to serve us!

What truths are embedded in suffering!

Suffering Instructs Us Life is not meant to be something we just live, without much thought as to its meaning and purpose. Nor is it meant to be something we callously spurn or recklessly destroy. Suffering is like a wake-up call. It calls us to attention; it calls us to account. Suffering corners us with the very question of the meaning of our lives, why we have it, what we are to do with it. If we are open to the lessons of suffering and do not rebelliously close our ears to it, we become very aware of what is good about life, precious about living it. If we have a heart for the value of life at all, we want to preserve life, not lose it or cause its destruction. Suffering is meant to make us aware of the good we had or hope to have; of the good we *want* and are now being deprived of. Faced with actual loss, like the death of a loved one, we are made aware of just how precious such a person was to us—we remember them lovingly, all the good about them, how good life was with them. We see the preciousness of life, life with those we love, life with all its opportunities and blessings, the great privilege to have been gifted with it. Through suffering life is meant to take on new meaning, become more valued by us. We are to be more careful not to spoil it, not to turn it sour and ugly, but to be committed to it in a deeper way. We are meant to learn to revere life, to love life and to be in awe of it!

Suffering Humbles Us   Suffering makes us aware that just as life has been given to us, it can be taken away. Life is not ours to possess and manipulate; it cannot be made to bend the knee to us. We cannot force it to give us what we demand from it. It is not ours to control at will. Therefore, it is in suffering that we become more awesomely aware of the fact that something is expected of us; that there is something we have to do and achieve with our lives. Suffering strips the callousness of pride and the complacency of arrogance from us!

Suffering Confronts Us   Suffering enjoins us to live an *accountable* life. We are to do unto others as we would want them to do unto us. Suffering commands us to fulfill life's duties, muster life's challenges; appreciate what life has to give. We are expected to fill our lives with meaningful content. There comes a day when we have to *return* our lives, give it back, and hopefully, with our life's mission accomplished!

Suffering Shapes Us   Suffering is a call to responsibility, also to bear and deal with the suffering in a required way. Refusing to learn its lessons, suffering can make us hard and callous. We need to become soft and yielded under its blows. It is then that we discover that suffering *serves* us. It transforms us into more sensitive, caring and decent human beings; our humanity is shown forth in a more admirable way. In our own pain we feel moved to reach out to others in their pain.

Suffering Commissions Us!   With what a sense of destiny, a vocation in life, we eventually emerge from our suffering!

Suffering Inspires us   We begin to experience a zeal for life. We want to live our lives in a much fuller and more passionate, infinitely more committed way. We become *there* for others, ready to heed any and every call to service.

Suffering Empowers Us With a heightened sense of what is meaningful and *right* in this world, we become more resolutely opposed to what is meaningless and *wrong* in this world. We experience the defiant power of the human spirit. This aroused strength of purpose in us provokes a *protest* against the abuse of life. We abhor violence and cruelty, the callous use and abuse of the lives of others, the taking of the lives of others for some or other spurious cause, or out of some or other twisted and evil motive. We have a strong desire to alleviate suffering, to combat its causes in all the help we offer, in all the endeavors to lighten the load and suffering of others. Filled with compassion and love of our fellow-man, we can stand up against those who callously and maliciously inflict suffering upon innocent others. We can defy the perpetrators of evil in this world, confront and expose them, call them to book. We can lay down our lives for the sake of those whom we seek to protect, whose senseless suffering at the hands of cruel others we vigorously oppose. We serve worthy causes with a passion and combat suffering with zeal.

Suffering Leads Us to Our Destinies in Life What spiritual triumph, what victory over every threat contained in suffering of any and every kind, when we are free of the fear of it, when we have transcended the state of distress, the victimization caused by it! All of our lives, every aspect it, become supremely meaningful when we become masters over fate. When we rise above our fate, that very fate becomes destiny. We have learnt from it, have become instructed in how to deal with and overcome it, have turned it into something supremely meaningful. Adversity becomes a triumph when we have wrested meaning out of suffering. Someone who has suffered sexual abuse as a child can, as an adult, wrest meaning out of that suffering by combatting sexual abuse as an adult in counseling and ministering to those who still suffer from the effects of it and by working for organizations that seek to rescue women and children from those who are abusing them or by reporting sexual abuse to authorities with the power to arrest and bring sexual offenders to justice. The combat of sexual abuse has become a life's mission. Our particular fates or areas of suffering can become our destinies, our callings in life!

Suffering Frees Us Evil is rendered powerless when it no longer has a hold on us. It is clearly outside of and not part of us. It cannot touch us, even if such evil is still very operative in the world and even when we still find ourselves in the midst of and assailed by it. A table is prepared for us *in the presence of our enemies*. We find ourselves blessed, our cups of joy running over—we having nothing to fear anymore (Psalm 23)! We have the power and courage to oppose and overcome evil with good. Our stand is clear and resolute. We will have nothing to do with what is wrong and will have everything to do with what is right. When our own suffering has served its purpose in our lives, we are free of its forebodings and its victimizing effects forever.

Suffering Makes Us Witnesses for Life! Even in the white heat of suffering or in a suffering situation that is fateful, that is, beyond change (e.g. being crippled for life), we can victoriously *transcend* the situation in a radical change of attitude, a reorientation towards life. To what moral heights we can rise, despite and even *because* of the suffering we had to or have to endure! The outcome is in the direction of a deepened appreciation of all that makes life so very worth the living; a more mature and resolute faith that our lives were destined to be; and a more awesome sense of responsibility in living it with greater care and commitment. Suffering, having found such a reason, Frankl stated, somehow ceases to be suffering. It loses its sting and its trauma. It is the sweet triumph expressed in Scripture:

> Where, O death, is your sting? Where, O death, is your victory? (Hosea 13:14/1Corinthians 15:55).

Suffering is turned on its head when we triumph over it in coming out of it beautified and *refined*, chastised and taught by it to be the kind of person that life has all along *intended* and *commissioned* us to be!

The following true account of a client of mine, illustrates the above wondrous truth.

Where Happy Little Bluebirds Fly

My client, a tourist guide in Israel, was the survivor of a terrorist attack. Guiding an American friend through a beautiful forest on the outskirts of Jerusalem, they were accosted and savagely attacked by two men. The American lady was stabbed to death despite her pleading. Stabbed time and again, my client was at last left for dead.

My client was advised to see me by her friend, another client of mine, in order to deal with the stress she was experiencing after that terribly traumatic incident.

We had only two sessions together.

In the first, the focus was on the terrorist attack, graphically captured in a booklet she wrote some time afterwards called: *Where happy little bluebirds fly: Memoirs of a terrible, yet very sacred, day.*

It was a beautiful day. Winding their way through the forest, they ventured off the main trail. No-one was to be seen anywhere. They felt they had the forest all to themselves. There was the peace of quiet but for the bird song, so audible in that otherwise deserted part of the forest.

Suddenly, out of nowhere, two men appeared, men that were later identified and apprehended as Palestinian terrorists, members of a terrorist group vowed to Israel's destruction. They walked crouched, stealthily, as if they tried not to be seen. Their whole appearance looked menacing. My client whispered to her friend to avoid their glance and to walk past them, ignoring them. But the men stopped them, standing in their path. They asked for directions in a broken Hebrew. The client answered them in Hebrew, immediately recognizing her mistake. The terrorists wanted to establish whether they were foreigners or Israelis and she had fallen into the trap. One of the terrorists grabbed her and the other her friend. They both struggled to free themselves but were overpowered.

Our client heard her American friend, dragged off some distance away from her, screaming and pleading for mercy till her throttled cry was finally silenced. She was stabbed to death. My client, however, after the initial and futile struggle, kept absolutely still, pretending to be dead, the grotesque shouting of her assailant: "Allah Akbar!", ringing in her ears.

As she was struck, again and again, she could still hear the birds singing. Her mind raced. She was being killed. Then, out of some deep source inside herself, she felt a strong surge of energy, a will to survive. Out of her heart leapt the Jewish prayer, the *Shema: "Hear, O Israel, the Lord your God is the One and Only"*, as a cry to be saved.

After 12 stab wounds and bleeding profusely, she was left for dead. The assailants took off, as quickly and as stealthily as they had appeared. When she felt sure they had gone, she managed to drag herself down the hill to where she heard the sound of voices. She was seen tumbling down the hill by the visitors to the area. They ran to her, others called for an ambulance. Their swift intervention saved her life.

We pondered the whole terrible event. She kept on coming back to the bird songs. They were singing before, during and after the attack. The song of the little birds meant something deep to her, like a comfort, a reassurance, a hope. It was like the presence of the precious meaning of her life that was always there. It had never left her and was still there for her to reach out to.

"In Your Blood, Live!" (Ezekiel 16:6)

The second session consisted of an overview of her entire life. How did this traumatic event as an adult relate to all that she had gone through in her life? What was she called upon to do now?

She recalled the great surge of meaning that she experienced some years before in coming to Israel, her homeland, from England where she had been born and where she lived; the joy she felt as she took off her shoes on the day of her arrival, just to feel the ground of Israel, its soil, under her feet. It was her love of the land, her gratitude for it, that made her take up her calling as a tourist guide; a vocation she was giving shape to on that very day that she took her American tourist friend hiking through the forest.

She told me that she was an orphan and that an English couple in London had adopted her. Her adoptive father turned out to be a most abusive and cruel man that liked to torture her with the accusation that she was an orphan. Growing up in that abusive home, a deep desire to trace her own family roots and establish her own identity took shape. As soon as she was able to leave the home where she was treated so badly, she began the search for her background and eventually discovered that her parents, who had both died in an accident, were Jewish. That motivated her to move to Israel, her Jewish homeland.

During our session, she realized that through being orphaned by life and given over to unloving and abusive adoptive parents, she had lost every sense of entitlement. The one sole desire to join herself to her people in her own promised land was being shaped in her as an irrepressible will to find her own destiny and meaning in life. How true, she agreed, was the saying of Frankl: "It is not what we expect from life, but what life expects from us."

She also marveled at the fact that, during her adoptive father's frequent and terrible beatings of her, she had learnt to keep very still so as to not incite his violent anger any further, and that it was this behavior during her childhood that had saved her life in adulthood! Only in being able to keep absolutely still, without any sign of resistance, limp in the grip of her assailant, did she deceive him into thinking that she was dead.

However, my client felt strongly that it was the prayer that had leapt from her heart that had empowered her to survive 12 stab wounds, one in the nape of her neck where her necklace with a little Star of David (the symbol of being Jewish) hung.

We discussed the similarity between her experience and the experience of Viktor Frankl when he entered the death camp, Auschwitz. After his own coat from which the manuscript of his life's work, hidden in it, was snatched away from him, Frankl found, in the coat pocket of an inmate that was sent to the gas chambers, a torn-out page from the Jewish prayer book (Siddur). It was the same prayer that my client prayed in her hour of desperate need.

Frankl interpreted his reading of this prayer as a call to say: "Yes!" to life despite the horror he was facing and would be going through. He had to learn, first-hand and *personally*, that life retains its meaning and *is* meaningful under *all* circumstances. Life, even in the face of death and despite the most horrific circumstances, retains its meaning. Life is and *remains* precious. And it will outlast death. Not even the grave would destroy it!

My client had a rivetingly similar experience. Life became extremely precious to her when she was at the point of losing it. As with Frankl, the horror of my client's experience commissioned her with a most meaningful task, one she started performing sometime after our sessions: to triumph over all she went through by becoming a source of great inspiration through her talks and writings to the countless families in Israel who had lost loved ones through terrorist attacks and the wars waged against the people of Israel.

"In your blood, live," is the inscription on the gates leading to Yad Vashem, the Holocaust Memorial Museum in Jerusalem; a commission she now felt challenged to accept.

From Senselessness to Meaning

Far from the terrorist attack being just a senseless tragedy she, like Frankl, "was chosen in the fire of affliction" for a mission of consolation to the people of Israel, a people constantly threatened with annihilation by terrorist groups, rogue countries and regimes. So very many families in Israel have suffered the grief of losing a loved one in a war or in a terrorist attack. Bereaved families flocked to her talks as her story became headline news in Israel. As in the case of Frankl, the meaning of her life became all the more deeply directed to bringing meaning to the lives of others by giving them hope and the faith to persevere, no matter what and despite everything.

My client was inspired to take up her life again, guiding tourists through the length and breadth of the State of Israel.

The Triumph of Good over Evil: The Story of a Rabbi

After the Nazis invaded the small village of Klausenberg, they began to celebrate in their usual sadistic fashion. They gathered the Jews of the town and made them stand in a circle to watch the following scene. The town's Rebbe, Rabbi Yekusiel Yehuda Halberstam, was dragged to the center. They began taunting and teasing him, pulling his beard and pushing him around. The jeering soldiers trained their guns on him as the commander began to speak.

"Tell us Rabbi," sneered the officer, "do you really believe that you are the Chosen People?" The soldiers guarding the crowd howled with laughter. But the Rebbe did not. In a serene voice, he answered loudly and clearly: "Most certainly."

The officer became enraged. He lifted his rifle above his head and sent it crashing down on the head of the Rebbe. The Rebbe fell to the ground. There was rage in the officer's voice. "Do you still think you are the Chosen People?" he yelled. Once again, the Rebbe nodded his bloodied head and said, "Yes, we are."

The officer became infuriated. He kicked the Rebbe and repeated. "You stupid Jew, you lie here on the ground, beaten and humiliated. What makes you think that you are the Chosen People?"

From the depths of humiliation, covered in blood and dust, the Rebbe replied:

"As long as we are not the ones kicking and beating innocent people, we can call ourselves chosen."

Witnesses for Life

Writing my doctorate on what Frankl called *the defiant power of the human spirit,* I had the great privilege to get to intimately know and interview a number of Holocaust survivors (Shantall, 2002). One of them was, **Leah Leibovitz**.

She was the survivor of six ghettos and camps stretching over 4 years. Her husband, baby boy, mother- and father-in-law, her own mother and father, sister and brother and many other extended family members, perished in the camps. Hers is a lament that is voiced in the book of Lamentations (1:12): *"Behold and see if there is any sorrow like my sorrow, which has been brought on me."*

Yet, how magnificently she rose above her fate!

After being rounded up to be sent to the camps after a most tragic stay in the Kovno ghetto, she was taken to Vaivara, a concentration camp in Estonia. There she was assigned the job of being the cleaning lady of her barrack. She told me the following story (Shantall 2002: 184):

> My barrack had a hundred women. They had diarrhea and were locked up the whole night, so you can imagine what the barrack looked like in the morning. By ten o'clock it had to be clean. Every day sixty to sixty-five women were taken out to work. There were some older women, and some very young girls. The Kapos came in the morning and broke arms and ribs with sticks in chasing the women because they didn't want to go to work. So there was disorder. I discussed this with the girls. I said, 'let us make a list. The younger and stronger ones can go, and let the others stay and work in and around the barracks—there was always something to do. After two days, I promise you, those who had worked two days, can have one day of rest on the third day, and then we'll change. I will rotate it in such a way that everyone will have rest in between two days of work.' They agreed. So I had the names, and every morning at seven o'clock, my group was outside without any screams and without any cries and without any damage done to people.

This dramatic change in the common scenes of screaming and chaos at the other barracks impressed the camp authorities. They appointed Leah into the position of a *Blockalteste* (a person in charge of a block of barracks). Three barracks of a 100 women each were placed in her care. These 300 women, with a young girl whom Leah "adopted" as her daughter, became Leah's charge throughout the following years of suffering. They followed her into other camps and were kept under her leadership and care. All of them were finally sent to Bergen-Belsen in February, 1945.

> We could not believe what was happening there. You could not live there for more than three months. There was typhus, death, almost no food, no work, nothing. Hundreds, perhaps thousands, were dying every night. There were mountains of dead bodies that were lying there, half rotten. It was terrible. Then at twelve o'clock on the 15th of April, the first British motorbike with two people on it rode through the fence. We jumped through the windows. The guards hit us with batons to force us back. They were all arrested. We weren't quite in our minds to appreciate what was happening. Some fell down and kissed the wheels of the tank and the tires of the motorbikes and all that. I don't much remember now because my mind was so numb at the time. All that I remember is going back to the barracks and getting my girls, **all** of them.

Leah was instrumental in saving 300 lives, including the life of her "adopted" daughter. A surviving brother had made his way to South Africa. It was there that Leah eventually settled.

> I had these breaks. In every camp, after some weeks, I was chosen for some position without my doing anything about it. I don't know why, maybe it was Providence, God's will, I don't know, but this happened in every camp. In all the four years that I was in camps, I was always given a chance of some leading job.

Having something productive to do, especially since what she was doing proved helpful to her girls, had strong survival value.

We always had our inner selves. This was our one and only possession. It was to guide us and sustain us spiritually through the camp period. The girls were my family. They are today also my family. When I go to Israel, I meet them. I meet my 'daughter', with their children and grandchildren. It is a reunion.

Leah eventually made her way to Australia where she was employed as a guide at the Holocaust Memorial Museum in Sydney and remained active as, what she called, "a witness to yesteryear" until the day of her death.

How convincingly she displayed the defiant power of the human spirit, a power that sustained, took her through and brought her to a place of spiritual triumph after all she had suffered, in being able to say this to me:

> I have a very clear conscience. I like myself. I have not failed myself. I can live with my own conscience. If I could do something, I did. I put myself out to help others. I did what I knew was the right thing to do!

Another passionate witness for life was **Dinah Benedikt.**

Dinah was only a young girl when she was among those rounded up and taken to the Kovno ghetto. Her imprisonment also covered a period of 4 years. She lost her mother, father, sister, a brother and his wife and their two children, and many extended family members during the Holocaust. She came to South Africa after the war to join her two surviving brothers who had fled to that country at the outbreak of the war. They were her only remaining family. It was in South Africa that I interviewed her (Shantall 2002: 192–216).

> It is such a painful and long history. I wouldn't even know how to start. It took years. And shall I tell you something? I am still not rid of it, it remains with you. It is perhaps not in the front of your life, not in the straightforward mind, but in the back of your mind, your sub-conscious life; it's there. It's something you can never get rid of, it rests there; it lies there. It is forever there. If I can describe it to you today, what I felt and what I went through, isn't it a testimony to you that it is still alive, and that it is still in me? It is not a dim memory at all, it's as fresh as anything.

In the Kovno ghetto, because she looked Aryan, she was chosen to work for the underground. When she was caught doing so, she was brought to the Gestapo head-quarters. After spending 3 days and nights in a death-cell, she was brought before the commander, a man notorious for his sadism and cruelty. He said to her:

> Don't you realize I have authority over life and death? Why don't you kiss my boots and beg for your life?

Struggling in her weak state to stand upright, she answered him, "Whether I live or die is your decision, yes. But that I do not beg for my life is mine."

So taken aback was he by the bravery of a mere slip of a girl that he ordered her to be taken back to the ghetto! But there was a greater trial of suffering awaiting her: Auschwitz, the camp in which she spent the remaining years of the Holocaust.

> In Auschwitz physical resistance was impossible. If you will chain a man's arms and legs, no matter how much of a fighter he is, he can do nothing. They put us in such a state that there was not any way of fighting back. **They tried to break our spirit—that was where our fight was.** To remain human beings, to retain your dignity, to remain Jews, and to remain alive—that was the battle. Their system was not only to attack you physically. Their

aim was to attack you morally. They wanted to break you into pieces. They wanted to convert you into an animal. They wanted to prove to themselves that they could break the Jewish nation, that they could break our spirit, our values, to break anything which is human. To convert us to the level of nothingness, that is what their aim was. Shall I tell you something? They did not achieve It! I used to take up debates with myself, or if I found somebody with whom I could debate, we used to elevate ourselves out of the dirt of everything around us, **much higher up, much more above. They could not do a thing to me inwardly**. All that they could do to me was physically, but they could not get me **there**. They could not kill my way of thinking, seeing, hearing. We were heaps of skin and bone, heaps of dead bodies, but they could not somehow get at us. In my mind I used to say to them: 'Come and get me! In me I have got all my values, in me I am above you. You are the nothing! You've got the gun but you are the nothing!' What kept some of us, I would not say all, the more we were depressed, the more we were converted into nothing, the more were our higher thoughts. **I think I never ever thought so nobly and so high emotionally and intellectually as then in hunger, degradation and in cold and in sufferings**.

What peaks of spiritual growth, wisdom, maturity, unshakeable integrity, what a powerful stand in faith that evil could not touch the dignity of her person and the beauty of her right to life, did this delicately built Jewess manage to achieve! When I first met her at a meeting of the She'erith Hapletah, a Holocaust survivors association in Johannesburg, she made the following remark. It was a statement that inspired me to undertake my doctorate research into the meaning of suffering:

Hitler could turn us into a heap of dead bodies, but he could not get at us. **We remain**.

What her terrible sufferings, both before and during this almost 4 year stay in Auschwitz, and her struggle after her release to come back to normal life, meant to her, is graphically described in her following comments to me:

Suffering gives you something, you grow. I think that the compensation for my suffering, for all my going through hell and back, is that it gave me a new look. It gave me depth. It has taught me to know myself. It mellowed me down in many a respect. It made me wiser, much wiser, if not cleverer. It is hard for me to tell you what depth I have achieved. And that is the compensation for my sufferings.

Turning a Tragedy into a Triumph

Suffering happens, indiscriminately. It has no favorites and spares no man. Everyone suffers in one way or another. But its true witnesses, its messengers, those who have found meaning even in their suffering, are few and far between. Most people just suffer without ever finding its meaning. The instinct is to escape it, deny its existence or turn bitter about it. Not even apathy, a bland acceptance of it as our lot, will dissipate it. Suffering will remain, a miserable fact of life. Its senselessness, if at all considered, will depress us, even frighten us. We fall into a state of darkness, confusion, even desperation. Everything looks futile, feels hopeless. We lose any sense of control and are just blindly taken along.

We need to hear from those who have somehow broken the stranglehold of misery; those who have found their way out of the pit of despair.

We want to hear stories with the promise of a happy ending.

"I Broke My Neck But My Neck Did Not Break Me"

The above is a statement often referred to by Frankl to describe a person who overcame his suffering through the defiant power of the human spirit. This person is Dr Jerry Long, a renowned logotherapist, who passed away not long after I had the privilege to meet and listen to him at the Logotherapy World Congresses in Dallas in 2005 and 2007. At a World Congress that followed, his wife gave me video recordings made of his life and public performances. His recorded story is called: *A Journey into Suffering* (recorded on You Tube, 2013). Quoting excerpts from it, I will let him tell it to you.

Our lives need to reach beyond ourselves, make an impact for the greater good; move the human story towards its completion in victory, one step closer, if we are to lift ourselves above feelings of incapacity, futility and defeat.

"On July 24, 1977, the course of my life was irrevocably altered. While swimming with friends in an irrigation canal, I dived in and broke my neck. The forceful impact of my head upon the hard canal bottom resulted in a compression fracture of the fourth cervical vertebrae, which caused instantaneous paralysis from the neck down. There then ensued several long, grueling, and sometimes painful months of rehabilitation which in essence has not, nor ever will be, ended.

Before the injury I was a strong 160-pound, athletically-built young man whose primary, though not total, source of meaning was physical prowess. And yet now, as I look down on my emaciated 115-pound frame, I am keenly aware of the deeper meaning and strong constitution which I have achieved as a result of my suffering. Without initially knowing it, I drew upon that uniquely human spiritual realm, the noetic dimension, and then began a journey into meaning.

Since learning about logotherapy (and logophilosophy), I have found that I unknowingly employed at least two of its primary techniques to facilitate my initial recovery and subsequent rehabilitation. By dereflecting away from myself, my immediate 'psychophysical' sense of pain was transcended. Dereflection was helpful not only then in coping with pain, but has continued to be beneficial in all aspects of my life. I have found that, whatever the situation, the degree to which I focus upon something or someone other than myself is, paradoxically, the degree to which I am enhanced by transcending myself. I would be lying if I said that I have never felt discouraged, but these times are rare because I view my life as being abundant with meaning and purpose. The purpose that I adopted (intuitively) on that fateful day has become my personal credo for life: *I broke my neck, it didn't break me.*

(continued)

I first learned about logotherapy while reading *Man's Search for Meaning* as a part of a general psychology course which I was taking at the local junior college. This book evoked profound feelings within me because, although my suffering was of a far lesser magnitude than that of Dr. Frankl and his comrades, I nevertheless saw many similarities between his experience and my own.

I wrote Dr. Frankl a letter expressing my appreciation for his book and how I personally related to it. His reply stated that I was an excellent example of 'the defiant power of the human spirit'. We have continued our correspondence, and I was elated to read in his most recent letter that I have been used as an example in his lectures and even in a European television interview. These acts touch me deeply, and I have found additional meaning by the hope that other persons, as a result of my arduous trek toward meaning, might be helped.

I believe my future to be a bright one. I am majoring in psychology, and plan to continue my education at least through the Master's level, perhaps to the Ph.D. My vocational desire is to be a psychological counsellor, teach, and write articles and books" (all of which he proceeded to do!). "But, in whatever I do, I feel that my physical handicap will have a positive influence upon my life, enabling me to have a deeper, more meaningful and further reaching impact, than would have been otherwise possible."

Enabling the Disabled

People who don't live with meaning in their lives are the really disabled.
The above are the words of one of the most exemplary sufferers that I know, Derick Brumer, who enrolled and completed his courses in Logotherapy with us at the University of South Africa. He has also given me his permission to share his story with you. He entitled it:

The Other 95%
"On a February day in 1986, which was my matric year, I was riding my 50cc motorbike through the streets of Pretoria, on my way to arrange a drama lesson for the school play in which I had the leading role. I can't remember the name of the play, just as I can't remember what happened to me that afternoon. All I know for sure is that my whole life changed in a second.

A passing taxi connected with me, sending me flying across the face of two houses. I landed on the tarmac. But I also suffered what is known as TBI, a traumatic brain injury.

(continued)

As I later found out, one of the motorists who stopped at the scene was a medical doctor, who just happened to be specializing in neurosurgery at the time. He didn't have medical equipment with him, but he cleared my airways, allowing oxygen to flow through to my brain.

An ambulance arrived and I was rushed to hospital where my chances of surviving that night in the intensive care unit was rated at no more than 5%.

I was in a coma. As I now understand, the reason a person falls into a coma is because of the pain that the body is experiencing at that moment. The brain decides to 'switch off' all non-essential functions, such as consciousness, so that it can concentrate all its energy on the vital business of survival.

Statistically speaking, a 5% chance of survival is more like 0%. But doctors never say 0% because something unexpected could happen. As it did in my case.

Several months later, I regained consciousness. I'm pretty sure that I remember waking up in a darkish room—like the room I shared with my grandmother when I was a small child. I seem to remember asking myself, 'what has happened to me? Why am I in this darkened room?'

Apparently, one of the amazing things is that I spoke in full sentences from the time I regained consciousness. And so I began my slow, laborious journey back to health and happiness. Without the constant support I received from my parents—my mother especially—I doubt if I would have been able to write this today.

I spent the next year doing initial rehabilitation, four times a week to begin with for an hour-long. Added to that I did approximately 1 h a day of independent exercise at home.

Music played an important role here because my late mother was a music teacher. It was natural that when I did my physio exercises independently at home, I 'jived' to the accompaniment of music from a radio-audio player. Actually 'jive' is a wrong word. A more accurate word would be 'wriggle' on the floor, because of my balance problems, spasticity and hemiplegia, a condition in which half of the body is paralyzed.

I believe music helped because it is controlled by the opposite side of the brain to the side that controls your logical thinking. Given the fact that our schooling emphasizes our logical 'left-brain' thinking, I'm sure that lateral thinking also played a role in my recovery, because it enabled me to think 'out of the box'.

In 1988, 2 years after my accident, I went back to matric. I passed five subjects, including three I had never taken before. Who says that people can't learn anything new after they've suffered brain-damage? In 1992 I did a word-processing course, and the year after that I went to Midrand Campus, which runs University of South Africa courses.

(continued)

I passed psychology 1 in the first year. In 1994 I tried to take two subjects—and failed them both! But in 1995 I was accepted into my hometown university, graduating 6 years later with a BA-degree.

Today I hold six tertiary qualifications, including a distinction for the advanced course in logotherapy, offered by the Centre of Applied Psychology of the University of South Africa. I had an article placed in the International Forum for Logotherapy Journal. It was entitled *Some Personal Comments on Perseverance.*

I am a sought-after speaker on the public circuit, and I believe that I'm a role model for all people as I demonstrate the potential 'recoverability' of anyone even after they've survived a traumatic brain injury. They will definitely need support, which differs in every case. In my case it was physiotherapy (as it taught me how to walk again) and speech therapy (as it taught me how to think and communicate again).

I tell my inspiring story as a Discovery Medical Aid organization member who has learned that whatever happens to you in your life should be seen as nothing more than a challenge. A challenge? Yes, provided that you are prepared to give 100% to make the most of your life, and you have the necessary *chutzpah* (guts) to make your most cherished dreams and ambitions come true. All it takes for anyone to be involved in an accident is for them to be in the wrong place at the wrong time. But that's looking very simplistically at the whole issue.

If one person gets involved in a traumatic incident, it's not only them that gets affected. Their whole direct family gets affected. For good reason, because the moment any person gets labeled 'disabled', they automatically become 'unemployable' as well.

This doesn't make any sense, because after a person has recovered from being disabled, even if only to some extent, they have achieved a triumph over and show a strength in the face of what would make most people feel is an insurmountable task. But people can overcome anything in life if they can just give it some meaning.

My mother used to that say 'when the Lord closes a door, He leaves open a window!' All you have to do is find that window.

Don't we all deserve the opportunity to make something of our lives?"

Suffering as a Task

We suffer alone. Nowhere are we more faced with the personal meaning of our lives, of life itself, than when tragedy befalls us. Life questions us, nowhere more sharply, than when have to suffer; when there is no way out but to bear our sufferings.

After the initial shock responses to what they had to face in the Nazi concentration and death camps, Frankl realized that suffering presented itself as a life task.

"How much suffering there is to get through!" he and his comrades told themselves once they accepted the challenge to suffer bravely and to endure it with dignity. When a man finds that it is his destiny to suffer, Frankl stated, he will have to accept his suffering as his task, his single and unique task. He will have to acknowledge the fact that even in suffering he is unique and alone in the universe. No one can relieve him of his suffering or suffer in his place. His unique opportunity lies in the way in which he bears his burden.

When the tragedy of suffering hits us, we are forced to answer inescapable questions if that suffering is not to engulf us. If we cannot escape suffering, we must endure it. And enduring it is to live and reach out to everything that makes life meaningful and precious. If we do not find a meaning in our suffering, our suffering will make us waste away. We will lose all grip on life itself. Then there is only way one way to go: on the decline towards the grave.

Only by leading meaningful lives can we remove "the sting of death", our fear of losing life forever. Nothing and no-one can cancel out what we have achieved and realized in life. Death may remove our physical existence but the impact of our lives continues. Our memory lives on. Who we have succeeded in being, the incalculable positive effect we have had on others and on the very course of human history, cannot be eradicated!

What a victorious cry to be able to say when our lives have accomplished its mission:

It is done! (John 19:30)

It is a privilege to carry a cross! Carrying our burden of suffering with faith is the path to human greatness.

The way in which man accepts his fate and all the suffering it entails, the way in which he takes up his cross, gives him ample opportunity—even under the most difficult circumstances—to add deeper meaning to his life (Frankl 1988: 76).

The truth of Frankl's statement is illuminated in the following account by another of our logotherapy students.

The Testimony of a Sufferer of Multiple Sclerosis

"What have I learnt? My empathy and understanding of other people's pain and suffering deepened. I learnt to be brave; having to go through all the procedures and injecting myself three times a week and surviving chemo. I have learnt that bad things happen to good people, no one is safe or excluded from pain and suffering in their lives. I have learnt to depend on other people when I am sick. A chronic illness affects your whole world, not just you. I have learnt to say 'no' and respect my limitations. I have learnt that being 'selfish' is not always a bad thing, sometimes we need to be selfish to look after ourselves.

It has given me new tasks and challenges. My life has changed overnight. I had to start looking after my body, trying to eat right, doing the right exercise

(continued)

for my MS, taking loads of new medications. My lifestyle is not a normal 30 year old person's. I have boundaries in everything I do and limits. Every day is a battle. I fight to get through the day. If I live an irresponsible lifestyle I would pay the price for it through my MS. Stairs and working full time, dancing—all this has become either impossible for now or somewhat of a battle for me. **Every step I take in this lifetime is a calculated, a well thought through decision.**

It has made me a stronger, more perceptive person. It did however really shake me to the core when I was diagnosed as having MS and that there is no cure for it. It still shakes me to my core sometimes. But I understand sickness, I understand darkness, my empathy for people has changed and I have empathy for people losing the use of their legs or their sight. The things I used to view as important are not important anymore. I can use this experience to help others in similar situations. A person with MS does not listen to people who do not have MS. We do not put our trust in other people easily since they cannot understand what this disease does to us. So, if I can overcome the obstacles in my life that MS affected and manage symptoms in a way that I can give people hope, this is my heart's desire.

The way I endure my situation can serve as an example to others. MS is a chronic disease and your day to day living has a big impact and **I think that is what counts: how you fight the battle day by day.** The outcome for me is meaningless if you haven't figured out how to live victoriously in your day to day living. What is the point then of it all? It is the day to day living and victories that change you and make the difference in your life.

This experience made me appreciate things I have taken for granted. This was and still is the biggest thing I have learnt. I realized that if I am walking it is grace, if I can climb up a step, if I can read, if I can use my hands, etc., it is grace. I do not take anything for granted and I am so very grateful for what I have left and what I can still do.

What choices do I still have? **My biggest choice I have is my attitude and what goes on in my heart.** I can choose not to be bitter or angry the whole time. I can choose if I control my MS or if it controls me. I am aware that in a way everyone has some burden, mine just has a name: MS. I choose how to be and live my life, even if there are things outside of my control – I can control my attitude and my relationship with God."

Passing on the Torch

Suffering establishes a fruitful, one might say a revolutionary tension, Frankl pointed out. It is **the tension of direction**. Those who have found their way in suffering, are those who can help us to find our way in life.

We need the *Ecce Homo*—"Behold the man!"—figures in our lives!

It is through the suffering of her client and later close friend, that Matthea Pretorius, another of our logotherapy students, a counselor herself, found greater meaning in her own life. Here is what she related:

Vicarious Suffering

"My dear friend Richard was diagnosed with motor neuron disease just before we met. He was first a client of mine and eventually became a good personal friend. The disease slowly stripped him of his ability to walk, to talk and eventually breathe. I saw him on a weekly basis before his death and when he could no longer come to our house, I went to his house, and eventually to the intensive care unit after he had to be hospitalized. I watched him deteriorate weekly, but I saw his spirit growing stronger as time passed and as we journeyed together through his pain and suffering. He found meaning and hope in the midst of living with the consequences of his degenerative disease and the dire prospects which the medical practitioners had laid out for him.

During the time of Richard's suffering, I learned that we should appreciate our loved ones. I learned that people will not be with us forever. We have to live life to the full and embrace every chance we get. His suffering made me aware of my own vulnerability and helplessness. I learned that we should not take our health for granted. Our lives are so fragile and can easily be lost or damaged. Motor neuron disease did not give him a second chance.

It was a very challenging task to visit Richard in hospital and at his home. Watching him grow weaker daily, was incredibly difficult for me. However, I had the opportunity of looking into his brilliant eyes and could tell him that there was meaning to his suffering. I could assure him that his suffering helped in changing me and that I was growing as a person because of him.

It definitely transformed me into a much more mature, stronger and enriched person with much more perceptiveness. I never thought that I would be able to ever do something like this. I felt honored to have had the opportunity to have met someone like Richard and to have spent time with him during his last days on earth. Assuring him of my love and appreciation was a privilege and an honor."

The Face of Compassion

Logotherapy is a therapy of compassion. Even its confrontational challenges are compassionate. We meet the client at his or her level. We never expect more than what a present problem situation requires of the client. But we do not expect less of the client either. Our compassion is expressed through the invitational message imbedded in the situation clients are faced with: "you can do it; your doing will prove how capable you really are; you will be expressing your person, emerge into being more of who you really are." **Compassion is the reassurance that nothing**

is lost; that all is still there, and that there is more waiting. There is no need for depression or despair. How consoling this is for someone who feels wounded, hurt, humiliated and alone!

There was the case of Mariana Pretorius, a student in logotherapy, facing yet another operation in the struggle to get the better of her particular affliction. She wrote to me about how tired she was of having to concentrate so much on just dealing with her energies so sapped by what was happening to her body, and her need to medicate and look after it. She had something very thought-provoking to say and it was this: ill, exhausted and drained of all energy as she was, she would feel misunderstood if, in a session with a logotherapist, premature focus was put on the need to exercise courage, have a positive attitude and see the challenge for action embedded in her suffering.

Reading the above as part of her submitted assignment, I felt compelled to write to her.

Dear Mariana,

Your experience has a tremendous amount to say to anyone involved in doing logotherapy. How absolutely right you are that you would feel misunderstood if the logotherapist should prematurely put the focus on the need for courage, a positive attitude etc. etc. You express the need to be held, to be comforted and soothed, to experience what Frankl called **a pre-reflective and pre-moral understanding and experience of meaning.** You would not want to feel in any way lectured to or even challenged to come out of your illness and its morbidity. It would feel so insensitive, so cruel and harsh to be approached in that way. Who can understand how it feels to be so drained of energy, so utterly unable to actively engage in doing something about the situation in which you find yourself?

What then, dear Mariana, is the meaning of your kind of suffering? Is it not a call for a deeper faith than the one exercised by a person that still has the energy to transcend a suffering situation and change his or her attitude towards it? The faith you are asked to have is the kind of just looking up in hope, waiting for a deliverance that you yourself cannot bring about. It is a deeper faith than the one called upon by the Ecce Homo technique. It is far less rational, far less analytical. It is the faith of a child, a faith that Frankl called **a core trust in Being.** Someone is watching over you. Someone is carrying you through a situation in which you cannot feel anything but helpless. It is **the faith of trust,** of being totally reliant on someone other than yourself. You can do nothing but entrust yourself to those who brought you into the world and to those in whose hands you have been placed. It is the kind of comfort of being looked after when you are unable to look after yourself. It is **the soothing faith of reliance upon more than you can even comprehend.**

(continued)

So relax into these everlasting arms, Mariana. You have a unique suffering to bear and a unique mission that is to flow from it. You will be able, once the enablement of healing comes, to bring a new voice into logotherapy, a voice not heard and little understood by therapists that are far too eager to help and not aware and trusting enough that the healing they are trying to facilitate is certainly not in their own hands."

"Till Death Do Us Part"

Frankl quoted from Isaiah 40:1 as an instruction to us: "Comfort ye, comfort ye My people." This is the approach of so many of our logotherapy students doing hospice work. One such student is a medical doctor, Izak Maree. He rightly calls his work in working with the terminally ill, "medical ministry". Palliative care aims to achieve the best qualify life for patients and their families in the time they have left together. Like so many other logotherapists in the field, Dr. Maree has questioned the completeness of the famous stages of dying as formulated by Elizabeth Kubler Ross (1997). The stages are those of Denial, Anger, Bargaining, Depression and Acceptance. Is there a further stage, one that the terminally ill patient is grappling through all of those stages to find? Is the Finding of Meaning in the very face of impending death not the final stage resulting in the kind of **peaceful surrender, not to death, but to the very meaning of life in the face of death**? Is there this kind of conclusion that somehow carries hope beyond the grave? Is there this kind of Sabbath or final rest that brings some kind of "happy ever after" ending to the story? Is there this kind of consolation; a kind of fulfillment; a profound kind of faith that embraces life, holds it close and dear forever at the end of it?

In the light of the above Dr. Maree has combined his insights into logotherapy with what is known as *dignity therapy* (Chochinov 2012). This therapy is based on four questions/discussion points that are explored during the sessions with the terminally ill:

- The telling of the person's life story and exploring which parts the patient felt were most important;
- What specific things do patients want their families and loved ones to know about them and how they would like to be remembered;
- What have the patients learned from life?
- What words and memories do the patients want to pass on to their loved ones?

The counselling sessions are then recorded verbatim, transcribed, and a new way may be used to present the counselling session results and progress to the patient. A collage may be made of photos/stories and memories that the patient can present to his or her loved ones; a story (literal or allegorical) may be written by the patient as something the family may remember them by; or even video recordings or recordings of songs and stories important to the patient may be made to leave as a "memento" to loved ones.

Dr. Maree wrote the following:

> **"Life Is Pleasant. Death Is Peaceful. It's the Transition That's Troublesome" (Isaac Asimov)**
> "Frankl believed that humans can find true meaning in life up to the very last moment. It holds true therefore that counselling the terminally ill may be of enormous benefit to the individual still suffering with existential questions, questioning his/her religious beliefs or questioning the meaning or purpose of their sufferings.
>
> Frankl teaches us not to ask what life offers us, but what we have to offer life. The curtain of death will eventually fall on every life on earth and for those destined to know of its imminent ending, there may be a no more appropriate time for the person to ask: What have I offered life and what are the meaningful contributions I will leave behind for others to remember me by?"

Having Been Is the Surest Way of Being (Frankl)

What a gracious opportunity is given those who have been granted the time to contemplate the meaning of their lives in the face of imminent death!

But what about those who were taken off guard, whose lives came to a sudden and swift end? Hospice work highlights the importance, upon our death beds, of the feeling that we have left something of worth behind us. Great meaning is derived from the consolation that we will be remembered; that the torch of our lives is to be passed on. There is no more meaningful and soothing place to deposit our lives than in the fond and loving memories of those who have greatly mattered to us in our lives. Partners, family members, especially our children, if we are blessed to have had them, can hold us close to their hearts in always remembering us with gratitude and love. What an acknowledgement of the worth of our lives this is! We meant a great deal to them, and to most of us, that is the greatest source of consolation we can have in the face of our own deaths. We are invested and live on in them.

Our lives are deposited in memory!

Is there a Memory that does not forget? Frankl certainly believed this to be so. Every life has meaning and its meaning, if realized, is recorded in a Book of Life which is to be opened for the affirmations that as rewards, await it. "Well done, my good and faithful servant; you were faithful over a few things, I will make you master over many things. Enter into the joy of your Lord" (Matthew 25:21). The latter Scripture applies particularly to those who have no-one to remember them and who may die a very lonely death.

The below message is the one Frankl (1988) gave to a schizophrenic girl with artistic talent, called Anna. It is from a session recorded in a previous chapter but worth mentioning here again.

> **Witnessed by Life**
> "Imagine there are about a dozen great things, works which wait to be created by Anna, and there is no one who could achieve and accomplish it but Anna. No one can replace her in this endeavor. They will be your creations, and if you don't create them, they will remain uncreated forever. If you create them, however, even the devil will be powerless to annihilate them. Then you have rescued them by bringing them to reality. **And even if your works were smashed to pieces in the museum of the past, as I should like to call it, they will remain forever. From this museum, nothing can be stolen since nothing we have done in the past can be undone."**
>
> To this, Anna replied: "Doctor, I believe in what you say. **It is a message which makes me happy."**

No life, if lived meaningfully, will ever be forgotten!

Unfinished Lives

The meaning of lives that are suddenly cut short are to be found wherever they had made meaningful impact. There they live on. Even an aborted fetus, a baby dying in infancy, a young child's life tragically lost, can hold such meaning. Frankl spoke about "survivor responsibility." The greatest monument that can be built in memory of the deceased is the monument of the lives of those who, in memory of the deceased, have devoted their lives in service to others. Frankl wrote an entire book in memory of his unborn child that was aborted shortly before his and his wife's deportation to the Nazi concentration and death camps. Frankl had arranged for this abortion. It was known that pregnant women, upon arrival at a death camp, were immediately sent to the gas chambers. He wanted to save the life of his beloved wife, Tilly. Upon the news of her death, Frankl wrote *Man's Search for Meaning*. He slept under a picture of Tilly above his bed for the rest of his life. And in memory of their unborn child he wrote the book: *The Unheard Cry for Meaning*.

Unfished lives may sometimes be the most beautiful.

Pathetiques

Not only are the unfinished symphonies among the finest, so also are the 'pathetiques', Frankl contended. The pathetiques refer to lives that seemed to have been wasted or a failure or of no productive use whatsoever. But who are we to judge, asked Frankl? The tragic fate of such loved ones often give those who survive them a mission to make these unfinished or incapacitated lives count. A mother of an autistic boy started schools for autistic children in South Africa. If life had been 'kinder' to her in giving her a normal child, the tremendous service she rendered in the field of autism would never have taken place. Society would have been the poorer! How many welfare organizations and campaigns have had their origins where a dire need was perceived through the fate of those who suffered or still suffer it!

We are sometimes unable to understand the meaning of some tragic event or suffering. Frankl (1988: 145) asked: **"Is it not conceivable that there is still another dimension possible, a world beyond the human world, a world in which the question of an ultimate meaning of human suffering will find an answer?"**

A Hundredfold in This World (Matthew 19:29)

Prof. Alexander Batthyany (2018) related the case of a woman who had known only rejection in her childhood but who, retroactively, came to understand this suffering in a meaningful way. The story was told to him by Elizabeth Lukas, whose client she was.

The client was an unwanted child born to an unmarried mother who tried to abort her in any way she could possibly think of: with a pin, with poison and other desperate measures. The mother did not succeed. Once born, her mother had little or no time for her and there was no father to help. The girl recalled a few flashlight episodes in her life: Her mother often left her alone in her push chair. One day, the push chair was standing on a hill and a sudden gust of wind caused the push chair to roll down the hill. She fell out and broke her leg, although much worse could have happened to her. Another time she played in the street, unsupervised. She came to a frozen pond, walked onto it, and the ice broke. People who happened to pass by rescued her. She had almost drowned and was drenched and shivering with cold.

The session unfolded as follows:

Fit for Life
Patient: "You see, I am unwanted. From the very beginning, I was unwanted. Nobody wanted me."

Therapist: "Yes, your mother did not want you. But, when I look at your childhood, I must honestly tell you: In the midst of all this tragedy, all of this rejection and neglect, it almost looks as if something or someone was watching over you and protected you. What a guarding angel you had! Just look at the many coincidences which saved you, all the coincidences through which you were protected; saved.

- Your mother tried to abort you, took poison to get rid of you, and she did not succeed. You survived.

(continued)

- The push chair rolls down the hill, and you, as a little fragile child, broke your leg—you know how much worse the accident could have ended.
- And when you walk onto a frozen pond and the ice breaks, and you fall into the ice-cold water, you could so easily have drowned, or could have suffered a cold shock. But as if someone was watching over you, you were not let down, you were not alone. Coincidence, or whatever you would like to call it, saw to it that you were rescued by people who just happened to walk by. Five minutes later, and they would have only found your corpse.

So yes, you are right, your mother conceived you under what must have been very difficult circumstances for her. Yes, she was unable to welcome you, to care and nourish you as every child deserves. We do not know which dramatic circumstances had overshadowed her life—but even if your mother did not welcome you, it looks as if you were nonetheless wanted and looked after, watched over—basically and fundamentally, existentially wanted. Or how would you interpret these remarkable coincidences?"

Patient: (The patient stared at the therapist and was silent for a few moments. She was obviously moved. Then she spoke.) "My God, I never saw it this way. I always thought of myself as someone who was utterly and completely unwanted, who disturbed others by my mere being there. But what you tell me … I cannot explain these coincidences … and it makes sense. It almost looked like I have been spared, saved, yes, spared would perhaps be the better word. You know, for my whole life I had this idea that nothing and nobody wanted me, that I should not exist.

You know—I understand that my mother was really overwhelmed by my arrival. That she was too young, that she was a victim of social constraints in her village, that she herself did not receive any support from her family, her neighbors and her village, when she got pregnant. I can understand the situation she found herself in. It is not that I cannot forgive her.

It is really mainly the idea that I was unwanted, that I should not have been born, which haunted me throughout my life. But now that we have talked about this … I never saw it that way: I was saved, I was spared.

– And after a pause –

But what for? Why would fate, with such a wealth of graceful coincidences, protect me? What could I be needed for, what could I be good for?"

The patient who always viewed herself as nothing but an unwanted person, looked at the therapist, with tears in her eyes and yet fascinated, and said:

'Now I can see that I am wanted after all. But for what has fate spared me?'

This question was pursued by both therapist and client as a journey into the freedom of so many choices, possibilities, and of pride.

For You, the Reader: Reflections

Having considered so many riveting accounts of those who have overcome even severe forms of suffering victoriously, we are reminded of the words of Helen Keller, born deaf and blind: *"All the world is full of suffering, it is also full of overcoming it."*

This is a truth, the testimony of the life and suffering of the expounder of logotherapy, Viktor Frankl. In 1945, 4 weeks after being back in Vienna after his release from the last concentration camp, Turkheim (part of the Dachau complex), Frankl received the news of his mother's death in Auschwitz and the death of his beloved wife, Tilly, in Bergen Belsen. In a letter to friends, published in Batthyany (editor) (2016: 23), Frankl wrote:

"So now I'm all alone. Whoever has not shared a similar fate cannot understand me. I am terribly tired, terribly sad; terribly lonely. I have nothing more to hope for, and nothing more to fear. I have no pleasure in life, only duties, and I live out of conscience. And so I have re-established myself, and now I am re-dictating my manuscript, both for publication and for my own rehabilitation. But no success can make me happy, everything is weightless, void; vain in my eyes. I feel distant from everything. It all says nothing to me, means nothing. The best have not returned and they have left me alone. In the camp, we believed that we had reached the lowest point—and then, when we returned, we saw that nothing has survived, that that which had kept us standing has been destroyed, that at the same time as we were becoming human again, it was possible to fall deeper, into an even more boundless suffering. **There remains perhaps, nothing more to do than cry a little and browse a little through the Psalms.**

I do not contradict myself in the slightest, I take nothing away from my former affirmation of life when I experience the things I have described. On the contrary, if I had not had this **rock-solid, positive view of life**—what would have become of me in these last weeks, in those months in the camp?

But **I now see things in a larger dimension. I see increasingly that life is so very meaningful, that in suffering and even in failure, there must still be meaning. And my only consolation lies in the fact that I can say in all good conscience that I realized the opportunities that presented themselves to me, I mean to say, that I turned them into reality.** This is the case with respect to my short marriage to Tilly. **What we have experienced cannot be undone, it has been, but this having been is perhaps the most certain form of being."**

References

Batthyany, A. (2016). *Logotherapy and existential analysis: Proceedings of the Viktor Frankl Institute Vienna* (Vol. Vol. 1). Cham: Springer.

Batthyany, Alexander (2018). *Paper at First World Congress of Logotherapy.* Haifa, Israel.

Chochinov, H. M. (2012). *Dignity therapy: Final words for final days.* New York: Oxford University Press.

Frankl, V. E. (1988). *The will to meaning. Foundations and applications of logotherapy.* New York: Penguin Books.

Kubler Ross, E. (1997). *On death and dying: Hemel Hempstead, United Kingdom.* Upper Saddle River: Prentice Hall.

Long, Jerry (2013). *A journey into suffering.* You Tube.

Shantall, T. (2002). *Life's meaning in the face of suffering: Testimonies of Holocaust survivors.* Jerusalem: The Hebrew University Magnes Press.

Chapter 11
Ultimate Meaning: Your Destiny in Life

Abstract The deepest quest in all of our lives is for meaning. To simply exist is not enough. The struggle to live well is not enough either. The quest for meaning is only *satisfied* and can only become an exhilarating force in our lives when we feel that our lives were destined and ordained to be. We are here for a purpose. We have a unique role to play. What is set aside for us to do, is set aside for nobody else. We are *irreplaceable*. Only such a conviction can remove feelings of unworthiness, envy, anger and despair. We are not excluded but *included* in the deepest sense of the word. Our life matters. Life needs us. We have an assigned place in this world. *In this specific space,* our destiny is to be played out. The chapter follows the exciting theme that we are destined to be; that our calling pursues, corners and confronts us, never gives up on us. Having and fulfilling a preordained spiritual mission in life is an *imperative* for spiritual growth towards its highest peaks of mental vitality and well-being.

Keywords To exist is not enough · The quest for destiny · We are irreplaceable · Life needs us · An assigned place in life · Our calling pursues us · A preordained mission in life · The peaks of mental well-being

The Quest for Destiny

The deepest quest in all of our lives is for meaning. To simply exist is not enough. The struggle to live well is not enough either. The quest for meaning is only *satisfied* and can only become an exhilarating force in our lives when we feel that our lives were destined and ordained to be. We are here for a purpose. We have a unique role to play. What is set aside for us to do, is set aside for nobody else. We are *irreplaceable*. Only such a conviction can remove feelings of unworthiness, envy, anger and despair. We are not excluded but *included* in the deepest sense of the word. Our life matters.

T. Shantall, *The Life-changing Impact of Viktor Frankl's Logotherapy*,
https://doi.org/10.1007/978-3-030-30770-7_11

Life Needs Us

Meaning is embedded in the very realization that our lives are not accidental. We begin to see just how important we are. There are people who depend on us and who love us. Those closest to us top the list: our spouses, our children and grandchildren, our parents, other close family members, dear friends, and down the list to people in our community and nation. We have an assigned place in this world. Duties, responsibilities, work to do, services to render, causes to serve—these are the requirements of living, part of what we are expected to do with our lives, the space that *we, personally and uniquely,* are expected to occupy. *In this specific space,* our destiny is to be played out. Faithfully performing what is required of us to the best of our abilities, despite the limitations we face, despite all our failures and mistakes, despite what may hold us back and what we have to struggle through and suffer, our lives, at the end of it, would have made a difference for the better.

We would have played our part in the meaningful unfolding of the human story!

A Once and Only

We are all an "only begotten," a once and only and a never again. We are given our lives with the call to perform what has been planned for us; each in our own circumstances, places and time in history. That call is held out to us, signaling to us the part we are expected to play. The role is ours; reserved for us only. The opportunity to play it is there, waiting for us to play it. The play has been written, the script exists. The Director is waiting. It is up to us to come onto the stage of history and fill the role that has been written for us.

But what is our say in the matter? Do we have a choice? Who is the Playwright? Are we not able to change the plot; define our own role in it? What about writing our own play; feature ourselves in it the way *we* would like to play out our lives?

Oh yes, we *do* have a say and we *do* have a choice. We can say: "Yes!" or "No" to our callings in life!

We have the freedom to shut our ears to the call. We can try and ignore it; lay the blame for the way things in our lives are on something or someone else. Or we can try and work things out for ourselves; live according to what makes us feel good and happy and contented without reference to anyone or anything outside of what best serves our own interests. We *can* work out our own destiny. We can laugh derisively at having a calling, a destiny to fulfill. We can claim that we are free agents. Or we can choose to simply go along with the flow; to let things be as they happen to be and to take things as they come. We can give life our best shot and leave the rest to chance. Why all the fuss and bother, we may ask? Why delve into mysteries, try and know the Unknown?

Another way to escape the call upon our lives is to theorize, write books about our view of things, and even teach our way of seeing things to others as some kind of gospel truth. In this way we can stay removed from any personal encounter, one we dread as some kind of unsettling confrontation. Interpreting life by distancing from it, gives us a sense of intellectual impartiality and with it, a sense of objectivity and importance. We do not have to lower ourselves into a position of having to live out our theories in the tests and trails of real life. Who can fail if never exposed to the possibility of failure, and if the escape from scrutiny can prove successful?

But the fact of the matter is that we feel kind of lost if we leave things to mere chance; restless if we feel unconvinced that we have any special part to play; if we believe that there is no real purpose in our being here, that whether we were born or not born is beside the point. There is nothing special or inspirational about coming from nowhere and going nowhere; nothing really beautiful or impressive if we get birthed like an animal and die like one, here today and gone tomorrow.

And who can deny that nothing really works or truly satisfies when we separate ourselves from a sense of calling in our lives; if we resist, even violently oppose the fact that we are being called to task? Discounting and ignoring what we uncannily sense is required of us, leave us with the loose ends of so many unanswered questions. Nothing holds or is neatly tied together. There is no real harmony. A deep sense contentment, lasting happiness, a joy in feeling truly fulfilled and at peace with ourselves, all of this evades us!

Who Snaps at Our Heels?

Can we deny the fact that we feel "hounded" sometimes, as if something or someone is dogging our footsteps? People suffer from persecutory anxieties and can worry themselves sick. What is at the base of our restless hearts? Why can we not escape an uncanny sense of accountability; succeed in somehow stilling the nagging and tugging of conscience, that restlessness of heart, the consciousness that something *more* is required of us? And most poignant of all is that we really *do* want something more in our lives!

Are we fighting ourselves?

What is tugging at our hearts? How do we explain the restless yearning after something?

In Hot Pursuit

The truth of the matter is that our destiny *pursues* us. We cannot escape it. We find ourselves cornered, time and time again. We are brought to a halt; things boomerang on us. We fall into difficulties. Everything that we fail at and that fails to go our way makes us aware that we are off course somehow; that we are not finding our feet, that we have lost our way in life; that there *is* another way!

Who can escape a *profoundly personal* confrontation some time or other, in one way or another?

Who can escape the call: "Adam, where are you?"

The Freedom to Be

The freedom to be is absolute. We have the say over our lives. We can strive to be whatever we desire to be. But how exasperating this freedom! It turns out to be a freedom to either align our lives with the call made upon it or not to do so. That is all there is to it! Try as we may, we cannot create a paradise for ourselves; make the world what we want it to be; force our own plans and imaginations upon the course of history. We are either part of a story that works towards a meaningful conclusion or we are out of the picture!

Our freedom has disconcerting limitations. It is a freedom within the narrow confines of either a Yes or a No or the nebulous and unsatisfactory: "I don't know or care to know"—these are the only alternatives or choices we have!

Our power is either something *empowered* by exercising our will to do what we uncannily know is required of us; or it is a power with destructive effects. Yes, we are free. We *can* turn a deaf ear. We *can* refuse the peculiar call addressed to us and to nobody else. We *can* spurn our destiny.

But whose fault would that be? Even if, at the end of our lives, judgment is passed on us for having missed our calling, even wasted or thrown away our lives, destroyed its very meaning, we will *have* to acknowledge that *we* refused to become all that we were meant to be; that *we* wasted our lives in so many ways, even threw it away, minimizing or even destroying whatever meaning it could have had. What is this but an acknowledgement that we *did* have a calling; that we *were* expected to fulfill the unique purpose of our lives but that *we* refused to do so?

How true the following statement:

"God judges a person based not only on his deeds, but on his success in fulfilling his personal mission. We must always feel that we are on a divinely ordained mission. This is a central point in man's growth, for there is a vast difference between a person who lives with a sense of being on a mission and one who feels he is randomly here with no purpose. The latter, many times, feels no responsibility to himself or the world around him."

(Rabbi Yitzchak Shurin, Rosh Midrasha).

The Joy of Living

Having and fulfilling a preordained spiritual mission in life is an *imperative* for spiritual growth towards its highest peaks of mental vitality and well-being. Here is a truth: We have not plumbed the depths nor have we scaled the heights of human destiny. Its intent is magnificent and its outcome glorious. How tragic that we fail to see and realize this and make it a truth in our own lives!

There is a wonderful treasure hidden in the fact of our limitations, in our being constricted, unable to force life to go our way. There is another kind of freedom that keeps on beckoning us; a promise of true liberation from the shackles we place upon ourselves. This is a *true* freedom to be found in the face of the unpredictability and uncertainties of life. The following is from a letter written by someone who experienced this kind of freedom:

"I am at the end of my life with not too many years left. How precious time has thus become—every moment is to be savored! The panic of midlife is over. Reality is far more wonderful then our fondest imaginations. Life unfolds a story that we could never have thought to write ourselves! Midlife is often a crisis of worry over time lost and not used or wasted and forever gone and how much time is left for us to do what we still yearn to accomplish? For me, that strain is over now. A new kind of contentment, what Frankl called: a Basic Trust in Being, has taken over. It is calm and happy and, in a way, more brimming over with life and zeal and pleasure and joy and appreciation and inspiration and faith and gratitude than at any time before! I feel more really myself than ever before in my life. All self-consciousness, all the stress and strain of having to be like this or that, or of trying to achieve this or that, has gone. Our times are not in our hands. There is a deeper stage of meaning than the last of Kubler Ross's famous stages of dying. In our bargaining with life in the face of death, she described this last stage in life as one of acceptance.

What I am experiencing is not acceptance, it is pure living: full, wholesome, vibrant and FOREVER ONGOING. Death is a transition to where? No-one knows. How marvelous!

The Pursuer

Here is something awesome: our destinies do not give up on us. Failing to realize it, seeking our fortunes elsewhere, *nothing,* but *nothing*, will work for us. It will be one restless thing on top of another, even misery upon misery, failure after failure, one mishap after another. If everything is never quite right or keeps on going wrong, is it not an indication that something *is* amiss or wrong, that we are to determine what it is and put a stop to it? Where does the sense of disappointment and restlessness come from but from what we are refusing to face and are trying to escape? Who does the punishing but all the wrong people we keep on mixing with; all the wrong situations we keep on putting ourselves in; all the meaningless or bad things we keep on doing? It is the consequences of our evasiveness or wrong actions that condemn us, nothing else! The injunction of destiny remains:

"Get yourselves a new heart and a new spirit. For why should you die, O house of Israel?" (Ezekiel 18:31).

Why feel shame at the end of our lives, why die with regret? Is there pleasure in the face of an unrealized destiny, in a life's mission avoided, a life thrown away and gone to waste?

Should we not rather "turn and live"? (Ezekiel 18:32).

A destiny is a destiny. It is a *given*. It *is,* and it is as certain and as absolute as the irrefutable fact that God *is*. We cannot get away from having to acknowledge this truth, if not now, then at the time when our time is up!

Did we give birth to ourselves; did we place ourselves where we find ourselves placed? Can we determine the course of our lives, get it to bend the knee to our stubborn will?

Can we stop ourselves from dying?

So where have we come from and where are we going?

Can we really escape these fundamental questions so part and parcel of the fact that we have free will; that we can think and decide, judge and know?

Can we escape who we are meant to be?

How confining but yet wonderful the freedom of responsibility, the only freedom we have!

From Start to Finish

For life to be meaningful in any ultimate sense, it must have been given to us with an end-point, a climax of achieved purpose in mind. Looking back, we recognize that this plan or purpose of our lives was interwoven into all that we went through, learnt and experienced. There was a constant call made upon us to give shape to what we were destined to be. We see why things had to happen the way they did, how they shaped and challenged us, how by some unfathomable grace we managed to achieve what we did, could come to the place where we are now. We recognize that it was not just about achieving physical and emotional well-being. A happy enough life would not have been enough. We wanted, struggled and searched for a spiritual destiny, a beyond and somewhere that would flood all of our lives, in all of its moments, with a sense of ultimate meaning. Nothing was for naught, none of our efforts and struggles were in vain.

For those of us who never really gave up on life but somehow kept on searching to embrace its meaning, everything worked together to help us achieve what our lives were meant to accomplish. What is ultimate is ultimately secured! The temporal is taken out of it. Our lives, all of its meaning, have been sealed into existence forever!

There must be this ultimate to the human story, to the story of our own lives. There must be a forever after!

A Hope That Endures

Let's face it. It is so true what Frankl testified from painful personal experience: life is basically tragic. We suffer. All is not well. In fact, without the promise of a better world, future fulfillment, all is pretty senseless and cruel. Even the best and most beautiful of lives end in death. What for? We also know so well that few of us have the courage to look the tragic side of life fully in the eye. We want to carry on, regardless. Things are not so bad, we try to tell ourselves. That is not my problem, let the world carry on the way it is without me. I just want some kind of island of happiness, away from it all. Who knows what's what anyhow? None of us have any final answers. So let's just do the best we can.

All too and most often, "the best we can" is "to take from life what we can." The effort of struggle, of trying to find answers, of questioning things, of questioning ourselves, of being questioned and challenged to think a bit deeper than the obvious and to look below the surface of the "this is the way things are" or "this is the way I want things to be for me", is avoided by most.

Far from blaming those who give up the struggle in the sole pursuit of happiness wherever, whenever and with whosoever it can be found, be it fleetingly and never in fully satisfying ways, we understand them. Is this not a temptation we feel inclined to follow ourselves? We may have less empathy for the power seekers. In fact, they most often fill us with revulsion. But there are those who reach positions at the top in terms of success, happy living, wealth and popularity that we find hard not to envy.

We turn to religion for ultimate answers and seek to take shelter under its reassuring wings. "You are safe, saved, will have heaven if not on earth then somewhere else and someday there" wherever that "there" is made out to be. Streets of gold, heavenly glory, spiritual bliss, the mystical never ending of being, a paradise of fulfillment and pleasure, a new earth and World to Come, a Messiah to reign and bring peaceful order, an "as it is in heaven" one fine day upon earth, how all of these different projections of the future sooth us! How we need it! Atheists on their death beds may still want to believe that they had it right, that their opinions held water; that it stood for something.

But the ultimate point is that we need to believe in ourselves and that *our* lives mean something in the bigger scheme of things. Life must be real. It must be real *to us*. If life was given to us to live it, we need to fill it out; give it shape. We need to believe that our lives are effecting something of ongoing worth. At the end of it, our lives must say:

"We were here!"

This is the breath of human intelligence.

A Basic Trust in Being

"It is my contention that man really could not move a limb unless, deep down to the foundations of existence, and out of the depths of being, he is imbued by a basic trust in ultimate meaning. Without it he would have to stop breathing. The trust in meaning and faith in being, no matter how dormant they may be, are transcendental and hence indispensable" (Frankl, 1988:150/1).

Trust is a surrender in faith that we will not be abandoned, left to fend for ourselves on our own. We are being looked after. Trust is a reliance on more than ourselves. This is the trust we express as to the ultimate meaning of life as well. We do not quite know where our lives came from nor what is to happen to it when it is taken away from us, but we trust that the final answers to our questions will be good, even astoundingly wonderful ones! Even if we fail to grasp the exact details of what life may mean in the ultimate sense of the word, true also of the devoutly religious, our very experiences testify to the reality of a Transcendent, what Frankl called: **the Supra-human**, called this exactly because it *is* beyond human grasp.

"Perhaps religion may be said to be ultimately man's experience of his own fragmentariness and relativity against a background which must properly be called 'the Absolute'—although it is somewhat arrogant to do so, so *absolutely* must the Absolute be conceived. Perhaps we may at most speak of something which is non-fragmentary, non-relative. But then what is this experience of fragmentariness and relativity in its relation to something 'irrelatable'? It is simple: **the sense of being sheltered, safe**. The religious person feels his shelter and safety lie in the realm of transcendence. **But for the seeker there is always what he has sought. And so this 'what he has sought' is nevertheless 'given' to the seeker—given not in its 'whatness' (as something found would be) but in its pure 'thatness'.** Thus intentionality breaks through immanence, and nevertheless come to a halt when confronted with transcendence" (Frankl, 1986:270).

Rational thought cannot explain what is essentially spiritual, Frankl (1988:111) contended: "Ultimate meaning, or as I prefer to call it, the supra-meaning is no longer a matter of thinking but rather a matter of believing. We do not catch hold of it on intellectual grounds but on existential grounds, **out of our whole being**, i.e. through faith."

It is a fact, Frankl (2000:146) stated, that "where knowledge gives up, the torch is passed on to faith." A graphic description of faith is given in the book of Hebrews (11:1): "Now faith is the assurance of things hoped for, the conviction of things not seen." This is the kind of faith, Frankl contended, that floods *all* of life with meaning. It gives us a sense of *ultimate* reassurance and contentment, banishes from our minds the disturbing feelings of distrust, doubt and despair. Hope becomes a beacon, inspiring us with the vitality of commitment, perseverance and fortitude. "A genuine faith springing from inner strength adds immeasurably to human vitality. **To such a faith there is ultimately nothing that is meaningless. Nothing appears in vain, no act remains unaccounted for"** (Frankl 2000:146).

We reach out towards the ultimate. Reaching out beyond ourselves is and remains a search. How true the saying that the destination is in the journey; in the many wonderful stops along the way! It is to the measure that we overcome and remove the stumbling blocks along the way and press ahead, that we experience ever greater clarity, meaning, a growing closeness to the Ultimate that all the more pervades, encompasses, draws near to and envelops us. We are taken along, directed and guided towards ultimate ends, limitlessly!

The glory of the journey is that it is endless! And what wisdom we gain along the way!

> Recognizing the dimensional difference between the human world and the divine world not only detracts from but also adds to knowledge and makes for wisdom (Frankl, 1988:113).

The Ultimate

> "We cannot speak of God but we may speak to God. We may pray", Frankl (1988:146) stated.

We cannot drag God down to our level, make the Invisible visible. "God is a Spirit, and those who worship Him must worship Him in spirit and in truth," a Biblical saying goes (John 4:24). We cannot give God a human face. Yet, the manifestation of God is to be seen everywhere and nowhere more beautifully than in the human face and nowhere more awesomely and glorious than in the face of God's Messiah, the Man among men, the King among kings!

The spiritual cannot be made literal. We cannot pull the domain of the Transcendent, which Frankl called *the Supra-human dimension,* down to a human level. We cannot explain God in concrete terms; turn the profundity of His ways into deadening rules and punitive regulations. The letter of the Law *kills* (2 Corinthians 3:6), as evidenced by religions that cruelly judge, discriminate against, banish and persecute, punish and kill or doom to hell those outside their fanatical pale. "The Law is spiritual" (Romans 7:14). It needs endless reflection, interpretation, discovery and embrace. God's commandments are guidelines towards the achievement of a life with purpose and destination. "The Law is holy, and the commandment holy and just and good" (Romans 7:12). It *speaks to* our hearts. It is voiced to our innermost grasp, to the inner ear of conscience. It is an **ultimate dialogue** which provokes personal response. **Embedded in us is an awesome enabling, the very hope of glory:**

We Can Answer!

"God is the partner of our most intimate soliloquies. That is to say, whenever you are talking to yourself in utmost sincerity and ultimate solitude – he to whom you are addressing yourself may justifiably be called God" (Frankl 2000:151). God is experienced as **"a personal Being, in fact, as the very sum and prime image of personality, or—we might also say—as the first and last 'Thou'**. For a person religious in this sense, the experiencing of God means experiencing the ultimate 'Thou'" (Frankl, 1986:62).

An Extended Human Science

It is on the human level, on the level of the experience of the Transcendent in our down to earth lives, where Frankl chose to put the focus. Fact is, however, that these transmissions of the Transcendent in our awareness of the profound nature of personal responsibility form part of what is an extended concept of science, that is, of experiences that are undeniably *factual;* verifiably part and parcel of the human condition.

We should be very wary of mysticisms, vain speculation and of theory, as much as we should be very apprehensive about the final answers of dogmatic forms of religion. **We should stay with experience, with the proof of what we know must be true even if we cannot properly explain it or put it into words**. Nevertheless, as it is said in the Bible, again and again: "It is written.." Truths are expounded in the Book of books and in streams of writings of those who have reflected on and searched deep into the Written Word. We speak the truth to each other and transmit it, generation after generation. Our search for the Truth, since it is beyond human comprehension, is neverending!

We Must Retain an Open Mind!

Logotherapy is a science, the science of human experience. Logotherapy is the science of meaning. It explores and illuminates the meaning of human existence on the here and now plane of human experience. It is a fact of human existence that there is a limit to human knowledge. Faith, the leap between the human and the Divine, is an exact fact of human experience also! And here is another scientific conclusion:

The differentiation between the human and the Divine is absolute. The difference is total, it cannot be equalized, made the same. Only God is God. No created being, man or angel, can be elevated to a place of equality with God. God is a Sovereign, a One and Only. "For of Him and through Him and to Him are all things, to Whom be glory forever" (Romans 11:36). God's will is supreme. "Who has directed the

Spirit of God, or as His counsellor has taught Him? With whom did He take counsel, and who instructed Him, and taught Him in the path of justice?" (Isaiah 40:13,14).

A man may be perfectly at one with God in the performance of God's will for his life, but the unbridgeable gap of differentiation between the human and the Divine, between the created and the Creator, remains.

The Divide

"I have come to draw the line of demarcation between religion and psychiatry ever more sharply. I have learnt, and taught, that the difference between them is no more nor less than a difference between various dimensions. From the very analogy with dimensions, however, it should become clear that these realms are by no means mutually exclusive. A higher dimension, by definition, is a more inclusive one. The lower dimension is included in the higher one; it is subsumed in it and encompassed by it. Thus biology is overarched by psychology, psychology by noology, and noology by theology" (Frankl, 2000:16).

The Divine *manifests* on the human level. Of a truth, "great is the mystery of godliness: God was made manifest in the flesh" (1 Timothy 3:16)!

If a truth is a truth it must be demonstrated as a truth. It must *work*, have demonstrable effects as to its essence and nature in real life, otherwise faith in the Divine is a fantasy, a theory, an abstraction.

Faith Must Be Translated into Works

"Time and again I am asked the question, "Where is a place for grace in logotherapy?" And I answer that a doctor writing up a prescription or performing an operation should do so as attentively as possible, but he should not flirt with grace. The more he pays attention to what he is doing, **the less he cares for grace, the better a vehicle he will be for grace. The more human one is, the more he can be a tool for divine purposes**" (Frankl, 1988:143).

We Are to Stay Human!

Frankl (1988:145/6) categorically stated that "man cannot break through the dimensional difference between the human world and the divine world but he can reach out for ultimate meaning through faith which is mediated by trust in ultimate being. But God is 'high above all the blessings and hymns, praises and consolations, which are uttered in the world', as it is said in the famous Hebrew prayer for the dead, Kaddish."

Since the fact that man is confined to the human dimension and from where, **and from where only**, he can experience the presence of the Divine, experience life as divinely given, he cannot and dare not make a religion out of God, one that enforces (imposes) its interpreted truths on others!

"Logotherapy is not a Protestant, Catholic or Jewish psychotherapy. A religious psychotherapy in the proper sense is inconceivable because of the essential difference between
psychotherapy and religion which is a dimensional difference. The aims of the two are different. Psychotherapy aims at mental health. Religion aims at salvation. Moreover, logotherapy must be available for every patient and usable in the hands of every doctor, whether
his *Weltanshauung (world view)* is theistic or agnostic. This availability is essential on the
basis of the Hippocratic oath, if for no other reason" (Frankl, 1988:143).

Aryeh Siegel, a logotherapist and former student of our logotherapy training
program in Israel, presented a brilliant paper entitled: *Man's Search for Divinity*. In
a letter of congratulations, I wrote the following to him:

"The title is exactly it! But who truly realizes this? That is why Frankl spoke
of the Unconscious God: it is an unconscious motivation behind all the efforts
to find meaning in our existence, whoever we may be. Frankl called the full
manifestation of it on the theological plane: salvation. And that it is! He also
clearly designated that each and every one of us, if sincerely on the path and
not in violent rebellion against it, can find meaning. But not all of us break
through to the Ultimate of that search. Frankl clearly stated that, in such cases,
we stop short of the ultimate answer to our existence as human beings.

The question: are only those who experience salvation in the ultimate sense,
"saved"? Indeed no! **Logotherapy teaches the principles of the Concealed
God.** Frankl, a Jew, devoted his life to make the experience of meaning in life
available to whosoever. His desire was that logotherapy should be accessible
to all. Meaning, he believed, is not exclusive but inclusive.

Grace is extended to everyone!

An Open Search

Frankl (2000:17) defined religion in the broadest of terms as man's search for ultimate meaning. "Once we have conceived of religion in this way—that is, in the
widest possible sense—there is no doubt that psychiatrists are entitled to investigate
this phenomenon, although **only its human aspect is accessible to a psychological
exploration.**"

This exploration of man's inherent religiosity reveals that the very *meaning* of
faith is an *openness* to the dimension of the Divine. It is a willingness to admit to the
existence of the Divine. The greater that openness, the more receptive or open-
minded we are, the more clearly can we discern what is being required of us. As
Frankl stated, the voice of the Transcendent can "sound through" to our conscience
(Frankl, 2000:60). We can more clearly "hear", become more acutely aware of what
we are being called upon to do and to be in every situation of our lives.

"The concept of religion in its widest possible sense as *trust* in ultimate meaning, certainly goes far beyond the narrow concepts of God promulgated by many representatives of denominational and institutional religion. They often depict, not to say denigrate, God as a being who is primarily concerned with being believed in by the greatest possible number of believers, and along the lines of a specific creed, at that" (Frankl, 2000:17/8).

It is an observable fact that "people who regard themselves as irreligious are no less capable of finding meaning in their lives than those who consider themselves to be religious" (Frankl, 2000:152). It is also observable fact that "man may go astray, ironically, by obeying the precepts of moral reason that, as such, deal only with generalities, whereas the ethical instinct alone enables him to discover the unique requirement of a unique situation. **Only conscience is capable of adjusting the 'eternal', generally agreed-upon moral law to the specific situation in which a concrete person is engaged.** Living one's conscience always means living on a highly personalized level, aware of the full concreteness of each situation" (Frankl, 2000:42).

An Unconscious Possession

Frankl (2000:68) pointed out that "God may be unconscious to man and man's relation to God may be unconscious." Even so, "man has always stood in an intentional relation to Transcendence, even if only on an unconscious level". Fact is, however, that "there is a religious sense deeply rooted in each and every man's unconscious depths" (Frankl, 2000:14).

Our latent relation to Transcendence, inherent to our nature and which Frankl called the "unconscious God", has far more chance of breaking through to consciousness in a therapy that puts the focus on the inherent meaningfulness of the life of every patient. "Psychotherapy, handled correctly, will release a patient's religiosity, even if that religiosity was dormant and its release was not at all intended by the therapist" (Frankl, 1968:166). In fact, if a logotherapist is a logotherapist, that logotherapist "will only be interested in a spontaneous breakthrough of religiousness on the part of the patient. And he will be patient enough to wait for such a spontaneous development to take place" (Frankl, 2000:77).

A Confirmation of Faith on the Human Level

Logotherapy is a science because it explores *all* human phenomena, including faith, spirituality and the quest for ultimate meaning, as *real,* as *indisputable facts of human experience.* Logotherapy strengthens our spirituality. It affirms and inspires our faith; makes it more real! And above all, it keeps the door open to the higher dimension of the Transcendent.

Unstinted spiritual growth is possible!

"It is the business of existential analysis to furnish and to adorn as far as possible the chamber of immanence—while being careful not to block the door to Transcendence. It aims to do no more than the former; that it do more than the latter cannot be asked of it. It practices, then, if we may use the term, an 'open-door policy'" (Frankl, 1986:275).

Faith goes *beyond* immanence into the glorious Unknown. Our hearts know our destination, not our minds! But we are here, now. It is therefore *vital* that we think and explore, search out meaning, seek to understand the "why and what for?" of our lives as it is given to us to live it right now. Such knowledge and the experience of *the truth of it* in our day to day living, *deepens* our faith. It grounds it, makes it real. Since we *are* fallible creatures, since conscience *does* err, since human understanding *is* limited, since we *do* get things wrong, it is *imperative* that we sort out the truth from its misconceptions; dispute the downright destructive distortions of thought, and try to make greater sane, rational, and more deep and abiding sense of things!

We *must* question beliefs. We must question our own beliefs! How else do we arrive at some closer point to the real truth of things, the real meaning and purpose of our lives?

What is real *lasts*. It stands the test of time and of rigorous scrutiny. In fact, it becomes all the more real. Truth emerges in inevitable triumph from the barrage of lies and deceptions, enforced rules and regulations and from efforts to oppose and disprove it. Truth prevails. Falsehood fails. How liberating this factuality: "It is true! I can trust what proved to be true exactly because it stood every test of opposition to it!" Who wants fantasy, the fantastic, the dogmatic if it proves to be unreal? Who wants to be deluded, led horribly astray, kept away from what will hold and prove to be true?

Who wants to live a lie or live with half-truths?

If faith is faith, it must work right here where we are and in the factual here and now of our existence!

"What is 'unknowable' need not be unbelievable. In fact", said Frankl (2000:146), "where knowledge gives up, the torch is passed on to faith."

The Just Shall Live by Faith (Habakkuk 2:4/Hebrews 10:38)
"And where are the great and wise men who do not merely talk about the meaning of life and of the world, but really possess it? Human thought cannot conceive any system of final truth that could give the patient what he needs in order to live: that is, faith, hope, love and insight. These four achievements of human effort are so many gifts of grace, which are neither to be taught nor learned, neither given nor taken, neither withheld or earned, since they come through experience, which is something *given* and therefore beyond the reach of human caprice. Experiences cannot be made. They happen. It is a venture which requires us to commit ourselves with our whole being."
Carl Gustav Jung (2001): *The Spiritual Problem of Modern Man.*

Destined Lives

The richest experiences of meaning, of faith in ultimate being and destiny, come not only from personal experiences. In fact, personal experience alone will not suffice. It lacks the factual, the 'proven true' of scientific observation, experimentation, validation and conclusion. What is experienced in personal life as true, is validated by the experiences of others. What is true for me, proves to be true for you also. Greater validity is lent to those things we hold in common. We are heading in the same direction! It is at this shared point that common knowledge becomes wisdom. We agree that we grasp more than we can possibly know or that we can adequately put into words. In this way, the way we relate to one another remains open to sharing, discovery and correction. What we can commonly share as a truth becomes shared inspiration to even greater heights of understanding by our ever more enlightened minds!

It is therefore with open and receptive minds that we share our own experience of issues of faith and destiny. Such open ended sharing generates rich dividends. We find that we are enriching one another's lives; that we are complementing each other; that our grasp of the meaning of our own lives deepens as we allow another to look into our personal stories and to give their take on it. This is how personal meanings begin to reflect universal values. A world conscience emerges. More and more people come together in joint understanding that enables them to develop a unity of purpose. **A common will to common meaning** pushes the darkness of closed mindedness, prejudice, bias, twisted truths, falsehoods, fake news, propaganda and slander, aside. Clearer understanding emerges and, as it does, a more pronounced judgement rests on the wicked and the deceitful. The oppressive hold on the minds of men becomes weaker to the point of a total collapse in the face of the glorious light and manifestation of the Oneness, the Unity and Glory of Ultimate Truth!

In that day the Lord will be One and His Name One (Zechariah 14:9).

A truth, even if it starts small, accumulates into greatness. More and more lives, in unity, testify to the truth of human destiny!

Arise, Shine, for Your Light Has Come (Isaiah 60:1)

Let us celebrate our shared experiences of coming into the light of ultimate truth. In my book: *Life's meaning in the face of suffering*, I have recorded a turnabout experience in my own life in my meeting with Viktor Frankl. Students in logotherapy were given the assignment to comment on the following sentence from the above section in my book.

As much as it was a point of utter determination, it was also a point of surrender (Shantall, 2002:14).

A Jewish student in one of our courses in Israel wrote the following:

"The beginning of a change took place when, during her own psychoanalyses, the focus on self and needs, just wasn't doing it for her. It wasn't getting her to whatever she might be looking for. She was feeling what was 'not me', which is often easier to discern before we figure out what 'is me'. She was also bothered by the passage of time; she did not want to waste any more time. She felt life was passing her by. When Teria's father died, here was someone she loved whose time had run out. It accentuated her need to be on some clear path, going forward. Feeling intense 'remorse over lost opportunities' (related to her Dad and her own life), Teria reached a turning point—where an utter determination to 'live fully and with care' (a directed and more deliberate life, one of decision and considered action) went hand in hand with surrendering (giving up) her old way of 'self-centered living'. This was a turning point, not a beginning—because the beginning of thoughts, conscious or subconscious, started long before this. The turning point is when a person knows in their deepest self that what occurs from here on is going to be different. **It is where thoughts become action**.

Interestingly, when I first read the words: 'it was also a point of surrender', it conjured up something different from what I think Teria was saying. It made me think that her determination to live differently and purposefully was in fact a surrender to forces bigger than her, outside of herself; a call she felt before on some level when things gnawed at her but which at the point of the crisis of her father's death, broke through in such a way that they could no longer be ignored. She surrendered to THAT call.

Living on a dimension of meaning is going from 3-D to 4-D. **It is a dimension that fills things out. It is something that adds awe and wonder. It is hope in that, if I have faith in Ultimate Meaning, I can carry out my life despite things happening in the world that are very frightening or deeply tragic**."

Pursue Versus Ensue

Candida Millar, a logotherapy student in South Africa, wrote this about her own strain towards the light of ultimate meaning:

"Living in the affluent society of Johannesburg, I have many times found myself in pursuit of being a better Christian by chasing after spirituality, health, financial balance, successful relationships, and love. The disappointments and stress have risen. As I ponder Frankl's *The Will to Meaning*, I have begun to ask myself if the focus of the pursuit is in fact faulty. How many of the aforementioned ideals are in fact not ideals that would ensue if my energy was directed purposefully? Have I fully explored meaning, and what it is that I am called for, or invited to be, as opposed to telling myself and idolizing the quest with extensive introspection and obsessive self-analysis? Finding fault and investing vast quantities of precious (and scarce) personal energy sources into 'fix it' activities, have left me exhausted and disillusioned, the results of which merely pointed to the next fault, a spiral continuing slowly, almost slyly silencing the magnificent calling of life that I crave to embrace.

So often I have ventured out looking for answers to the boredom that I have filled with endless shallow tasks, frustrating myself as I see my purpose drifting further from grasp, inviting depression, exhaustion and anger into the void. To the untrained eye, these tasks may even appear to be purposeful and what we call 'good deeds' in the Christian community. But alas, it is far from it. I had convinced myself that the search for meaning was good enough, meaning was the end goal. It is not. **It is a very important beginning, a genesis of questioning, and the inception of true auditory capacity. This is the beginning of conscience regaining its voice, and life's invitations becoming clearer and more direct, illuminating the next right thing to do**.

Is there, therefore, anything to pursue or is our existence based on answering the call, breathing life into each moment brought to us, thereby fulfilling the purpose of our journey on earth, and experiencing the abundant life (both good and seemingly bad, though also good) that ensues?

In response to Candida's assignment, I wrote the following feedback:

"What a major shift from pursue to ensue! The self-absorbed strain towards moral perfection, seemingly such a worthy goal, and the hyper intention involved in making that right and called-for contribution to life, are still efforts to manipulate life to bend the knee to us in acknowledgement and praise. We have proved ourselves worthy. What an effort! Instead of experiencing meaning, meaning is forced into existence. The effort depletes and exhausts us! The focus is still on self, on what we can get out of life in terms of well-earned reward. Where is the surrender to the call coming to us in every situation in exactly the way that life, and not us, determines it? Where is the yielded receptiveness to the voice of the Transcendent sounding through to our conscience, that is, our awareness of responsibility to answer the situation in the one and only right way it is being demanded of us?

Straining towards making ourselves what we think we should be, however moral and lofty this aim is, we miss **the transformative effect of grace**, of being shaped like clay under the expert Hand of the Potter! Faith floods all of life with meaning, Frankl contended. Faith is an act, and a very courageous and self-sacrificing one. It is a surrender to something or Someone other and greater than ourselves. That is the life-giving, invigorating, growth-provoking connection that envelops and embraces us and changes us from 'glory to glory'. We move from one rung of Jacob's ladder to an ever higher one. The angels moved up and down the ladder that Jacob, re-named Israel, saw (Genesis 28:12). This is the place where you are now! It is this vital and unique give-and-take and interactive relationship between an 'I and a Thou' around the meaning of the moment!"

We can conclude this chapter with what another South African logotherapy student shared about her own experience of ultimate meaning and that she described as a returning to the source of who we fundamentally are. It is given to you, dear reader, as a final reflection.

Reflection for You, the Reader: Back to the Source

Cowboys and Crooks

"The other day, after reading through Viktor's Frankl's writings on logotherapy, I took a break and went to see a movie called 'Cowboys and Aliens' and I was inspired. Whilst watching actors Daniel Craig and Harrison Ford do their thing, I kept hearing a sentence being repeated in my head over and over again, filtering itself into my consciousness. And the line was 'Try and remember where you came from.'

Now one of the reasons why this phrase was so spookily and beautifully poignant for me is because of something that happened when I gave birth to my first son. For all intents and purposes I was lonely in my marriage. And not solely because of external circumstances, but because I was lonely within myself. I suppose, in retrospect, I was in some kind of existential abyss, experiencing what Frankl might term as noogenic neuroses. When I fell pregnant, I was consumed with a warm and fuzzy feeling that I was sure was not just the onset of maternal hormones. The moment I looked at that pregnancy tester kit and saw the blue lines signaling a miracle, I was struck with a feeling of wholeness and joy. And the joy came with the knowledge that this little being was inside me and for 9 months I would not be alone. What is even more significant was that when I gave birth, I whispered something to my son. Now you have to understand this, back then I was a lost lonely soul, entrenched within my own self-inflicted narcolepsy. I was sleepwalking through my life. The dimensions from which I was living were ultimately not fulfilling me. Happiness, Success, Peace, Security and Love were eluding me, no matter how much I tried to will them into my life. But as my newly birthed son was taken from me and cleaned, I felt this surge of connection. Within seconds of him being placed on my chest, as his skin touched mine, his crying stopped. And I whispered words to him that I did not understand, until now. And the whisper was this:

'Welcome, little one. Try not to forget where you came from.'

We spend our whole lives trying to remember where we came from. And if we conduct that search in a proactive conscious manner, then we realize that the remembrance of where we came from is created by a desire to reconnect and reunite with our 'I am-ness', our purpose. Some may call it Source, God, Spirit, Divine Being, Love. I believe Frankl sees it as A Will to Meaning which in turn brings us to The Meaning of our Life. It's a will to reach out beyond ourselves and grasp hold of the essence that makes us 'Human'; the need as Frankl puts it, to transcend the biological and psychological dimensions of ourselves. A subhuman existence may numb the existential abyss

(continued)

temporarily. But in the end the wish to 'remember' and the desire for purpose always sounds through. The illusion is the trap of making us think and feel like we are in a state of love. It's that blue hypnotic light that the cowboy folk all stare at in the movie. It's the stress free euphoria of drugs or alcohol, the instant gratification of binging on food. It is the self-righteous gratification of following religious dogma, not because of the realness of love and worship, but because it makes us feel 'right'. It is the feeling of validation you receive from being 'famous', the giddiness of 'power'. It is the neediness of being seen as desirable, the romanticism around ourselves; the sexual high that we mistake for love.

When the cowboy folk are set free from the blue light, they are confused as to who they are. But one by one, as they meet up with their loved ones, they start to remember. Love helps raise them from their noogenic sleepwalking. The Blue Light is the illusion. And just like the moment when I gave birth to my son and he stopped crying when his skin touched mine, and I whispered those words into his ears, so will we cease to search vacuously when we start to remember where we came from!"

References

Frankl, V. E. (1968). *Man's search for meaning: An introduction to logotherapy.* London: Hodder & Stroughton.
Frankl, V. E. (1986). *The doctor and the soul. From psychotherapy to logotherapy.* New York: Vintage Books.
Frankl, V. E. (1988). *The will to meaning. Foundations and applications of logotherapy.* New York: Penguin Books.
Frankl, V. E. (2000). *Man's search for ultimate meaning.* New York: Basic Books.
Jung, C. G. (2001). *Modern man in search of a soul.* London/New York: Routledge Classics.
Shantall, Teria (2002). *Life's meaning in the face of suffering.* Testimonies of Holocaust survivors. Magness Press: Jerusalem.

Chapter 12
The Choice Is Yours: Become What You Have Been Created to Be!

Abstract We have seen the necessity of searching for and coming to know the very meaning of our lives. We have considered that we need to believe in the ultimate worth of our persons, come to embrace our ultimate destiny: our reason for being, if we are to make any final sense of our lives. It is because our calling in life is both inherently given and presented to us as a task that it has such a profound power in drawing us in its direction. We are nudged and challenged to respond at the same time. Each of us has our own space to fill, Frankl asserted. And it does not matter how big or small that space is. That is beside the point. The only thing that matters is that the space is filled. We can conclude our explorations into the meaning of our lives with a reflection on the meaning of the Biblical story of the creation. Its commission to us is to come out of hiding and to revere and embrace the Tree of Life, the principles of meaningful living.

Keywords Divine being · An attitude of gratitude · A focused life · Man with a mission · The evil of evil · Holy unbelief · The end of the matter · A monument to weal or to woe

Divine Being

> Great are the accomplishments of the Lord, **accessible to all who want them** (Psalm 11:2).

When life can be so divine, so incredibly beautiful and precious, that we weep at the sheer marvel of it, why, oh why, is our vision so clouded over? Why be downcast, so embroiled in our own problems, so pressurized and busy, that we do not give ourselves the time to think what life is all about?

Why not look up at what is approaching us, coming nearer and nearer, and make our destined way towards it?

© Springer Nature Switzerland AG 2020
T. Shantall, *The Life-changing Impact of Viktor Frankl's Logotherapy*,
https://doi.org/10.1007/978-3-030-30770-7_12

Life is a gift. That we can experience its meaning in ever greater depth, a miracle. Why rob our lives of meaning when meaning is all around us, waiting to be found?

Why let our attention be captured by things that, in the end, prove futile? Why put our focus on what detracts, disillusions, twists things out of all proportion?

Why feel miserable and depressed, bored or frustrated?

What is life expecting of us? It is expecting us to revere, appreciate and enjoy it, to be in awe of it and serve it.

A change of attitude changes everything!

An Attitude of Gratitude

The Jewish custom is to express gratitude immediately upon waking. Let us consider the meaning of this custom.

"We thank before we think", comments Rabbi Jonathan Sacks. He points out that, in Hebrew, the word order is changed, not 'I' (*ani*) 'thank' (*Modeh*) but *Modeh ani*. In Hebrew the 'thanks' comes before the 'I'. The thanks is for life, before any personal and pressing need comes to mind.

"For me", says Rabbi Sacks, "**the almost universal instinct to give thanks is one of the signals of transcendence in the human condition.** It is not just the pilot we want to thank when we land safely after a hazardous flight; not just the surgeon when we survive an operation; not just the judge or politician when we are released from prison or captivity. It is as if some larger force was operative, as if the hand that moves the pieces on the human chessboard was thinking of us; as if Heaven itself had reached down and come to our aid."

He makes the statement: "Giving thanks is beneficial to the body and the soul. It contributes to both happiness and health. It is also a self-fulfilling attitude: *the more we celebrate the good, the more good we discover that is worthy of celebration.*"

(From *Tzav*, the Hebrew name for one of the weekly Sabbath's Torah reading portions).

How do we possess our souls and not lose it? How do we foster its well-being; find a well of happiness springing up from our innermost beings and spilling over?

It is all a matter of where we put the focus.

The Focus of Meaning

"Whatever things are true, whatever things are noble, whatever things are just, whatever things are pure, whatever things are lovely, whatever things are of good report, if there is any virtue and if there is anything praiseworthy, think on these things" (Philippians 4:8,9).

We are to direct our attention to whatever we find pleasing around us. We are not to miss a moment to delight in all the wonders of nature, big and small, to take note of things we can appreciate and enjoy and be grateful for in our surroundings and in the experiences of every day. *We are to open our eyes and see what is there to be seen*, and waiting for us to see it. We are to acknowledge the kindness and goodness in other people, even if there is only a glimmer of it. What is more, we are to relate to those who are withdrawn, aloof, hostile or morose, even when they are indifferent to us or treat us unkindly, in a way that will provoke their own, if hidden, goodness. We are to see it as a challenge to win them over, the same way as it is a task to commend and affirm, respond appreciatively to those who relate to us in kind and caring ways.

We are to remember everyone of importance to us, consider how we are impacting their lives, what our attitudes and actions are or will be doing to them. We must be there for them, never lose contact with and preciously preserve our loving relationships with them.

We are to have time for ourselves, times of meditative study, quiet thought and reflection. We are to give evaulative attention to what we are like, where we are, where we are going—the meaning of what we are experiencing every day.

Here is a vivid description of where all our lives should be moving, even straining towards:

"He who injures none and assists all in accordance with the best of his abilities—he is a true human being. The truly human personality, unchangeable almost as Deity itself, sees in every gain or loss solely another summons to react to it in the right way" (Rabbi Samson Raphael Hirsch, 1990).

The Journey

From heaven God gazed down upon mankind to see if there be one who reflects; one who seeks out God (Psalm 53:3).

To reach the level of optimal being is a journey, one earmarked by constant study and reflection; an ever deepening and more profound grasp of the meaning of life.

We have an inherent will to find meaning, a will that makes us question and contemplate what is meaningful in life and what not. Experience teaches us. This is the journey of discovery of Mark Wilson, a South African logotherapy student, one he recounts in answering a series of assignment questions.

"Thinking about my life, how do I feel about it?

When thinking about my life, I am confronted with a myriad of feelings. Until relatively recently emotions such as regret, anger, despondence and heartache overwhelmingly dominated my reflections on and my responses to my existence. In the last few years those emotions have encountered some opposition in the form of feelings of hope, optimism, a sense of fulfilment and moments of happiness and even joy. The 'negative' emotions still persist, largely due to an inability to let go of the regret and anger I constantly direct at myself for what I still experience as the wasted years of the first four-fifths of my existence. I am, as yet, emotionally unable to accept the past as a treasure trove of memories and experience and still perceive it as time frittered away in the pursuit of success which, once achieved, would inevitably result in 'happiness'.

In recent years I have had to, through a series of life circumstances, make choices which led to the abandonment of the pursuits of success and happiness in favor of responsibilities. Ironically, the very abandonment of the things which I believed I held dear and the embracing of responsibility (which I had always actively avoided as far as possible) were what brought about the arrival of the hitherto unknown feelings of hope, optimism, fulfilment and happiness.

Am I satisfied with my life?

I doubt that it is possible for any thinking human being to be completely 'satisfied' with their life. Perhaps it would be truer to say that one can be satisfied with how one's life is progressing, but to say that one is satisfied with one's life as a whole implies an arrival at a point beyond which one no longer needs to strive for anything. Only someone with extremely limited imagination could ever believe that it is possible to arrive at a point at which no further quest or development was required or necessary. So, in terms of how my life is progressing, I can say that I am more satisfied with it than I have ever been. For the first time I have a sense of purpose and am able to recognize that sense is what gives rise to the positive emotions I now experience. **The taste of fulfilment has led to the desire for more**. I am beginning to have the sense that dissatisfaction with one's life is not a bad thing; it is in fact the spur which drives us to pursue satisfaction which, because it is an unattainable goal, ensures constant searching and striving.

My, as yet, brief journey with logotherapy has set me on the right path but the path needs to be trodden much harder and further before I will be able to emotionally and spiritually fully actualize the principles of living which I recognize and understand intellectually.

Is my life going somewhere?

(continued)

> While I was relentlessly (and sometimes ruthlessly) pursuing success, I believed whole heartedly that the journey towards it meant that my life was 'going somewhere'. It was only when I abandoned that journey in favor of the responsibilities which presented themselves to me, that I realized that the journey to success was going nowhere at all. It was simply a means through which I hoped that the Holy Grail of happiness would ultimately be delivered to me. From the point at which I made the choice to accept responsibility, albeit that it was an initially not fully committed choice, I became aware of a real sense of 'going somewhere'. Feelings of resentment at having to give up some of my former life were soon nullified as a sense of purpose, which gave my life direction, started to take over. I became aware of a clarity of direction which, very surprisingly, sometimes even brought me to a state of happiness the likes of which I had never experienced while I have been actively pursuing it. A fulfilled life can only come about as the byproduct of a life that has tangible meaning; meaning which can be experienced and understood. I wish never to return to the state of unconsciousness of true meaning in which I existed for so many years."

Man With a Mission

How can the wonder of life, so vast, so rich, so exquisite in all of its manifestations, so given to all of us in a world, a universe, a creation so vast and magnificent, flowing and coming from a Source so beyond human comprehension, be channeled through to and somehow be contained in human form?

What is man, created in the image of the Divine?

It is a man with a mission. He will have to sort out his life; find what path he is meant to follow. He must find his way. He is commissioned to become what he has been created to be: in the very image of the Divine. It is a potential he has to make manifest in all that he is and does and contributes to the world. He has to clear the air; to make space for a World yet to come in all that creation was ordained and, therefore, destined to be.

He is a work in progress!

"What Man Is, He Is Not Yet, But Ought to Be and Should Become" (Frankl, 1968/2006:67)

The tension and strain between what is and what ought to be, as Frankl described it, is at the heart of an inspired and goal-directed life. It is also to be found in *a restlessness of heart*. We all uncannily sense what we are meant to be like; what kind of life we are expected to lead. This comes to us as a call to become what we have been given the potential or capability to be. Responding to the call in living *responsibly,* we give true shape to ourselves: we become who we are meant to be. Our lives are achieving their purpose; are directed in the intended direction. How graphic Frankl's following statement:

Meaning is the tension of direction!

The End of The Matter

So where are you in this overall picture, in your particular journey in life, dear reader? Where am I? Where do we find ourselves at the end of this book, after all we have reflected on and considered?

Let us go back to the beginning and conclude with a closing answer to the question:

"Adam, where are you?"

We have seen the necessity of searching for and coming to know the very meaning of our lives. We have considered that we need to believe in the ultimate worth of our persons, come to embrace our ultimate destiny: our reason for being, if we are to make any final sense of our lives.

There is a call made upon us; yes. That call is embedded in our very will to meaning. It is a call that beckons us to search:

> What is lost in so many lives and what must be recovered is a sense of personal calling, that there is a reason I am alive, the feeling that the world somehow wants me to be here, that **I am answerable to an innate image, which I am filling out in my biography** (Hillman 1997:285).

Hillman (1997), a post-modern thinker and psychoanalyst, describes Frankl's concept of a will to meaning as **"a condition of want beyond personal needs"**. This restless, yet inspired strain between what is and what ought to be, is graphically stated by Hillman as **"being inherently ahead of ourselves**; our future lives that come to us in the present moment."

> "As for the heavens – the heavens are the Lord's, but the earth He has given to mankind" (Psalm 115:16).

It is because a calling is both inherently given and presented to us as a task that it has such a profound power in drawing us in its direction. We are nudged and challenged to respond at the same time. Hillman (1997:278) described this process as a slow *awakening.*

> Awakening to the original seed of one's soul and hearing it speak may not be easy. How do we recognize its voice; what signals does it give? Before we can discern its voice we have to notice our own deafness, the obstructions that make us hard of hearing: the reductionism, the literalism, the scientism or our so-called common sense. Meanings don't slide in fast, free, and easy, but are encoded particularly in the painful pathologized events that perhaps are the only ways we can wake up to a timeless, everlasting, yet fragile connection with the invisible other world, the undeniable call of fate.

Life as a call to live it in the way it is meant to be lived is a call that is addressed to each of us *personally*.

"I have called you by your name; you are *Mine*" (Isaiah 43:1). (Italics mine)

Hillman (1997:6) describes this sense of calling as "that essential mystery at the heart of each human life. Each person bears a uniqueness that asks to be lived and that is already present before it can be lived. **Each person enters the world called**."

A calling is, as Hillman (ibid.) states, "something intensely personal to myself, or rather to some future self of my own."

Each of us has our own space to fill, Frankl asserted. And it does not matter how big or small that space is. That is beside the point. The only thing that matters is that the space is filled.

> Rabbi Aryeh Frimer relates the famous story about the Rabbi, Reb Zushe of Anapoli. His friends, finding him troubled before he passed away, asked him: "Reb Zusche, of what do you have to be fearful?" He replied: "I am not worried that I will be asked at the gates of heaven why I was not like Moses, or like Rambam or the Ba'al Shem Tov" (famous Jewish sages). "I clearly did not have their intellectual or spiritual skills. I am worried that I will be asked: 'Zushe, why weren't you Reb Zushe?' I am worried that I have talents and potential that have not been used fully."

To Each His Own

How strongly Frankl accentuated the fact that life's meaning must be personalized, discovered by each and every one of us in our own lives! I have the responsibility to give expression to what is meaningful in life, in *my* life, and you have the same responsibility to manifest the truly meaningful things in life as operant, given voice to, in *your* life.

Our lives are very different. I have had my own experiences in life, you in yours. Things happened differently in my life than in yours. We were and are faced with our own set-ups, our own loved ones and circumstances; have our own tasks and duties; are given our own opportunities, challenges to face, problems to overcome, difficult situations to handle, sufferings to bear.

> "Life ultimately means taking the responsibility to find the right answer to its problems and to fulfil the tasks which it constantly sets for each individual. These tasks, and therefore the meaning of life, differ from man to man, and from moment to moment. Thus it is impossible to define the meaning of life in a general way. Life does not mean something vague, but something very real and concrete. They form man's destiny, which is different and unique for each individual" (Frankl, 2006:109).

A Common Will to Common Meaning

What we *do* have in common is the commission to live our individual lives meaningfully, each giving heed to **the immutable values of meaningful living** in every concrete and real situation of our own lives.

Will we live up to what is required of us? Do we give expression to the values that hold true for all of us, values that are truly humane, that transcend and, at the same time, address every one of us in a profoundly personal way?

"Adam, where are *you?*"

The call is timeless and unchanging. It remains and is the same in every single moment of our lives. We live in the very Presence of this call upon our lives in each unique situation and at every particular moment in time.

We are meant to be on course with our lives towards the climax point of release from and victory over every hurdle, every blockage, every painful event and suffering, every effort to deter our way towards the fulfillment of our own destinies in life.

There may be an all-out effort made by the distorting influences of bad and hurtful, tempting and wrong situations in our lives to slow down our progress, to "strike at our heel" (Genesis 3:15), but we have the greater power: the power to overcome every adversity triumphantly. We can strike at the head of what seeks to delude and get us off course (Psalm 91:13; Luke 10:19).

> "Man has been given more power over his lusts" (his wrong inclinations as a result of his misled perceptions) "than his lusts have over him. Man is capable of 'striking at the head' of lust, while lust, at most, can catch him on his heel. And only when man is off his guard will the serpent, or lust, be able to catch him by his heel. If man is constantly alert and on guard he will be able to elude both" (Rabbi Samson Raphael Hirsch (1990:19).

We are to treasure our destiny in heeding the call to fulfill it with conscientious and alert awareness!

The Essence of Human Existence

The commission to take up the particular reigns of our own lives by living it accountably, is vividly illustrated by another South African logotherapy student, Andre Swanepoel.

He stated: "In order to steer away from vagueness and generalizing, it needs to be kept in mind that 'meaning questions' come from life and are directed to each of us *individually* and *differently* and are requiring a *responsible* response". He captured the thoughts of Frankl in the following way:

There is something fearful about our responsibility:

- At this moment we bear the responsibility for the next;
- Every decision from the smallest to the largest is a decision for all eternity;
- At every moment we bring to reality—or miss—a possibility that exists only for that particular moment;
- Every moment holds more than one possibility, but we can choose only a single of these—all the others are lost—also for all eternity.
- There is also something glorious about our responsibility. It is glorious to know that the future is dependent, even if only to a tiny extent, upon how we decide at any given moment. What we actualize by that decision, what we thereby bring into the world, is saved. We have conferred reality upon it and preserved it from passing. Having done what we needed to do, the future, the next step, opens up before us. We can move on.

Quoting Frankl, he wrote: "How can we learn to know ourselves? Never just by reflection, but also by action. Try to do your duty and you will soon find out who you are. But what is your duty? The demands of each day."

Writing about his own experiences, he related:

"I have been deeply questioned by my logotherapy studies. I realized that I was busy paying attention to *real life, my own life*, questioning me and demanding a response from me (it was a phenomenological investigation—the data of my actual life experience). I was transformed by the process of bringing what was presented and required in terms of logotherapy theory in line with my own life, resulting in personal growth way beyond what I expected. I understood that I had to start living a meaning-centered life before attempting to become a logotherapist. The following statement made by Frankl had a strong and lasting motivational effect on my search for meaning:"

'You can't persuade others of anything of which you are not convinced of yourself!'

I became aware of my spiritual realities and started to discover and understand consciousness of responsibility. Up to now, I was urgently questioning the meaning of life, never realizing that indeed I was subjected to *spiritual distress*—suffering over philosophical problems with which life confronts human beings. Of great benefit to me was the realization that the spiritual dimensions cannot be ignored for it is what makes us human!"

We cannot ignore the spiritual intent or meaning embedded in all the practical and concrete, the here and now happenings and situations in our lives. The deepest quest in our lives is for meaning! We will remain in distress until we have quenched our spiritual thirst for ultimate meaning in our lives.

The spiritual thirst for meaning in life is at the very heart of human existence!

Sir Laurens van der Post wrote the following about the Bushman in the Kalahari Desert in Southern Africa:

"The Bushman in the Kalahari desert talk about the two 'hungers'. There is the Great Hunger and there is the Little Hunger. The Little Hunger wants food for the belly; but the Great Hunger, the greatest hunger of all, is the hunger for meaning."

The True North

This is how Andrea Trope, our South African logotherapist, highlighted the meaning dimension of being:

"Living self-transcendentally is a state of being that I will strive for my entire life. It is when we endeavor to focus on something greater than ourselves, and to move from self-centeredness to a point of selfless sharing. Self-transcendence, for me, is about finding my 'true north'. It is about rising above any limitations and finding my purpose in this world. I believe my purpose is about giving something back to the world. Rav Berg writes that when we are self-involved, we are blind. The paradox is that only when we step outside of ourselves can we really see: see who we are, see what we need to do, see what is really happening around us. These words take us in a full circle to the concept of awareness and choice. When we are aware, we make the right choices, and our soul's yearning for harmony is in synchronization with the beautiful order or the universe. It is when we are not self-seeking, but rather looking beyond our needs, that healing from suffering occurs. It is only in our wakefulness that we can grasp our passions. Being 'awake' is when we are truly alive. When I am most responsive to life, is when I am on my quest."

Sacred Missions

Frankl categorically stated : "I would not be willing to live for the sake of my 'defense mechanisms' much less to die for the sake of my reaction formations" (1968:11). Are we to walk around forever with a fig leaf in trying to cover our shame? Must we continue to be on the defensive, always seeking self-justification, as we complain that life is unfair or as we put the blame for our own shortcomings on others? Will we find peace and happiness by insisting on having it, by claiming it from life that we perceive as withholding it from us? Self-absorption is a prisoner of spiritual freedom and growth! The truth, stated Frankl (1968:4), is that "man is not primarily interested in any psychic conditions of his own but rather is oriented toward the world, toward the world of potential meaning and values which, so to speak, are waiting to be fulfilled and actualized by him." Driven by a will to pleasure and power leaves the will to meaning inoperative, our lives empty of values and meaning.

The existential vacuum is, according to Frankl, the collective neurosis of our times.

This view is echoed by Rabbi Nathan Lopes Cardozo, a famous scholar and teacher of our times:

"One of the greatest tragedies of modern times is that millions of people live and die without ever being aware that there is supreme meaning to their lives. Only if we understand that life is of invaluable importance—and not merely a matter of physical survival—can we live a life of grand spiritual import" (*The Jerusalem Post, January 25, 2018, p. 16*). Rabbi Cardozo goes on to say:

> "To be truly alive is possible only when one lives for some supreme goal. The ultimate question regarding our lives is whether there is anything worth dying for. If the answer is no, then we must ask ourselves whether there is anything to live for. For most people, there is more to life than our physical survival, or having a great time. It is the exaltation of existence and the ability to hear a perpetual murmur emitted by the waves beyond the shore of worldliness that give us the feeling of life's utmost significance. If not for that, we would agree with French philosopher and novelist Albert Camus who said that the only serious philosophical problem is whether or not to commit suicide. There are values in life that surpass our concern for the mundane, and many of us are prepared to make highly uncomfortable and even painful sacrifices in order to live by those values. It is these sacrifices that give our lives a notion of belonging, of being part of something much larger than the sum of the components that make up our physical existence."

Missionaries of Transcendence

The above is the title that Hillman (1997:283) gave to those outstanding personalities who have heard the call and realized it in their lives. "We may comprehend more, by studying an extraordinary person, about the depths of human nature than by studying even the largest sample of accumulated cases. A single anecdote lights up the whole field of vision" (ibid: 33). Frankl called upon us to join the outstanding remnant whose lives are beacons of light for those still struggling through the darkness in a world void of meaning.

What light does the life of an extraordinarily decent human being cast? It is the light of hope, of possibility. We all have it in us to rise to the great heights of human stature. We *can* overcome, outlive and move on from even the worst of situations. We can also lift ourselves out of a mindless, petty and mundane level of living. No matter how helpless or incapable we may feel ourselves to be, we can, by a very change of attitude, change our situations into situations that serve rather than destroy us or simply make us fade out of the picture. Human greatness is to show what *can* be achieved in the very face of even the darkest of fates; the most boring and lifeless of situations. It is this defiant power of the human spirit that is being called out of hiding by those who become missionaries, witnesses of the transcendent power invested in the human breast.

What a magnificent commission!

> "Man's task in the world is to transform fate into destiny; a passive existence into an active existence; an existence of compulsion, perplexity and muteness into an existence replete with powerful will, with resourcefulness, daring, and imagination" (Rabbi Joseph B. Solovetchik).

The possibility of human greatness is at the fingertips of faith. Real faith is exercised by a change of direction in attitude and action. It is an *exercised will* to meaning resolutely *separated from*, with *a back turned* on, everything that pulls us down and draws us away from what keeps our spirits uplifted and thriving.

> "The righteous do no complain of the dark, but increase the light; they do not complain of evil, but increase justice; they do not complain of heresy, but increase faith; they do not complain of ignorance, but increase wisdom" (Rav Kook, "Arpilei Tohar", p. 27–28).

"But the Greatest of These Is Love" (1 Corinthians 13:13)

As bearers of the light of meaning in life, we are meant to shed light into the darkness of a suffering world. On the strong is the obligation to assist the weak. This is the prime yardstick of our humanity. "The entire Law is fulfilled in this one command: 'You shall love your neighbor as yourself'" (Galatians 5:14).

There are those in the concentration and death camps of Nazi Europe who capitulated under the monstrous and inhumane suffering inflicted upon them. Eva Weisz, a Holocaust survivor, one of my doctorate research participants, had the following to say about what she had experienced:

"Many survivors could not bounce back and return to normality because they were crushed—it was enough to crush anybody. But it is because I was brought up with so much love, that I survived in the way I did. They were not able to destroy me. So many people's emotions have been destroyed completely and utterly. They could not destroy my finer feelings, my humanity. *This* is my story!" (in Shantall, 2002:152,259).

The Evil of Evil

Judgment rests on those who killed the faith of their victims through the relentless suffering that they had inflicted upon them. Evil relishes in evil-doing. It can never get enough of it. Evil is stripped of its facades and shows itself most fully for the evil that it is in its vicious efforts to degrade human beings to the level where all that is left for them is a frenzied effort to hold onto the last little shreds of life, way past caring about anyone or anything anymore. On such satanically cruel and heartless actions will rest the irrevocable judgement of damnation forevermore!

> And they shall go forth and look upon the corpses of the men who have transgressed against me. For their worm does not die, and their fire is not quenched. They shall be an abhorrence to all flesh (Isaiah 66:24).

Holy Unbelief

Eliezer Berkovits wrote two books on the Holocaust: *With God in Hell* (1970) and *Faith after the Holocaust* (1973), He described what he called: the ***holy unbelief*** of those whose suffering in the Nazi death camps became intolerable. Elie Wiesel (1982:32), in his book *Night*, gave a vivid portrayal of holy unbelief in the face of what they were forced to observe and endure as the victims of history's greatest crime, the Holocaust.

There is a suffering that goes beyond endurance.

"Never shall I forget that night, the first night in camp, which has turned my life into one long night, seven times cursed and seven times sealed. Never shall I forget that smoke. Never shall I forget the little faces of the children, whose bodies I saw turned into wreaths of smoke beneath a silent blue sky.

Never shall I forget those flames which consumed my faith forever.

Never shall I forget that nocturnal silence which deprived me, for all eternity, of the desire to live. Never shall I forget those moments which murdered my God and my soul and turned my dreams to dust. Never shall I forget these things, even if I am condemned to live as long as God Himself. Never."

What a shock of incomprehension when he witnessed a truck load of Jewish babies and children, some of them still alive, being tipped over into the flames of a burning mass grave of bodies! In ever worsening situations, Elie clung to what still gave him a sense of meaning amidst all the horror: his love for his elderly father. Far greater than the horror of what they were being subjected to, was the horror when even this hold onto meaning weakened and his concern for his father began to slip away. Men had begun to lose their human face. They had reached a point of suffering where the spirit of hope and faith, their humanity, was at last extinguished. All that was left of them was their bodies, automatically struggling and straining to stay alive.

From the hell of such unbearable suffering could only come the wailing cry:

> My God, my God, why have you forsaken me? (Matthew 27:46; Psalm 22:1)

"Though He Slay Me, Yet Will I Trust in Him" (Job 13:15)

But can hope really be extinguished? How precious life is as it is still clung to by those who are already in the process of dying! How hope is expressed in that last gasp of breath with the words: *"Into Your hands I commit my spirit!"* (Luke 23:46; Psalm 31:6)

Apart from what Berkovits (1973:4) described as holy unbelief, there was also the phenomenon in the Nazi death camps of what he called: **holy faith.** "The faith affirmed was **superhuman**, the loss of faith—in the circumstances—**human**."

Dare we condemn those who sunk to the level of mere animal existence under the relentless torture of circumstances such as those imposed on them in the Nazi concentration and death camps? Such victims may well say to us:

> "How dare you speak about loss of faith; what do you know about losing faith, you who have never known what we have known, who never experienced what we have experienced?"

Under abnormal circumstances abnormal reactions are normal, Frankl observed. How he warned against judging anyone who acted less than heroically by those who were not in their shoes! The same accusation is leveled by Berkovits (1973:5):

> "In the presence of the holy faith of the crematoria, the ready faith of those who were not there, is vulgarity. But the disbelief of the sophisticated intellectual in the midst of an affluent society—in the light of the holy disbelief of the crematoria—is obscenity."

Yom Kippur
"The Day of Atonement. Should we fast? The question was hotly debated. The fast would mean a surer, swifter death. We fasted here the whole year round. The whole year was Yom Kippur. But others said that we should fast simply because it was dangerous to do so. We should show God that even here, in this enclosed hell, we were capable of singing His praises.

I did not fast, mainly to please my father, who had forbidden me to do so. But further, there was no longer any reason why I should fast. I no longer accepted God's silence. As I swallowed my bowl of soup, I saw in the gesture an act of rebellion and protest against Him. And I nibbled my crust of bread.

In the depths of my heart, I felt a great void" (Elie Wiesel, 1982:66).

Righteous Anger

Anger is what we should feel when we read the accounts of or see what is happening to those who are cruelly subjected to suffering. Protest is what we should be expressing, not against God, but against the evil of those who willfully perpetrate it. This is the conclusion of some other Holocaust survivors that I have interviewed.:

> "I do not hold God accountable, basically because I have taken God out of the picture. I do not say there is no Creator, but the God that we understand, sitting in judgment on us, I do not accept anymore. What I do accept is that there is man" (**Don Krausz**, quoted in Shantall, 2002:239).
>
> "You would say that I am looking for too much, for too high, and too big. Perhaps it is not too much and not too high and not too big. It is the world that is at fault. Humanity is at fault. The world was guilty of our Holocaust" (**Dinah Benedikt**, quoted in Shantall, 2002:216).

A Monument to Weal or to Woe

With our lives, what we do with it and how we live it, we build a monument, Frankl asserted. Some monuments are to be toppled, torn down, its rubble removed. Others are to rise out of the dust, magnificent and wonderful to behold:

Ecce Homo!

There are opposites, stark contrasts, between what should never have been and what was always intended to be.

Rabbi Samson Raphael Hirsch wrote about the stark contrast between the character traits which the Jewish nation, as **a called out people**, is expected to realize in ever growing measure, and those of Amalek (the nation that attacked the weak and the floundering as the Israelites travelled through the wilderness).

"The nation is to walk the earth as the most perfect incarnation of the ideal. Through all times and amidst all trails, the saving remnant of Israel is to endure and move steadily forward to the goal of ultimate perfection; men who 'do no wrong, speak no deceit' and 'in whose mouth there is no tongue of deception'. They shall find their pasture and peace on earth; they alone will have no cause to fear anything or anyone. The final leaf will drop from Amalek's sham laurels only when Amalek's sword will be broken by a mightier weapon, a national entity that flourish only by virtue of its loyalty to God's moral law—a nation upheld solely by its obedience to God."

The calling of the Jewish people was and is to serve as a call to **the decent minority in each nation** that Frankl spoke about. "In those days it will happen that ten men of all the different languages of the nations will take hold, they will take hold of the corner of the garment of a Jewish man, saying, 'Let us go with you, for we have heard that God is with you!" (Zechariah 8:23; see also Revelation 6:4–9).

Free-Willed Obedience

Whether our faith in the meaningfulness of life is expressed in Biblical terms or not, each one of us will be measured by the yardsticks of our own conscience. It is here where we will stand or fall: "I lived up to or failed to live up to what I was meant and had the capacity to become."

We will pass judgment on ourselves; the yardsticks for living a meaningful life are in our own hands.

What we as human beings are commissioned to achieve is given to us in potential that we are tasked to bring to full realization. Potential is *a promise of realization*. It is a *capability* given to us as a *possibility put before us as a choice*; no, more than that, as a *command*:

"Become what you have been created to be!"

We have the freedom to become what we were graced with the ability to be: utterly decent, good and moral human beings.

Evil, therefore, is a dis-grace!

A most perceptive young woman, who qualified as a logotherapist in South Africa, Birgitta Nel, and faced with all the perplexities and challenging difficulties in her own life, put it this way:

"I can become bitter or better."

Every situation is a choice, she writes. The issue is and remains the following: In which way will you or I deal with it?

"Do not ask with shock and lament and a complaining: 'Why?' if something goes wrong or something bad happens to you. Rather ask: 'What must I do about this situation, how am I going to deal with it? What is the *best* and therefore the *only* right response?

- Calm your emotions and tune into the situation;
- Face the full facts;
- Consider the options if you do not immediately know what to do or how to react;
- What is being asked of you? The answer or the meaning of the situation may not be immediately clear;
- Make the one right or best choice, even if it is a difficult or costly choice;
- Stay committed to that choice with the trust that if you should have reacted differently, that will be made clear to you."

There is a right way or an out-of-the-way response.

A right choice of action is a responsible response: "I am living up to what is expected of me in giving expression to abilities I *do* have. I *can* be what I am expected to be!"

The choice is therefore sovereignly mine. The call addresses *me*. No-one can answer for me. But this too is the nature of my freedom: no-one, nothing can rob me of my freedom of choice either!

The Power of Hope Has Been Invested in Me!

When I act in a way that I can approve of and not feel ashamed or embarrassed about, I am out in the open. This kind of openness, the revelation of my true self, establishes my identity. I am **recognizably** myself: someone others can take note of, like and love, respect and admire. Every time I act with full will behind it, I grow in human stature.

I am who I am, relentlessly!

> "This free-willed, joyous obedience, this freedom in obedience and this obedience in freedom, which makes one most happily aware of one's own strength precisely by subordinating one's personality completely to the will of God—these constitute the most important characteristic of sublime moral perfection" (Rabbi Samson Raphael Hirsch).

To react badly: with frustration, irritability, anger or complaint and bitterness, is to be defeatist: I am letting myself down. I am spoiling my image. I have an ugly face. I cannot be seen for who I really am. I disappoint and dishearten people. They dislike me and stay out of my way. No interaction of note, no real encounter takes place. I have missed the moment. The meaning it could and should have had, is gone. The opportunity is lost. The next step in my emergence as a person did not happen. What now? What am I to do after having slipped up so badly?

Shame and guilt work regressively. I move backward, fall behind.

Conviction of wrong must therefore be swift and decisive. The cords pulling me into retreat must be snapped and quickly. I will have to move away from the wrong at a faster pace to make up for lost time. I must regain lost ground! I have to go to those I have wronged and set things right.

To repent is to make restitution!

Graced with Life

We have been gifted with life. What grace! Grace is something unearned, undeserved. But is grace what it is if it expects nothing from us; if it just lets us be, drift along, get lost or go the wrong way?

Will it never stop us in our tracks, confront and challenge us, reprimand or warn us; reason with us, even very fiercely?

Will it just leave us, not accompany us or hover over us and be lovingly concerned about us, even if we fail to be aware of it?

Will it not want to commune with us, share things with and instruct us, even when we refuse or fail to listen?

Will it not help us, send relief our way when we can't take it anymore, show a way out of a tricky situation, lift us up when we fall, rescue us when we are held hostage or faced with danger, even if we believed we were totally abandoned? Often a resurrection of hope occurs long after a catastrophic event, sometimes only beyond the grave!

Will it not care about us, be saddened by our foolish mistakes, be righteously angry at our rebellious and willful ways?

Will it not wait, even eagerly, and again and again, to forgive us?

Will it not do everything to save us from disaster, fight and resist those set out to harm us, step in for us; intervene on our behalf, even if that intervention happens long after the injustice has been inflicted upon us?

Grace being grace, will never give up on us, desert us or leave us destitute. This the end of the matter will ultimately prove.

But grace being grace will also never force a response from us.

Being free, with no force exercised upon us, we can deny grace, spurn and discount it. We can throw our lives away, willfully destroy it. We can disconnect from the spirit of life within us.

We can lose our human face.

Even so, grace does not pass judgment. That only we can do.

Evildoing self-destructs. Its time runs out. It reaches its end, one of utter defeat. But time, the opportunity to be forgiven and change, is drawn out in uttermost mercy!

The Legacy

There is only *one* way of being: having been!

This truth has been beautifully captured by another logotherapy student in South Africa, Vivien Chomse:

> "When I was about 12 years old, I struggled desperately with feelings of inferiority, futility and felt myself to be incompetent and even worthless. I was in a car with a couple of friends and for some reason I was expressing my miser-

(continued)

able concerns about myself. One of the girls, whom I really respected, uttered the words, 'Gosh Vivien, look at all you have mastered to get to where you are now. No-one can take that away. You should be proud!'

Since then my perspective began to change and I began to respect and appreciate myself more by regarding my efforts and successes to overcome hardships as meaningful. I began to have a sense of my life being somewhat victorious, giving me hope for a future: nothing of my past was lost, of no value or insignificant. It was my story. The past was past. However, I had the choice to review the past in a new light. And I gained perspective. By capturing my past as part of my story, I was able to transform it from being something non-existent, wasted or simply gone and useless, to something of value, to be treasured.

"My past is part of my legacy".

The Final Injunction

Here is the final consolation, injunction and promise of glory:

You, yes you, and me, yes me—we were meant to be!

"There is no greater distinction and no greater bliss than to be among those who have been counted for and by God, to take one's place on God's roster even though one be in the most humble circumstances, and even in the most transient moment of life on earth, to be counted as a member of the hosts of God. Only after having become aware of the full extent of his duty and after having resolved to perform it fully can one pass from the nondescript crowd of the selfish multitudes into the ennobled circle of those who have been counted by God, and attain the blissful awareness that he is now among those whom God has numbered as His own." (Rabbi Samson Raphael Hirsch, 1990: 331).

The Moment Is Now

Life is always immediate. What was significant in the past, in both the negative (the still painful or problematic) and positive sense of the word (the love, the blessings, the strengths shown, the battles overcome)—all the continued hindrances and all that we have gained, all our achievements—are right here and with us in the present moment of being.

Life is always an encounter. Right now there is a present challenge and confrontation, a present meeting with life that calls us one step further into our waiting futures. All of our lives have brought us to *this* moment and seek to meet with us right now.

It is how our pasts and our futures meet right at this moment that calls us to action.

An Israeli student of logotherapy, a most spiritually perceptive and gifted person, Haya Winiarz, sent me some thoughts on the importance of the immediate moment. It provoked my following reply.

"How we choose to act is recorded for eternity. **A wrong choice, a "No" to life**, is to retreat into the past, to still hold onto old habits, stay in familiar places of security. There is even safety to be found in nurturing our pathologies, in not risking the change that our healing will bring. The future asks too much of us. Projecting ourselves into the future with foreboding, anxiety and worry that we will not make it, that we will fail to live up to the high standard of responsible living held out to us, we skip over what is being asked of and offered to us as a step forward us, right now. **A right choice is a "Yes" to life**, right here and where we are, right now, no matter what may have gone before or what may come afterwards. We are in the moment. "Here I am, send me!" (Isaiah 6:8) is the only stance that changes us, and the world around us, for the better. This is the stance that makes progress. Here we stand on holy ground. We take possession of our ordained places in life, little by little. We increase our boundaries, little by little, until we fully achieve what has been given to us as our inheritance forever!"

Lesley Witt, a trained logotherapist in South Africa, had this most remarkable statement to make:

"Faith does not demand the final outcome."

Divine Enablement

Becoming who you are meant to be is a process. It is never a neat and easy straight line. There are ups and downs, sometimes extremely low downs, but the ups keep on moving upward beyond the downs. You change, but in the right and intended way: you *grow*, take on more and more of the features that make you unique, more singularly yourself. You become more expressively the kind of person that makes an impact on others

By becoming who you have been created to be, you gain a presence that leaves a lasting impression.

"By breathing into man a tiny spark from the infinite fullness of His own spirit that fills the world with His thoughts, from His own holy, unfettered will, from His own creative power that freely dominates the world which He himself freely created, God has raised man high to Himself beyond the bounds of the physical world. God has thereby elevated man, made in God's image, to become a free personality, ruling freely over the world in the service of God and God's purposes. Precisely by implementing this power in his daily personal life does man fulfill the will of his God; only in this manner, uplifted and encouraged by God Himself, can man render his service to God in this world." (Rabbi Samson Raphael Hirsch, 1990:393).

What will you be doing in heeding the call spelt out in this book?
You will be realizing your divinely given potential!

A Final Reflection, for You, the Reader: The Tree in the Midst of the Garden

The creation story has to be *retold* in each of our lives. Let us in conclusion consider the meaning of our lives in its Biblical context.

"It is finished!"
Man was created on the sixth day. There was a seventh day ahead, a day of accomplished intent; a day of rest: "It is done! I am the Alpha and the Omega, the Beginning and the End. I will give of the fountain of the water of life freely to him who thirsts. He who overcomes shall inherit all things, and I will be his God and he shall be my son" (Revelations 21: 6,7).

As mankind we were given work to do! There was overcoming to be done. What we were created to be: in God's image, we were given the capability to become. We were to attain a *likeness* to God, to be *like Him*. We were created to reflect His glory, His holiness, His goodness, His attributes of mercy, lovingkindness, tolerance, justice, a desire for peace; we were to have the spirit of forgiveness among us (Exodus 34:6–7).

Paradise was our birthright and our intended destination. The in between period was designated as a task: to overcome evil with good.

Sent out of paradise with the mission to correct what is wrong with what is right, we were meant to return to it in the triumph of an accomplished task. We too, could then enter the rest of a work well done and exclaim:

"It is finished!" (John 19:28–30). "I have fought the good fight, I have finished the race, I have kept the faith" (1 Timothy 4:7).

We believed that we were able to fulfill our mission with God's empowerment invested in us. We proved that it was possible.

We did what we were commanded to do!

The commission

God walked with our first forebears in the cool of the evening. They were graced with freedom. All things, the fruits from every tree in the garden, were theirs to richly enjoy (Genesis 2:16; 1 Timothy 6:17). Meaning was there to be found, in everything. They were in paradise.

But there was a condition. "From every tree of the garden you may freely eat; but from the tree of the knowledge of good and evil you shall not eat, for it the day you eat the fruit of it, you shall surely die" (Genesis 2:16, 17).

Man was not to try and create his own meaning independent of finding and embracing it as an awesome gift *not* of his own making!

Can we steal from life, carry its treasures away from where it belongs? Do we have the right to distort the truth, take the Law in our own hands and twist it to suit our view of things? Can we change the Law, even abolish it? Can we rob life of its meaning? To try and do so is to rob ourselves of the experience of meaning! We lose paradise, that heaven on earth state of existence and are left with nothing but strain and effort in a world that fails to yield to us by giving us what we demand of it!

Who can declare himself sovereign, a heroic self-man man, at last in need of nothing and accountable to no-one, his own god in a world *he* rules to his own liking?

Either we embrace life or we lose the very right to breathe it!

> Since we are the offspring of God, we ought not to think that the divine nature is like gold or silver or stone, something shaped by art and man's devising (Acts 17:29).

This was God's warning to the first humans He created to be conformed into His own image. Adam was an earthly creature but he had the breath of God breathed into him. He became a *living soul,* a *spiritual* creature. The human soul is above the animal soul. In Adam's soul was invested the messianic mission: to play his part in bringing everything in harmony with God's intended will so that "God may be all in all" (1 Corinthians 15:28).

A case to settle

The first members of humankind were tempted and faced with deception: "Did God really say?" The sin of unbelief was slyly seeking to slither into their minds. Deceived by it, they did what they were forbidden to do. A will to pleasure: "the tree was good for food" and a will to power: "it was desired to make one wise", both of which, the former and the latter, suppressed and overcame their will to meaning. They were enticed to lay claim to what was given to them freely! God was their Provider. He was their Enabler. To demand a gift and take it, is to rob it of its meaning as a gift, freely and lovingly given. What was to be beautiful, would turn ugly. Life that was meant to be sweet, would turn biter.

Adam and Eve had no shameful self-awareness before they became tempted to try out what they were warned against: not to stretch out their own hands to take what they, in their provoked lust, were given to preserve and uphold.

Man does not live by bread alone but by every word that proceeds from the mouth of God (Matthew 4:4).

Rejecting God's loving injunction to uphold a godly way of life, the first human couple became partakers in what was to poison their existence with a sense of shame. Not only did they have to hide away from scrutiny and self-defensively justify their guilty actions, but they also became alienated from one another.

The blame game began!

Once trapped by the lure of the illicit, lying at the door, waiting for entry and the destruction of what Frankl called a Basic Trust in Being, there would be the loss of the spontaneous and innocent joy in living. Fear and doubt, disillusionment and resentment, would enter the picture and mar a sense of well-being.

Was that the dismal end of the matter? Or was it the beginning of our human story? No, it was not an end but a beginning: the beginning of the story of redemption! Death, the inevitable result of disconnecting from God, the very Source of our lives, was to be swallowed up in victory! God's intent for our perfection, our achieved and total oneness with Him, with one another and with our world, was there from the very beginning. We may have brought the suffering consequences of our wrongdoing upon our own heads. But that very suffering was meant to instruct and not to destroy us.

Adam and Eve were enwrapped by God's love. Their exposed nakedness was covered by the skins of a slain, a Sacrificial Lamb before they were sent out of paradise. Their sins were covered by forgiveness! The promise of redemption was that they would be carried through all their sufferings, chastised and refined through it, towards the ultimate end of the victory of overcoming everything that caused them to stumble and lose their way!

The Tree of Life

In the very midst of the garden, the paradise state of being, was the Tree of Life. **Central to human existence are the Laws of meaningful living, the instructions about what should and should not be, what we should and should not do. Taking these injunctions to heart, we gain wisdom and understanding—we grasp the very meaning of life!**

The Lord will magnify the Law and make it great and glorious. It is a tree of life for those who grasp (truly understand) it and happy are all who retain her. Its ways are ways of pleasantness and all its paths are peace (Isaiah 42:21; Proverbs 3:17, 18).

It may have been a Tree whose instruction we have spurned, whose knowledge of what is good and what is evil we may have distorted and failed to give heed to. But it is a Tree that is untouchable. The meaning of life is indestructible. Its injunction to wholeheartedly say: "Yes!" to life and an absolute: "No!" to what harms and destroys it, is forever held out to us.

We can be born again!

> God placed Cherubim at the east of the Garden of Eden, and a flaming sword which turned every way, to guard the way to the tree of life (Genesis 3:24).

Cherubim, the second highest order of angels, are distinguished by the faculty of knowledge. They rank just below the seraphim, the highest order of angels, angels of a warm, loving nature. The sword and the cherubim, symbols of affliction and divine revelation, were set at the entrance to paradise, not to keep us out, but **to guard the way to the Tree of Life!**

The way back to our originally intended paradise existence on earth is not lost to us. We find that way back through the instruction of affliction: the painful consequences of wrongdoing and evil in the world and divine revelation: a heightened understanding of meaningful and conscientious living.

The set-out journey

Evil is to be overcome in this world. Its prominence is not to endure, however boastfully those who have chosen its ways may still strut the earth:

> Why do you boast in evil, O mighty man? **The goodness of God endures continually.** Your tongue devises destruction, like a sharp razor, working deceitfully. You love evil more than good, and lying rather than speaking righteousness. You love all devouring words, you deceitful tongue. God shall likewise destroy you forever; He shall take you away, and pluck you out of your dwelling place. **But I am like an olive tree flourishing in the house of God; I trust in God's unfailing love for ever and ever** (Psalm 52:1–5;8, 9).

We are on a commissioned journey: "To him who overcomes, I will give to eat from the Tree of Life, which is in the midst of the paradise of God" (Revelations 2:7).

Adam's fall was his moment of grace! It paved the way to repentance, a deepened awareness of right living: "Blessed are those who do God's commandments that they may have the right to the Tree of Life, and may enter through the gates of the city" (Revelations 22:14).

Innocence is to become holy: instructed and wise, able to overcome, stand up against and refute evil.

A final stand

We are fed so many false facts; there are so many lying tongues out there in the world and more so now than ever. But why? Is it because the truth is dawning in ever brighter light?

> Arise, shine, for your light has come and the glory of the Lord is risen upon you (Isaiah 60:1).

> Who can resist this kind of light? Who can stop the sun from rising? How fake and, therefore, incredibly weak and puny is the lie which, after all, is nothing but a twisting or a hiding of, or a futile attack on the truth. It has no solid ground to stand on!
>
> We have to preserve our minds; keep it lucid and clear. We are to take our stand in not letting any lying distortion of the truth of human dignity and worth, of the sacred beauty and meaning of life, enter our minds and poison our thinking.
>
>> Remove from me the way of falsehood, and graciously endow me with Your Law. I have chosen the way of faith, I have submitted to Your judgements. I clung to Your testimonies, O Lord, do not put me to shame! I will run on the way of Your commandments, when You will broaden my understanding. **Teach me, O Lord, the way of Your statutes, and I will cherish it step by step**. Make me understand so that I may cherish Your Law, and I shall observe it with all my heart. **Lead me on the trail of Your commandments, for that is my desire**. Incline my heart toward Your testimonies and not to covetousness. Avert my eyes from seeing futility, through Your ways preserve me. Fulfill Your promise to your servant, regarding fear of You. My life is always at risk, but I did not forget Your Law. The wicked laid a snare for me, but I did not stray from Your precepts. Your testimonies are my eternal heritage, for they are the joy of my heart. **I have inclined my heart to perform Your statues, forever, to the utmost** (Psalm 119:29–38, 109–112).

Postscript

Thank you, dear reader, for sharing all the thoughts set out in this book with me. Having come this far, you and I are well on our destined way!

References

Berkovits, E. (1970). *With God in Hell*. New York: Ktav Publishing House.

Berkovits, E. (1973). *Faith after the Holocaust*. New York: Ktav Publishing House.

Frankl, V.E. (1968, 2006). Man's search for meaning: An introduction to logotherapy. London: Hodder & Stroughton.

Hillman, J. (1997). *The soul's code: In search of character and calling*. Great Britain: Bantam Books.

Hirsch, S. R. (1990). *The Hirsch commentary: The Pentateuch*. New York: The Judaica Press, Inc.

Shantall, T. (2002). *Life's meaning in the face of suffering. The testimony of Holocaust survivors*. Jerusalem: The Hebrew University Magnes Press.

Wiesel, E. (1982). *Night*. New York: Bantam Books.

References

Batthyani, A. (2016). *Logotherapy and Existential Analysis: Proceedings of the Viktor Frankl Institute Vienna* (Vol. 1). Cham: Springer.

Batthyany, A. (2018). *Paper at First World Congress of Logotherapy*. Haifa, Israel.

Berkovits, E. (1970). *With God in Hell*. New York: Ktav Publishing House, Inc.

Berkovits, E. (1973). *Faith after the Holocaust*. New York: Ktav Publishing House, Inc.

Bettelheim, B. (1967). *The Empty Fortress: Infantile Autism and the birth of self*. New York: The Free Press.

Bowlby, J. (1967a). *Maternal care and mental health*. New York: Schocken Books.

Bowlby, J. (1967b). *Child care and the growth of love*. London: Whitefriars.

Bowlby, J. (1969). *Attachment and loss. Volume 1: Attachment*. London: The Hogarth Press.

Buber, M. (1958). *I and Thou*. New York: Scribner.

Cantello, M. (2004). *Communing with music*. Los Angeles: Devorss and Company.

Cavalletti, S. (1992). *The religious potential of the child*. Chicago: Cathechesis of the Good Shepherd Publications.

Chochinov, H. M. (2012). *Dignity therapy: Final words for final days*. New York: Oxford University Press.

Crumbaugh, J. C., & Henrion, R. (1994). The Ecce homo technique: A special case of dereflection. *International Forum for logotherapy, 17*, 1.

DesLauriers, A. M., & Carlson, C. F. (1969). *Your child is asleep: Early Infantile Autism*. Homewood: The Dorsey Press.

Frankl, V. E. (1958). The will to meaning. *Journal of Pastoral Care, 12*, 82–88.

Frankl, V. E. (1967). *Psychotherapy and existentialism. Selected papers on logotherapy*. New York: Simon and Schuster.

Frankl, V. E. (1968). *Man's search for meaning: An introduction to logotherapy*. London: Hodder & Stroughton.

Frankl, V. E. (1985). *The unheard cry for meaning: Psychotherapy and theology*. New York: Simon and Schuster.

Frankl, V. E. (1986). *The doctor and the soul. From psychotherapy to logotherapy*. New York: Vintage Books.

Frankl, V. E. (1988). *The will to meaning. Foundations and applications of logotherapy*. New York: Penguin Books.

Frankl, V. E. (1997). *Viktor Frankl Recollections: an autobiography*. New York: Plenum Press.

Frankl, V. E. (2000). *Man's search for ultimate meaning*. New York: Basic Books.

Frankl, V. E. (2004). *On the theory and therapy of mental disorders: An introduction to logotherapy and existential analysis*. New York: Brunnner-Routledge.

Frankl, V. E. (2006). *Man's search for meaning*. Boston: Beacon Press.

© Springer Nature Switzerland AG 2020
T. Shantall, *The Life-changing Impact of Viktor Frankl's Logotherapy*,
https://doi.org/10.1007/978-3-030-30770-7

Freud, S. (1927). *The future of an illusion: The standard edition* (Vol. XXI). London: Hogarth Press.

Freud, S. (1930). *Civilization and its discontents: The standard edition* (Vol. XXI). London: Hogarth Press.

Freud, S. (1971). *Introductory lectures on psychoanalysis. The complete introductory lectures on psychoanalysis*. Oxford: Alden Press.

Fugard, A. (1984). *The road to Mecca*. Cape Town: Fugard Theatre Production.

Krasko, G. (2004). *The unbearable boredom of being: A crisis of meaning in America*. New York: Universe Press.

Jones, E. (1967). *The life and work of Sigmund Freud*. London: Penguin Books.

Hillman, J. (1997). *The soul's code: In search of character and calling*. Great Britain: Bantam Books.

Hitler, A. (1992). *Mein Kampf*. London: Pimlico.

Hirsch, S. R. (1990). *The Hirsch commentary: The Pentateuch*. New York: The Judaica Press, Inc.

Keller, H. (1933). Three days to see. *The Atlantic Monthly, 151(1)*, 35–42.

Koren Siddur. (2010). Jerusalem: Koren Publishers.

Krauthammer, C. (2015). *Things that matter: Three decades of passions, pastimes and politics*. New York: Crown Forum.

Kubler Ross, E. (1997). *On death and dying*. Hemel Hempstead: Prentice Hall.

Long, J. (2013). *A Journey into suffering*. You Tube.

Leslie, R. C. (1965). *Jesus and logotherapy*. New York: Abingdon Press.

Leslie, R. C. (1994). Frankl's case of Elfriede G. *International Forum for Logotherapyy, 17(2)*, 114–120.

Lukas, E. (2000). *Logotherapy textbook: Meaning-centered psychotherapy*. Toronto: Liberty Press.

Lusseyran, J. (2006). *And there was light*. Canada: Morning Light Press.

Miller, A. (1988). *The drama of being a child and the search for the true self*. London: Virago Press.

Montessori, M. (1964). *The Montessori method*. New York: Schoken Books.

Montessori, M. (1996). *The discovery of the child*. Madras: Kalakshetra Press.

Montessori, M. (1974). *Education for a new world*. Madras: Kalakshetra Press.

Montessori, M. (1992). *The secret of childhood*. Orient Longman Ltd: Mumbai.

Montessori, M. (2006). *The child, society and the world: Unpublished speeches and writings*. Oxford: Cleo Press.

Moore, C. (1998). The use of visible metaphor in logotherapy. *The International Forum for Logotherapy, 21(2)*, 85–90.

Pattakos, A. (2010). *Prisoners of our thoughts*. San Francisco: Berrett-Koehler Publishers, Inc.

Pattison, S. (2000). *Shame: Theory, therapy, theology*. Cambridge: Cambridge University Press.

Sacks, J. (2000). *A letter in the scroll*. New York: Free Press.

Shantall, T. (2002). *Life's earning in the face of suffering: Testimonies of Holocaust survivors*. Jerusalem: The Hebrew University Magnes Press.

Shantall, T. (2003). *The quest for destiny: A logotherapeutic guide to meaning-centered living, therapy and counselling*. Pretoria: University of South Africa Press.

Spiro, K. (2002). *World perfect: The Jewish impact on civilization*. Bookdepository.com.

Wiesel, E. (1982). *Night*. New York: Bantam Books.

Wistrich, R. S. (1983). Antisemitism as a 'radical' ideology in the 19th century. *The Jerusalem Quarterly, 28*, 83–94.

Wistrich, R. (1991). *Antisemitism: The longest hatred*. New York: Pantheon Books.

Wistrich, R. (2010). *A lethal obsession*. New York: Random House.

YouTube: *The life and times of Charles Krauthammer.* https://ww.youtube.com/watch?v=pH5yZxCvNOs

Consulted Sources

Ainsworth, M. D. (1967). The effects of maternal deprivation. In M. D. Ainsworth, R. G. Andry, H. F. Harlow, S. Lebovici, M. Mead, D. G. Prugh, & B. Wootton (Eds.), *Deprivation of maternal care: A reassessment of its effects* (pp. 289–351). New York: Schoken Books.

Allport, J. S. (1961). *Pattern and growth in personality*. New York: Holt, Rinehart & Winston.

Allport, G. W. (1966). *Becoming: Basic considerations for a psychology of personality*. New Haven: Yale University Press.

Allport, G. W. (1971). *The individual and his religion: A psychological interpretation*. New York: Macmillan.

Allport, G. W. (1979). *The nature of prejudice*. Reading: Adison-Wesley.

Bowlby, J. (1967a). *Child care and the growth of love*. Middlesex: Penguin Books.

Bowlby, J. (1967b). *Maternal care and mental health*. New York: Schocken Books.

Bowlby, J. (1969). *Attachment and loss*. London: The Hogarth Press.

Bugental, J. F. T. (1965). *The search for authenticity: An existential-analytic approach*. New York: Holt, Rinehart & Winston.

Bugental, J. F. T. (1972). The challenge that is man. In J. F. T. Bugental (Ed.), *Challenges of humanistic psychology* (pp. 5–11). New York: Mc Graw Hill.

Bulka, R. P. (1972a). Logotherapy and Judaism: Some philosophical comparisons. *Tradition, 12*, 72–89.

Bulka, R. P. (1972b). Logotherapy and Judaism. *Jewish Spectator, 37*(37), 17–19.

Bulka, R. P. (1974). Death in life: Talmudic and logotherapeutic affirmations. *Humanitas, 1*, 33–42.

Bulka, R. P. (1975a). Logotherapy as a response to the Holocaust. *Tradition, 15*, 89–96.

Bulka, R. P. (1975b). Logotherapy and Talmudic Judaism. *Journal of Religion and Health, 14*(4), 277–283.

Bulka, R. P. (1977). Logotherapy and the Talmud on suffering: Clinical and meta-clinical perspective. *Journal of Psychology and Judaism, 2*(1), 31–44.

Bulka, R. P. (1979). *The quest for ultimate meaning: Principles and applications of logotherapy*. New York: Philosophical Library.

Bulka, R. P. (1980). Frankl's impact on Jewish life and thought. *International Forum for Logotherapy, 2*(3), 41–43.

Crous, F., Havenga-Coetzer, A. A., & Van den Heever, G. (1997). *On the way to meaning: Essays in remembrance of Viktor Frankl*. Western Cape: National Commercial Printers.

Crumbaugh, J. C. (1979). Logotherapy as a bridge between religion and psychotherapy. *Journal of Religion and Health, 18, 188–191*.

Crumbaugh, J. C., & Henrion, R. P. (2004). *The power of meaningful intimacy: Key to successful relationships*. USA: Xlibris Corporation.

Dawidowicz, L. S. (1975). *The war against the Jews: 1033-1945*. New York: Holt, Rinehart & Winston.

Des Pres, T. (1976). *The survivor: An anatomy of life in the death camps*. New York: Oxford University Press.

Dimont, M. I. (1962). *Jews, God and history*. New York: Signet Books.

Dimont, M. I. (1973). *The indestructible Jews*. New York: New American Library.

Dimsdale, J. E. (1980). The coping behavior of Nazi concentration camp survivors. In J. E. Dimsdale (Ed.), *Survivors, victims, and perpetrators: Essays on the Nazi Holocaust* (pp. 163–174). New York: Hemisphere.

Erikson, E. H. (1974). *Identity: Youth and crisis*. London: Faber & Faber.

Erikson, E. H. (1977). *Childhood and society*. New York: Norton.

Erikson, E. H. (1981). *Identity and the life cycle*. New York: International University Press.

Fabry, J. (1988). *Guideposts to meaning: Discovering what really matters*. Oakland: New Harbinger Publications.

Fabry, J. B. (1987). *The pursuit of meaning*. Berkeley: Institute of Logotherapy Press.

Fabry, J. B. (2013). *The pursuit of meaning: Viktor Frankl, logotherapy, and life*. Charlottesville: Purpose Research.

Fravell, J. H. (1963). *The developmental psychology of Jean Piaget*. Toronto: D. Van Nostrand Company, Inc.

Frankl, V. E. (1960). Beyond self-actualization and self-expression. *Journal of Existential Psychiatry, 1*, 1–17.

Frankl, V. E. (1962a). Logotherapy and the challenge of suffering. *Pastoraql Psychology, 8*, 25–28.

Frankl, V. E. (1962b). Psychiatry and man's quest for meaning. *Journal of Religion and Health, 1*, 93–103.

Frankl, V. E. (1966a). Logotherapy and existential analysis: A review. *American Journal of Psychotherapy, 20*, 252–260.

Frankl, V. E. (1966b). Self-transcendence as a human phenomena. *Journal of Humanistic Psychology, 6*(2), 97–104.

Frankl, V. E. (1974). Logotherapeutic approach to personality. In W. S. Sahakian (Ed.), *Psychology of personality: Readings in theory* (Vol. 99, pp. 184–203). Chicago: Rand McNally.

Frankl, V. E. (2010). *The feeling of meaninglessness*. Princeton: Marquette University Press.

Freud, S. (1961). *Beyond the pleasure principle*. London: The Hogarth Press.

Freud, S. (1968). *Civilization, was and death*. London: The Hogarth Press.

Freud, S. (1985). *Volume 13: The origins of religion*. Middlesex: Penguin Books.

Fromm, E. (1966). *The art of loving*. London: Unwin Books.

Fromm, E. (1967). *Psychoanalysis and religion*. London: Yale University Press.

Hadfield, J. A. (1964). *Psychology and morals*. London: Methuen and Co. Ltd.

Harlow, H. F. (1958). The nature of love. *American Psychologist, 13*, 673–685.

Harlow, H. F. (1967). The maternal affectional system. In *Determinants of infant behavior II*. London: Methuen.

Heidegger, M. (1962). *Being and time*. New York: Harper & Row.

Hirsch, S. M. (1969). *The nineteen letters*. Jerusalem: Feldheim Publishers.

Hussserl, E. (1970). *The crisis of European sciences and transcendental phenomenology: An introduction to phenomenological philosophy*. Evanston: Northwestern University Press.

Jaffe, D. T. (1985). Self-renewal: Persosnal transformation following extreme trauma. *Journal of Humanistic Psychology, 25*(4), 99–124.

Jaspers, K. (1961). *The future of mankind*. Chicago: The University of Chicago Press.

Jacobson, S. (1995). *Toward a meaningful life: The wisdom of the Sages*. New York: William Morrow.

Kant, I. (1959). *Critique of pure reason*. London: J.M. Dent & Sons Ltd.

Kierkegaard, S. (1980). *The sickness unto death*. Princeton: Princeton University Press.

Lukas, E. (2015). *The therapist and the soul: From fate to freedom*. Charlotessville: Purpose Research.

Lukas, E. (1986). *Meaningful living: Logotherapeutic guide to health*. New York: Grove Press.

Lukas, E. (2014). *Meaning in suffering: Comfort in crisis through logotherapy*. Charlottesville: Purpose Research.

Jung, C. G. (1969). *Psychology and religion*. London: Yale University Press.

Klein, M., Heimann, P., Isaacs, S., & Riviere, J. (1952). *Developments in psychoanalysis*. London: The Hogarth Press.

Klein, M. (1957). *Envy and gratitude: A study of unconscious sources*. London: Tavistock Publications.

Klein, M. (1963). *Our adult world and other essays*. London: William Heinemann.

Laing, R. D. (1965). *The divided self: An existential study in sanity and madness*. Middlesex: Penguin Books.

Marshall, M., & Marshall, E. (2012). *Logotherapy revisited: Review of the tenets of Viktor E. Frankl's logotherapy*. Ottawa: Ottawa Institute of Logotherapy.

Maslow, A. H. (1958a). Self-actualizing people: A study of psychological health. In C. E. Moustakas (Ed.), *The self: Explorations in personal growth* (pp. 160–194). New York: Macmillan.

Maslow, A. H. (1958b). Personality problems and personality growth. In C. E. Moustakes (Ed.), *The self-explorations in personal growth* (pp. 232–246). New York: Macmillan.

Maslow, A. H. (1964). *Religion, values and peak experiences*. Columbus: Ohio State University Press.

Maslow, A. H. (1966). Comments on Dr. Frankl's paper. *Journal of Humanistic Psycholoty, 6,* 107–112.

Maslow, A. H. (1967). Self-actualization and beyond. In J. F. T. Bugental (Ed.), *Challenges of humanistic psychology* (pp. 279–286). New York: McGraw-Hill.

Maslow, A. H. (1968). *Toward a psychology of being*. Princeton: Van Nostrand.

Maslow, A. H. (1972). *The father reaches of human nature*. New York: Viking Press.

Maslow, A. H. (1974). Self-actualization: Meta-motivational theory of personality. In W. S. Sahaskian (Ed.), *Psychology of personality: Reading in theory* (pp. 325–343). Chicago: Rnad MacNally.

Maslow, A. H. (1981). The psychology of science. In P. Reason & J. Rowan (Eds.), *Human inquiry: A sourcebook of new paradigm research* (pp. 83–92). Chichester: Wiley.

Maslow, A. H. (1987). *Motivation and personality*. New York: Harper & Row.

May, R. (1958a). The origins and significance of the existential movement in psychology. In R. May, E. Angel, & H. F. Ellenberger (Eds.), *Existence: A new dimension in psychiatry and psychology* (pp. 3–36). New York: Basic Books.

May, R. (1958b). Contributions of existential psychotherapy. In R. May, E. Angel, & H. F. Ellenberger (Eds.), *Existence: A new dimension in psychiatry and psychology* (pp. 37–91). New York: Basic Books.

May, R. (1965). Intentionality, the heart of human will. *Journal of Humanistic Psychology, 5,* 202–209.

May, R. (1983). *The discovery of being: Writings in existential psychology*. New York: Norton.

Moustakas, C. E. (1958a). Summary: Explorations in essential being and personal growth. In C. E. Moustakas (Ed.), *The self: Explorations in personal growth* (pp. 271–284). New York: Macmillan.

Moustakas, C. E. (1958b). True experience and the self. In C. E. Moustakas (Ed.), *The self: Explorations in personal growth* (pp. 3–14). New York: Macmillan.

Moustakas, C. E. (1971). *Individuality and encounter: A brief journey into loneliness and sensitivity groups*. Massachusetts: Doyle.

Rogers, C. R. (1956). What it means to become a person. In C. E. Moustakas (Ed.), *The self: Explorations in personal growth* (pp. 195–211). New York: Macmillan.

Rogers, C. R. (1957). The necessary and sufficient conditions of therapeutic personality change. *Journal of Counseling Psychology, 21*(2), 95–103.

Rogers, C. R. (1972). *On becoming a person: A therapist's view of psychotherapy*. London: Constable.

Rogers, C. R. (1980). *A way of being*. Boston: Houghton Mifflin.

Rogers, C. R. (1985). Toward a more humans science of the person. *Journal of Humanistic Psychology, 25*(4), 7–24.

Rogers, C. R. (1989a). A note on 'the nature of man'. In Kirschenbaum & V. L. Henderson (Eds.), *The Carl Rogers reader* (pp. 401–408). Boston: Houghton Mifflin.

Rogers, C. R. (1989b). A therapist's view of the good life: The fully functioning person. In Kirschenbaum & V. L. Henderson (Eds.), *The Carl Rogers reader* (pp. 409–420). Boston: Houghton Mifflin.

May, R. (1969). *Existential psychology*. New York: Random House.

Piaget, J. (1968). *The construction of reality in the child*. London: Routledge & Kegan Paul Ltd.

Robbins, A. (1992). *Awakening the giant within*. New York: A Fireside Book.

Sartre, J. P. (1957). *Being and nothingness: An essay on phenomenological ontology*. London: Methuen.

Sartre, J.-P. (1967a). *Existential psychoanalysis*. New York: Philosophical Library.

Sartre, J.-P. (1967b). *Essays in existentialism*. New York: Citadel Press.

Schultz, D. (1977). *Growth psychology: Models of the healthy personality.*

Segal, H. (1964). *Introduction to the work of Melanie Klein*. London: William Heinemann.

Southwick, S. M., & Carney, D. S. (2012). *Resilience: The science of mastering life's greatest challenges*. New York: Cambridge University Press.

Soloveitchik, J. B. (1965). *The lonely man of faith*. New York: Three Leaves Press.

Tweedie, D. F. (1965). *Logotherapy and the Christian faith: An evaluation of Frankl's existential approach to psychotherapy*. Michigan: Baker Book House.

Sullivan, H. S. (1953). *The interpersonal theory of psychiatry*. London: Tavistock Publications.

Tillich, P. (1961). Existentialism and psychotherapy. *Review of Existential Psychology and Psychiatry, 1*, 5–20.

Tillich, P. (1965). *The courage to be*. London: The Fontana Library.

Winnicott, D. W. (1957). *The child and the outside world: Studies in developing relationships*. London: Tavistock Publications.

Winnicot, D. W. (1958). *Collected papers: Through paediatrics to psychoanalysis*. London: Tavistock Publications.

Winnicot, D. W. (1964). *The child, the family, and the outside world*. Middlesex: Penguin Books.

Author Index

© Springer Nature Switzerland AG 2020
T. Shantall, *The Life-changing Impact of Viktor Frankl's Logotherapy*,
https://doi.org/10.1007/978-3-030-30770-7

Subject Index

A
Anticipatory anxiety, 102, 164
Attitude of gratitude, 268
Attitudinal values, 22, 24, 25, 112,
 162–164, 186

B
Basic trust in being, 75, 251, 254–255, 289

C
Collective neurosis, 277
Common will to common meaning,
 31, 261, 274
Connection/sense of connectedness/meaning
 as connection, 2, 29, 30, 35, 57–59, 81,
 100, 111, 112, 121, 122
Conscience, 12, 21, 29–36, 40, 43, 45, 77, 92,
 135, 176, 178, 180, 181, 201–203, 210,
 213–216, 244, 249, 255, 258, 259, 261,
 264, 282
Created to be/meant to be/ought to be, 6, 8, 21,
 22, 29, 30, 34, 36, 38, 45, 47, 48, 54,
 56, 75, 93, 94, 121, 123, 125, 135, 177,
 178, 195, 199, 210, 215, 250, 252, 271,
 272, 282, 285–288
Creative values, 22, 24, 28, 112, 185

D
Defense mechanisms, 207, 209, 276
Defiant power of the human spirit, 130, 134,
 164, 223, 227, 229, 231, 232, 278
Dereflection, 142, 159–164, 168

D (cont.)
Dimension of meaning/Supra-human
 dimension/The Transcendent
 dimension, 15–16, 30, 42, 77, 100, 114,
 170, 200, 212, 255, 257, 262
Dimensional ontology/different levels of
 being, 41–42

E
Ecce Homo technique, 162–164, 238
Ecce Homo/Behold the man, 25–26, 163,
 236, 281
Enablement/empowerment, 55, 175–176,
 286, 287
Existential vacuum/existential frustration, 6,
 117, 133, 179, 277
Experiential values, 22–24, 106, 108–109, 186
Extended human science, 37, 256

F
Faith, 4, 25, 27, 35, 37, 42, 75, 91, 101, 120,
 121, 131, 165, 186, 191, 210, 224, 227,
 230, 251, 254, 278–280
Freedom of will/freedom of choice, 1, 17, 42,
 44, 136, 139, 159, 186, 202, 283
Free-willed obedience, 282–283

G
Grace, 54, 107, 125, 154, 186, 192, 193, 215,
 236, 252, 257, 258, 264, 282, 284
Guilt, 6, 8, 13, 21, 44, 88, 121, 135, 182,
 190–192, 201–203, 205–207,
 209, 281

© Springer Nature Switzerland AG 2020
T. Shantall, *The Life-changing Impact of Viktor Frankl's Logotherapy*,
https://doi.org/10.1007/978-3-030-30770-7

Printed in Great Britain
by Amazon

16626918R00190